LOTTE LEHMANN

A Life In Opera & Song

Lotte Lehmann

A LIFE IN OPERA & SONG

Beaumont Glass

Capra Press
Santa Barbara · 1988

Library of Congress Cataloging-in-Publication Data

Glass, Beaumont, 1925–
    Lotte Lehmann, a life in opera and song

    Discography: p. 303
    Includes index.
    1. Lehmann, Lotte, 1888–1976. 2. Singers—Biography.
I. Title
ML420.L33G6 1988   782.1'092'4 [B]   87-32574
ISBN 0-88496-277-6

Excerpts from the following books and publications are reprinted by permission:
"Profile," *Song and Sentiment*, by Marcia Davenport, 1935, 1963, The New Yorker
Magazine, Inc.; *Time*, January 22, 1934; "The Listening Post," *Esquire*, June 1935; *Five
Operas and Richard Strauss* by Lotte Lehmann, 1964, Macmillan, New York; *First and Last
Love* by Vincent Sheean, 1956, Random House, New York; *At the Piano—Ivor Newton* by
Ivor Newton, 1966, Hamish Hamilton, London; "Goering, the Lioness and I" by Lotte
Lehmann, *Opera* 66, edited by Charles Osborne, 1966, Alan Ross, London; *Toscanini* by
George Marek, 1975, Atheneum, New York; *Lotte Lehmann...Mehr als eine Sängerin* by
Berndt W. Wessling, 1969, Residenz Verlag, Salzburg; The Richard Strauss-Ludwig
Karpath Correspondence 1902–1933, edited by Günter Brosche, part 2: 1926–1933, in
Richard Strauss-Blätter Nr. 7 (May 1978), p. 1-18, from the Internationale Richard Strauss
Gesellschaft, Vienna.

Cover and book design by Judy Sutcliffe. Cover portrait of Lotte Lehmann as the
Marschallin by Schattenstein, courtesy of Metropolitan Opera, New York, and *Opera
News*. Title-page drawing of the Marschallin by Lotte Lehmann.

Photo credits where known: Benque & Kindermann, Hamburg (p. I, t.r.); E. Bieber, Hamburg (p. II, b.r.; p. II, t.r.; p. IV, t.l.); Hans Dietrich & Co., Vienna (p. VI, t.r.); Rudolf Dührkoop
(p. VI, b.r.); Ellinger, Salzburg (p. IV, t.l.; p. IX; p. XIII, b.; p. XIV, t.l.; p. XVI, t.l.);
Foka, Vienna (p.V, t.l.); Charles Glass (p. XXIII, t.r.); Frances Holden (p. XIII, t.r.;
p. XVI, t.r.; p. XX, t., ctr. l.; p. XXI, t.l., t.r.); Leonard McCombe (Life) (p. XXII, b., p. XXIII,
b.l.); Lotte Meitner-Graf, London (p. XXIII, t.l., p. XXIV); A. Mocsigay, Hamburg
(p. I, b.l.; p. II, t.l., b.l.; p. VI, b.l.); Ruth Orkin, New York (p. XVI, ctr., b.); Rothmaier, Salzburg (p. X & XI, series); Otto Skall, Vienna (p. III, b.l.; p. IV, b.r.; p. VIII, b.r.); Telegraph
Feature Service, Brisbane (p. XIV, b.); Tschiedel-Setzer, Vienna (p. III, t.l., t.r., b.l.; p.V, t.l.,
t.r., b.r.; p. VI, t.l.; p. VII, t.l., b.l., b.r.; p. VIII, t.l., t.r., b.l.)

CAPRA PRESS

P.O. Box 2068, Santa Barbara, California 93120

To Frances Holden

Foreword

A PERSONAL NOTE

FOR TWO AND A HALF YEARS I was Lotte Lehmann's assistant at the Music Academy of the West in Santa Barbara. I accompanied master classes in lieder and opera, coached students, and occasionally assisted with staging. During those years Mme. Lehmann presented complete productions of *Der Rosenkavalier* and *Fidelio*. I was privileged to observe how she built up every role, detail by illuminating detail. I cherish my *Rosenkavalier* score, scribbled full of her stage directions and comments.

In the summer of 1961 I was Mme. Lehmann's assistant stage director for *Fidelio*, her last production. She asked me to block and direct the ensemble scenes so that she could save her energy for the individual characterizations and the crucially important dialogue.

I am old enough, and lucky enough, to have seen Lehmann's Marschallin several times at the Metropolitan Opera and to have heard a number of her lieder recitals. Those were unforgettable experiences.

During my years in Europe with the Zurich Opera, I had a chance to visit Mme. Lehmann nearly every summer in Salzburg, Vienna, Schrunz, or Bad Gastein. She often came to Switzerland as well.

I saw her for the last time in Santa Barbara, a year before she died, bent and barely able to walk with two canes, but still a fascinating woman.

More than any other artist I ever knew, she incorporated a genius for interpretation, uniquely combined with the rare ability to articulate her insights and to pass them on to others.

This book is my attempt to offer my thanks to Lotte Lehmann for the precious gifts she has given to me and to so many. Its form was determined by the special nature of the documents available. I wished wherever feasible to preserve the actual words of Lotte Lehmann and of those who heard her in her major roles and in recital at various stages of her career. I am the translator of all the materials in German, French, and Italian that have not already been published in English. In the case of Lehmann's early letters I might better say I am the cryptographer, since they were written in a now-obsolete form of German script and, especially in her letters to her brother, dashed off in a nearly indecipherable scrawl. Her typewritten letters, bristling with numerous corrections scribbled in ink, are often almost as hard to read as her earlier German script. The orthography and syntax of her later letters in English, except where otherwise noted, have occasionally been corrected; but basically a considerable portion of this biography is Lotte Lehmann speaking in her own words and in her own characteristic way.

This book would not have been possible without the indispensable cooperation of Dr. Frances Holden, Lotte Lehmann's longtime companion, who graciously invited my wife and me to live with her for five months, giving us what had been Lotte's own apartment. We were surrounded by the mementos of a great career and of a most productive friendship. Everywhere there were samples of Lehmann's prolific creativity: her felt pictures, her paintings, her glass mosaics, her ceramics. Her opera scores, her volumes of lieder were there. Hundreds of photos. A nearly complete collection of her records. The parrot and the dog that survived her. Outside our window the Pacific, framed by hibiscus and jacaranda. Hummingbirds, butterflies, and a pair of amorous owls. No would-be author could ask for a more inspiring setting in which to write a book about Lotte Lehmann.

Frances was indefatigable in tracking down letters, old date books, all sorts of random bits of information that might be usable. Her enormous library alone had the answer somewhere to almost any conceivable question.

Much as she hated speaking into a tape recorder, she gamely submitted when the mood was right. Her recorded reminiscences, though punctuated by screams from Suzy, the parrot, are fascinating and suggest a gift for total recall.

The Lotte Lehmann Archives at the University of California, Santa Barbara, contain thousands of letters to and from Lehmann, along with telegrams, manuscripts, photos, press books, scrapbooks, and paintings, to which I was given unlimited access through the courtesy of Dr. Joseph A. Boissé, University Librarian, and Christian Brun, Head of the Special Collections Department.

Hertha Schuch of Vienna and Gary Hickling of Hawaii have been particularly helpful in sending me interesting and hard-to-find material on Lotte Lehmann. Mr. Hickling has compiled the definitive Lehmann discography, a mammoth, complicated task.

I wish to thank Judy Sutcliffe for finding me a publisher, for setting the type, and for loaning me a car; Dr. Daniel C. Jacobson for teaching me how to use a computer; Charles Edward Glass, my brother, for lending me his printer; and my wife for helping me read through mountains of letters and clippings.

I would like to express my gratitude to Margaret Specht, who took the trouble to read my first draft, and to Roger Levenson for his editing and proofreading.

Special thanks also to Risë Stevens and Rose Bampton for their graciousness in granting me interviews.

Contents

Photographs follow pages 76, 140 and 204.

INTRODUCTION

ARTURO TOSCANINI called her "the greatest artist in the world."
Richard Strauss uttered the words that are now engraved
on her tombstone: *"Sie hat gesungen, daß es Sterne rührte"* —
her singing moved the stars. Puccini preferred her *"soavissima"*
Suor Angelica to all others. Thomas Mann addressed her as *"liebe
Frau Sonne"* — dear Lady Sunshine. Bruno Walter accompanied
her in lieder recitals which became an annual feature of the Salzburg Festivals until the Nazi annexation of Austria.

Lotte Lehmann was probably the most beloved—and is certainly still one of the best remembered—of all the stars of the
Vienna State Opera during its most resplendent era. In all the
capitals of opera her Marschallin in *Der Rosenkavalier* reigned supreme for twenty-two years and set standards for all her successors. She was the greatest Sieglinde, Elisabeth, and Fidelio of
her time.

Toward the end of her thirty-six-year operatic career, as one by
one her other roles began to disappear from her active repertoire
and only the Marschallin still lured her back to the opera stage,
she found a second career in every way as great and important
and beautiful as the first: she opened the door to the marvelous
world of German lieder to far greater audiences than ever before.
In America, at least, her name became practically synonymous
with the word lieder. She used to sing *three* Town Hall recitals
every year in New York, and they were always quickly sold out,
including every one of the many extra seats packed onto the recital platform. Her concert tours and her recordings awakened an
unprecedented appreciation for German lieder in audiences all
over the country.

Then, after she no longer sang in public herself, she evolved a
new forum of activity. The master classes in which, before an au-

dience, she imparted to young singers her priceless insights into the interpretation of opera and art song were at that time both original and unique. The atmosphere was alive and exciting, like a performance. Mme. Lehmann would often step before the piano herself to demonstrate the interpretation of a song, or would act out part of an operatic scene. Particularly fascinating was the eloquent way she could verbalize what she was doing, what the piano introduction—for instance—was expressing, or what an operatic character was feeling "between the lines." How often are we granted an opportunity to witness the creative process in action, to hear a great artist put his or her thoughts into words? How many great artists are even *able* to do so? Lotte Lehmann's master classes were a powerful inspiration to all those participants who had the sensitivity to grasp her suggestions and the sense to profit from them. For the audience, too, the master classes were a revelation. Thanks to Lehmann's unfailing sense of humor, they were also great entertainment.

Two generations of singers have benefited from study with her. Her former students are singing in opera houses all over the world. Yet she never taught singing as such—or, more exactly, never since her own student days. What she taught was interpretation, how to bring a song to life, how to express its deepest meanings, how to make a living human being out of an operatic character.

Besides what was uniquely her own, she passed on a great and noble tradition. She had studied voice with Mathilde Mallinger, Wagner's first Eva in *Die Meistersinger*. She coached Strauss roles—and Strauss songs—with Richard Strauss himself. One of her early accompanists, Ferdinand Foll, was a friend of Hugo Wolf's. She sang with most of the leading conductors of her time. The great three in her life were Franz Schalk, Bruno Walter, and Arturo Toscanini. She shared the stage with many other brilliant artists. She knew the authentic style and the most valid traditions that had evolved under the guidance of Wagner, Strauss, and Puccini, to name just some of the composers who continued to mold their operas in rehearsal after the scores had been printed and published. What she absorbed from great predecessors and contemporaries she passed on, both consciously and unconsciously, to her students.

Her voice, or at least a fair facsimile of her voice, can be heard on records. It had a unique, haunting quality, instantly recognizable but hard to define. What one notices right away is the immediacy of her response to the emotional content of the words and music. Not for her the concept of poetry as "emotion recollected in tranquillity." The poem is alive in her at that very moment of uttering it, with all the vividness of an actual experience, as if she herself were poet and composer, combined, in an ecstasy of inspiration. The older records, made when her voice was in its prime, suffer from the technological limitations of early recording equipment. The later records capture her singing somewhat more faithfully, but by that time her voice had understandably lost something of its youthful glow. No records, however, can recapture the visual component, the overwhelming impression she created through the combination of facial expression, personal magnetism, and stage presence—a kind of magic—which remained hers as long as she lived and which came across as effectively in her master classes as it had at the height of her career. Her whole being became the song.

As a singing-actress her identification with the role she was singing was total while she was performing—no other singer surpassed her in bringing those ladies of the imagination to such vivid life. Yet when the performance came to an end she could throw off the aura of the character and the mood of the final scene—however tragic, exalted, or nostalgic—with an instantaneousness that often startled her friends. Elsa, Sieglinde, the Marschallin—and all the roles she wrote about in *My Many Lives*—disappeared in Lotte Lehmann, the woman. Yet in another way those many lives were all there inside of her, constituting a woman of many sides and many moods.

What was she like, that woman? Her companion since the death of her husband in 1939, Frances Holden, has declined the many requests to write a biography of Lehmann. Dr. Holden, who had been so close to Lotte, declares herself daunted by the apparent contradictions in the character of her friend. "Almost any characteristic I might think of could be countered by its opposite; but in one way Lotte was absolutely consistent: there was no meanness in her." Perhaps a picture of the woman will emerge in this book through the words of her friends and colleagues, through excerpts from her hitherto private correspondence, through quotations from her writings both published and unpublished, through reviews, interviews, and photographs.

She was incessantly creative. When not singing or teaching she was writing or painting or making ceramics, glass mosaics, colorful felt cutouts, or illustrated jokes in verse. A number of her writings have been published, including a novel, an autobiography (up to 1937), two books on song interpretation, two on the interpretation of her operatic roles, and two volumes of poetry. There was a One-Woman-Show in New York of some of her paintings, including her pictorial versions of Schubert's *Die Winterreise*. She also made a film in Hollywood and read German poetry for Caedmon Records, all of this while maintaining a world-wide correspondence with friends and students, former colleagues, fans from the old days in Hamburg and Vienna, and with such luminaries as Bruno Walter, Thomas Mann, and Toscanini.

Though safely Aryan herself (her stepchildren had a Jewish mother), she was staunchly anti-Nazi from the very beginning and stopped singing in Germany soon after Hitler came to power. When he took Austria into the Third Reich, she—German by birth and Viennese by adoption—applied for American citizenship. After the war she spent far more money than she could actually afford on parcels of food and clothing and other necessities for her friends in Europe who had suffered great privations during that terrible time. Until the end of her life she contributed generously to a home for needy retired performers in Austria. The generosity of spirit that radiated through her singing found its counterpart in many deeds of kindness (often secret) in her private life. As just one touching example, one of her letters makes clear that she had arranged to teach a talented student for nothing and even to contribute a generous sum each month toward living expenses, while insisting that the student not be told the name of her unknown sponsor. There were many such gestures.

She herself would be the first, however, to laugh at any sug gestion that she was a saint. There *was* a saint in her, yes, and one felt that side of her in her portrayal of Elisabeth in *Tannhäuser*, which, like all her great interpretations, went far beyond mere play-acting; but there were plenty of other less hallowed personae in her fascinating personality. She was, after all, a very famous Manon in the earlier years of her career and always a wildly passionate Sieglinde. Like all great artists she was self-absorbed. A great diva almost *has* to be, to protect herself. The career has to come first if it is to become—and stay—a world career. The competition at the top is enormous; the strains and hazards of a singing career—one that depends upon the health of a delicate pair of membranes in the throat—are exceedingly nerve-wracking. Perhaps Lehmann was not always an angel; but neither was she the sort of prima donna who would ever stab a rival in the back. It is no secret that Maria Jeritza managed to keep her away from the Metropolitan for many years, or that Viorica Ursuleac made trouble for Lehmann in Vienna during the 30's and spread malicious, grossly distorted stories about her to the very end. But those ladies were in direct competition with Lehmann in many roles they sang in common; most of her colleagues, such as Elisabeth Schumann and—in the next generation—Risë Stevens, loved her dearly. Elisabeth Rethberg, who shared several of the same roles at the Met, had a close and very cordial relationship with Lehmann. Among the male colleagues there was not, of course, the element of rivalry; from the very beginning they could be numbered among her most enthusiastic friends and supporters. Among her favorites were Richard Mayr, Alfred Jerger, Alfred Piccaver, Leo Slezak, Karl Aagard-Oestwig, and Lauritz Melchior.

In all her writings she maintained a dignified reticence in discussing her unkinder rivals; on the contrary she graciously—and sincerely—praised their artistic accomplishments, unprejudiced by bitter memories of personal injuries behind the scenes.

Seemingly incompatible Lottes somehow managed to coexist in a surprising harmony of contrasts. During the busy years of her career, she often escaped to the isolation of lonely beaches on the island of Hiddensee in the Baltic Sea. Later, she retired to a sort of private paradise in Hope Ranch, Santa Barbara, remote from the bustle of the world—peaceful, perhaps, but not exactly quiet: she loved the barking dogs, talking Mynah birds, singing canaries, and screeching parrots that populated her Eden. Yet the same Lotte Lehmann thrived on excitement and stimulation. Bores were her principal aversion. She was witty, loved to laugh, and adored a funny joke. Highly impulsive by nature, she was quick to act on the whim of the moment, without a thought of possible consequences. If there was no excitement around her naturally, she was capable of stirring some up, deliberately, one way or the other, as when she might bring together two people who could not stand each other, just to watch the sparks fly.

In everyday life, in ordinary human relations, Lehmann could sometimes be wrong about people. Because she was so impulsive and quick, there could be misunderstandings, misjudgments. But she saw into the very souls of the characters she portrayed on the stage; hers was a phenomenal insight into every subtle nuance of the psychology of those creations of the poetic imagination; she made them totally real, gave them the breath and heartbeat of life. Fortunately she could articulate those insights. Mary Garden's book was a disappointment to those who hoped to find in it clues to her famous interpretations: "I was Mélisande" or "I was Thaïs." One looks in vain for any revelation. They say Maria Callas shied away from any analysis of her roles. But in *My Many Lives* Lotte Lehmann has written indispensable chapters on the heroines she portrayed. That book should be required reading for anyone interested in performing those roles or studying those operas. It is also to be recommended to anyone who cares about opera at all.

For those who were there, a Lehmann performance was something very special and quite unforgettable. The love that flowed back and forth between artist and audience was something wonderful to feel. Nothing was ever routine, not even for a moment; every moment was an experience, intimately shared.

Chapter One

A DROP OF THEATRE BLOOD

THE FIRST LEHMANN TONES—not *bel canto* but surely expressive—rang out on February 27, 1888, in Perleberg, in the northern part of Germany, a middle-sized town about halfway between Berlin and Hamburg. The new arrival received a string of names: Charlotte Sophie Pauline Lehmann. The ten syllables quickly dwindled down to two.

With the same inimitable relish that made a little jewel out of every song she sang, Lotte Lehmann in her memoirs and early letters takes us back into another century and another world, the world of her childhood, and recreates its atmosphere with her flair for characteristic detail.

She remembers the night watchman calling the hours, the Gypsies who passed through the town, the linen lady whose visits cheered Lotte's ailing mother, *Lumpenmatz*, the rag man, who fished out of his rag bag foul-smelling bits of St. John's bread (a popular seasonal delicacy in German-speaking countries still today) as a reward for the children who brought him pieces of used clothing they had begged from their mothers. Here, in her own words, is the organ-grinder:

> There was always great excitement when a special genius of the barrel-organ came down the street with his cart.... Above the organ-mechanism there was a large box with pictures in lurid colors pasted all around it. The series of pictures told a story, and the horrible "thrillers" of today are tame compared to the blood-thirstiness of those wild tales. They always started with some cruel murder. Blood flowed in streams. One saw the poor victim, usually a beautiful woman, quite dead, long yellow hair hanging down in improbable glory, dripping with blood. Then came the murderer; and one was convinced that he was a killer, for his face spoke volumes. At the end one had

1

> *the relief of seeing him beheaded, and the pleasure of admiring with
> a shiver the lifted axe. I could never sleep after one of those exciting
> performances.... Sometimes the hoarse voice of the "Director" was
> drowned out by the barrel-organ, but always enough of his narration
> stuck in my head for me to act it all out later for Mama, in a dra-
> matic performance that generally netted a box on the ears, for I had
> been forbidden to watch those horror stories.*

Now and then an acting troupe would come to town, and
Lehmann remembered the leading lady, behind the scenes, wan
without her grease-paint, wearily sewing spangles on a robe that
later, on the stage, would conjure up all the glamour of the theatre for those people of Perleberg who could not afford to visit
Hamburg or Berlin.

Her father, Carl Lehmann, was a proper German official, upright, industrious, methodical, orderly. He was a secretary of the
Ritterschaft, a kind of benevolent society, with branches in various
parts of Germany, that also functioned as a bank and managed
estate matters for the landed gentry of the area. The rent-free
house in which Lotte and her brother, Fritz, grew up belonged
to the *Ritterschaft*. It was a fine two-story house, overgrown with
vines. There was an acacia tree in the little front garden, a big
garden in back and a poultry yard. The garden was her father's
pride and joy. Part of it was given to Lotte, for her to look after
herself. Her father had also set up a playground for the children,
with a swing, parallel bars, and a roundabout.

Her mother, Marie, suffered very poor health through most of
her life. Although Carl Lehmann's salary was a respectable one
for those days, his wife's medical needs were such that money
was always in short supply and the family had to watch every
penny. Money was a serious problem—sometimes a desperate
one—well into Lotte's first engagement as an opera singer. It
was the cause of endless disputes at home; and the relationship
between her parents, good people both, was often marred by
disharmony where money was concerned.

Music was a common bond—not classical music, for they
knew next to nothing about that—but the folk songs that were
so much a part of the average German's life in those days. Papa
played the zither and sang tenor in the Perleberg glee club—

Fritz called it "the Half-a-Lung." Mama had a beautiful, mellow contralto which was never heard in public but which played a formative part in Lotte's love of singing. It was a voice that should have been trained; but Marie's father was sternly opposed to any idea that his daughter might ever be a performer.

Lotte loved to chirp along with the rest of the family, but when company came (which was seldom, for Mama was usually ill) it was Fritz who was asked to sing, first as a boy soprano, later as a promising tenor. Unfortunately his voice was ruined by an over-eager choir director who made him sing soprano, tenor, or bass according to the need of the moment while his voice was still changing.

Whereas Lehmann always saw herself as having been quite an ordinary little girl—her mother used to say that Lotte had never given her a moment's trouble as a child—Fritz, who was six years older, was the wild one, the adventurer, the unpredictable artist. He loved to dress up as an Indian—with the scalps of Lotte's dolls hanging from his belt—to scare the good burghers, out for their Sunday walk in the woods. He was always up to something, the ringleader in many an escapade, and Lotte looked up to him with awe and admiration. She would have loved to join the fun—and sometimes did when they were alone together— but no proper schoolboy would have anything to do with a little sister in front of his friends. Fritz was always in and out of trouble, especially around report-card time, and caused his mother no end of worry; yet, perhaps for that very reason, it always seemed to Lotte that Fritz was Mama's favorite. Long after she was a grown woman and a famous opera star, it still hurt her that Mama would make more fuss over a violet from Fritz than over a new car from her.

Lotte adored her mother, a woman who was kind, full of concern, always forgiving. Unfortunately, she was also frequently ill. Lotte's closeness to her mother was a dominating factor in her life as long as her mother lived. Separation from one another always brought on many tears. When Lotte, grown up, went on tour, first to South America, then, years later, to North America, her mother missed her painfully and wrote touching letters full of the fear of "wild Indians" and other imagined dangers. When

Lotte sang a new role or a première or a particularly important
concert, Mama would put garlands of flowers around her picture
and "hold her thumbs" (the European version of crossing one's
fingers) until they ached. Lotte was very much under her
influence. Mama was always very sweet and kind, but some
need of Lotte's seemed ever unfulfilled, nevertheless. She was
over-anxious to please her mother and yearned for constant reassurance of her love. Mama cried easily and often. She suffered
from chronic gastric pains; reading or writing inflamed her eyes
severely. Even in her picture as a lovely young woman one can
sense the melancholy strain. Lotte, looking at that picture, describes hers as a sombre beauty, without light. She had loved a
young lieutenant who fell in the Franco-Prussian War; sometimes she had the tactlessness to refer to that "love of her life" in
the presence of Lotte's father. Both of Lotte's parents came from
the same town, Prenzlau, to the north of Berlin, where Marie's
parents had owned a mill. Her family had been quite well off until
her father died, leaving them suddenly without means. Carl Lehmann was a handsome young man, with good prospects. They
married, moved to Perleberg, and settled down to raising their
two children.

At Easter there were egg-hunts. At Christmas, Mama would
dress up as the *Weihnachtsmann*—the German version of Santa
Claus—and distribute presents. Every summer the family would
go off to Warnemünde on the Baltic Sea for a vacation at the
beach. There Mama, almost a recluse at home, would be surrounded by friends, adding a cello-like alto to the familiar old
songs they all loved to sing.

There were always pets at the *Ritterschaftshaus*. Lotte Lehmann
had a life-long passion for animals that began with Mohr, an old
poodle, and Mauzi, a yellow tom-cat. They were the first in an
unbroken line. She loved animals and animals loved her. Even
deer, normally so shy, would eat out of her hands. Lotte hated to
see any animal suffer. She would run away when she learned a
hen was to be killed. Years later in Chicago, then the meat capital
of America, the thought of the animals brought there to be
slaughtered filled her with revulsion. She even "hated" Meta, the

maid-of-all-work, for killing a fish. The hatred, however, did not last very long for Meta was a favorite playmate in the fascinating dress-up game they called "countesses."

Lotte, Meta, and Selma Betz, a friend from school, would wrap old bedsheets around their waists, give each other flowery names, mince around the house with dainty steps, and make up the kind of high-flown talk they had picked up from Meta's mystery novelettes. The really thrilling parts of those stories, however, were just too scarey to act out; bits like this would keep Lotte awake at night: "And suddenly the coffin-lid was lifted and the pale Countess Elvira stepped out...." Meta tried to convince Lotte that the *Ritterschaftshaus* was haunted. She had seen a ghost on the stairs. Perhaps Meta is to blame for Lotte's lifelong fear of being alone in the dark.

Playing countesses was a sort of embryonic step toward opera. Soon Lotte was "Queen Louise" in a school operetta. Her still-tiny voice was nevertheless the best in the school and already there was talk of training for a singing career. But Papa would have none of that. She would have a proper, practical profession. Still, he let her put on plays in the vine-covered summerhouse in the garden. He even supplied paper lanterns and, afterwards, led the dancing and singing. On that stage Lotte played her first trouser role, in one of her brother's hand-me-downs and a false mustache, good practice, no doubt, for the Octavians, Composers, and Fidelios that lay in the future. The first play she ever saw had been *Cinderella*, performed by a troupe of midgets. Then came Camillo von Kunzendorff and his traveling players. According to family legend, Papa was descended from an illegitimate son of Sophie Arnould, the great French singing-actress. That drop of theatre blood was beginning to stir in Lotte's veins.

There were secret piano lessons, paid for out of Mama's household allowance, to surprise Papa on his silver wedding anniversary. Then came dancing lessons and Lotte's first admirer, a sturdy farmboy from Fritz's class at school. Her first love, when she was twelve, was her music teacher at school. Her first engagement—it lasted perhaps five minutes—was to the boy next door.

Another talent began to flourish about this time: she loved to paint. Her specialty was an appropriately flamboyant rendition of Hell.

Mama was never very happy at Perleberg and longed to live near her relatives in Berlin. Eventually she persuaded Papa to apply for a transfer to a Berlin branch of the *Ritterschaft*—a real sacrifice for him, for he loved the garden he had cultivated so often between dawn and the start of office hours at the *Ritterschaft* next door.

In 1902, soon after Lotte's confirmation, the Lehmanns moved to Berlin. Fritz had gone on ahead to begin his training for the humdrum routine of officialdom. To please his worried mother, he had given up his dream of going to sea. The family found an apartment on Hochmeister Street in the cheap northern sector of Berlin. It was very different from the spacious house and garden and the clean air of Perleberg.

Chapter Two

A DOOR TO WONDERLAND

BERLIN WAS EXCITING. Mama was happy to be among her relatives. Papa was able to add *Ober* (chief) to the string of words that made up his title. Fritz formed a secret society with the lofty name, Justice. Mostly the members drank a lot of beer. Lotte felt at first like a country mouse among big city cats. But soon she had many good friends. There were some disappointments however. The *Tiergarten*—the name implies a zoo—turned out to be autos instead of animals; and the linden trees of *Unter den Linden* — a famous boulevard — seemed "miserable, stunted, and insignificant" compared to those in Perleberg.

Lotte was enrolled in the Ulrich Lyceum. It was a school for girls and every one of them—including Lotte—was madly in love with "Ulli," as they called Headmaster Ulrich. He gave them advice that she never forgot: "Go your own way, don't run with the herd. Be a personality. Become what you are, that is the best thing in life." The girls also had a crush on their classroom teacher, who encouraged Lotte's very evident talent as a writer. The check for ten marks she received when one of her poems was accepted by a Berlin paper, *Der Tag*, meant more to Lotte than many a splendid fee she later earned with her singing.

Lotte loved that school, especially play-reading and declamation. "To be able strangely to transform oneself, suddenly to be able to express what someone else had felt and to make it one's own, so that it seemed to come out of one's very self—how fascinating! To be an actress was my quiet, secret dream...." Mathematics, however, remained a thorn in her side. She never did learn how to balance a checkbook.

A triple romance began to blossom. The neighbors had two girls and a boy. The Lehmanns had one girl and—temporarily—

two boys, for Erich, a friend of Fritz's, was boarding with them. For some time six young people were finding excuses to pose near a window. All sorts of signals were intended or imagined—and sometimes intercepted by an irritated mother. Finally the two families got together for a Sunday outing at a suburban concert-garden where the bandmaster was celebrated for a particularly choice rendition of "Glow, Little Glowworm." The customers consumed coffee and cake, danced, or talked politics. Since in this case both fathers were staunchly conservative, their conversations were more a mutual ratification than a stimulating exchange of ideas. There was a series of such outings. On the way home from one of them Lotte received her first kiss and a proposal of marriage. Willi Hilke asked if Lotte would wait five years for him. First there would be his year of military service— in the Cockchafers, a guards regiment with a particularly dashing uniform—and then four years at the university, studying philology. Lotte said yes. Marriage with Willi seemed infinitely preferable to the lot of a secretary at the *Ritterschaft*, pension or no, that Papa was planning for her. A job with a pension—that was what any good German official would wish for his child. First Papa had hoped that Lotte might become a schoolteacher. Her dismal marks in math soon burst that bubble. But a practical profession would in any case be necessary. Sometimes Lotte struggled against Papa's principles; sometimes she submitted. Her relationship with her father was often adversarial. Papa, the sensible one, generally found himself outnumbered, three to one. Fritz always sided with Lotte and Mama always sided with Fritz. It was only in later years that Lotte came to understand and to appreciate her father's special ways of showing his deep love for her.

About the time Lotte graduated from school, the Lehmanns moved to Gross-Lichterfelde, a pretty garden suburb of Berlin, where the air was better for Mama, whose health, always precarious, was on one of its downward curves. With their new apartment came the right to use the garden, a special blessing for Papa. Lotte, freed from schoolwork, helped with the household chores. To pass the time she would sing folk songs and the latest hits while she dusted or swept (cooking was ruled out; she would be too extravagant in the kitchen).

One day the lady in the flat upstairs, Frau Kühnen, who had often complimented Lotte on her singing, decided that Lotte's lovely natural voice deserved to be properly trained. She was shocked to learn that Papa had already enrolled Lotte in a commercial school. She prophesied a glamorous operatic career, maybe even marriage to a prince. Frau Kühnen had a contact. Her uncle ran the canteen at the Royal High School of Music. That uncle of hers turned out to be very helpful. He arranged for one of the advanced singing students, Fräulein Erna Tiedke, to prepare Lotte for the entrance examinations which, as luck would have it, were only a week away.

Lotte had been twice to the opera, standing in the top gallery with Willi and Fritz. Her first opera was *Lohengrin*, a work that was later to be a major milestone in her career. Then came *Mignon* with Emmy Destinn, who became, with Geraldine Farrar, one of Lotte's early idols.

But still she had absolutely no repertoire of classical music, nothing at all to sing at an audition.

With Mama's blessing, but behind Papa's back (for the lessons cost two marks each), Lotte worked with Fraulein Tiedke on Siebel's aria from *Faust* and "Jerusalem" from Mendelssohn's *St. Paul*. Here is her impression of her mentor:

> ...She loved behaving like a prima donna, wore a whole shopwindowful of imitation jewelry on her person and a shawl with long fringes decorated with ostrich feathers.... A door to wonderland had opened to me in which shone the glorified form of Erna Tiedke, singing her brilliant trills and bewildering coloraturas and relating her dizzying conquests on her path to fame...It seemed to me that every other coloratura-singer in the world was done for, and when I shyly asked Frl. Tiedke who sang her parts in the Royal Opera House, she would answer with proud modesty: "As yet, Frau Herzog...."

It was a frantic attempt to pack a year or two of vocal lessons and musical training into six days; but it worked. Lotte sang Siebel's aria at her very first audition. She was accepted. But there could be no scholarship for the first term. That was a fixed policy.

Papa had accompanied her to the audition, presumably unaware of the cram-course that had proceeded it. To his ears none of the contestants sang as beautifully as his Lotte. He saw the necessity of raising the tuition money and somehow he managed it. As long as he lived no one else ever sang like his Lotte.

She was now a Student of Music. That was at least a minor distinction in title-loving Germany. And an inner transformation went along with it. When Willi wrote to congratulate her but expressed the hope that her future professional activities would not conflict with her duties to house and home, she was deeply offended. "Does he mean me to beat carpets in the morning and give concerts at night?" She thought of Erna's high-minded maxims: "I must dedicate my life to Art. Nothing must divert me from my lofty goal!" There was a farewell letter. It cost a few hot tears. A turning point had been reached.

At the Royal High School of Music Lotte studied with Helene Jordan, one of the voice teachers. Progress seemed painfully slow. Lotte was impatient for results and all too aware that she was just a rank beginner. When a bass from the opera class called out: "Well, little lamb, can you say baa yet?" she burst into tears. There were classes in theory—there she felt quite hopeless—as well as in Italian and piano. Her favorite was elocution and she gives to her teacher, Elise Bartels, the credit for the clear enunciation that was consistently praised throughout her career. Every vowel, every consonant was carefully and consciously shaped and drilled and polished. At term end Lotte won a scholarship.

Unfortunately Mama became seriously ill with a severe gastric hemorrhage. Lotte had to take leave from school and take care of her. She also had to do the cooking. No matter how conscientiously she tried to stick to the recipe there were long faces at the table; but everyone was kind enough to pretend to Mama that Lotte's concoctions had been delicious. Her friend of later years, Frances Holden, claims that when Lotte took it into her head to cook, it was as if there had been an explosion in the kitchen. She had—as the whole world knows—other, compensating talents.

One summer the family discovered the enchanting island of Hiddensee, in the Baltic, north of Stralsund. In those days the island—from then on one of Lotte's favorite haunts—was inhabited mostly by artists. It was cheaper to live there than in Berlin and the family had wonderful, healthy vacations in the invigorating sea-air.

During Lotte's second year at the Royal High School of Music, Helene Jordan became seriously ill. Lotte was given to another teacher with whom all progress soon came to a standstill. The school director kept urging Lotte in the direction of oratorio; but the ambition for opera had begun to take hold of her, heart and soul. Her old scrapbooks from that period are full of penciled comments on the clippings of newspaper reviews. She must have managed to see quite a few performances of opera in Berlin, and her scribbled criticisms show considerable discernment. She became discouraged at the Royal High School and decided to make a change.

After an audition, she was accepted into the Etelka Gerster School of Singing. Mme. Gerster had studied with the legendary Mathilde Marchesi and was for a while Adelina Patti's principal rival. Her school was packed with rich young ladies from all over the world. Lotte received free tuition, a great exception, and was assigned to Frl. Eva Reinhold for voice training. The Gerster School method was disastrously unsuited to Lotte's voice. The students were made to hold small wooden sticks between their jaws to keep the mouth opening always the same for every tone, for every vowel, at every pitch. Vocalises were specially printed in three colors, to emphasize the various registers. Such methods went counter to Lotte's healthy vocal instincts, as well as to her musical sense. The little stick kept the jaw muscles rigid; the emphasis on different registers impeded the development of an even scale. Woe to the poor unfortunate whose stick slipped out! The rest of the class would break up with the giggles and Eva Reinhold was not noted for a sense of humor. For a few months, however, Lotte's relationship with her teacher was a reasonably positive one. In the summer of 1908—Lotte was now twenty years old—Frl. Reinhold arranged for her to stay with aristocratic friends of hers at their beautiful estate. They called Lotte their nightingale and were very kind to her. She began to feel less awkward in society. The future Marschallin kept her eyes open.

Meanwhile, in Perleberg, another contact was working for

her good, with the help of highly placed connections. The wife of
the director of the *Ritterschaft* there, Frau von Saldern, had heard
of Lotte's beautiful voice and arranged, through Baron Konrad zu
Putlitz, the president of an agricultural society that often had
dealings with the *Ritterschaft*, to sing for his brother, the *Intendant*
of the Stuttgart Court Theatre, another Baron Putlitz.

The exciting news reached Lotte while she was still on vacation and she was quick to share it with her teacher, who happened to be taking a cure at Bad Kissingen. Frl. Reinhold— who
was swathed in wet compresses as she wrote—took a very chilly
view of such an audition, feeling that Lotte was far from ready,
but giving a grudging consent. She referred Lotte to Professor
Otto Bake, a well-known concert accompanist, for coaching. The
good professor sweat a bit of blood over Lotte's rhythmical insecurity; but with his help she prepared "Elsa's Dream" and
Agathe's aria from *Der Freischütz*. The audition took place at the
Excelsior Hotel in Berlin, where Baron Putlitz happened to be
staying, on September 28, 1908; he was very favorably impressed
with her voice and agreed to hear her again when she felt ready
to accept an engagement.

When she returned to the Gerster School, however, things
took a discouraging turn. Lotte was having difficulties with the
Countess's second aria from *The Marriage of Figaro*. Eva Reinhold
was determined that Lotte should get it right. Week after week,
at every lesson, she insisted upon hammering away at that same
aria. Lotte grew more and more tense and more and more frustrated. It would not come. For years afterward her knees would
shake at the mere mention of the opening words. It became a
complex, a paralysis. She never really enjoyed the role of the
Countess, even though her singing of that very aria was highly
praised, later, in Hamburg, Vienna, and London.

Frl. Reinhold was convinced that Lotte was not working hard
enough. Instead of trying any other approach, she kept forcing
Lotte to struggle through the Countess's aria. Her attitude toward her pupil seemed to have changed drastically ever since the
audition with the *Intendant* from Stuttgart.

One day—it was New Year's Eve—Lotte was summoned before Etelka Gerster herself. The great lady listened with ice in

her eyes. Once again it had to be the Countess's aria. Her verdict
was a harsh one and there was no appeal: she was most dissatisfied; Lotte had sung very badly and done her no credit. Lotte's
studies at the Gerster School were at an end.

It was the blackest day in Lotte's life. She went home numb
and silent. A package was delivered with a cushion she had made
for Frl. Reinhold as a Christmas gift. It was accompanied by the
following letter:

> Dear Fräulein Lehmann:
>
> ...I am sorry that your singing instruction at the Gerster School has
> come to an end in this way, but alas! I have seen this coming for
> months. I can only say that none of my pupils has ever been such a
> disappointment as you have, and this has given me many a dark
> hour. I believe that, if you want to and have to achieve something in
> the future, you should take up a practical career. Only then will you
> come to know the real meaning of hard work, and perhaps you will
> realize later that you weren't doing your duty with all your might.
> Whether you were considered a hard worker at the Hochschule you
> will know best yourself. Finally, I have one request to make. It is
> very painful for me to keep this cushion you gave me, now that you
> are no longer my pupil. You have taken great trouble over it and I
> am sure you will be able to make use of it elsewhere. I don't want to
> hurt your feelings, Fräulein Lehmann, but I really cannot keep it.
> The feeling that you had made any sacrifice for me would be painful
> to me. Now I know that the only sacrifice that you and your parents
> made during your year's study at Frau Gerster's School of Singing
> was only a matter of ten or twelve marks, and that you were unfor-
> tunately unable to appreciate the value of your tuition—for which
> others pay sixty marks a month—its true worth. Frau Gerster re-
> quests me to tell you that your progress is not even that of a mediocre
> pupil, and that even as a paying pupil you would have been expelled.
> Free tuition in her school is only for girls of exceptional attainments;
> moreover Frau Gerster was extremely surprised at the tone of your
> letter to me. She says that I have done more with you by my great
> patience in teaching you than she could have expected, for otherwise
> you would have been dismissed from her School of Singing several
> months ago. How could you expect me to recommend you to any oth-
> er member of the staff in the school when Herr Bake found your in-
> dustry unsatisfactory?
>
> I am, yours sincerely,   Eva Reinhold.

Chapter Three

A PAIR OF MIRACLES

WHAT TO DO NOW? Lotte and Fritz searched the want ads. Perhaps she could be a companion to some older lady and sing to her now and then. At least her voice would be good enough for that. Papa enrolled Lotte in the next starting session of a commercial course. Lotte rallied from her depression and rebelled. She poured out her troubles and hopes in a desperate letter to Mathilde Mallinger, begging for a chance to study with her. Mallinger had been Richard Wagner's first Eva in *Die Meistersinger*—she had even helped him "compose" it, having playfully added a trill to the phrase that closes the ensemble at the end of the Prize Song (Wagner was delighted and wrote that trill into his score). King Ludwig II of Bavaria called her his "immortal Elsa." She had been a star in Berlin and Bayreuth. Now she had a singing class in Berlin. Lotte put her whole heart and soul into that letter.

Papa had never been so angry. How could she be so stubborn? Did she think that all those experts were wrong? Such a letter would surely be the waste of a stamp. Lotte made up her mind that if this letter failed to help, she would never ask her father to invest another penny in her voice. The letter—to the "Royal Prussian *Kammersängerin* and Professor Mathilde Mallinger"— was dated January 9, 1909.

There were long weeks of suspense. Lotte shuddered as the deadline for the commercial school drew near. Finally there came a reply, written on February 18th; it was brief, simple, and offered to hear Lotte and "get acquainted."

Mallinger was a kind of miracle. Lotte's voice began to blossom and grow. She felt free. That was the way she had always dreamed that singing could be. Mallinger had lots of tempera-

14

ment; when impatient with Lotte she was quite capable of
throwing things around—she was after all a prima donna—but
her annoyance was never more than momentary. Basically she
was very kind and motherly. Lotte loved her dearly and thought
of her always with deep gratitude.

Baron Konrad zu Putlitz paid for the lessons, another miracle.
Her letter thanking His Excellency lead to an invitation from his
wife to meet the family at their home. Thus began a close relationship with the Putlitz family that was to play an important part
in Lotte's life. The baroness became a second mother, advising
Lotte on appropriate clothes and many such matters and guiding
her through the intricate social codes of the day. Lotte made
friends with the two daughters, Erika—who was about Lotte's
age—and Elisabeth. As for the baron, Lotte wrote of him as
"goodness personified." He is rumored to have later been in love
with her; but there is no hint of that in her correspondence or in
her warm friendship with the baroness.

The following August, while Frau Mallinger was on vacation
by Starnberg Lake, Lotte was invited to Gross-Pankow, the
Putlitz family estate at Retzin-Prignitz. The other Baron Putlitz,
Rudolf's brother Joachim (the *Intendant* of the Stuttgart Court
Theatre for whom Lotte had auditioned while still at the Etelka
Gerster School), happened to be there as well, with his wife and
daughters, Dora and Adrianna. One morning he asked her to
sing for him again and specifically requested the piece that had so
impressed him before, Agathe's aria from *Der Freischütz*. Lotte's
heart sank. She hadn't looked at that music for months. Here is
her description of that day as she wrote it to her family:

> I sat there totally turned to stone and stared at him in horror. He
> immediately turned a degree or two cooler and asked: "Don't you
> want to?" I stammered something about being "unprepared." But
> the baron [Konrad] was making anxious signals at me from the back-
> ground, so I quickly added "yes." I felt as if I were condemned to
> death. I was dreadfully sure that all would now be over, because how
> could I get up and sing the great Freischütz aria, knowing it would
> be all rusty and full of mistakes? I went inside to practise feverishly.
> The Putlitzes were touchingly kind. Baron Konrad comforted me by
> saying that the Intendant is actually quite unmusical, that he can

only hear through experience whether a voice is effective or not. Little mistakes slip by him completely unnoticed. If I had refused to sing for him I would have ruined his impression of me forever. By evening I was half dead from fear. Both daughters of the Intendant were charming to me. Dora kept holding my hand. Erika gave me a glass of heavy, old Malaga. I sang exceptionally well, without an atom of anxiety. Everyone was enthusiastic. Especially the wife and daughters of the Intendant. Erika told me in confidence that they are the actual "Intendant"... well, I have them entirely on my side. Dora gave me a picture of herself, she's enormously fond of me. The other one, Adrianna, threw her arms around me, and as we were getting ready to drive home she wrapped me so snugly in covers that I could scarcely breathe.

Lotte's vocal progress soon reached the point where she was encouraged to start learning entire operatic roles. Her first was Agathe in *Der Freischütz*, the very prototype of a German heavy lyric soprano (*jugendlich-dramatisch*, young-dramatic, Lotte Lehmann's voice type throughout her career). Her coach for repertoire was Arthur Arndt, who also provided help and advice. Lotte gave singing lessons herself to two or three pupils. That way she could earn a little pocket money (at one mark a lesson).

On October 24, 1909, Lotte sang in a charity concert in Perleberg. It was the first time she had returned to her old home town since the family had moved to Berlin. She sang eleven numbers, including two excerpts from *Lohengrin* and two Schubert lieder. Already in this first recital the reviewers mentioned the warmth of feeling for which she was later so famous:

> ...Miss Lotte Lehmann develops more and more into an exceptionally promising artist. As a result of the noble timbre of her voice, which is pleasing to the ear even in the highest register, she was able not only to interest us outwardly but to touch us more deeply through her warmly felt interpretations, which are always kept within the limits of artistic discipline and refined taste.

Although the reviewer was on the staff of a provincial newspaper, his observations foreshadow the impressions of many a leading critic in the future.

After about a year, Mallinger sent Lotte around to the agents. Accustomed to singing teachers' recommendations, they tended to ignore her. Mallinger told her she should put on a few prima donna airs. Lotte was too natural and down-to-earth to even think of trying to bring *that* off.

Meanwhile, she needed dramatic training. Mallinger sent her to Felix Dahn, stage director at the Royal Opera House in Berlin. With him she studied the role of Agathe from the actor's point of view. The part includes a good deal of spoken dialogue. Lotte, who had always loved reciting plays in her elocution classes with the text in front of her, felt naked and clumsy without the book in her hand. Then there was the visual, the physical side of acting. "Here I stood helpless in an empty space and suddenly had two arms too many and two legs getting in my way." Lotte always thought of herself as having been terribly awkward and self-conscious during her early efforts to act. If there was a step or two on the stage she felt sure she would stumble. Yet her efforts must finally have been pleasing to Herr Dahn, for he wrote to a number of theatres on her behalf and recommended her to Carl Harder, director of the very important E. Drenker Theatrical Agency.

Frau Mallinger and Herr Dahn considered Lotte to be ready now for a first engagement. Baron Konrad zu Putlitz advised her against accepting his brother's offer of a beginner's contract at Stuttgart. Her colleagues would suspect favoritism, in view of her friendship with the family of the *Intendant*, and would resent her. The theatre at Rostock expressed an interest; but Lotte would have had to supply her own costumes, and they would have been too expensive, considering the more than modest salary she would receive there.

Suddenly, an exciting prospect materialized. An entrepreneur with grandiose ideas and—as it turned out—shaky financial support, a certain Max Halpern, arranged to take a company of German singers on tour to Rumania and Bulgaria to present a series of German operas for the first time in those countries. Among the singers were two stars, Rudolf Berger, from the Royal Opera of Berlin, and Marie Rappold, from the Metropolitan in New York. Lotte would be engaged to sing small roles; but Halpern was so taken with her that he spoke of the possibility of Marguerite and Micaëla as well. Dahn was responsible for this offer. Both he and Mallinger were strongly in favor of accepting it.

Papa, on the other hand, was not so sure. Understandably, he wanted assurance that his inexperienced young daughter would be safe in far-off lands among free-and-easy theatrical types. Lotte tried to convince him and the baron that this would be a fabulous opportunity to make up for her lack of ensemble training, and to get stage experience singing with an orchestra among seasoned professionals. The baron wrote to the German ambassador in Bucharest, who made inquiries as to suitable, safe lodgings for a young lady there. Finally Papa asked the conductor, Edmund von Strauss, who had been signed for the tour, whether on his honor as a father he would give his consent to his own daughter. At that gentleman's "decided negative" everyone in the family but Lotte breathed a long sigh of relief. And a good thing too. The entire enterprise collapsed in Sofia. The death of King Edward VII of England put the other courts of Europe into official mourning and kept influential society out of the theatres. Without their patronage neither Bucharest nor Sofia was large enough to support a season of foreign opera. The tour ended in scandal and ruin. Lotte would have found herself out of funds and stranded far from home.

There was an audition in June with the director of the Hamburg opera, Herr *Geheimrat* (Privy Councillor) Max Bachur. In July came the signed contract, her first ever. A landmark. It was of course a beginner's contract. That meant small roles and corresponding pay (three years at 200 marks a month the first year, increasing by 100 each of the next two years).

Her parents would not dream of letting her live in Hamburg all alone. They had heard hair-raising tales of the pitfalls of theatrical life. It was decided that Papa would retire—although that meant a sacrifice of part of the pension that had been his goal throughout his working life—and that the family would move with her to Hamburg. Only Fritz would have to stay behind in Berlin for the sake of his job. He moved into shabby quarters, always ready to put Lotte first, to sacrifice his own ambitions for what he recognized to be her greater talent. No one appreciated her achievements and her successes more than Fritz. No one was happier about her freshly launched career.

Chapter Four

A CHAMBERMAID IN VALHALLA

AUGUST 25, 1910. First rehearsal: Gerhilde in *Die Walküre*.
Felix Landau, the coach, thundered out the "Ride of the
Valkyries" at the piano and Lotte, with a quick prayer and
a big breath, let loose a hearty "Hojotoho!" Since there are nine
Valkyries in the opera, eight of them often singing at once, it is
understandable that Lotte could have been slightly confused as to
which one she was trying to sight-read:

> I am to sing Gerlinde, one of the Valkyries. Good Lord, is that a lot
> of shrieking! I can't say I'm crazy about the part. But it's quite nice,
> not at all easy, and one can at least show something.

Lotte meant Gerhilde, though she was later to sing Ortlinde, too.
It was actually a long time before she sang either one.

Wanting to arrive prepared, Lotte had written to ask which
roles she would be singing. She was told she would find out
when rehearsals started. A raw beginner could generally count
on small parts only; they would be quickly learned in a few coaching sessions.

> So much is expected. I had to sight-read everything. Although my
> heart was beating fearfully, I plowed right in with death-defying
> recklessness—and even though I sometimes strayed hideously far off
> the field—it turned out better than I had feared. I was praised with
> a smile: "Well, at least you have courage." Yes, that I have. And the
> happy feeling of hope.

The day before she had ventured bravely into the director's
office, armed with warnings about the casting couch from worried aunts and uncles. Herr Bachur's "absent-minded look of fatherly benevolence" was a great relief to her. "This was no
seducer...my virtue seemed assured...."

19

*He introduced me to the conductor, Gustav Brecher, the assistant
general manager, Siegfried Jelenko, and the new conductor, Otto
Klemperer. They are all quite friendly and nice. Let's say: condes-
cendingly kind. I feel a bit like a baby, rather helpless. People are
running this way and that, everywhere groups of chattering, laughing theatre people are standing about, nonchalantly staring at me—
but they seem to be a cheerful lot.*

*I sang for Brecher and Klemperer. They found my voice very
lovely—but too sentimental. I've noticed already that the singers sing
quite differently here. They belt it out a bit brutally. Frau Mallinger
always insisted that a tone sound beautiful and round. Landau, the
coach, said to me today: "You are singing too much. Not so softly. You
have to shout against a full orchestra playing ff—so please sing loudly and with a cutting edge!" Well, I'm going to guard against that.
I'm not going to force. I shall do it as Frau Mallinger told me to.
Something is wrong if you have to try to "shout."*

There were serious financial problems for the family. The
apartment where they had hoped to stay rent-free was not available after all. Lotte's first pay check (200 marks) would not be due
until October. Moving had been expensive. The apartment they
found for 160 marks "with central heating" was four flights up, a
disadvantage for Mama, who had over-exerted herself and was ill
again. Papa had asked for an advance on his pension; it came as a
shock to learn that the entire amount would be deducted on the
first of October, instead of bit by bit over several quarters. Lotte's
first exciting months in the theatre were overshadowed by constant stress at home. Mama was painfully worried about Fritz,
living on his own in Berlin in what she was sure must be great
disorder and privation. Papa was in despair about how to pay the
bills. Lotte felt that the decision of her parents to move with her
to Hamburg had been a great mistake. It was humiliating to have
to ask Baron Putlitz for help, but there was nowhere else to turn.
The baron came to the rescue with cash for the most pressing
needs and a load of potatoes and apples to keep hunger at bay.

Meanwhile, each new day brought new experiences at the
theatre which Lotte was quick to share with Fritz by letter. The
role of her debut was the Second Boy in *The Magic Flute*.

*I'm getting more and more accustomed to theatre routine. Today
was the orchestra rehearsal for Zauberflöte. It went very well.*

*Brecher conducted. Everyone was so nice, you have no idea. I
hadn't imagined it like this at all…. Incidentally, it is quite helpful to
play the child for the time being…. They always call me "die Kleine"
[the little one]! "Have you heard, die Kleine has never sung with
an orchestra before." I am naturally scared to death and lament to
everyone within earshot that I am dying from fear of the orchestra.
And I encounter only smiling, kindly faces.*

Elisabeth Schumann, who turned out to be one of Lotte's
dearest life-long friends, had been in the theatre for a year already and showed her the ropes. They went shopping for make-
up together. *"Die kleine Schumann,"* as Lotte called her in the letters to Fritz, brought her up-to-date on theatre gossip—Brecher,
for example, was the lover of Edyth Walker, the star soprano
from America, who indirectly ran the opera house. Lotte was unaccustomed to the free-and-easy ways of her male colleagues at
rehearsal. Schumann advised her not to appear to be a prude.

Lotte to Fritz:

*You can't imagine anything more gemütlich than those rehearsals.
What a lot of tomfoolery they are all up to! They act so familiar. If
one of them pinches your cheek or puts his arm around your waist it
doesn't mean a thing. If a girl would make a fuss about it she'd be
finished.*

The great night arrived, September 2, 1910, the debut of Lotte
Lehmann. According to the program that has been preserved,
Elisabeth Schumann (not Magda Lohse, as Lehmann remembered it years later in her autobiography) was the First Boy, Annemarie Birkenström the Third. Putting on the makeup was a
new experience and great fun. Everyone told Lotte that her features were of a type that would project very well on the stage.

The theatre supplied the costumes, but the soloists had to buy
their own footwear and rent the wigs, an unanticipated expense
for Lotte. She felt painfully self-conscious in her Second Boy's
skimpy tunic; she kept pulling it down to cover as much of herself as possible until the seams nearly split. The tights she had
been given were practically worn through; she had had to buy
new ones, another irritating outlay. She must have been braver
than she later remembered; or perhaps she just wanted her
brother to be proud of her courage:

Well, yesterday was the eventful first night! My first debut. It went very well. My part came off without a hitch, Brecher came up after the first act and shook hands with me as he passed by, saying, "very good, Miss Lehmann, keep it up." The stage director also praised me. Mama and Papa think I "acted wonderfully," they thought my movements were "so distinguished!" Well, for the Second Boy that's about all you can do. I felt no trace of fear, we had been joking around so much in the wings. Singing with an orchestra is a great feeling; I can't understand why the other beginners all groan about it. You wouldn't believe how nice everyone is. They all came up to me and asked how I felt the first time; naturally I pretended to be in mortal terror, which everyone found very "sweet." One thing is very good: it is definitely not the custom to go out somewhere after a performance. Everyone goes home. Unless, of course, there is a special occasion. When Caruso comes in October, for instance, there will probably be some sort of banquet to honor him…I looked very good in my makeup. Everyone was surprised how well I made myself up the first time. The costumes are charming, all silk (Egyptian). The decor is really quite magnificent!…Incidentally, there is no envy among the singers of the little roles. Schumann begged me to take over the part of Pepa in Tiefland, which she doesn't want to sing, and [Helene] Brandes asked me to study Frasquita [in Carmen], which of course I shall do. I will also learn the part of Siebel in Margarethe [Faust], just in case….

Lotte took full advantage of every opportunity to learn by watching and listening. When she was not singing she was generally in the audience, in the artists' box or in complimentary seats with her father or mother, learning the repertoire. She was thrilled with Edith Walker's Brünnhilde:

I tell you, she is not to be described. There is just one word: phenomenal. Yesterday [the evening before the Zauberflöte rehearsal] I saw Die Walküre. It is overwhelming. And what a cast…it was all glorious. And Walker! She is as great an actress as she is a singer. When Wotan cast her out, she screamed and fell. I tell you, such a scream! I feel as if it is still ringing in my ears. It penetrated to the very marrow of my bones; I was all tense with concentration, that's how it affected me. Horrifying. Simply marvelous. Who in Berlin can duplicate this Brünnhilde?

Lotte was always direct and straight-forward by nature. She

generally said what she thought, and that sometimes caused her
trouble, later in Vienna among all the *Kammersängerinnen*, and
even here in Hamburg. Frau Hindermann, who sang the Queen
of the Night at Lotte's debut, was a friend of a friend of Lita zu
Putlitz. She took Lotte under her wing and tried to keep her
from putting her foot in her mouth:

> *She counteracted a stupidity of mine. I was saying in front of others
> that Councillor Bachur had held out to me the possibility of singing
> Mignon. She quickly interrupted: "I consider it out of the question
> that you should sing Mignon." Afterwards she took me aside and
> said: "But child, you have to be more diplomatic. You said that in
> front of a singer, Frl. Brandes, who has been longing for the part of
> Mignon for ages. Something like that could do you damage. One has
> to be very discreet in the theatre." Often I say something that seems
> to me utterly harmless and safe—and later I notice: oh, that was
> careless again! But I'll learn, all right. Next summer when I come to
> Gross-Pankow, I shall probably have become quite false!! That may
> be practical for the theatre—but I would find it horrible if deviousness
> ever became a habit with me.*

Lotte took her work very seriously, and that bothered some of
her colleagues. They struck her as a rather frivolous crew, but she
was grateful for their friendliness, nevertheless, and enjoyed the
relaxed atmosphere at rehearsals:

> *I'm simply amazed how jolly they all are. I am used to being so dead-
> ly earnest about my work—at Frau Mallinger's it would have been
> unthinkable for us to cut up during our lessons. But here! I can't be
> quite that merry myself, it's all too strange and new to me. Recently
> someone said to me: "This must be your first engagement. Your ex-
> pression is so naive and astonished." — One learns unbelievably
> much at rehearsals. I go to every orchestra rehearsal. The others all
> say: "Ha, she'll soon get over her eagerness." But I won't...I am so
> firmly convinced that honest effort will lead me to my goal. All the
> conductors like my voice—if I only had the chance to sing something
> that suits me, like Micaëla or Mignon. But I shall train myself to be
> a heroine of diplomacy, and that means above all: wait patiently.
> Fatal words! And yet unavoidably necessary. First I have to prove
> myself in little parts, before they will trust me with bigger ones. Ah,
> I'm so happy to be here in Hamburg....*

Lotte's second role was all of four words long: "*Wolfram von*

Eschenbach, beginne!" Not even solo; three others shared the line with her. She sang the Second Page in *Tannhäuser* on September 6th, the first in a series of *Edelknaben* (pages) for the Inseparable Four, Lotte, Magda Lohse, Grete Schlegel, and Annemarie Birkenström, who were later to perform the same distinguished service in *Lohengrin*, with twice as many words (eight) for the same fee. As a matter of fact, Lotte almost lost the chance to sing in *Tannhäuser*; at one of the rehearsals the Second Page made a mistake:

"Wolfram von Eschenbach, beginne!" *was a discord—and what a furious look Brecher gave me.*

"Give that part to someone else," *he declared categorically.*

It was my first painful experience at the theatre. I wept bitter tears. Annemarie *comforted me:*

"You should be glad," *she said, "that you've got out of that silly Page's part. It's the sort of part that can stick with you for years. Brecher will soon forget that you went wrong—and you needn't sing it any longer."*

But I wanted to sing it...I wanted to sing absolutely anything just to learn not to regard the stage as foreign territory. So I waited for Brecher outside the rehearsal room and when he came out I burst into tears and begged him to give me back my Page's part. He looked surprised and amused. It was certainly the first time a soloist had ever begged for that little part that everyone is glad not to have to sing.

"Very well," *he said, keeping a straight face with difficulty, "if you promise never to sing a wrong note again, I shall let mercy temper justice."*

Every now and then there would be talk of a small solo part, like Flora in *La traviata*—Lotte arranged to borrow a party gown and some stage jewelry, for it was the custom in those days to play that opera in contemporary dress. But Flora never materialized.

Finally, after being a second boy and a second page, she was cast in a female part that even had a name: her first real solo role, Freia in *Das Rheingold*, with the great Arthur Nikisch as guest conductor. The performance date was exactly three weeks after her debut. Lotte was torn to shreds in the newspapers:

...Fräulein Lehmann played Freia with touching clumsiness...about

the vocal qualities of the young performer, whose throat seemed to be constricted with nervousness, nothing can be said... (Fremdenblatt)

...With resignation one had to make the best of the vocally as well as dramatically helpless Freia of Frl. Lehmann... (Correspondent)

Another reviewer amused some of his readers with the opinion that among the gods of Valhalla Fräulein Lehmann's Freia seemed to be a chambermaid.

Such reviews are understandably devastating to a young and insecure performer. But Lotte showed amazing spunk and spirit. After quoting every dismal word in a letter to Fritz, she went on to say:

I am not at all discouraged by the bad reviews, though I was furious at first. I pleased Brecher, that is the main thing. He said I did very well for a beginner and surpassed his expectations...

Lotte's reign as a goddess turned out to be brief. Soon she was back with the page boys. Her repertoire was enriched with one of the bridesmaids in *Der Freischütz* (at least a small solo), an apprentice in *Die Meistersinger*, and a choirboy in *Der Prophet* (Meyerbeer, in German, of course).

She began to pester the directors, conductors, and coaches—in fact any one who would listen—for better parts. Otto Klemperer fascinated her.

That is a wonderful human being; he looks like a mad genius. I found him enormously interesting, this thin young man as tall as a lamppost with the mournful, burning eyes and pale cheeks. I invested him with romantic glamour and had quite a passion for him...

Apparently she began to fascinate Klemperer too. Soon she was fighting him off in deserted stair wells and he was chasing her around the furniture in empty rehearsal rooms. The passion on her part, referred to above, actually came much later, after he was hotly pursuing Elisabeth Schumann. Lehmann and Klemperer shared a long friendship, but never a simultaneous passion. In 1910 she may have found him "fascinating," but his passes were most unwelcome.

This Klemperer is a disgustingly fresh fellow. Yesterday I had a rehearsal with him, with three other singers. I happened to come a bit too early and was alone with him. Naturally he swept me into his arms with that stormy "temperament" of his. I fought him off with all my strength. And then he asked me with deep surprise whether I didn't love him. I said: "No, Herr Kapellmeister, not the least bit— not at all." And he simply didn't believe it. It's really laughable. Fortunately, he does not hold my resistance against me. He was very friendly afterwards.

I could laugh myself sick over Klemperer. He looks so melancholy whenever he sees me. If he were not such a brutal type, for whom a harmless "flirt" is out of the question, it might be very pleasant for me; as it is, he is a much too dangerous human being.

Four weeks later:

Lately Klemperer impressed me very much. He is a remarkable person. As I was looking at the rehearsal schedule one evening, he came up to me and said: "Sing something for me." I went with him into a rehearsal room. As usual, he tried to embrace me again. As usual, I resisted, for Klemperer is the kind of man against whom one has to defend oneself—he is like a beast. Then I sang the Micaëla for him. He praised many things about it. And then he said: "What do you want now from me? You want the part? And you think I will give it to you without further ado. You overestimate my power. I have nothing to say. I never do the casting for the operas I conduct. I shall propose it, but I cannot guarantee the result." And he looked at me with something like contempt. Too bad that I have so little to do with him. I must now try to convince him that I don't want to take advantage of his weakness for me. Though in fact I do. But I like that about him.

There was constant tension back home. Lotte regretted that her parents had ever decided to move with her to Hamburg. They were always complaining and Lotte, already nervous over her work at the theatre, confessed to Fritz that she was ready to "climb up the wall" at the eternal "back to Berlin!" Kindly Mama had become "the incarnation of reproach." She felt that Lotte had changed.

And I have changed. Do you know, I'm often amazed at the toughness and the energy that keep me above water. I had been afraid that I would lose heart a little. But no, I feel what I am tempted to call an almost frivolous optimism, a goal-conscious certainty. And that is foreign to Mama. She cannot understand that I no longer need to "seek refuge in the bosom of my parents," weeping and longing for help, as I used to now and then.

On November 18th, members of the Hamburg Opera ensemble presented a concert in Altona, one of the suburbs. Lotte sang Micaëla's aria, along with lieder by Franz and Reger, and had her first taste of local applause. The word spread around at the opera house, how beautifully she had sung and how enthusiastically the audience had responded. Soon she had a chance at a Sunday matinée to sing a really grateful role, Anna in *Die lustigen Weiber von Windsor*. Anna has a big aria and a delightful love-duet, besides the ensembles and the dialogue. The audience took her to its heart. This time her father describes it all to Fritz:

> *Dear Fritz! Today Lotte had a great day that will probably be decisive for her whole life. Whereas her vocal qualities as Freia in Rheingold could scarcely be judged, the Anna in Lustige Weiber gave her a most beautiful chance to shine. Her success was—to skip to the point—sensational, especially so when one considers the usual attitude of the Hamburg audiences toward newcomers. Lotte looked enchanting, bringing, in her whole personality and her voice, everything to the role that was called for. From her first entrance she seemed to be as sure of herself as if she were a seasoned artist, and without an orchestra rehearsal she made no mistakes, either in acting or in singing...Lotte passed the test brilliantly. A stone fell from all our hearts. Now I no longer have to worry about Lotte's future; she has a fine career in front of her.*

A rather different view was expressed, years later, by Siegfried Jelenko, the assistant general manager of the Hamburg Opera, in an article he wrote after Lotte Lehmann had become a beloved star:

> *Finally she was entrusted with the part of Anna...which she sang satisfactorily, but, but—during the aria she continually beat time with her left hand and sang, so to speak, with her legs. It was touching and side-splitting. But the brilliance of her glorious soprano won a triumph.*

In spite of Jelenko's negative impressions, the reviews were without exception very encouraging:

> *...Frl. Lehmann charmed the eye and the ear equally, with a highly graceful portrayal of Jungfer Anna, born of the spirit of the Biedermeier era... (Hamburger Fremdenblatt)*

> *...Frl. Lehmann was a charming Jungfer Anna in every way. As*

she sang it, the duet with Fenton was a high point of yesterday's per-
formance... (Hamburger Correspondent)

...and Frl. Lehmann as a charming Jungfer Anna, whose loveliness
of appearance and refinement and purity of vocalism were equally
pleasing... (Hamburger Nachrichten)

Nevertheless Lehmann herself often referred to her early
awkwardness on stage. Those who saw her act, or saw her direct
singing actors, can hardly imagine her as ever having been clumsy as an actress. She was often called "the singing Duse." Yet in
1910 that particular talent was far from evident. Jelenko's article
describes what must have been a real problem at first:

> At her audition we were struck by the warm timbre of her bright so-
> prano. She appeared uncommonly unassuming, even tim-
> id...Wherever one placed her, there she stuck, with a touching lack
> of concern or affectation. After the first rehearsals...conductors
> shook their heads, saying she had no sense of rhythm in her body,
> and doubting whether she would be adequate even in little roles. The
> sensuous sound of her voice seduced me; I pleaded for patience..."one
> can, one *must* try her out for a year!"
> The winter went by, and spring had brought no great progress;
> her singing was probably more secure, but her acting ability?!—
> Attempts to infuse a little dramatic life into her would be answered
> with such an uncomprehending, naïve cheerfulness that one would
> have been brought to the point of despair, had not the beautiful sound
> of her voice cautioned further patience.

Even before her successful performance as Anna, Lotte had
shared an exciting secret with Fritz. Brecher, the leading conductor at the opera, had promised her the part of Sophie in *Der
Rosenkavalier* in the première, at which Strauss himself would be
present. She was to say nothing to her colleagues but to study
the difficult role very diligently. Every day she was given at least
one musical rehearsal. It seemed a sure thing. She fell in love
with the enchanting new music, and threw herself into the part
with enormous dedication and energy.

> *Dear Fritz! A great piece of luck! I mustn't rejoice too much—it is so*
> *great, that it's almost unbelievable. I have been given a LEADING*
> *role in Rosenkavalier by Strauss...The part is as if it had been writ-*
> *ten for me. Naïve-sentimental. Captivating. But difficult—madly*

difficult...I am speechless that I should get such a part. The music is wonderful. Completely delightful. It all sounds colossally playful and elegant. Edyth Walker will play the Rosenkavalier. Imagine that, me with such a partner! The Rosenkavalier is a very young prince [sic] whom I marry at the end...

Lotte did not realize that the role would be double cast; that she would be competing with Elisabeth Schumann for the première; and that everything would depend upon the staging rehearsals scheduled for January. Lotte was generally thought to have the more beautiful voice. But Elisabeth was at that time a much more graceful actress; she also had come to the theatre a year earlier than Lotte and had far more experience, far more "routine." Jelenko was the stage director, and we know what *he* thought of Lotte as an actress. Edyth Walker, the Octavian, wanted Schumann as her Sophie and that was that. So Elisabeth Schumann sang Sophie in the Hamburg première of *Der Rosenkavalier*—a role which she practically owned for the next quarter-century—and Lotte had a crushing disappointment.

> *At the time, of course, I thought it an atrocious injustice that I hadn't been allowed to do the first performance. I regarded Elisabeth as the world's greatest intriguer—a role which, Heaven knows, was quite foreign to her nature—and felt myself misunderstood and ousted from my rightful place...Elisabeth, always a good colleague, was well aware of my unjustified mistrust. She took great pains to be especially nice to me...*

That was a very short-lived shadow in a very long and happy friendship.

Back to the pants parts. Max in *Fortunios Lied* (by Offenbach) and the Sandman in *Hänsel und Gretel*. Then came Lola in *Cavalleria rusticana*.

> *When I was just a beginner I had to learn the part of Lola rather quickly and substitute for a fellow-singer who was taken ill. It was one of the first roles which I had to "portray." I was so clumsy and so horribly inhibited that I could scarcely move or stand on the stage, and the self-assured Lola was the very last person whom I was capable of representing. In deathly fear I stared at the conductor, possessed by the single desire to sing "correctly," fearing that otherwise I would never be given another role. Why under these circumstances*

I had any desire for another role is not clear to me, for the tortures which I endured I wouldn't wish on any enemy. I really must have been something catastrophic, for after this performance even a very good friend advised me to give up the stage for ever.

It is hard to imagine that her acting could have been quite as hopeless as she paints it. Before the end of her first season she was given the chance to sing Agathe in *Der Freischütz* for one performance in Altona. That was a major leading role for her *Fach* (voice type) and an important step forward. Her fun-loving colleagues, knowing she would be nervous in her insecurity, did whatever they could to befuddle her backstage. At her last entrance she is supposed to cry out: "Do not shoot! I am the dove!" They pretended to be prompting her and whispered from the wings: "I am the goose, I am the goose." Fortunately, she did not fall into their trap.

Chapter Five

LIKE FLYING IN A DREAM

LOTTE'S SECOND SEASON in Hamburg was again dominated by page boys, fourteen times in *Tannhäuser* and ten times in *Lohengrin*, apprentices in *Meistersinger* (eight times) and a choirboy in *The Prophet*, plus such new variations as one of the *Friedensboten* (Messengers of Peace) in *Rienzi* and—a promotion—the First instead of the Second Boy in *Die Zauberflöte* (five times). To the Sandman was added the Dewman (*Hänsel und Gretel*). Petticoats replaced the pants for repeats of Jungfer Anna and Agathe. On October 14th she sang the attractive role of May in *Das Heimchen am Herd* by Karl Goldmark (based on *The Cricket on the Hearth* by Dickens), opposite Elisabeth Schumann as Heimchen, to quite gratifying reviews, such as: "Frl. Lehmann was a lovely May."

But the really special event of her second season took place the very next day. Lotte sang Eurydice in *Orpheus* (Gluck) on a double bill with Caruso in *I pagliacci*. Caruso stood in the wings to hear her and was obviously very much impressed. He came up to her afterwards, saying, "*Brava, brava! Che bella, magnifica voce! Una voce italiana!*" At supper later she was seated next to the great *divo*; he signed his name on her fan and drew her a caricature of himself, later sending her a photograph inscribed: *à Mlle Lotte Lehmann (la charmante et jolie Euridice) très sincèrement Enrico Caruso Hamburg 1911*. In Lotte's presence he promptly asked the direction to cast her as Micaëla opposite his Don José in the next performance of *Carmen*. Since she had not yet sung the role and there was no time for rehearsals, that request had to be denied; but when he asked that she be his Mimi in Leoncavallo's version of *La Bohème* the following season, the assistant general manager gave his promise (which, by the way, was never kept).

31

There is a piquant epilogue to Lotte's contact with Caruso:

> The next day I received a telegram from his secretary: Signor Com-
> mendatore Enrico Caruso invited me to have supper with him at his
> hotel after the Carmen performance. I sat with the wire before me,
> frozen with terror.
>
> I was just a great baby and imagined that temptation had come
> to me in the guise of the loveliest voice in the world.... So I fetched
> my French dictionary and wrote a polite refusal. Quickly, before I
> could regret it, I took it round myself to the hotel. On the way there I
> passed the theatre and heard Hindermann saying to Fleischer-Edel:
> "Will you be at Caruso's after the performance tonight?" I stopped
> and asked whether Caruso was giving a party today. Yes! an enor-
> mous dinner at his hotel.... Oh, what luck that I had found out in
> time! So it was not for me alone—my dark yet dangerously alluring
> presentiments of a chambre separé were quite unjustified. My letter
> of refusal fluttered to the ground in little pieces!

The part of Micaëla finally did come her way, but only after Caruso had left.

At the end of Lotte's second season Bachur retired and a new
director, Dr. Hans Loewenfeld, took his place, bringing with him
Felix von Weingartner as his first conductor. Along with Weingartner came his wife, Lucille Marcel, as star soprano. Brecher
and Walker were gone. Klemperer, fortunately, was still there
and had persistent faith in Lotte's voice. Loewenfeld, on the other hand, soon lost interest in her. He was a well-known stage director, primarily concerned with the dramatic side of his productions. As an actress, Lotte failed to meet his expectations in her
new role as Martha in Der Evangelimann by Wilhelm Kienzl. Furthermore, he was not particularly impressed with her voice,
which he found lovely in quality but not quite big enough. Lotte
had already decided to do some work on her voice, having had almost daily lessons with Katharina Fleischer-Edel, one of the
singers at the Hamburg Opera that she most admired. Then she
went to a teacher, Alma Schadow, who, though not the artist
that Mallinger had been, was noted as a brilliant technician and
voice builder. During the summer vacation before her third season, she worked very intensively with Frau Schadow, following

her teacher to a lakeside resort, where she took her singing lessons in a bathing suit. Lotte was thrilled with her progress.

Tensions at home had not diminished. It was decided that Lotte would get a room of her own, across the street from the theatre, and that her parents would also move, into another apartment. Mama was sick, as usual; moving was a strain; and again, as usual, there were money problems and messages of distress to Fritz, who always tried to help as best he could, though it invariably meant stinting on his own needs. Lotte asked for an advance on her salary; it was refused. Then she tried to borrow from a bank; but none of her colleagues was willing to co-sign the loan. Once again the baron saved the day. And again he also sent sacks of potatoes, fruit, and vegetables. Lotte, by the way, became expert at sewing her own clothes at this time.

The third season offered another round of page boys (the last!), with five times each in *Lohengrin* and *Tannhäuser*. More gratefully, there were also several Annas, Agathes, and Micaëlas (though not with Caruso). Soon a Rhinemaiden, two Valkyries, and the Shepherd Boy in *Tannhäuser* were added to her chores, the last bringing her some nice reviews. But Lotte was ambitious and yearned for the opportunity to grow as an artist through the chance to perform more challenging parts. Klemperer advised her to try to get an engagement at a smaller theatre, where she would regularly be able to sing the leading roles that belong to her *Fach*. Since she was under contract, that meant getting a release from Loewenfeld. Lotte suspected he would be only too glad to be rid of her. She was scheduled, finally, to sing Sophie in *Rosenkavalier*, with Elisabeth Schumann as Octavian. Klemperer had arranged for the director of the Wiesbaden Opera to come and hear Lotte in the performance. Her agent also sent her provisional contracts with several theatres (Königsberg, Düsseldorf, Chemnitz, Magdeburg, and Freiburg) and told her she could sign whichever one she preferred. Suddenly Loewenberg, who had agreed to let her go, changed his mind and refused to release her. Unconsciously, she had pulled off an age-old theatre trick: if you want something from the director ask for your dismissal. No doubt Loewenfeld was impressed that those other five theatres were interested in her. He offered to work on the acting of Elsa with her, and spoke of later giving her Eva as well. Now her prospects began to look a little brighter.

The *Rosenkavalier* went very well for Lotte, with mostly very decent reviews (though Schumann fared rather poorly in the papers).

> ...*Fräulein Lehmann sang and played "die Fräulein Faninal" very delightfully—the high notes were of an unbelievable lightness and ease, with blinding brilliance....* (Hamburgischer Correspondent)

> ...*The young singer, Frl. Lehmann, stood out all the more sympathetically, who, through the gracefulness of her appearance as well as her clear soprano, gave to the character of Sophie, along with a light hint of cloister incense, all the charm and all the sweetness of her being....* (Hamburger Nachrichten)

There was one negative one too:

> ...*Frl. Lehmann is still too stuck in beginner's diapers to have grown into a Sophie, in spite of relatively beautiful vocal resources.That was a casting mistake which should be rectified in repeat performances.*

Then came the breakthrough.

> *One day Klemperer called me..."Do you think you could manage to take on Elsa's part? You'd only have a week...we're in a fix. I've persuaded Dr. Loewenfeld to let you risk it. Well—do you think you can do it?"*
>
> *Did I think I could do it!*
>
> *I had, of course, studied Elsa's part by myself and came proudly to the rehearsal. But if I thought I knew the part, I realized my mistake after the first five minutes. Klemperer sat at the piano like an evil spirit, thumping on it with long hands like tiger's claws, dragging my terrified voice into the fiery vortex of his fanatical will. Elsa's dreamy serenity became a rapturous ecstasy, her anxious pleading a challenging demand. For the first time I felt my nervous inhibitions fall from me, and I sank into the flame of inner experience. I had always wanted to sing like this—it was like flying in a dream: a bodiless gliding through blissful eternity.... But usually one wakens from this lovely kind of dream with the terror of falling. And so I was dragged back from those ecstasies by Klemperer's voice saying: "No idea of the part. We must work hard if you're to manage it."*
>
> *I managed it.*

*I sang Elsa in spite of the indignant looks of Pennarini, my Lo-
hengrin, in spite of the producer's shrugged shoulders, in spite of
Klemperer's discouraging interpolations at the orchestral rehearsal....*

*Theo Drill-Orridge was singing Ortrud on a visiting engagement,
and her eyes grew wider as she noticed at the rehearsal how simply
everyone was against me—even Klemperer, who grew furious every
time I forgot anything, seemed to lose all confidence in me and shouted up: "What's the matter? Has the big part gone to your head?"*

Then came the performance. Lotte's letter to Baroness Putlitz
captures her elation:

*Now, I believe, much has been reached. The Elsa was such a great
and unusual success, the audience applauded in a frenzy and kept
calling "Elsa," there were about eighteen curtain calls! Dr. Loewenfeld, Weingartner, everyone expressed appreciation. Naturally now
there is no more talk of any engagement elsewhere. I believe that it
was the most beautiful day of my life. It was as if I had drunk too
much wine, everything was spinning around before my eyes.
Wherever I looked there were hands reaching out to me in congrat-
ulation, all I could hear were voices shouting "bravo." There is something very special about applause.*

*And that the role was Elsa! I sang with such enjoyment! The
nervousness melted away in a few minutes—I forgot the stage and
the audience. How remarkable that was, as I was coming down the
steps on my way to the cathedral and everyone was singing "Hail to
thee, Elsa of Brabant!" That was so festive and so beautiful. It was
a great day.*

The critics confirmed her success:

*...At last an Elsa who was only Elsa and could not just as well have
been Ortrud. To many it may have seemed a risk to entrust this
great role to the young, inexperienced Lotte Lehmann. And it was a
risk; but not an experiment, for the basic prerequisites, which offered
at least the possibility of success, were in this case present. The swan
knights we have known here have seldom rushed to rescue a more
enchanting, more tender Elsa, so touched with romantic magic, as
she was outwardly portrayed by Frl. Lehmann. An Elsa without the
excesses of the usual prima donna, an Elsa who was all innocence
and guilelessness. Artistically too, Frl. Lehmann fulfills her task for*

the present in a way that is entirely her own. She forgets most of what she had planned and what others have prompted her to do; she gives herself up completely to the impressions of the moment and to the dramatic situation. That is very good, for in that way she keeps for her Elsa a perfect, almost touching unaffectedness; in that way she is not tempted to make what is already complicated appear to be even more so than it really is, and in that way she avoids any farfetched philosophical obscurities and any false theatricality.... (Hamburger Fremdenblatt)

...That new Elsa was Fräulein Lotte Lehmann. Outwardly a picture that could assure sympathy and support for the role she was to portray, through the warmth of her feelings and through the profusion of youthfully fresh, beautiful tones at her disposal, at least as much as through her appearance. A slight nervousness that was noticeable at the very beginning—understandable in the heavy reponsibility of a first appearance in a leading role—was soon suppressed. Thus the careful treatment of the text and that of the melodic line came into their own, no less the agreeable evenness of her vocal resources.... (Neue Hamburger Zeitung)

...When one considers what it means for such a young singer to be suddenly at the center of interest, her performance was of astounding assurance.... (Hamburger Neueste Nachrichten)

...An Elsa...of touching grace in her appearance and in her singing...An Elsa so human, so unpretentious, such as one does not often get to see and hear.... They will tell her that this or that must be done differently, they will try to instill in her all the experiences of all the Elsas who ever stood on a stage. If she relies entirely upon her own experiences, she will be the Elsa that Elsa should be and must be.... (Hamburgischer Correspondent)

The next performance of *Lohengrin* created a sensation of a different sort. It was the day after Christmas and Lotte was again the Elsa. The husband of Elisabeth Schumann was sitting in the first row, directly behind Klemperer, who had just finished conducting the last measures. Schumann's husband shouted: "Klemperer, turn around!" and struck him across the face with a riding crop so forcefully that he was knocked to the ground. Klemperer picked himself up, turned to the audience, and said: "Herr Puritz struck me because I am in love with his wife." The incident became a famous theatre scandal. Here is the back-ground, as Lotte reported it to her baroness:

> After the performance [Lotte's first Elsa] Klemperer ran away with [Elisabeth] Schumann! She leaves a splendid position, a nice, kind husband who worships her, to whom she owes her operatic training, who bought her everything, her trousseau, her furniture. She was married for six months and everyone thought that she loved him sincerely. As an architect he had a good social position, earned about 30,000 marks a year. And she takes off into the blue with a man who has nothing but his genius, which however goes hand in hand with a nervousness that borders on madness. He wooed her for a long, long time with stubborn persistence. Three months ago she said to me: "This can't go on. Klemperer pursues me in a very compromising way. I love my husband and do not want Klemperer to come between us." And then the day before her flight she said to our mutual singing teacher: "I love Klemperer to the point of madness. I have to leave my husband. Even if I am destroyed, I must go with Klemperer." I feel so sorry for her that I almost forget her lack of conscience where her husband is concerned....

After a few days Schumann and Klemperer came back together and moved into a hotel.

> Her husband then took her away by force, had her committed to a hospital for observation of her mental condition. After fourteen days she was declared to be healthy, released and—went back to Klemperer. Her husband sent him a challenge to a duel, which he rejected.

There follows the story of the notorious *Lohengrin* incident; then the aftermath:

> For me it was an unforgettably horrifying evening. Klemperer has now been dismissed and yesterday evening he ran away with Schumann. She was supposed to be dismissed as well, but at the pleading of her husband her dismissal was changed to four weeks' leave of absence. He maintains that she is sick. And when she comes back to her senses he wants to take her back!! Whether Dr. Loewenfeld will ever let her perform here again, however, is very questionable. Isn't it all frightful? I feel sorry for all three in my heart. I cannot condemn Schumann, as so many do. This sort of thing, after all, is not exactly child's play. She must have honestly struggled against her feelings. Oh, the awakening will be terrible for her.

Fritz's widow, Theresia Lehmann, recalls a final vignette, as he described it: Lotte, dusting herself off onstage after her final swoon, had heard the commotion out in the audience; she could not resist peeking out to satisfy her curiosity. Fritz (who had been in Hamburg for Christmas) never forgot the sight of Elsa's blonde head, crown and all, thrust between the curtains, nor her look of stunned amazement at the pandemonium that was rocking the opera house.

The success of Lotte's Elsa insured that she would generally be cast in grateful leading roles. Besides such smaller parts as the Mermaid in *Oberon* and Echo in *Ariadne auf Naxos*, for both of which she received very favorable mention in the press, she appeared as Irene in Wagner's *Rienzi*, Antonia in *The Tales of Hoffman* (to use the familiar English title), and Dorabella in *Così fan tutte* before the season was over.

Besides the success of her own achievements, luck was on her side in another way as well: the woman who had been engaged as "first" young-dramatic soprano had a fiasco. Her failure meant that Lotte could move up a notch. "Thus one rises up over others," she ruefully wrote to the baroness, "and unlearns compassion and thinks only of one's own advantage."

She began to prepare Elisabeth and Sieglinde, two roles that would soon become highlights of her repertoire and remain so throughout her career. She started to accumulate a following. There were requests for interviews, then disappointed reporters who had hoped for something sensational or spicy in her story. But audiences were falling in love with Lotte. Her star was rising. She was most definitely on her way.

Chapter Six

RAINING GOLD

LOTTE HAD GOOD LUCK with Gluck. His *Eurydice* brought her to the attention of Caruso. The title role in *Iphigenia in Aulis*, which opened the new season 1913-1914, her fourth, won her new laurels and wonderful reviews:

...Only the Iphigenia of Fräulein Lehmann stayed entirely within the classical framework. The heartfelt warmth of her dew-fresh voice, the perfectly beautiful tone-production, the utterly convincing naturalness in action and gesture together created an unusually enchanting totality....

...Among the performers...Frl. Lehmann deserved the palm. The talented artist, who still grows with each greater assignment, offered us an absolutely ideal Iphigenia, because here the touching simplicity of a powerful but unforced art again becomes nature....

The director of the Vienna Court Opera, Hans Gregor, came to Hamburg to hear a certain tenor sing Don José; Lehmann was the Micaëla...

The next day Norbert Salter, the agent, summoned me to his hotel....I listened in amazement to several telephone conversations in which fees of thousands were bandied about like colored balls. Then, radiating good will, Salter turned his smiling face to me and said: "I'm going to tell you a story. You know who Director Gregor is, don't you? Well, he came to Hamburg to engage a tenor and was at the Carmen performance yesterday. He listened very attentively to the tenor. And then, when we met after the performance, he pushed aside the contract I had already made out, and just said: 'I'm going to engage Micaëla for Vienna. Lehmann is her name, isn't it? All right then.'" Salter made a dramatic pause. "And here is your contract."

I looked at him—speechless.

"Well—have you nothing to say?"

39

No, I had nothing to say.

I seized the pen and would have signed then and there without having read the contract at all. I saw the lengthy figure of the salary, the long term of years—did I need to think it over? Yet I did stop.

I took my Vienna contract first to Jelenko.... Jelle, who wanted to keep me at the Hamburg Opera at any cost, rushed off to Dr. Loewenfeld.

"If you give her 12,000 marks a year, she'll stay in Hamburg."

"Twelve thousand marks! Has she become a megalomaniac? I shouldn't dream of it."

Two obstinate people at loggerheads!

Jelenko returned, scarlet with rage.

"He won't do it.... He thinks the Vienna contract is just bluff. But wait, little Lehmann.... He'll have to give in."

...I went home defiantly, to find a telegram from Salter urging an immediate decision.

So I signed the Vienna contract.

After she had signed, Lotte continued to agonize over the decision and negotiations went back and forth for most of the following year. On the one hand, Vienna was a sort of Mecca for any singer in the German-speaking part of the world. An engagement there would mean a great leap forward in her career. On the other hand, she felt at home in Hamburg, where her parents seemed now so well settled. She had won the love of the Hamburg audiences and was finally in a position to get the roles she had always longed to sing. If Hamburg had come close to meeting the salary Vienna was offering, she would have stayed, in spite of the greater prestige of a Viennese engagement.

During this period Dr. Loewenfeld amassed a sizeable collection of scathing letters from Lotte. Fortunately they only made him laugh. Later, when she was leaving Hamburg, he told her he would take them out and read them whenever he was in a bad mood. "Now I know," she quipped, "that you'll think of me often."

Meanwhile, important new roles entered her repertoire. The Countess in *The Marriage of Figaro* was an inner victory, considering her terror of the big aria that had nearly destroyed all her self-confidence at the Etelka Gerster school, the dread aria she had been forced to sing, lesson after lesson, week after week, until her throat was paralyzed with tension. Although she later confessed that she had never completely overcome her complex about that piece, she managed to hide any trace of trepidation:

> ... Lotte Lemann ... sang the first aria with movingly beautiful vocal quality, with cultivated taste, with genuine warmth. And she also showed her mastery of the second aria, which is very specially tricky, with an assurance that made one forget that she was singing the role for the first time.... (Hamburg critic M. L.)

> ... The technically difficult aria in the third act was excellently managed by the artist, as if it were a familiar possession of long standing.... (Hamburg critic M.)

Twelve days later came her first Sieglinde, a role she quickly made her own. She sometimes felt that of all her roles Sieglinde came closest to her own inner nature. Her identification with the part was almost magical. It was later to become her calling card in South America, Chicago, New York, and San Francisco.

She was scheduled to sing Chrysothemis in *Elektra*—the sort of role that can wear out high notes—but she wriggled out of it:

> As much as the part challenged me, I was afraid of overtaxing my voice. It is a crazy role. I encouraged one of my colleagues to ask the director for it. He has the idea she is intriguing behind my back.... I hope I can get out of it. I know myself well enough to know that I'll regret it later, but the regret will do less harm to my voice than the part.

Lotte was so happy as Pamina in *The Magic Flute* that she wished it could be her debut role in Vienna. Her contract there depended upon a successful guest performance. Gregor wanted her to sing Eva in *Die Meistersinger* near the end of April. Loewenfeld refused to give her leave. Her guest performance in Vienna was postponed until the fall. She had not yet sung the part of Eva; that came her way near the end of the season. Meanwhile, Pamina won raves for Lotte and a scolding for Loewenfeld:

> ... Frl. Lehmann portrayed Pamina with winning naturalness, sang the part with her own sort of refined musical conception and with an innerness of tone and expression that make it painfully regrettable that Dr. Loewenfeld was not capable of keeping at his institute for many years to come such an outstanding talent.... (M.)

...Fräulein Lehmann is the best Pamina one can imagine...(M. L.)

Lotte's next assignment was much less to her taste. In *Orpheus in the Underworld*, Offenbach's parody of Gluck, Greek mythology, and the Second Empire, she was cast as Eurydice. At that point in her blossoming career, she felt no affinity at all with the operetta style.

I can't tell you how tired I am. It's just too much now with this eternal, horrible Orpheus. I still have ten more performances to sing! That's too much for anybody...mornings endless rehearsals and then to have to sing in the evenings!

But she rose to the challenge with a flair she had never suspected. The critics found her charming.

I am blissful that even this part, which is so alien to me, came off so well. It was also a great success with the audience.

She was, of course, predestined for the role of Eva in *Die Meistersinger*. That was recognized from the start.

...If in yesterday's performance this side [the deeper relationship between Eva and Sachs] of the profound Meistersinger poetry came especially into its own, then the credit must go primarily to Fräulein Lotte Lehmann, who sang the part of Evchen for the first time and who already at this first attempt gave the figure the sharpness of outline that is essential for the goldsmith's daughter. Eva Pogner is neither lyrical nor sentimental: she is a perfectly healthy daughter of Eve with a slight touch of thoroughly natural sensuality, and she sees things as they are.... She is...aware of the pain that she causes Sachs, and therefore Fräulein Lehmann...imbues with all possible warmth...that moving passage in the workshop scene in which Evchen inwardly releases herself from Sachs's heart with an almost passionate spiritual exultation.... (H. Ch.)

...Frl. Lotte Lehmann appeared in the role of Pogner's daughter, striking us right away with her grace, and clearly establishing her right to undisputed possession of the part. She fulfilled her task with feeling and understanding, with warmly appealing wholeheartedness and sincerity, all qualities that are needed for Evchen. Even the conscious cunning and charming slyness—in worming out of Sachs what she wants to know—found in Frl. Lehmann favorable qualifications. The tone of irritation with Sachs (in the second act)

sounded for once like the expression of an upright personality. The excessive impudence and aggressiveness recently noticed here in other interpreters of the role...were this time absent. To the adornment of the part, besides the slenderness of the outward line, were added yesterday the attractive vocal qualities, the naturalness of delivery, and musical tact.... Extraordinarily well-realized [was] the delicacy with which she revealed her suspicion of the sorrowful secret that Sachs was hiding in his soul...(W. Z.)

Meanwhile Salter, her agent, had not been idle. He had secured for her lucrative guest contracts in Cologne, in Zoppot, and—her first step outside Germany—in London. To make room for those engagements she had to be released from an agreement to sing in Bayreuth. Siegfried Wagner had offered her one of the Valkyries (Ortlinde) and a Flower Maiden. Lotte Lehmann never sang at the Wagner shrine, even though much of her international repertoire consisted of Wagnerian roles.

For Lotte it would be "raining gold," as she put it, in the summer of 1914. The lean years, the constant financial stress, seemed over. At last she could do something special for her mother. That was almost an obsession as long as Mama was alive. That constant preoccupation runs through her letters like a *Leitmotiv.* For some time she had wanted Mama to take the cure at Neuenahr. Now that could be combined with the engagement at Cologne and Mama could be with her on her travels through Germany and do a little sightseeing on the Rhine. But first came England. Lotte had sung at a lavish party in honor of the chairman of the Hamburg-American Line. There she had met John Naht, one of the directors of the company. Mr. Naht and his wife spontaneously offered to accompany Lotte to London and look after her while she was there. That was a great relief to both Lotte and her parents. She sang two performances of Sophie in *Rosenkavalier* at the Drury Lane. Thomas Beecham was the conductor, Frieda Hempel the Marschallin, and Michael Bohnen the Ochs. Lotte did not set London on fire—yet—but she claimed "a pleasing success."

The Nahts kindly took her back to Germany as well, to Cologne, in time for her next engagement. There she sang Agathe, in a production of *Der Freischütz* conducted and staged by

Hans Pfitzner, and Eva, both very successfully. To thank him for
his work with her at rehearsals, Lotte gave Pfitzner some white
roses, a reference to those in *Freischütz*. Here are some excerpts
from his letter of acknowledgment:

> I would also like to say that I am very happy to have met in you one
> of the greatest hopes for the German stage. Never become—when
> your fees become higher—a rehearsal-shy prima donna, but remain
> always an artist who is there to serve the work of art.... Now sing a
> beautiful Evchen, for which I wish I were your coach and conductor.

Mama's intense, chronic gastric problems were further complicated by an ulcer. The specialist in Hamburg had wanted to op-
erate, but the Lehmanns were afraid of that. Then the doctor
found a way to give her blessed relief: an oil that coated her
stomach-lining so that food would not irritate the ulcer. Now, after the cure at Neuenahr, she looked better than Lotte had ever
seen her and mother and daughter enjoyed the little luxuries that
the "golden rain" had brought them.

On the way to Zoppot Lotte stopped at Berlin to make her
first phonograph records, for Pathé. They were two arias from *Lohengrin*, "Elsa's Dream" and the "Song to the Breezes."

Zoppot, a sea-side resort near Danzig, is now called Sopot
and is presently a part of Poland. In those days it was famous for
its festival of opera out in the woods, the perfect setting for that
celebration of the German forest, *Der Freischütz*. Lotte, of course,
sang the Agathe. Her partner was Richard Tauber and thereby
hangs a tale:

> I have hardly ever seen the Freischütz so enchantingly produced as
> it was there by the greatest of all producers—Nature. Again and
> again we were thrilled by the enchanting poetry of our forest setting.
> Only once I cursed the darkness of the pines when with the cry of
> joy, "Sweetly enraptured, to him!" I had to rush into Max's arms
> [Max is the name of Richard Tauber's role]. I had won a forfeit
> from Tauber, and the uncommonly tempting reward was to be a bar
> of chocolate.
>   "Where is my chocolate, Richard?" were my first words that even-
> ing as I took my place behind the two screens made of interwoven
> pine branches which hid us from the audience.

"You'll get it when you least expect it." Max prophesied with a
mischievous smile....
    The music started.... *"Sweetly enraptured, to him!"* I exulted and
ran into the dark pines where my Max awaited his entry.
    He pressed something into my hand, murmured, *"j'y pense,"* and
dragged me onto the scene, into the blinding glare of the footlights.
    Now wasn't that thoughtful of him? Max had brought a bar of
chocolate for his Agathe.... I quickly laid the marvelous present on a
bench.... Ännchen [the soubrette] sat on it and couldn't be moved
from her place all the rest of the act.

The first performance was marred by rain and drizzle for an
hour; but the show went on as a damp Agathe sang her first aria
for five thousand soggy spectators. "Instant Opera," by the way,
was not unknown in those days. One of the features of Lotte's
contract that had pleased her most, after a particularly strenuous
season in Hamburg, was the clause that excused her from rehearsals. In those days the singers had much more freedom for individual dramatic interpretation within a traditional framework that
tended to be the same from theatre to theatre. The age of the
stage director was yet to dawn.

By now she was growing accustomed to beautiful reviews;
nevertheless, no artist can take them for granted and it must
have been rather gratifying to read words like these: "A finely
schooled voice that gushed forth comfort, a heartfelt interpretation, a highly sympathetic appearance" or "Lotte Lehmann...has
at her disposal a magnificent voice."

What to do with a handful of melting chocolate, whether to
sing in the rain or cancel—such questions soon became totally
trivial. A world war broke out while Lotte and her mother were
in Zoppot. All the performers were in a state of panic. No one
knew what was going on. At the station they had to wait for
many hours as, one after another, all the trains were being di-
verted to carry troops to the front. Lotte stood on the platform
and watched trainloads of eager young men, singing lusty patri-
otic songs as they went off to the reality of bloody battlefields.

Back in Hamburg, Lotte was almost shocked to find the theatre packed at every performance, in spite of the war. There were
two main differences: more operetta was played than ever be-

fore, the more frivolous the better; and salaries were uniformly cut in half. The opera performed for countless charitable causes and the singers were in ever-increasing demand at the hospitals. No family was unaffected. Fritz was called up, but his weak heart kept him from the front. First he did garrison duty; then came an assignment at the war ministry in Berlin. The sons of Baron Putlitz were all sent to the war zone, where one of them was later badly wounded. Erika zu Putlitz served as a Red Cross nurse. For Lotte the war years were no interruption in her steady artistic growth and her series of successes. She felt almost guilty that her personal life was going so well while so much of the world was suffering.

> Life for me flows on as usual, as if the frightful world war were not raging outside. My troubles and my joys are still those of everyday. One feels so small and oh so inconsequential, speaking of one's every-day world while so much blood is flowing and so many tears.

Despite the cut in salary, Lotte was able to pay off all her debts except the debt to Baron Putlitz (and even that—at least the monetary part—was paid off very soon; not one of the surviving forty-seven letters she wrote to Baron or Baroness Putlitz fails to express her deep and enduring gratitude for their ever-ready help). Her successes outside of Hamburg had raised her prestige in her home theatre. Now all the leading German opera houses were open to her if she should choose to leave.

Mama moved with Lotte into the *pension* across from the thea-tre. Poor Papa stayed alone in the apartment, but joined them for meals. Strange to say, this arrangement turned out to be a harmonious solution to domestic tensions and father, mother, and daughter enjoyed each other's company in a more relaxed way. Mama thrived on the new freedom from household cares. Her health was vastly improved, to Lotte's enormous relief.

October of 1914 brought Octavian into Lotte's repertoire. After Sophie, the *Rosenkavalier* himself. She relished the part.

> How the public loves me here! One could see that again yesterday in the fabulous success I had as Octavian in Rosenkavalier, which I sang for the first time. The audience kept calling out my name. In Vienna I will have to try to win such love, starting from scratch. They say, though, that the Viennese like to spoil their artists. I leave

it up to destiny. That will guide me to what is best.

Lotte never lost that sense of being guided. She always felt a higher power at work, molding her career in accordance with some mysterious, divine plan.

The critics confirmed her newest success:

> ... *With the musical conscientiousness, with the strong artistic instinct and unerring taste which belong to her, Lotte Lehmann has now taken possession of the part of Octavian as well. Her way, which imitates no model and which no one else will find easy to imitate after her, is apart from anything that smacks of routine or conventionality and yet just as far removed from any striving for effect, from any oddity. The simple result of a sure artistic instinct which lets nothing divert it and therefore always finds the right way. Lotte Lehmann has the rare ability, the rare courage, to stand still on the stage— perfectly still, without pose, without the meaningless movements with which "routine" tries to cover embarrassment, without grimaces, without the surrogates of true temperament. And in this simple repose, which is quite natural in life and only strange to the stage, she produces a more genuine, stronger effect, than any pause-filling routine was ever able to do. Quite aside from her vocally brilliant performance ... her Rosenkavalier was dramatically a thoroughly distinguished achievement—independent, full of temperament and high-spirited humor. Furthermore, all that is supported by a dazzlingly attractive outward appearance.... (M. L.)*

The great Arthur Nikisch, who had conducted her first, bashful Freia years before, now heard her as Sieglinde and Eva and was deeply impressed. His enthusiasm earned her a more than welcome raise from the management.

Then, on October 30, 1914, came her first performance in Vienna, the guest appearance upon which her engagement would depend. In spite of the war, the imperial city seemed bustling with life and gaiety. Lotte encountered starry names at her first rehearsal. Wilhelm von Wymetal, one of the first great stage directors in opera, personally showed her around the house. Franz Schalk, the first of Lotte's three musical gods, was the conductor, Friedrich Weidemann the Sachs, and Richard Mayr, who became an especially treasured colleague as well as *the* Baron Ochs in *Rosenkavalier*, was the Pogner. This was a company of giants.

There was only one slightly sour note:

...a man came to my door at the hotel and addressed me urgently and mysteriously through the dividing wall. At first I didn't know what he wanted until at last I heard the word "claque."

I burst out laughing. So they did have that here, as my Hamburg colleagues had predicted.

"No, no, I don't want a claque," I cried to him, "I won't pay for my applause. It's a frightful idea...."

"Think of your career," came the urgent whisper behind the door. But I remained deaf to his entreaties and at last his ghostly tread took a hesitating departure.

An hour later, smuggled in in some cunning way, a man with a smug, foxy face stood before me, with orders and medals hanging curiously on his coat.

"I've come about the claque this evening," he said clicking his heels and bowing deeply.

"But, I've already told you I don't want it," I answered impatiently.

"Oh, that was Wessely. I haven't been here—so Wessely's been here...."

He shook his fists accusingly to Heaven at this infamous rival. No, he was the real "Chief of Staff Officer" of the claque, esteemed by all. Indeed it seemed to me from what he told me that he must be the chief person in the Opera House.... Under his arm he carried a packet of old newspapers, in every pocket gilt postcards and letters with contracts for applause which had been sent to him in strictest confidence, and which he only wanted to show me as a proof of his eminence. At last I had to acknowledge it—one must have him....

When, on the evening, among the enthusiastic calls for Weidemann, Miller, Mayr and Haydter, a few "Lehmanns" were mingled, I wished I could fall through some friendly trap door; "Freudenberger's doing his bit...." I thought with shame, and scarcely enjoyed my success at all.

The reviews next day must have consoled her, among them:

...A more charming portrayal would be hard to imagine. That was for once an Evchen such as Wagner must have pictured: of a pleasing cheerfulness, roguish, childlike and naïve, warm and full of feeling, completely natural. A lovely appearance and speaking eyes assist the artist in her finely detailed characterization.... ("rp," Neues Wiener Tagblatt, 31 October 1914)

There was some quibbling about her voice, difficult to judge fairly in a partly *parlando* role like Eva, and two critics annoyed Lotte by using the word, "soubrettish;" but all in all the reviews were very encouraging, for Vienna was accustomed to the very highest standards. Most mentioned the friendly reception given her by the audience. The successful guest performance put the seal upon her contract with Vienna.

Lotte shared her first, fresh impressions with Baroness Putlitz:

> *I am now looking forward to the engagement in Vienna. Everything made such a great impression on me. And in Hamburg my voice would surely be over-exerted [by too frequent performances]. What a fabulously beautiful orchestra [the Vienna Philharmonic]! It simply carries one's voice. And the audience! So enthusiastic, quite different from the cool, reserved Hamburgers. And though my dear colleagues tried hard to talk me out of it [the contract with Vienna] and painted everything there gray on gray, I can see nevertheless that through this engagement I have climbed high as a tower.*

After Vienna, Lotte had a guest engagement in Rostock, singing Sieglinde with great success in a cast that included Edyth Walker, the Brünnhilde who had thrilled her so much when she heard *Die Walküre* for the first time in Hamburg. Brecher was the conductor, a happy reunion. In Rostock Lotte also sang Gutrune.

Back in Hamburg the busy round of rehearsals and performances resumed. There were always new roles to be studied, coached, learned by heart, and staged, always old ones to be revived. In December came Margiana in *Der Barbier von Bagdad* by Peter Cornelius. In March, 1915, Angèle in *Opernball*, another operetta (by Richard Heuberger), which Lotte found more congenial than Offenbach's *Orpheus*. Then, on March 29, her first Elisabeth in *Tannhäuser*, another landmark in her career, one of her very greatest achievements. "It was a beautiful day," she wrote the Baroness, "when I sang that glorious role for the first time."

The critics agreed with her:

> *...The Elisabeth was embodied for the first time by Frl. Lehmann. .... All the deep, spiritual empathy, the jubilation of a loving heart, the chaste excitement, the nobility of the young princess, the sudden pain of recognition, the fervor of the prayer, all of that vibrates and*

rings, rejoices and laments in this highly gifted voice, wins three-dimensional shape and touches us wondrously and enduringly…. The acting of the young artist was deeply moving and revealed again the sure instinct of a talent that penetrates with total accuracy into the being of each of the womanly characters she portrays…. (M.)

…Frl. Lehmann never offers us cheap theatricality; rather she knows how to surround each of her characters with a halo of true poetry, unfolded from within; and without affectation or anything forced she finds—as if of her own accord—the character and the form that express the inner being and the spirit of Wagner's art…. (R. Ph.)

Wherever she went, Lotte was pursued by a troop of adoring fans, most of them young females known as *Backfische* (literally, baked fish, the equivalent of flappers or teenagers in English). The shy ones would secretly press a couple of violets into her hand, for instance, and then disappear in the crowd. The bolder ones could be something of a trial. She would see the shadows of their feet through the crack under her hotel-room door, as they were waiting to besiege her the moment she might appear. Sometimes her maid, whose name was also Lotte, had to stand guard.

She [the maid] was very young and imaginative and, really only half a child like the others, was carried away on this whirl of adoration. On the many occasions when she was allowed to go to the opera, she would act like a madwoman the whole day. She particularly liked operas where I wore a crown. This seemed to her the only style worthy of me…. My young friends used to tell me that in the gallery she had whole crowds round her to whom she would proudly say: "You can see her now, but I see her every day. I see her in bed and simply everywhere. For she is my mistress."

…When she saw me as Recha [Rachel in La Juïve], she was deeply mortified at the rags I had to perish in. When the executioners threw me into the pot, she bellowed in despair: "They're throwing my mistress into boiling oil…."

Rachel (*Recha* in German) was one of her new roles in her last year as a regular member of the Hamburg Opera.

Her most popular role of all, however, turned out to be Myrtocle in *Die toten Augen* by Eugène d'Albert. It is the story of a young woman, blind since birth, who is miraculously given sight by the touch of Jesus Christ. The one thing she has longed to see is the face of her beloved husband who has always been very kind to her. She has never been told that he is monstrously ugly. When she sees him he is devastated. For his sake she stares at the sun until her eyes are blind again.

There are several extremely effective scenes and Lotte made the most of them. A *tour de force* was the moving pantomime in which she sacrifices the gift of sight which had shortly before filled her with such exultant ecstasy. Lotte showed in her face the enormous effort of will needed to keep looking into the sun in spite of searing pain, the bitter acceptance of the return of darkness, and the great love that motivated her renunciation. It was a scene of overwhelming spiritual power as she played it (and as she re-enacted it for her master classes in Santa Barbara forty-five years later).

There was one line that Lotte refused to sing. According to the score, when Myrtocle realizes that she can see, her first words are, "a mirror! a mirror!" Lotte could not accept that. She felt that vanity at such a moment diminished the character of Myrtocle and the glory of the miracle. D'Albert tried vainly to convince her that his libretto was psychologically right, that a blind person would first of all want to see what she looked like. But Lotte simply left out the line altogether and started with the ecstatic, hymn-like phrase, "Light! Light! Everywhere light!" Her performance was so deeply moving that d'Albert had gratefully to admit that she was right.

An aria from *Die toten Augen,* "*Amor und Psyche,*" practically became Lotte's theme song for a while. It was the most frequently requested encore at her concerts whenever she came back to Hamburg.

The successes of Lotte's last season in Hamburg, the love that welled up to her from the audience there, made her regret that she had signed with Vienna; she asked Gregor to release her from her contract. Fortunately for her future career he refused.

Myrtocle was the role of her farewell to Hamburg.

Chapter Seven

THAT SOMETHING EXTRA

Let Lotte Lehmann herself give the prelude to her long love affair with Vienna:

The year 1916 was a rather important one in my life; I left the Hamburg Municipal Theatre for what at that time still bore the proud name of "Royal and Imperial Court Opera" at Vienna. The clouds of war, however, had by now cast their long shadows over the once gay city, and the Emperor's throne was manifestly doomed. Thus I never really came to know the glamour of Old Vienna about which I had heard so much—flower parades in the Prater or the procession of brightly resplendent carriages in the petal-covered Hauptallee. This to me was already part of the past, a glorious fairy tale; for the Vienna I came to know looked very different indeed. We lived in modest circumstances, with no more food than our regular ration cards entitled us to, and I still vividly remember suffering from acute hunger for the first time in my life. My fairly substantial income proved of scant help in the matter, because what one needed in Vienna was "contacts;" we knew no one and had no access to sources for butter, eggs, and milk outside the city. I shall never forget the kindness shown me by the singer Richard Mayr. When I once confessed that I was hungry and simply did not know how to go about finding more than my allotted ration, he immediately began to have food sent to us regularly from his farm, and life brightened considerably. I have often blessed him for his generosity.

Lotte's official debut as a regular member of the Vienna Court Opera took place on the traditional opening night of the season, the Emperor's birthday, August 18, 1916. The opera was *Der Freischütz*. The reviews were magnificent for Lotte:

...The first evening introduced a new member of the company: Fräulein Lotte Lehmann as Agathe. That was a case of "she came, she conquered," a total victory!.... Fräulein Lehmann, of winning

52

appearance, is poetry incarnate and her singing is poetry too, as is also the simplicity of her acting, free of any artificiality. The glorious soprano of the young artist must have been trained by a master. Seldom has one encountered such vocal culture, faultless in every way, which, transmitted through a voice saturated with beautiful sound, is permeated as well with an artistic sensibility of the noblest kind. And to crown the whole, Fräulein Lehmann is mistress of the most model enunciation of the text one can imagine. Many great singers will be placed in the shade by the young artist through that quality alone. Fräulein Lehmann was stormily and most heartily applauded after her first aria as well as repeatedly during the performance and at the end of the acts. It is now understandable that she was the darling of Hamburg and that they let her go with deep regrets. The Vienna Court Opera has made in her…a major discovery …. (Sch—r., Deutsches Volksblatt, August 19, 1916)

…A singer with magnificent resources, an actress full of feeling and taste…. She glided past all the weaknesses in Agathe's overly delicate virginality with an adroitness that revealed the thinking artist…. (Neues Wiener Journal, August 19, 1916)

…an excellent new member, Fräulein Lehmann, sang the Agathe with the greatest success…. Fräulein Lehmann can quickly become a darling of our opera audience…. (Die Zeit, August 19, 1916)

…Lotte Lehmann has every prospect of becoming a Vienna favorite…. Yesterday she took the public by storm…. It is quite an accomplishment to literally electrify a sleepy audience with Agathe's prayer…. (another Viennese paper, unidentified in the clipping)

Other roles followed swiftly: Elisabeth, Antonia and Giulietta (the latter new), and Micaëla. The reviews were favorable, the audiences were enthusiastic; and yet Lotte sensed that something was missing.

The Vienna Opera…was alien territory, and whereas in Hamburg I had been everybody's spoiled darling, in Vienna I was merely one among many. Great stars reigned in individual splendor among the soloists…and though I did have some gratifying success, I seemed to lack that something extra which would put me in a class with the others….

Then came the "something extra," the needed sensation. Lotte was assigned to the second cast of a Strauss première, the

new version of *Ariadne auf Naxos*. In its original form, the opera
had been conceived as the climactic final scene of a Molière play
(*Le bourgeois gentilhomme*), adapted and translated into German as
Der Bürger als Edelmann by Hugo von Hofmannsthal. The combination of play and opera proved to be unwieldy, and highly im-
practical for most theatres. Hofmannsthal fashioned a prologue to
replace the play. The opera thus became an opera within an opera.
Strauss was fascinated by the challenge of setting quick, realistic
conversation to music, without the loss of musical interest characteristic, for example, of the old *secco*—dry—recitative. Certain
conversational scenes in *Der Rosenkavalier* had suggested the pos-
sibilities; now he was keen to exploit them and refine them. The
key role in the new prologue was that of the Composer. Strauss,
over Hofmannsthal's original objections, had conceived of the
part as a trouser role, for a soprano (or high mezzo-soprano) playing a young man, another *Rosenkavalier*, so to speak. And the performer he had in mind was Marie Gutheil-Schoder, a brilliant
singing-actress, who had delighted him as Octavian in the
Viennese première. Gutheil-Schoder, of course, was chosen to
create the role. Lotte was, in effect, her understudy. She would
no doubt have sung some performances eventually, long after
the glamour of the première. She fell in love with the part and
worked hard to master it. Then fate stepped in. Gutheil-Schoder
had to miss an important rehearsal because of a cold. Strauss was
there. The rehearsal could not be canceled, the performance was
only a few days off.

Lehmann was called. Expecting nothing, she was not even
nervous. She threw her whole heart and soul into the beautiful
role she had been studying so long and with so much love.

Strauss was enthralled. He asked her to come to a solo musical
rehearsal that afternoon. Franz Schalk, the conductor, and Hans
Gregor, the *Intendant*, were also present. After another run-
through Strauss made up his mind. Lotte Lehmann would sing
the world première.

Lotte objected. Marie Gutheil-Schoder had always been one of
her idols. She was upset to think that such a great artist should be
hurt on her account. Strauss, Gregor, and Schalk told her this was
their business and she would do as she was told. Later, in his me-

moirs, Schalk wrote that this was the only time in his experience when one singer had turned down a juicy role for the sake of another. Lotte, in telling the story, always disclaimed any right to a halo: when they insisted, she was very quick to overcome her compunctions.

Gutheil-Schoder never held it against her. She graciously claimed that Lotte's performances as the Composer were among her loveliest memories of the Vienna Opera.

Among Lotte's mementos there is a touching note from one of the great Wagnerian tenors of the day:

> Dear Fräulein Lehmann,
>
> I was at the dress rehearsal today [of Ariadne]. Your singing was wonderfully beautiful. I had to tell you that.
>
> Best greetings. Your devoted colleague,
>
> Erik Schmedes.

The première took place on Wednesday, October 4, 1916, starting at 7 p.m. Maria Jeritza sang Ariadne, Selma Kurz was Zerbinetta. They were two of Vienna's top favorites.

"At 7:40 all Vienna knew who Lotte Lehmann is." So wrote Ludwig Karpath, a leading critic. That tells it all. It was the sort of sensation necessary to launch a really great career.

Now that all Vienna knew who Lehmann was, she was in demand everywhere, especially for charities (the Red Cross, disabled soldiers, breakfasts for school children, etc., etc.). She fulfilled an enormous number of such requests, and made several special recordings for the war-effort. Furthermore, all the agents were jostling each other out of the way to sign her up for guest contracts.

After one of Lotte's charity concerts the critic who signed himself H. W. nearly burst into song:

> ... this God-gifted artist became a tumultuously applauded darling of our concert audience, entirely through the heartfelt, nobly natural rendition of a few songs, with which she won all hearts. At the same time her glorious, youthful tones rang like the bells that welcome May, effortlessly, as the song of the lark ascends to blue heights, and penetrated to the most intimate depths of our hearts like the first ray of sun in spring. Now we have again a singer in Vienna such as we

have not had since [Bertha] Ehnn [a Viennese favorite in the 1870's].

There were of course numerous interviews, and the following excerpts from one of them give us an idea of how Lotte Lehmann the woman impressed the Viennese:

> ...*She had enjoyed unusual popularity in Hamburg, not just through her magnificent voice and her noble artistry; she also quickly won all hearts through her gracious and friendly nature.... Since I had the pleasure of spending an hour in stimulating conversation with the artist at her home, I felt the winning magic of her personality, which lies in the simplicity, naturalness, and almost child-like sincerity of her character....* (Paul Wilhelm, WWZ, October 29, 1916)

The star did not yet feel at home in the Viennese heaven. A letter to Baron Putlitz gives vent to her nostalgia for the North. Though written before her success in *Ariadne*, it expresses what she continued to feel about her new environment for a while longer:

> *I am not happy here. Vienna is a great disappointment to me. Everything about life here, it seems to me, is calculated for outer "effect." Editors of scandal sheets, photographers, members of the claque...I find all of that frightful. I yearn for Hamburg, for pure sea air—here it is dusty and all purity is stifled in an atmosphere that robs me of breath. Perhaps I am being sentimental. My calling, after all, is not to be happy but to go forward. And that is happening. I'm sure that I shall overcome my home-sickness....*

On November 21, 1916, Emperor Franz Josef died. The theatres were closed and no one knew when the new emperor, Karl I, would order their reopening. Lotte longed to accept offers of guest performances in Hamburg but permission was not granted. Lotte lost her temper over all the red tape, stirring up quite a storm. The unfortunate recipient of her wrath was Secretary Lyon (later assistant director)...

> *Lyon suddenly became very serious. He picked up the telephone and asked to be put through to Prince Montenuovo.*
> *Then I got thoroughly frightened.*
> *"Herr Lyon, I didn't really mean it...you're not going to report me, are you?"*

"That was lèse-majesté," he said, as solemn as a judge, and related word for word through the telephone what I had said....
In those moments of fear I simply couldn't imagine what the consequences of my thoughtless words might be. I didn't see that with his other hand Lyon was pressing down the receiver so that the line was dead, and it was only when he said: "What was that, Your Excellency? I'm to send for a mental doctor and have Fräulein Lehmann taken away in a straight jacket?" that I noticed it had all been a joke, and breathed again....

To celebrate the first official appearance of the new emperor and empress, a Gala Concert was given (at the *Konzerthaus*). Along with Maria Jeritza, Selma Kurz, Lucie Weidt, Leo Slezak, Richard Mayr, and Alfred Piccaver, Lotte Lehmann was asked to sing. She happened to overhear some snide remarks about her dress.

It simply hadn't occurred to me that this was an evening to which one must come "in all one's grandeur"—clothes just didn't interest me and I wore some old thing that had originated in Hamburg—so I probably did look like Cinderella among my colleagues. But it was a lesson to me. Never again would I stand among the others looking like an interloper.... So I went the very next day to a great salon and ordered something expensive and grand.

As far as public and press were concerned, it seemed as if the new favorite could do no wrong. Backstage, things looked a little different.

All in all, I felt rather out of place in Vienna, being myself terribly German in those days, utterly Prussian in my background and so alien to the natural geniality of the Viennese that I mistook for hypocrisy what I later learned to appreciate as a charming and graceful way of life....
The general manager received a great many complaints about me, and I rather suspect that in those days he must have found me downright obnoxious.... At rehearsals he used to drop sarcastic remarks about both my musical abilities and my ill-mannered behavior toward my colleagues.... One day our [stage] director, Wilhelm von Wymetal, took me aside to inquire if I could not possibly indulge my colleagues' hankering for somewhat more elaborate formalities."For instance," he pointed out, "all you ever say is a simple 'Good morning' instead of 'Good morning, Frau Kammersängerin.' Further-

more, what would it cost you to add a 'How do you do?'" With devastating candor I replied that it would not cost me anything, but that
I saw no reason for asking, since I really was not, after all, the least
bit interested in how she was or was not doing. Wymetal had to
laugh in spite of himself, wondering out loud what he was going to do
with such an obstinate and confirmed Prussian.

Yet things did not always end in good-natured banter, and I was
to discover time and again that a touch of charm and graceful diplo-
macy tends to oil the wheels and pay off in the long run.

Lotte's outspoken informality got her in trouble more than
once. In January of 1917, only a few months after her engagement had begun, she was briefly suspended and, for a while, incredibly, dismissal was a definite possibility. The following report
appeared in the *Neues Wiener Journal* on January 20:.

> ...Fräulein Lotte Lehmann had to submit to an official disciplinary
> investigation which ended in a verdict of guilty. This verdict is not so
> tragic, however, for the sentence is not likely to have exceeded a fine
> or a reprimand. The occasion for this penalty was a little affair, in
> which Fräulein Jeritza is said also to have played a part, in a dress-
> ing room of the Court Opera. During the course of a somewhat
> vehement scene Fräulein Lehmann, who calls a spade a spade in
> good North-German fashion, is said to have made a remark which
> Director Gregor took personally, after it had been repeated to him, by
> "good friends," of course. He ordered an official disciplinary investiga-
> tion according to the regulations. Now everything is all right again.
> Fräulein Lotte Lehmann, who during the proceedings against her
> was not permitted to sing at the Court Opera, is now singing
> again....

Another version was reported by Siegfried Jelenko as he remembered the incident years later in an article for one of the
Hamburg papers. That he took credit for the satisfactory conclusion appears to have been typical of "Jelle."

> ...I was on a business trip to Vienna and was really looking for-
> ward to seeing her there. A funereal voice answered my telephone
> call: "Oh God, how good that you are here! I am terribly upset and
> must speak to you as soon as possible." We agreed to meet the next
> morning at nine at a coffee house near the opera. And there she came,
> looking like a wilted lily, a weeping willow, which gave me quite a
> start. What had happened? She had had to take over the role of Elis-

abeth for a sick colleague. While dressing, on the evening of the per-
formance, she sent for Assistant Director Lyon because of some quite
minor matter that was bothering her; and since he couldn't comply
right away, she made use of some authentic Lehmannisms against
him and the institute, in the presence of the wardrobe mistress and
the hairdresser. Lyon made an official complaint to Director Gregor
and now she was to be punished with disciplinary action, possibly
even with immediate dismissal. My first thought was: "Hurrah,
then she'll come back to us!" (Shame on me!) Then, however, I said
to her: "Director Gregor used to act under my direction at the Hel-
den Theatre in Berlin, years ago, in the Saxon dialect. I'll go to him
and try to get rid of this conflict." And I succeeded too. Needless to
say, he received me warmly. As I introduced my concern, he put on
his official face: [the following in broad Saxon dialect] "No, listen,
that just doesn't go here, such a lack of discipline at our institute,
that's never yet been seen here. Poor Lyon was totally out of his
head! No, and furthermore in front of witnesses, and he told me
officially there would have to be a trial!" I tried to calm him down
and little by little I managed it. "Yes, but she must get a punishment.
She'd better report to me. No, at such an institute!" I thanked him
and hurried away to impart the result to the poor delinquent who
was waiting all-a-tremble near by....

Paul Schwarz, one of Lotte's early colleagues at the Hamburg
Opera, later remarked about "Jelle:" "This curious gentleman
liked to cast himself in the part of the Promoter of Lotte Lehmann's Promising Talent, without in fact ever having lifted a
finger for her."

By the end of her first season Lotte had sung twenty-one roles
in Vienna, including, among the new ones, Mignon, Manon
(one of her favorites), Marguerite, Frau Fluth in *The Merry Wives
of Windsor* (a promotion from her early Hamburg Anna), and,
from her former repertoire, Pamina, Elsa, and Octavian (besides
the Agathes, Evas, Elisabeths, Antonias, and Micaëlas already
mentioned above). In the spring a pair of one-act operas by the
Viennese boy wonder, Erich Wolfgang Korngold, was premièred. Lotte sang Laura in *Der Ring des Polykrates* (though not in
the first performances) and Jeritza had the lead in *Violanta*. It is
remarkable that anyone could have studied, memorized, and rehearsed so many major roles in such a short time.

Of her Laura in the Korngold piece one critic wrote: "She is delightful. Pure sunshine on the stage."

Lotte's second season in Vienna brought new successes as "Lotte" (Charlotte) in *Werther*, as Sieglinde, as the Countess in *The Marriage of Figaro*, and as Margiana in *The Barber of Bagdad*, as well as in concert:

> ...When she sings... one feels that each aria, each song is radiating new colors, new flashes of light. Her ever-blossoming talent carries the magic of the most modest simplicity. To the stage or to the recital platform she brings the same utter naturalness and credibility, along with human warmth and emotions that spring from deepest musical understanding. One hears and sees in her an artistic talent gifted with six senses. The sixth: a most pure, inborn musicality, refined and easy in the execution, delicate and poetic with rare subtlety. She feels and lives her renditions with high culture and nobility. That bell-like, silvery voice sounds forth from a deep-feeling soul. That voice bears a piece of her heart. The pure, noble, soft poetry of that singing, the legato line, the delicate sentiment of that dreamy, warm voice, are very rare phenomena. Lotte Lehmann has beyond a doubt one of the most beautiful female voices we have ever heard.... The whole evening was one great jubilation over the beloved and celebrated artist.... (a. e., *Wiener Fremdenblatt*, January 14, 1918)

...and rapturously received guest performances in Hamburg:

> ...Once more the opportunity to listen to the nobly lovely art of our Lotte Lehmann...and as she lent to the little songs her captivatingly sweet, wonderful voice, a jubilation, a thundering ovation broke loose such as never yet has shaken these walls. Again and again we are forced to ask: was there really no way to keep this artist here? Must Vienna possess what rightly belongs to Hamburg? For us no golden cage could have been precious enough for this nightingale with the radiant voice.... (*Neue Hamburger Zeitung*, August 6, 1917)

In May of 1918 Lotte enclosed a number of clippings in a letter to Baroness Putlitz:

> Here—at random—are some reviews.... All the others Papa pasted into an album. That is an encouraging book! When I leaf through it I often feel it isn't I about whom all those beautiful things were said. How grateful I can be. And how happy and proud, that these successes are like a precious bouquet that I can offer to you as thanks for all that you once did for me.

In those days, when Lotte was not singing herself, she was in the artists' box, high up in the third gallery, listening to the others. That was an era of great singers.

> For years, in Vienna, I lived in the opera house.... I went to almost every performance there because I felt that I couldn't breathe without absorbing the atmosphere of the opera.... I wanted to hear every one, and see everything and decide for myself what I liked and what I didn't like—and wanted then to close my eyes and ears and with complete independence do what my feeling drove me to do...without wanting to copy—perhaps even without being <u>able</u> to copy: for imitation is a talent in itself—a dangerous talent which I fear almost more than a lack of talent [written in reference to her students].

Lotte Lehmann had the humility and the good sense to study the work of all the other great artists of her time, to draw the best of each into her inner self, and then to go her own way. Her art, like her voice, was totally individual and born out of her very individual personality and her very deepest feelings. Some reviewers referred to her "flawless" vocalism. But Lotte herself constantly disparaged her own command of technique, and—as she put it—relied on "the wings of emotion" to carry her safely over any technical hurdles. As long as her emotional response to the music and her artistic instincts were guiding her, she could forget about technique and give herself completely to the musical moment. If, on the other hand, something that had seemed to come easily to her, was thoughtlessly pointed out as being difficult, she would be in danger ever afterwards of a sudden attack of stage fright as that difficult note drew near.

> For example, as the Composer in Strauss's Ariadne auf Naxos I had to sing a lovely little song [Du, Venus' Sohn — gibst süssen Lohn]. I had always sung it with great ease and freedom.... One day a former singer said to me: "It surprises me again and again to see with what delicious ease you sing that difficult and exposed little song, as if it had no difficulties for you at all. And it is so very tricky...." I was very much astonished. "But it really isn't so difficult," I answered, more amazed at the moment by my technical surety than was my hostess. "But that is just what is so charming, Fräulein Lotte: you don't realize it at all."
>
> I had forgotten the conversation—but my subconscious mind recalled it at just the wrong moment: in the next performance of Ari-

adne *I sang this lovely song miserably and was never again able to sing it really well....*

Psychology plays an enormous part in singing. Because she felt her roles so vividly, Lotte was always in love with her stage lover—but only on stage and never (well, hardly ever) in private life. Perhaps handsome Karl Aagard-Oestwig, her dream-Lohengrin and Bacchus (after 1919), was an exception. As Manon she loved Alfred Piccaver. As Lotte Lehmann she adored his "heavenly" voice. But when his mother and her mother tried to make a match between them, Lotte rebelled. She was not at all interested in him as a man, only as one of her very favorite singers. On stage, no matter how foul a tenor's breath or how ungainly his girth, she saw only Siegmund (for instance), never the singer.

As for the ladies, there was trouble with only one, and that trouble lasted for decades. Fritz Lehmann put it very picturesquely: Maria Jeritza was forever throwing red-hot coals in front of Lotte's feet. Lotte, without mentioning names, put it like this:

> I was quickly pushed to the front, and one uncrowned queen of the Opera didn't like that.... For the first time in my life, I believe, I encountered veiled hostility. I learned that the way upward can also be an ugly and obnoxious competitive struggle, a struggle in which I must always be worsted, for when I am forced to fight I fight with open visor.... In my heart I have never had much sympathy with the idea of the prima   donna   assoluta...There is room for so many.... There is something undignified about this petty fighting for oneself.
>
> In general, artists are a great army fighting under one flag; ready to help one another, understanding, good comrades.

In her books, Lotte wrote often and with sincere generosity about her admiration for many aspects of Jeritza's art—the thrilling way she turned her back to the audience to greet the Hall of Song at the climax of her entrance aria in *Tannhäuser*, her moving characterization of Santuzza, her glorious singing as the Empress in *Die Frau ohne Schatten*—but privately there were bitterness and hurt. Because they were for years the two top stars in Vienna, each with an enormous following, and because Vienna loved to watch the sparks fly on their opera stage, they were often cast together in the same opera: Brünnhilde and Sieglinde,

Ariadne and the Composer. Later, the Empress and the Dyer's Wife, Octavian and the Marschallin. They used to enter the house through different doors, flocks of fans waiting at each entrance. Lotte never knew when Jeritza's lightning would strike; but she could be fairly certain that if she had a soft, sustained high-note to sing, Jeritza would find a way—as if it were a part of the staging—to nudge Lotte off balance. Once Lotte asked the wardrobe department if she could borrow, for a guest engagement in London, a cloak that had been part of Elsa's costume in *Lohengrin*. Jeritza would be singing the role during Lotte's leave of absence and everyone in Vienna knew that Maria had recently added a magnificent cloak, all cloth-of-gold, with a spectacular long train, to her Elsa costume. The wardrobe mistress was sure there would be no need for the old costume and was about to pack it in a trunk for Lotte to take to London. Somehow Jeritza got wind of it and suddenly materialized at the scene. "Put that back!" she ordered, "I might just get a whim to wear it."

In June 1918 Lotte traveled to Constantinople to sing for the Sultan. She was much relieved when the war ministry requisitioned a private compartment for her on the over-crowded train (this was still World War I). She sang four concerts in three days, including two matinées (one for the ladies of the Sultan's harem). Lotte was fascinated by this other, exotic world, but ready for a restful vacation with her mother by the beautiful Königssee in the Bavarian alps, not far from Salzburg, where she hoped none of the *Backfische*—bless their hearts—would be able to find her.

Chapter Eight

ROLE SCREAMS FOR LEHMANN

THE HABSBURG EMPIRE was falling apart. In April 1918 Clemenceau had revealed that Karl I had made secret negotiations for a separate peace. Germany, furious, forced him to surrender all independent power of action. The German armies suffered defeat in August. The Bulgarian front collapsed in September. The Poles declared their independence; Czechoslovakia was born as a republic; and Yugoslavia proclaimed as a state, all in October. The dual monarchy was dissolved by Hungary in November. The army disintegrated rapidly. On November 11 Emperor Karl renounced all share in the government but refused to abdicate, taking his titles with him to Switzerland. On November 12, 1918, the Republic of German-Austria was proclaimed.

There were violent revolutionary disturbances in Vienna. Austria, too, was starting to fall apart: Vorarlberg sought union with Switzerland; Tirol wanted to secede. Major concessions had to be made to hold the already shrunken country together. The new government was held responsible for war reparations. A four-year rampage of inflation began.

Yet the Vienna Opera continued to flourish. Only its name was changed. *Hofoper* became *Staatsoper*. The old Court Opera was now the new State Opera. And to many Viennese the battles of the Lehmannites with the Jeritzians were of far more consuming interest than the clashes between Socialist Democrats and Bolsheviks.

The last act of the last imperial *Intendant* (Baron Leopold Andrian) had been to appoint a new double directorate: Franz Schalk and Richard Strauss. The new era turned out to be a glorious one for the Vienna Opera, in spite of the ferocious political unrest raging outside the opera house. And in spite of enormous

64

initial resistance to the appointment of Richard Strauss. The press fumed that their "poor city" could not afford such an expensive genius (at 80,000 crowns a year); did the Viennese want to see their new State Opera turned into a private showcase for Richard Strauss? Anti-Strauss partisans drummed up support for a letter of protest and managed to persuade nearly all the members of the company to sign, except for Selma Kurz and Jeritza. Yes, Lotte, too, was gullible, much as she loved singing Strauss.

Strauss himself relaxed at home in Garmisch, sanely biding his time, sure that the storm would blow over. Which, of course, it did. Schalk helped by saying publicly: "I am for Strauss... If there were *more* Strausses we'd have to hire them *all!*"

It was some months before Strauss actually took over his post. Meanwhile, Schalk gave Vienna a foretaste of high artistic events to come with the local première of Pfitzner's *Palestrina*, an opera of deeply serious spiritual and philosophical content, as well as considerable musical beauty. Lotte was cast as Silla, another trouser role.

Other new roles for her ever-growing repertoire were Lisa in Tchaikovsky's *Queen of Spades* and Friederike in *Der Musikant* by Julius Bittner.

Always there were numerous concerts and recitals as well. Often Lotte's accompanist was Professor Ferdinand Foll, who had been a friend of Hugo Wolf's and remained a champion of his wonderfully subtle songs.

Spring brought a whiff of romance. Lotte got herself engaged; then, three weeks later, *dis*-engaged. The briefly lucky man was Wilhelm Dessauer, a very talented, 36-year-old painter who happened to be doing her portrait as "Lotte" in *Werther* in pastels. His personal eccentricities, at first intriguingly attractive, showed up on better acquaintance as symptoms of a serious neurasthenia. Lotte's parents had sensed that all along. Since he was a well-known banker's son, and rich, and since she was the darling of press and public, it was only natural that photographers were following the couple everywhere. Lotte's new role as blushing bride was rapidly losing its charm. The constant need to keep smiling in society and for the camera, while signs of neuro-

sis were becoming ever clearer in her fiancé, went against
Lotte's characteristic openness. She broke the engagement. The
noble way he took the disappointment helped to soothe her re-
morse at having to hurt him:

> He accepted the break-up as only a truly extraordinary human being
> could do: by thanking me for a short time of happiness.... Ashamed
> and confused I stand in awe of the simple bigness of his character—
> and at the same time I know that I did the right thing in freeing
> myself, for it was indeed a "freeing".... I felt as if released from
> heavy chains.... Needless to say the whole affair has aroused enor-
> mous attention in Vienna. That they found everything marvelous—
> both engagement and dis-engagement—also goes without say-
> ing.... Here everyone is slippery as an eel [aalglatt].

After her season in Vienna, Lotte went to Hamburg for her
annual series of guest performances. Very weary from her strenuous schedule, she was looking forward to a complete rest at
Westerland on the island of Sylt, where her brother, now married, had a house. Sylt is still a favorite spot for nude bathing in
the North Sea. There she received an urgent message from
Richard Strauss. But first the background:

> One day a large package arrived unannounced. It turned out to be
> the piano score of Die Frau ohne Schatten [The Woman Without a
> Shadow, the new Strauss opera], along with a letter from Schalk,
> in which he implored me not to send it back by return of post, as was
> my custom (all my life I have suffered from an inferiority complex).
> That procedure would merely be a waste of time: I had to sing the
> role of the Dyer's Wife, if for no other reason than that it had been
> written especially for me. There was absolutely no point in my being
> difficult and making him get down on his knees before I gave in and
> accepted. In other words, he concluded, make believe that this score
> has already been sent to you once before.

Lotte took a peek at the part. It terrified her. She turned it
down (but kept the score). Then, barely settled down for her
well-earned rest at Westerland, she received the following letter from Strauss, dated June 27, 1919:

> My dear Fräulein!
>
> The piled up work for the festival [Strauss was vigorously involved

in the founding of the Salzburg Festival] *has unfortunately almost totally forestalled the preliminary work with the solo cast members of Die Frau ohne Schatten. If the already announced date of the première, October 1, is to be met [it was not; the first performance took place on October 10], then the staging rehearsals must start on August 28. I therefore address to you the respectful request that during the vacation you apply yourself to studying the role of the Dyer's Wife, who is the crucial figure in the external action, so that the part will be well memorized by the beginning of August; and I include the respectful question, whether you might not have the inclination and the time to come here in early August (about ten days before you travel to Vienna) and to study the role with me personally, to give it that last bit of polish.*

Frau Lucie Weidt [cast as the Nurse] will do the same and it would be of great use to you and make your work much easier, if you could have your role ready here with me alone before your arrival for the last [musical] rehearsals [in Vienna].

If you come from the north, Garmisch is right on the way to Vienna (i.e., a couple of hours from Munich), this is a lovely place for a sojourn and my wife would be especially happy if she could receive you here, honored lady. She sends her very best greetings.

So please come around the 5th of August and gladden with your visit your sincerely devoted

Dr. Richard Strauss.

Lotte dashed back to Austria to find the score, which had also just settled down quite snugly for a restful vacation in her mother's suitcase. By some miracle she managed to find in Gmunden (a lake-side resort between Salzburg and Linz) a pianist who could actually read the difficult music. She sweat blood over the score as she shed pounds at a sanatorium that specialized in weight-reduction. It was a strenuous summer. Drastic dieting (too much Viennese pastry in Lotte's recent past). Wild rides on an electric horse. Going nowhere fast on a rowing machine. Excess flesh melted away; but her fear of the part refused to do the same. She feared for the health of her voice. The part seemed just too dangerous. She decided again to turn it down.

Schalk responded with a telegram that must have warmed the wires:

IMPLORE YOU OVERCOME HYSTERICAL STATE OF

PANIC UPON FURTHER ACQUAINTANCE ALL TER-
RORS OF THE PART WILL FULLY DISAPPEAR AND
SHEER JOY TAKE THEIR PLACE ROLE SCREAMS FOR
LEHMANN AND ARTISTIC SPIRITUAL SALVATION ON
TO GARMISCH SINCERELY SCHALK

Strauss, apprised of her latest rebellion, also sent a telegram.
Lotte was still adamant:

> I answered that I did not want to sing the part because I had no in-
> tention of establishing myself as a match-seller on the Kärthner-
> strasse the day after the première....

The telegraph office in quiet little Gmunden was gradually going crazy. Here comes another telegram from Strauss:

DYER'S-WIFE-ROLE NEITHER LOW NOR HIGH NEI-
THER LONG NOR TAXING KEEP STUDYING AND 5
AUGUST COME HERE SO I CAN PERSONALLY CURE
YOU OF THE STUDY-SICKNESS DIAGNOSED IN ALL
SINGERS SINCE SALOME WITH TRIED AND TRUE
REMEDY OF ALTERATIONS LETTER FOLLOWS
GREETINGS RICHARD STRAUSS

Here is the letter (dated July 22) that followed:

> My dear Fräulein!
>
> I would be far more horrified over your letter if Die Frau ohne Schat-
> ten were my first opera. As it happens, however, I have known that
> kind of letter, such as yours is, for 15 years and the study-sickness, of
> which the symptoms are clearly recognizable in your words, has each
> time been cured before the première.
>
>   What ox, or let's say, which of your opera-composing colleagues
> put the idea into your head that this role is too taxing? At the piano,
> while studying, when a couple of high-lying phrases need to be prac-
> tised,—how often certain things seem taxing that later, on the stage,
> practically sing themselves. For God's sake, think of the frightful dis-
> grace if you—the top young-dramatic soprano—could not sing the
> most beautiful young-dramatic role. If Frl. Jeritza had to take over
> your role because Frl. Lehmann couldn't handle it. You surely don't
> want to do that to yourself! That would really be suicide! And you
> don't have to, either—the prescription for the remedy against this
> most harmless of all singers' illnesses, the climax of which you seem to

be *presently suffering, is already available here. You only need to come as soon as possible; I promise you, in 3 days you'll be healed, if you have gone through the lovely role with me (it is truly beautiful and fabulously grateful). If we have to we can change a few details, make a few alterations in the cut so that the dress will be a perfect fit!*

Your refusal, therefore, is hereby most politely, but most firmly rejected—we expect you very soon, my wife asks you please to stay as our guest (have you not received my last letter?) and then:

[He sketches in four bars from Zerlina's second aria in *Don Giovanni*; the words—not written—refer to a special remedy, unavailable through a pharmacist, which is sure to cure all ills.]

With cordial greetings! Your
For the time being still very indignant
Dr. Richard Strauss.

Apparently Lotte kept playing hard to get, for a few days later she received a letter from Ludwig Karpath that included these lines:

Strauss just telegraphed a third time: I am to drive to Gmunden, pack you into a trunk, and take you with me, so that you can't get out of it. You can see how much importance he gives to your participation. To let such a world-première slip away from you would be a crime against yourself....

Perhaps Lotte was more afraid of stifling in a suitcase than of singing the role. In any case, she finally found the courage to agree. The weeks she spent with Strauss in Garmisch were among the most artistically productive in her life. He professed to be astonished and pleased at her thorough preparation and actually had very little to change or to correct. Mostly he concentrated on the phrasing. He seemed to approve of her interpretation and made very few suggestions. Sometimes there seemed to be tears in his eyes. They worked long and hard every morning, more intensively than Lotte had ever thought possible. In the evening he accompanied Lotte in his lieder, a special joy for both of them, and also for his wife, Pauline, for whom most of them had been composed. There would be nostalgic tears and affectionate embraces and Lotte understood what few who knew the Strausses ever understood: that this marriage was a

truly happy one after all. To the world in general Frau Pauline
was the most notorious shrew since Xantippe, not excluding
Shakespeare's Kate. If a picnic had been planned and it started to
rain, Strauss would get the blame. If Lotte objected that he could
hardly be expected to stop the rain, Strauss would say: "Don't defend me—that always makes it worse." Her tantrums in public
made everyone shudder but Strauss. She often claimed that she
had married beneath her. She complained to Lotte that she could
have been the wife of a dashing young hussar. Lotte laughed and
said she could not work up much sympathy for the wife of the
world's greatest living composer. A typical response from
Pauline would be that Massenet and Lehár wrote far better music than her husband. Yet Strauss adored her and had already im-
mortalized her in such orchestral works as *Ein Heldenleben* and
Sinfonia domestica; now, in *Die Frau ohne Schatten* Lotte's role, the
Dyer's Wife, had been partly modeled on Pauline by Strauss's
great collaborator, Hugo von Hofmannsthal. Later, as we shall
see, Strauss was his own librettist for an opera entirely about
Pauline *(Intermezzo)*. Strauss had a placid nature and claimed that
he needed the goading of his wife to stimulate his inspiration.
"Believe me," he said to Lotte one day, "the admiration of the
whole world is less dear to me than one of Pauline's fits." Fortunately for Lotte, Pauline took a great liking to her. They did
strenuous calisthenics together every day, on the floor, for
Pauline felt that the sanatorium at Gmunden had not quite
finished the job of transforming Lotte into a sylph.

A letter to Baroness Putlitz gives Lotte's impressions while
they were still fresh:

> Those were very interesting and wonderful days which I spent in his
> delightful villa. We studied very much and in between I took "air
> baths" with the very earthy Frau Pauline Strauss…. There was a lot
> of fun and a lot of amazement, that I must say!! But I like her, she
> is such a character [sie ist so originell]. And she loves me ardently. I
> am on very friendly terms with her and her "Richardl." Back in
> Vienna, work poured down on me, so to speak; in the stupid heat of
> late summer we had unspeakably exhausting stage rehearsals from 10
> to 3 every day….

Lehmann had much to say about Strauss in several of her

books. She was asked about him in every interview. Here is an excerpt from one of her unpublished papers:

> The time spent at his house brought me nearer to him. But it would be an exaggeration if I said we were friends...one was simply not his friend: he drew a wall about himself and his family—and his works were the children of his spirit. Therefore I find it so wrong when people say he was too much the "businessman" and always only thinking about the royalties his operas would bring in.... No, he was like a father who naturally wanted to see his children admired and famous. Is that so wrong? That he happened to have a good sense for business has nothing to do, I find, with the ideal side of his genius....
>
> I always honored Strauss very much, also as a human being. And when in the terrible Nazi times most people did not understand him, I nevertheless always knew: he could not have been a Nazi. For political fanaticism was absolutely foreign to his nature. But if a member of his family was in danger, he would do anything to protect his loved ones [Strauss's daughter-in-law was Jewish].
>
> After all: who has the right to pry into the character of someone who has given so much beauty to the world?
>
> I have always honored him.... I think with gratitude of the glorious genius which gave so much richness to my life as a singer through his operas and through his songs.

Die Frau ohne Schatten makes enormous demands upon all the resources of a leading theatre. It received a lavish production, in spite of the miserable state of the economy. Then, as always, the opera was a symbol of all that was great in Austria's heritage. Almost everyone considered it worth every penny. The ingenious, magnificent sets were by Alfred Roller. Jeritza sang the Empress, Aagard-Oestwig the Emperor, Richard Mayr was Barak, Lucie Weidt the Nurse.

Incidentally, Lotte had always been told that the role of the Dyer's Wife had been written for her (as in the letter from Schalk, above). It was something of a shock for her to read a magazine article many decades later in which Jeritza was quoted as saying that the part had originally been offered to her, but that Strauss had changed his mind when he realized that the Empress was the more grateful role. Be that as it may, the subject came up in the vastly entertaining double interview that reunited the two arch-rivals during the intermission of a Metropolitan Opera broadcast in 1962.

The première was a glorious success, one of the most brilliant ever. Many critics felt that this was Richard Strauss's most beautiful, richly-textured opera (Strauss himself considered it his masterpiece). Everyone rejoiced in the exceptional cast of stars, all at their very brightest, and in the sumptuous settings and special, magical effects. Franz Schalk, who conducted, brought out all the beauties of the complex score.

Lotte's role was especially challenging because at first glance the Dyer's Wife seems rather unlikeable (as mentioned above, she was inspired partly by Hofmannsthal's impressions of Pauline). The character is a discontented, embittered young woman who seems sullen and selfish, forever reproaching her kindly, patient husband (Barak) and utterly lacking in any appreciation of his noble nature, let alone any feelings of gratitude for his understanding love. At least, that is how she appears in the first two-thirds of the opera. Lotte managed to win the sympathy of the audience for this poor, frustrated creature, and thereby to justify Barak's great love and add stature to the story, by discovering the jewel deeply buried under layers of grime. That is what Schalk knew she could do and what he meant in his telegram by "salvation." He saw that the part cried out for the sort of spiritual dimension she alone could find in it.

The rehearsals and performances presented a number of technical problems that had to be solved. Some of them are discussed in Lotte's book about the Strauss operas.

> I had been giving some thought to the problem of what I could possibly do [during the long, serene, and very beautiful musical interlude expressing the goodness of Barak]. The last preceeding phrase that I had sung consisted of a violent outburst against Barak, and immediately after the interlude I was to resume the same pitch of undiminished fury. Dramatically I felt somewhat at sea, and I asked Strauss what he thought I ought to do. "Do?" he asked in turn. "Nothing. Absolutely nothing at all. Why must you be doing something? After all, in real life people don't keep running back and forth all the time, do they? Just stand there quietly and think yourself into the meaning of your role. I'm sure you'll find the right sort of expression."

Strauss's simple explanation actually contained a valuable hint as to the nature of acting. One must have the courage to stand still, to "act" without "action," and one's thoughts must be so wholly concentrated and lucidly powerful as to be perceptibly convincing. To me, this was a revelation.

Then there were the quick changes. In one scene the Dyer's Wife is offered seductive temptations through magic.

This particular scene was staged with striking effect in Vienna. A huge glass platform rose out of the pit, with girls in slave costumes on it; multicolored lights played on it from below, and the vision was absolutely ravishing. The transformation [of the poor Dyer's Wife into a glamorous siren] came about after the brief moment of darkness which had to suffice for my change of costume. Two dressers stood by, ready and waiting; they quickly wrapped me in a brocade coat and fastened the diadem in my hair. Every movement had been practised to perfection, and my sudden reappearance as a queen must have been a rather impressive sight. A huge gold mirror was held up by the slave girls, and I stepped in front of it, kneeling slowly....

Then, after the vision of a handsome, half-naked young man, the Dyer's Wife is returned to her rags.

Once again...a brief moment of darkness and a change of costume accomplished in desperate haste. Somehow this race against time always came off without a hitch, but it invariably left me trembling from head to foot.

Lotte garnered many glorious reviews for Papa's scrapbook.

...It is not possible to portray a female creature more movingly, more compassionately, or more winsomely. With her seriously, sadly sung words, "You have not made me a mother. My craving for that I have had to put down," she casts a clarifying light over the riddles of the entire opera.... (Dr. Elsa Bienenfeld, Neues Wiener Journal, October 11, 1919]

...Lotte Lehmann was the Dyer's Wife. Already in appearance a magnificent, naturalistic character-study, her acting achieved rich nuances. Her vocal organ takes the complicated Straussian passages with effortless ease. The voice seems fuller and healthier.... (Armand Erdös, Wiener Mittags Zeitung, October 11, 1919]

Outside of the theatre, times were hard for everyone. The

new republic had been cut off from most of its former food and fuel supplies. A kilo of butter cost 180 crowns, sugar 65. Lotte and her aging parents needed servants. It was simply too expensive for them all to live together in the city. Lotte was receiving 50,000 crowns a year (Strauss as co-director 80,000). But, thanks to galloping inflation, that was just enough to house and feed one person. Though she had more than enough to do at the Opera, she had to accept as many guest engagements and sing as many concerts as possible to take care of her parents. She scored a great success in Prague. A popular variety theatre offered her 120,000 crowns to sing every evening in a 30-minute operetta to be composed especially for her by Franz Lehár. She fought for that with both directors, Schalk and Strauss, but they refused their permission. "Did she intend to sing while the customers were eating goulash?" They did not want a star of their opera to appear in cabaret. Lotte answered one question with another:"Did they intend to compensate her for the 120,000 crowns?"

In spite of glowing successes, Lotte was deeply depressed and very nervous. She confided her feelings to the baroness:

> Money seems to trickle away through my fingers. I have gone through weeks of a terrible depression that I can't seem to shake off. I have withdrawn from every social contact...I am always alone. Yesterday I gave in to the urging of a colleague and went to a supper at his house. Lots of people, champagne, happy chatter, laughter.... I sat among them like a stranger. I can't enjoy myself like that any more, or laugh so lightheartedly. I hope this will soon pass. How rarely a performance at the theatre makes me really happy. I am so nervous that I suffer stage-fright as never before....

To make matters worse, her father seemed to be failing and she had trouble getting on with him.

An apartment with a veranda and a garden was found for Mama and Papa in a villa in Baden, near the park. It turned out to be less expensive for them to take their main meal at a restaurant than to have it prepared at home. Mama was able to make breakfast, Jause (afternoon coffee snack), and Abendbrot (a simple supper) herself. Lotte moved into a Pension.

Next for Lotte were three Puccini operas in a row, the first in her career. Mimì in La Bohème, Madame Butterfly, and, in October

1920, Sister Angelica. Within a few years she also added Tosca, Manon Lescaut, and Turandot. Puccini himself came to Vienna to oversee the première of his *Trittico*, three one-act operas that had in common the theme of death, violent, transcendent, or satirical.

> He was accompanied, as usual, by his old friend, Riccardo Schnabel-Rossi (who served also as his interpreter). Puccini was not satisfied with the casting of the female role in Der Mantel (Il tabarro)—impatiently and in a sour mood he said to Riccardo, "Please go to the Angelica rehearsal and listen to the singer. Probably someone impossible, since I never heard of this Lehmann...." Riccardo told me that after five minutes of my piano-rehearsal he dashed back to Puccini, crying: "She is great!"
>
> "Oh, you with your partiality for anybody that happens to be singing in Vienna!" was the maestro's answer.
>
> The role in Der Mantel was then given to Jeritza and it is quite unnecessary to mention how enthusiastic Puccini was about the change. I too found him grateful and very delighted with my Angelica. I have a very flattering letter from him, and a picture...with the lovely inscription: "A la indimenticabile Angelica di Vienna."
>
> While he was in Vienna we also gave La Bohème. I sang Mimì.... After the performance he came to my dressing room, and when I asked him if he was satisfied with me, he answered: "Look into my eyes—there you see tears of gratitude...."
>
> Suor Angelica was given in Vienna at a memorial performance after Puccini's death, and my voice and my soul gave a greeting to the great master of cantilena. Perhaps they soared to those regions of light to which he was carried away.

Among his operas, *Suor Angelica* was Puccini's child of sorrows. Soon after the world première at the Metropolitan Opera, that centerpiece of the Triptych had been detached from the side-panels. The nun whose sin for love was forgiven by the Virgin was left to languish in semi-oblivion until Lotte Lehmann revealed what could be done with the part. For this, Puccini, who had never lost faith in his opera, was infinitely grateful. To those critics who belittled *Suor Angelica* he had this to say: "Go to Vienna!" According to his friend and sometime librettist, Giovacchino Forzano, he felt he had found a successor to his beloved Rosina Storchio in Lotte Lehmann who had "absolutely realized" his conception.

There are three letters from Puccini in the Lotte Lehmann Archive of the University of California, Santa Barbara. The first was written after he heard that she had canceled her first scheduled performance as Manon Lescaut; apparently she had expressed the fear he might be annoyed with her.

Gentile e cara Sig^{ina} Lehmann

How can I be angry with my soavissima [utterly lovely] Suor Angelica? With much sorrow I heard that you gave up the part of Manon because of illness. I asked about you, but they told me you were not in Vienna.

Be assured of my esteem for I recognize and appreciate your great qualities as an artist. You will sing Manon on some other occasion and I am absolutely certain that you will have a triumphant success.

With best wishes and affectionate greetings
Your devoted

Giacomo Puccini

Lotte finally did sing in Puccini's *Manon Lescaut*, three years after her first *Suor Angelica*, and once again the composer came to Vienna, this time especially to hear her.

Dear Signorina Lehmann   19. X. 23

I want to tell you how happy I am with your interpretation of Manon—your art, full of sentiment, together with your beautiful voice have given to my Manon a great vividness [un grande rilievo] and I thank you cordially and am very happy for the great success you have had.—a rivederci—with best greetings

Your affectionate

G. Puccini

Two months later she received a postcard from Italy:

Many good wishes and greetings to the gentle and exquisite Manon from G. Puccini

Less than a year later Puccini was dead. He never heard her Tosca, but he told Forzano he could well imagine that she would bring to the role "more womanliness" than other singers and through that quality make Tosca more believable.

When Lotte, then in her eighties, happened to read what Puccini had said about her, she burst into tears.

Top Left: The "inseparable four" as Pages in *Tannhäuser*, Hamburg, Lotte Lehmann on the right. Top Right: The role that won her a Vienna Court Opera contract, Micaëla in *Carmen*. Bottom Left: Lehmann (left) as Dorabella in *Così fan tutte* by Mozart. Bottom Right: Margiana in *Barbier von Bagdad* by Cornelius.

I

Top Left: An early leading role in Hamburg as Agathe in *Der Freischütz*. Top Right: Myrtocle, the blind heroine of *Die toten Augen*, one of Lehmann's greatest successes in Hamburg. Bottom Left: Her "break-through" role as Elsa in *Lohengrin*, Hamburg 1912. Bottom Right: Lehmann as Eurydice.

Top Left: Lehmann as Elsa in Act II of *Lohengrin*, Vienna. Top Right: As Eva in Act I of *Die Meistersinger*, Vienna. Bottom Left: As Elisabeth with Lauritz Melchior in *Tannhäuser*. Bottom Right: As Elisabeth in Act II of *Tannhäuser*, Vienna.

III

als „Sieglinde"

Top Left: Lehmann as Sieglinde in *Die Walküre*, Vienna. Top Right: Siegmund draws the sword from the tree, an ecstatic moment in *Die Walküre*, Act I. Bottom Left: Lehmann in the dungeon scene of *Fidelio*, Salzburg. Bottom Right: As Puccini's *Tosca*, with *Alfred Jerger*.

IV

Top Left: Lehmann as Manon in Puccini's *Manon Lescaut*. Top Right: Madame Butterfly. Bottom Left: Puccini's favorite interpreter of the role of Suor Angelica. Bottom Right: Lehmann as Turandot.

Top Left: Lehmann as "Lotte" (Charlotte) in *Werther* by Massenet, Vienna. Top Right: She sang the première of *Arabella* the day after her mother died, 1933. Bottom Left, Right: Preceding her consummate Marschallin role in Vienna, Lehmann played both Sophie and Octavian in Hamburg and Octavian in Vienna in Strauss' *Der Rosenkavalier.*

Top Left: The Composer in *Ariadne auf Naxos* by Richard Strauss, première 1916, the role that made Lehmann famous in Vienna. Top Right: As the poor Dyer's wife in *Die Frau ohne Schatten* by R. Strauss. Bottom Left: The Dyer's wife is tempted by jewels and rich fabric in a lightning change of costume. Bottom Right: As Christine in *Intermezzo* by R. Strauss.

Top Left: Lehmann as Frau Fluth in *The Merry Wives of Windsor* by Nicolai, Vienna. Top Right: As Blanchefleur in *Kuhreigen* by Kienzl, Vienna. Bottom Left: As Massenet's Manon. Bottom Right: Tatiana's letter scene from Eugen Onegin by Tchaikovsky.

Chapter Nine

SHE WAS HIS BIRTHDAY PRESENT

L OTTE LEHMANN MET OTTO KRAUSE, her handsome future husband, in a most unusual way: she was his birthday present.
A present from his wealthy wife, who wanted something
very special for that special occasion. He was a great opera-lover
and his favorite singer was Lotte Lehmann. His wife, for whom
money was no object, gave a splendid party and engaged
Fräulein Lehmann to sing. For Lotte, it was love at first sight.
She had never experienced that feeling so overwhelmingly before. Every note she sang became a *billet doux*. The recipient was
just as smitten as the gift. He left his wife and—temporarily—his
four children. The first Mrs. Krause deeply regretted her generous, extravagant impulse, which had turned out to be much more
expensive than she had ever dreamed. One can understand her
bitterness; but she rather overdid her fury as a woman scorned.
She adamantly refused to give Otto a divorce and began to make
Lotte's life as miserable as possible. Since she was very rich and
influential, she could afford to make Lotte very miserable indeed.
All Vienna was titillated at the scandal.

Lotte was torn apart by an ethical dilemma, a crisis of conscience, that would have been devastating enough as her private
problem; it was unbearably aggravated by the merciless glare of
unwanted publicity. She was on the verge of a nervous breakdown. She decided to leave Vienna and its opera. The following
story appeared in the *Neues Wiener Tagblatt* of February 13, 1922:

> ...*Frl. Lotte Lehmann yesterday submitted to the directors of the
> State Opera a request for release from her contract. We have been
> informed by competent authority that this decision is unrelated to any
> artistic matters or to the relationship between the artist and the di-
> rectors of the State Opera, and is attributable only to private person-
> al reasons. At present Frl. Lehmann is firmly determined to leave*

77

*Vienna permanently…. She is presently a patient at a sanatorium
in the vicinity of Vienna, undergoing treatment for a nervous disturbance which developed out of entirely private causes.*

The directors did not release her. She was at this point their
most beloved star, especially now that Maria Jeritza was spend-
ing more and more of her time at the Metropolitan Opera in
New York.

Before that fateful birthday party for Otto Krause and its stress-
ful aftermath, Lotte had long been depressed and very lonely,
shunning society. The following letter to Baroness Putlitz gives
a pathetic picture of her state of mind before he came into her
life:

*In Gross-Pankow you live in a lovelier, quieter world. The big city is
unbearable. You see nothing of the profiteering and graft that are
spreading everywhere here. I live withdrawn from the world like a
hermit. I literally never go out…. For next summer—June to September—I am in the midst of lively negotiations with South America.
If only something will come of it! Aside from the immense fees, the
long trip alone is enticing, the thought of not having to sit around like
a bird in the cage of this dying Austria. Horrible the day of rioting
lately, of which you surely must have read. Vienna was the picture of
terror. One lives here continually under a sword of Damocles. The
air is charged with fearful tension, rumors flutter everywhere…. The
inflation is so crazy that every salary-raise is overtaken by the rise in
prices before it is even paid out. I have tried to keep these fears from
Mama. She has no idea of the prices my brother and I are paying
for her. This is what pains me above everything: that she may yet
have to experience hard times, perhaps the horrors of a new and
terrible revolution, instead of enjoying a little peace at the end of a
life that was burdened with many cares. But hers is just one individual destiny! This so-called "great time" has turned men into a herd
of sheep and the wolves are attacking….*

The contrast between Lotte's private unhappiness and the
golden picture of Vienna's *Liebling,* basking in success after success, is rather shocking. Lotte needed something to lift her up, to
thrill her with beauty. She had given that thrill so often to others
from the stage. Now she found it, suddenly, in love.

But she imposed upon herself a painful expiation: an almost
crushing sense of guilt. Her loving mother, who had met Otto

and admired him, tried to reassure her in a touching letter:

> Dearest Lotte,
>
> Let me tell you, as your mother, that the Lord puts love into human
> hearts; it cannot be sinful that you love Otto. Such laws are made by
> humans, not by God! Otto is in my eyes a very good and honest
> man. He gave me his hand and promised that he will never again
> bring such unhappiness and misery to our family as he did before,
> nor make you, my dearest child, suffer—he will never do that again!
> Everything points to his great love for you. In case that woman puts
> up another act, don't despair, my dearest child; we shall find ways
> and means to make you happy. Just keep your trust in the Lord, He
> will lead you. Don't torture your nerves. And even if at the moment
> things look obscure and hopeless, the sun will soon come out again....
>
> Your loving Mama

The more sensational Viennese papers were doing their ut-
most to exploit the affair for all it was worth. Lotte was afraid
that Baroness Putlitz would sternly disapprove. It was a while before she summoned the courage to write to her about it.

> Forgive me, dearest Baroness, I was not sure that you would under-
> stand. Yours is such an upright nature, so sensitive to what is strictly
> right and proper. And that which has become my destiny departs
> from that straight path. It strikes at a marriage, separates husband
> and wife, father from children. I believed that you would condemn
> me. And I kiss your kindly hand that you do not. I have been
> through many, many trials and have stood upon that narrow bridge
> that leads into eternal night. If I were not so firmly convinced that it
> will turn to good, must turn to good—I would not have been able to
> live through this. So I go [to South America] with the deep faith that
> the man I love will be free when I return. I can do no more than
> put an ocean between us until he is free. For the inner reason that I
> can no longer bear to be here and for the outer reason that I do not
> want something to be branded as a deplorable adventure that to us is
> our destiny. One thing I beg you not to believe: that I was irrespons-
> ible or frivolous. Oh, Baroness, a heavy stone has fallen from my
> heart now that I have been able to speak of this freely.

Lotte was miserably unhappy during the voyage to South
America (in May 1922) and during the long months abroad. The
longing for Otto, her homesickness, and an overpowering sense

of guilt were tormenting her ceaselessly. Helene Wildbrunn, a great Wagnerian soprano and a warm, kindly human being, gave Lotte the mothering she badly missed. At the end of their tour, Lotte gave her a photograph with the following inscription: "Beloved Frau Wildbrunn, your friendship is the one very precious thing—the only thing—I gained from the South American tour." Here is how Helene Wildbrunn remembered those days:

> That inscription, so typical of her impulsive nature, sprang from a soul that was at that time deeply suffering, that could not quite rejoice over the unprecedented, brilliant successes of her thrilling Sieglinde which were being exuberantly celebrated by press and public. She could not get over her longing for Vienna, for her great love, her future husband, and the separation from her beloved parents; she was deaf to all the hymns of praise which were bestowed upon her art.
>
> Perhaps it was granted to me and to my husband to have a calming effect upon her during that time of daily contact, to give her comfort and hope, and to guide her thoughts toward the task that lay before her, to give to expectant audiences the blessing of her great art.
>
> As her partner I was captivated every evening anew by the magic of her so warmly radiant voice, that could effortlessly obey every inner impulse, and I was overwhelmed by the depth and truthfulness of her rich feelings, by her total surrender to the character she was to portray. In Lotte Lehmann nature truly became art and that art unfailingly led back to nature. The most precious thing that an artist can offer!

The ship, *Tomaso di Savoia*, carried two contingents, an Italian troupe under Pietro Mascagni, and a German one under Felix von Weingartner. Mascagni would have nothing to do with the Germans, perhaps because of bitter memories of wartime enmity; but the other Italians were more cordial to their German counterparts.

Lotte and her parents, who went to stay with Fritz and his wife at Westerland, had never been separated for such a long stretch. Her mother tried to be cheerful in her letters:

> My dearest, sweetest Lotte,
>
> My thoughts are always with you. Now I am worried how you are taking the trip and whether you are not sick. We shall be relieved once we know that you are there. And you will see so much beauty,

the country, the people.... Enjoy it all. Youth is such a wonderful time and you are so receptive to everything beautiful that comes your way. Later, when the gate to the future is closed, one can enjoy the memories. That is also something great, and you will one day experience that too, dearest Lotte. I can enjoy it now and it makes me, who am an old woman, very happy.... Soon you will be in America and see wild people, Negroes, Indians, and savages. Please be careful.... Come back safe and sound — that is the greatest wish of Mama who loves you.

Parsifal and the entire *Ring* were presented in Buenos Aires, with resounding success. It was the first time that Wagner had been performed in German in South America. There were also performances in Montevideo, Rio de Janeiro, and Sào Paolo. Lotte received glowing reviews as Freia, Sieglinde, and Gutrune. The following, from Buenos Aires, is typical:

...One of the most beautiful voices, fresh and radiant, belongs to Lotte Lehmann.... In sorrow, passion, in rapturous love and yielding femininity her Sieglinde was a perfect masterpiece, which will count as one of the greatest events of this year's Colón season.

Besides her operatic appearances, Lotte's contract called for a recital at Bahia Blanca. The audience there had never heard a German lieder-singer before.

They thought of a singer more as a castanet-snapping Spanish woman, and didn't understand it at all when a lady in a simple evening dress sang simple songs in a foreign language without any gestures or fuss.... At the beginning of the recital the audience scarcely applauded at all, but gradually the magic of the Lied conquered there too....

Lotte had to repeat the concert a few days later. Meanwhile, mournful letters were filling the mailbags bound for Europe. The I-told-you-so's began sailing in the opposite direction:

My darling Lotte,

Just now came your two letters with two pictures.... Your eyes and your whole expression so sad! My dearest Lotte, remember, we begged you to stay here, not to go; even the last day, dearest Lotte, there was still a chance! I was so worried about you and you got so angry and said, "Do stop!" And I started again, tried to convince you, but did not succeed. Then, when I saw that I could not move you, I tried to tell you that the sea voyage would be good for you and your

*nerves.... When you signed the contract for America I got so scared,
as if I would have a stroke, but I dared not tell you because you always think that I do not want you to have some pleasure or other,
that I would prefer to keep you always near me. Well, of course I am
only happy when I can see you, if only from afar!...*

*You wrote that you had sinned against Otto's wife, and that you
had to suffer; and you torture yourself with such thoughts as that your
going abroad was a punishment. How can you have such horrible
ideas? Your wish to spend a few months abroad has been fulfilled.
Well, you had other ideas in your imagination and now you do not
like it. But you are reasonable and must tell yourself that it is a great
disappointment, but not a punishment!*

Finally, Otto decided to join Lotte, sailing to South America at
the end of July. Mama was greatly relieved.

*He is such a wonderful man. And now we can be reassured, be-
cause nothing can happen to you when he is with you. Rest assured
that I am very fond of him, and that I hope your deepest wishes may
be fulfilled. This is the great wish of your loving Mama.*

Otto had come to Vienna as a child from Budapest, where he
was born in 1883. Before his marriage he had served as a cavalry
officer, having been an accomplished horseman since the age of
fourteen. Back in Vienna, Lotte had the thrill of seeing him ride
one of the famous *Lippizaner*, the white stallions of the Spanish
Riding School, still one of the most popular tourist attractions in
Austria. He taught Lotte to ride and some of their happiest times
were when they were galloping together over windswept
moors or through the shallow surf beside the sea. He was not,
however, a man of independent wealth.

It was four years before he was free, four years of trial, of passion and penitence, of private ups and downs, for Otto and
Lotte.

Artistically they were great years. She sang her first Desdemona, Tosca, Ariadne, and Manon Lescaut. There were guest performances in Berlin, Budapest, Prague. Raves and ovations everywhere. The Jeritza-Lehmann rivalry continued to sell newspapers (and theatre tickets):

*...Will Lotte Lehmann be a Tosca? Will Lotte Lehmann be no
Tosca? The riddle-game went 'round and 'round. Well-meaning fe-*

male colleagues prophesied a flop. The fans of Frau Jeritza smiled their superior smile; for them there is naturally only one Tosca.... The fans of Frau Gutheil-Schoder showed their skepticism; for them too there is but one singer and she is neither Jeritza (mocking smiles) nor Lehmann (smiles of condolence) but Gutheil (smiles of ecstasy). But even the Lehmannites themselves were unsure; for it was by no means certain that an ever-so-German Agathe, an Eva, the singer of blonde lyrical sentiments, the tender-hearted Lotte Lehmann, would turn out to be a good Tosca.... People shrugged their shoulders, put on an expression of deeply compassionate, painful regret and predicted the worst. We know how sympathetic colleagues are, especially those who crave to sing the same role. It literally breaks their hearts when a colleague risks disaster. Well, I can't help it.... The Tosca of Fräulein Lehmann was a success, in fact a great success. It cannot be denied that she pleased the public. [She] gave her own kind of Tosca, without any scenery-chewing, without virtuoso theatrical effects, simple, natural, with great warmth of feeling; she offered nothing but a loving woman who suffers torments.... Jeritza's Tosca has a bolder design, she is a singing she-devil with the smile of a child and the shriek of Messalina; she burns down the theatre. Lotte Lehmann is plainer, but captivating....

...A very nice Jeritza enthusiast sat next to me during yesterday's performance of Tosca—*in both intermissions and three times during the second act [she kept repeating]: "No, Lehmann is no Jeritza." The Jeritza enthusiast is right. Lehmann is no Jeritza; Lehmann is Lehmann. The great singer, the mistress of an incandescent voice, and the artist who can trust her blooming soprano to meet the outrageous requirements of Tosca. Elemental power, it must be admitted, is not her strong suit. And therefore the prayer in the second act is the highlight of her Tosca.... It is the artistic deed with which Lotte Lehmann has conquered the part.*

In Berlin Lotte sang the double role Marie/Marietta in *Die tote Stadt* by Erich Korngold, another Jeritza part. (George Szell, like the composer, a young prodigy, was the conductor; Richard Tauber, her partner.) Korngold wrote her his appreciation:

I cannot leave [Berlin] without expressing, apart from my general thanks to the director, my special gratitude to you for your unique achievement. You were marvelous—enchanting. With all the necessary immorality as required by this role. I would not want one bit

84 LOTTE LEHMANN

more of depravity or "verisimilitude." Your dramatic impersonation,
melodic accents and climaxes, the purity of outline in the death
scene—everything was there. Also passion, truthfulness of expression,
and devotion to the opera.... I thank you a thousand times and with
all my heart. In sincere admiration and devotion, your
Erich Wolfgang Korngold.

Lotte made every effort to be objective about her own strengths and weaknesses. She forwarded the above letter to Korngold's biographer with the comment: "Nevertheless, the real Marietta was Maria Jeritza. I shall never forget her portrayal of the part!" Be that as it may, "Marietta's Lute Song," recorded in its original form as a duet with Richard Tauber, was one of Lotte Lehmann's most popular records.

The artistic event of 1924 that had the most far-reaching importance for her career was without a doubt her first Marschallin in *Der Rosenkavalier*. She was the first singer (and for a long time the only one) to sing all three of the leading soprano parts in that opera. Lotte and the Marschallin grew together, she molding the role in her own unique way and the role molding her, until she became identified with the character. From then on an aura of the Marschallin never totally disappeared from her public persona. In the minds and hearts of many admirers she *was* the Marschallin.

It was almost through a fluke that she first sang the part. London's Covent Garden offered her a contract that was dependent upon her singing the Marschallin. They were under the impression that the role was already a part of her repertoire. Lotte was afraid that if she set them straight she might lose the chance to sing at such a prestigious opera house. So she signed the contract and studied the part. Actually, she practically knew it already, from having sung Octavian so many times. Still, as she has written, the Marschallin is not the sort of role one can master overnight.

Fortunately, the conductor of the London *Rosenkavalier* was Bruno Walter. He was an enormous help to her in polishing the role, in bringing out the thousand facets that make it uniquely fascinating. It was the first of their many collaborations. Lotte had always wanted to sing with him. It was partly because of him that she had signed the contract. She revered him ever afterward as a wonderful teacher and friend, as one of the guiding spirits in her artistic development. His approach was not just a musical one. He could have been a great stage director, if he had not been an even greater conductor. Talking through a role with him was worth a month of stage rehearsals.

The date was May 21, 1924, a Lehmann landmark. It was a dream cast: Richard Mayr as Baron Ochs, Elisabeth Schumann as Sophie, and Delia Reinhardt as Octavian. It was the first performance of *Der Rosenkavalier* in London since 1914 (those Beecham nights at Drury Lane with Lotte as Sophie), on account of the world war and its anti-German aftermath. The audience was so "indescribably" enthusiastic that two extra performances were hastily added to the originally scheduled six (Frida Leider sang one of the Marschallins). The critics of London were unanimously delighted with Lotte:

> ...It is impossible to praise too highly the performance of Mme. Lotte Lehmann; she was every inch a princess—voice and gesture alike held a dignity that raised the tone of the whole thing.... (The Telegraph)

> ...[Lotte Lehmann is] an exquisite singer with a voice capable of the most delicate inflections, and an actress whose quiet ease is the perfection of the art that conceals art.... (Ernest Newman)

> ...Lotte Lehmann's princess moves one as one scarcely expects to be moved in opera....

> ...The outstanding performance of the evening was that of Mme. Lotte Lehmann as the Marschallin. Vocally and histrionically finished to the smallest detail, it had a nobility of style and a depth and variety of emotion that made it seem the only ideal rendering of the part one may wish to hear in a lifetime.... [The last two quotations are from unidentified clippings in a Lehmann scrapbook.]

During the same guest engagement, Lotte sang Sieglinde and Ariadne. It was the first production of the revised version of *Ariadne auf Naxos* in England (Schumann was the Composer, Maria Ivogün the Zerbinetta). In spite of all the enthusiasm for Lotte's Marschallin, the audience stayed away. Ariadne's time had not yet come. There were only two performances.

Richard Strauss had tried to dissuade Lotte from signing the contract with London. He had wanted her to spend May and

June rehearsing his latest opera, *Intermezzo*, in Vienna. His letter of March 22, 1924, expressed his intention of personally working with her on the "very difficult" leading role. Four days later, while she was singing in Berlin, he sent an urgent telegram: *"PLEASE NOT SIGN LONDON BUT STAY VIENNA."* As luck would have it, the planned première of *Intermezzo* did not take place in Vienna. The dual directorship, Schalk and Strauss, had become increasingly strained. The two temperaments were poles apart. Opposing factions had formed around each of them and had gradually grown in force and belligerence. Finally, Strauss resigned his post. He agreed to continue conducting in Vienna and kept the beautiful town house he had built on a part of the historical Belvedere site that had been given to him by the city in a mood of gratitude for artistic glories. He gave the honor of the *Intermezzo* première to Dresden instead of Vienna, with the stipulation that Lotte Lehmann sing the part of Christine (alias Pauline; the role was obviously a portrait of his wife).

Dresden was not happy about that stipulation. They were proud of their ensemble and preferred to cast with their own stars a world première of such importance and prestige. Lotte encountered considerable resentment at first. For one thing, the conductor, Fritz Busch, was scandalized by her free-and-easy way with the notes. He complained to Strauss that she was always "swimming." That is the German way of saying she was not always singing exactly what the composer wrote. Strauss's answer was a classic: "I'd rather have Lehmann swim through my operas in that inspired way of hers than have any one else, however precise." He could be very indulgent if he felt that the singer was genuinely communicating the essence of the part, filling it with the breath of life. In later productions of *Intermezzo*, with other sopranos, he demanded a much stricter adherence to the printed notes.

Strauss wrote his own libretto for *Intermezzo*. It was based on a minor incident from his own life with Pauline. He wanted the naturalness of everyday conversation and devised a vocal line that would faithfully follow every inflection of the text. Sometimes the words were merely spoken rather than sung. Only rarely was the vocal line allowed to soar. Christine is represented as a holy

terror. It was Lotte's challenge to make her sympathetic. Strauss
knew that she would do just that, when he insisted upon her for
the première. She was not at all keen to do the part. For one
thing, it seemed fiendishly difficult to ears not yet attuned to
Wozzeck or Lulu. For another, it would take a bit of courage to portray a shrewish Pauline while aware that that rough diamond of a
lady would be sitting in the audience. Lotte on Christine-
Pauline:

> Pauline Strauss was incredibly rude on occasion, but fierce in her
> stubborn integrity. In Intermezzo [Strauss] certainly presented her
> in all her many-faceted and ever-contradictory complexity....
> Investing the role of Christine with a measure of charm proved to be
> a difficult task.... It is rather tricky to be charming if the libretto re-
> quires you to say what I can only translate as "Shut your big mouth."
>
> It was truly touching to witness the care that Strauss lavished at
> rehearsals upon making sure that his Pauline-Christine corresponded
> in every detail to the personality of his wife.... When he said to me,
> "Lotte, you're really so much like my wife in your whole being," I ac-
> cepted it as the greatest compliment ever paid me. In fact, I had to
> swallow hard a few times before I could trust myself to thank him.

The world première of this "bourgeois comedy with symphon-
ic interludes" took place on November 4, 1924. The work was
performed not in the opera house but in the more intimate
Schauspielhaus where spoken drama was generally presented. Lotte's inspired impersonation of the leading role was a major factor
in a brilliant success. A great future was predicted for the new
opera. Actually, it is only rather recently that it really came into its
own again, thanks mainly to a charming production in Munich
and an excellent recording.

Lotte added Dresden to her list of conquests:

> ...Lotte Lehmann—vocally and histrionically a sensation. Any man
> with a heart in his body would be glad to go home to this
> "Xantippe".... (Dr. Otto Reuter)
>
> ...In the role of the temperamental, passionate wife Lotte Lehmann
> offered an unsurpassable achievement of rare truthfulness and natu-
> ralness, with a thoroughly sympathetic undertone.
>
> ....No praise is too great for her feat.... That Frl. Lotte Lehmann
> was able to portray this complicated figure with such living warmth
> assures for her a reputation as a singer with unlimited abilities.

During her guest engagement in Dresden, Lotte sang some of her other roles as well, Desdemona, Elisabeth, Eva, and Mimì. Dresden, the "Florence of the North," was very proud of its culture, of its opera, of the great singers who belonged or had belonged to its ensemble, of the discriminating taste of its audiences. Therefore, these paeans of praise are doubly impressive:

> ...As Desdemona [she] surprised us with an abundance of new sides to her highly gifted artistry. In her costume and make-up, as if after a painting by Titian, she gave the figure utterly individual contours. She by no means yielded herself in grief to the treachery of Iago, but rather plunged actively into the drama and fought for her innocence up until the last moment. Her downfall attained the stature of incomparable tragedy. The glorious voice revels in the high-arched, late-Verdi cantilena, a magnificent, dramatically colored bel canto.... (C. J. P.)

> [Elisabeth]...The voice has the intoxication of youth, bubbling over with the blissful joy of singing. Then there is the great temperament, not just in the acting but also in the voice. Further, the fabulous high notes which soar so victoriously over the ensemble, dominating it effortlessly. It was already a magnificent achievement purely from the vocal point of view; it became even more so through the acting. The appearance alone was enough to win us over. One could believe her to be one of those lovely sculptured figures from the Naumburg Cathedral. But that was the external surface. High above that was what Lotte Lehmann accomplished with her portrayal.... Here was embodied humanity.... (Th.)

> [Eva]...She turned the evening into an event.... (C. J. P.)

> [Mimì]...Yesterday Lotte Lehmann sang Mimì in La Bohème. Those were precious hours that one experienced in the opera house. Hours of inner living.

Behind the scenes there were plenty of problems and frustrations, as usual. As soon as she returned from South America with a pocketful of hard cash, Lotte set about finding a suitable home for her parents. She wanted to buy them a house with land, where they could raise animals for food in those difficult times. Otto and Papa investigated all sorts of real estate in Germany and Austria. The search took many months. Finally, in April 1923, they found what they were looking for at Hinterbrühl, not far from Vienna. Mama could hardly express her relief:

My good, dearest Lotte and Otto,

Indescribable is my joy. I am so proud and happy to have my own home. Already now! This is the fulfillment of my greatest and most fervent wish. How lovely it will be to have my own household! I am so full of happiness and gratitude to you and Otto—you really did not rest until you fulfilled your mother's wishes! I can hardly believe it— a house and a garden—it will be ours till our death—Papa is so happy. He sees himself already working in the garden. He is laughing for joy....

Mama who loves you.

It was a full year before they could move into their new home because the tenants refused to move out after the property had been sold. There was a law to protect their rights. The only solution acceptable to them was that Lotte and Otto should find them a comparably advantageous place to live in Vienna, and that was more easily said than done. The search continued, this time for a home for the tenants.

Meanwhile, the inflation in Germany, where Lotte's parents were living until they could move to Hinterbrühl, was even wilder than in Austria. In April 1923, 125,000 marks to the dollar; in September 48 million! It cost six million, for instance, to rent a seat cushion in a third-class train car. A train ticket from Munich to Berlin, second class, cost 583 million marks.

Finally, after a year of waiting, Lotte's parents were able to enjoy their new home. Lotte, however, was mostly away, in London, Berlin, Dresden. Papa had very much wanted to go to Dresden for Lotte's first *Intermezzo*. She persuaded him not to come, fearing a fiasco. She asked him to wait for the opera to come to Vienna. When it finally did, a little over two years later, her dear father was dead. He did not live to see the day, April 28, 1926, when Lotte and Otto, free at last, were married.

Chapter Ten

I KISS HER AND SHE THANKS ME

THE MARSCHALLIN IN LONDON made Lotte a truly international star. From then on her career blossomed outward from its center in Vienna. Her seasons in London and Berlin became annual events. She sang in the Salzburg Festivals every summer from 1926 until 1937. Except for two seasons (1922/23, 1923/24), she remained loyal to Hamburg until 1929. There was also the Munich Festival of 1926, there were Budapest, Breslau, Prague. Paris was happy to be conquered in 1928, Stockholm and Brussels in 1929. She was the first German to sing in Belgium after the war; her triumph with three programs of German lieder (the first two at the Royal Theatre, the third at the Palace of Fine Arts) "was not only a great personal success but represented a significant step forward in establishing a better relationship between Belgium and Germany." At the start of the first of her recitals in Brussels, the audience was decidedly cool. Memories of wartime devastation left great bitterness against the Germans in many Belgian hearts. But the Lehmann magic quickly worked its spell. One elderly Belgian lady said: "I can't stand that language, but the singer sings so gloriously that I can't help applauding." (Both quotations are from the clipping in Lotte Lehmann's press book of an unidentified newspaper report.) Finally, in 1930, came the U.S.A.

During all this time she was also active in the recording studios. Arias, lieder (too often with wheezy salon orchestra accompaniments, but vocally beautiful), religious songs, and some appealing, lighter music, like her irresistably seductive version of *Eine kleine Liebelei*.

There were honors and decorations. Especially for her, Schalk revived the title of *Kammersängerin* (literally, Chamber Singer,

90

from the days of the monarchy when singers were honored by the appointment to sing for the emperor in his chamber, a sign of his highest esteem). Lotte was the first singer to receive that designation since the collapse of the monarchy. She officially became *Frau Kammersängerin* Lotte Lehmann on February 17, 1926. On September 26, 1928, she became an "Honor-Member of the Vienna State Opera."

Lotte was decorated by France, first with the Golden Palm, then on March 19, 1931, with the order of the Legion of Honor. At that time, she was one of the very few women who had received that honor. Former Premier Jean Louis Barthou (who happened to be a great Lehmann fan) kissed her on both cheeks in traditional French style as part of the ceremony. Lotte was so moved she could only stammer out, "*Merci.*" Barthou turned to the audience and said: "She is absolutely charming. I kiss her and she thanks me."

The King of Sweden conferred upon her the golden medal *Literis et Artibus* after a performance of *Fidelio* in February 1929 (Maria Nemeth was similarly honored for her performance as Donna Anna in *Don Giovanni*). After a difficult crossing of the ice-bound Baltic, the Vienna Opera had come to Stockholm for a guest engagement. Lotte started back independently, before the rest of the company. Her ship was stuck fast in the ice for twenty-two hours.

Fidelio! The next great landmark in Lotte's career after the Marschallin in *Der Rosenkavalier* was the role of Leonore ("Fidelio") in Beethoven's *Fidelio*, the supreme test of her endurance as well as of her artistry. Lehmann often said that the role demanded every bit of physical and spiritual strength that she could muster. It was her farthest excursion into "high-dramatic" territory. When she fell to the floor of the prison after the great rescue quartet, she felt as if she were not just *acting* a collapse; then, however, the flaming ecstasy of the following duet filled her instantly with new energy and life, from its very first notes. In *My Many Lives* she writes: "I found in [the role of Leonore] the most exalted moments of my opera career and was shaken by it to the depths of my being."

She sang the part for the first time on March 26, 1927, in a gala performance to celebrate the centennial of Beethoven's death. There was a cast of stars: Piccaver as Florestan, Alfred Jerger as Pizarro, Mayr as Rocco, Schumann as Marzelline. Lotte Lehmann reached new heights and set a new standard. Franz Schalk, who had guided her through the rehearsals and conducted the performance, wrote to a friend: "A great, overwhelming, radiant festival, and our Lotte Lehmann was its brilliant center." Anna Bahr-Mildenburg, a great singer of the previous generation, was in the audience. Her impressions of that night have been preserved:

> After the great Leonore aria I was seized with terror: that was such a deeply human, thrilling scene, so natural and full of feeling, that I thought my pulse had stopped beating. Everything that the young singer had done before was as if swept away through this achievement, which will signify a landmark in Lehmann's career. Her accomplishment is grander and more human, more detailed and well thought out than that of the great Lilli Lehmann.

The critics searched for new superlatives:

> ...Lotte Lehmann was an experience as Leonore. That is a Fidelio of whom they will still be singing in the most distant future. That is perfection.

> ...Lotte Lehmann was simply glorious; more than that, hers was great singing and a moving womanly creation.

> ...One can hardly imagine another performer of Leonore like Frau Lehmann. Perhaps she lacks heroic volume. But out of her words, whether spoken or sung, the tones sound as if they come from the depths of the feminine heart. So speaks and so sings the purest love, which is infinite in its joy of giving, only giving, and asks nothing, expects nothing in return. That tone, true to nature, unaffected, unadorned with any fancy nuances, penetrates movingly to our hearts.

Two months later Lotte sang Fidelio in Hamburg to similar acclaim:

> ...She is one of the few who have realized the mysterious something which this opera contains; she is in tune with the magical things in the Beethoven language, she has come inwardly near to the soul of Fidelio in an astonishing process of artistic travail. For years we have

experienced no Leonore in Hamburg who reached so deeply into our hearts.... In acting as in song this Leonore was the glowing flame of the evening.... Feeling was everything, guided vocally by powerful impulses, yet under emotions of the highest kind. A sound-miracle [ein Klangwunder].

Berlin was equally ecstatic:

...In a performance filled by Bruno Walter with the spirit of Beethoven, Lotte Lehmann sings Leonore, frees that image of the Ideal from the bonds of tradition. Intuitively conceived out of the fullness of a strong, individual femininity, a Leonore of pure human greatness emerges, to whom conventional operatic pathos and masculinized heroics are equally foreign. A womanly nature of pensive inner simplicity which does not give up its natural manner even in masculine dress, a true heroine of the heart.... This Leonore moves us and stirs us because she alone is fundamentally the genuinely felt Leonore of Beethoven. She sings her great aria, technically masterfully articulated, with moving sentiment, an outpouring of purest feeling. In the prison scene she finds just the tone of voice, the very gesture for the strongest possible dramatic accentuation. "Kill first his wife!" how deeply stirring that sounds from her mouth....

Leo Slezak sang Florestan to Lotte's Leonore in some of her later performances in Vienna, and had this to say about her in his autobiography:

Lotte Lehmann was my favorite of the many Leonores with whom I have sung. She had the secret, the only secret we have—the heart....

The production of Fidelio with Lehmann as Leonore was taken to Paris in 1928 and to Stockholm in 1929. During the guest performances of the Vienna Opera in Paris, Lotte also sang her Marschallin and Sieglinde. The composer, Reynaldo Hahn (whose songs she loved to sing), summarized his impressions of the season for one of the Paris papers:

...With a refined expertise [science], with admirable nobility and justness of expression, she molded, shaped, and adapted, to the most delicate nuances of feeling, the precious material of a voice rich in timbre, moving and pure. Her acting is worthy of her singing: clean, well-balanced [sobre], distinguished, without a gesture too much, and always in perfect harmony with the music. She understands when it *is necessary to become carried away, ardent, and as if heedless of any risk. Mme. Lehmann offers to the astonished spectator an absolutely perfect combination of the musical and dramatic elements, and it is she who constitutes the most important revelation of the Vienna Opera.*

Other Paris critics wrote: "Whoever has had the good fortune to see Mme. Lotte Lehmann in *Fidelio* knows that she is unique," and "I believe it is not possible to possess to a higher degree the art of singing."

To meet the vocal challenge of *Fidelio*, Lotte had studied with the distinguished teacher, Felicia Kaszowska, with whom she had also faced the stratospheric flights of the title role in *Turandot*. Puccini died before he had finished this, the last, grandest, most ambitious of his works. The opera was completed by Franco Alfano, using the composer's sketches. Vienna gave *Turandot* a double première. The first night featured Viennese *bel canto* and subtle acting, with well-established favorites Lotte Lehmann and Leo Slezak in the leading roles; the second "première" starred Maria Nemeth and a new Polish tenor, Jan Kiepura, both of whom made a sensation with their viscerally thrilling, powerful high notes. Nemeth made a name as one of the major Turandots; but Lotte also made her mark in the part, and had a fine success with it in Berlin as well as in Vienna. The following review comes from Berlin:

> ...I confess, I anticipated Lehmann's high notes with some trepidation. A more pleasant surprise is scarcely imaginable! This unbelievably difficult role, difficult because one has to sing almost constantly in the highest register, was as good as totally conquered by the artist. Unforced, free, clear, warm, her voice purled forth.... It was a top performance.

She recorded the two arias, the second of which includes material missing from the standard Ricordi score and only recently rediscovered and performed.

Turandot and Leonore were followed by the title role in *Das Wunder der Heliane* by Korngold. Lotte's recording of the soaring aria, *Ich ging zu ihm*, was one of her favorites. Jan Kiepura was her partner. He played a young man unjustly imprisoned who begs to see her unveiled beauty before he has to die. The critics were impressed with the tasteful way in which she gave the illusion of disrobing while preserving the essential purity of the character.

> ...Lotte Lehmann has deeply understood and captured the nature of Heliane, the magic of a naïve loveliness, an innocence threatened by the sweet torments of erotic arousal. Her first entrance, bathed in light, ethereal in appearance and expression, is unforgettable. The way in which she unbinds her hair, uncovers her feet, her body, that cannot be acted more movingly or at the same time with more purity. The aria in which she later defends herself before the court [the aria she recorded] comes out of burning emotion. It is masterfully expounded, building in intensity of feeling, without pose or exaggeration. The language of the heart, which is as shattering as the aria itself. Lotte Lehmann may place Heliane among her gallery of saints, which extends from Wagner's Elisabeth to Beethoven's Leonore.

Years later Lotte remembered Heliane in a letter:

> The rehearsal time of Wunder der Heliane is in my memory as a very happy one. I recall that it was rather difficult for me to appear in the first act almost naked, in the scene where, following the wishes of the tenor, I have to shed my garments—but it was done so discreetly, that I do not think anybody could have been shocked. Nowadays it would be no cause for blushing anymore!.... I also think that Heliane should have been given to the very young and lovely Margrit Angerer. I have never ceased to be objective with myself—and now in retrospect I cannot understand that I accepted parts which were really not right for me.

Self-criticism was often typical of Lotte. As her friend, Frances Holden, says, "she was always putting herself down." A letter, from the time of the Heliane rehearsals, to Mia Hecht, Lotte's faithful fan from Hamburg days, tells much about her attitude to her life as an artist:

> You, my dear Mia, would like to spare me the cares of every day. Oh, my child, who can do that? Lucky are they who can raise themselves for a time above those cares; and I belong to those who are blest in that way. Edyth Walker was right: we have to be thankful for that, we have to be good. I try to be. In the past, in my early youth, I did many things for which I now have to make up. Today, going through life more "consciously," every wrong deed would weigh doubly

heavily…. If only I could be more patient with Mama! My nerves so often let me down.

Lotte's next première in Vienna was Katharina (Kate) in *Der Widerspenstigen Zähmung* (*The Taming of the Shrew*) by Hermann Goetz. Marie Gutheil-Schoder had sung the part with great success three decades earlier; now, having just retired as a singer, she was engaged to be the stage director. Lotte had always been in awe of Gutheil-Schoder's remarkable technique as an actress. She was anxious to please her former idol and tried to do exactly what was asked of her. That turned out to be very inhibiting to Lotte's spontaneous, instinctive way of acting. Gutheil wanted to show her every tiny move. Lotte felt hamstrung:

> It was the only role in which I was really bad. Since I absolutely worshiped Gutheil-Schoder, I slavishly imitated everything she did. Now, what she did was all very great and wonderful for her own portrayal, but not for mine. I remember that I was to place my hand on the arm of a chair, and she explained to me long and exhaustively what I had to do with each of my fingers.
>
> …I was so under the spell of that woman that I did everything she wanted me to. After a rehearsal Strauss [who had returned to the Vienna Opera as guest conductor] came up to me and said: "Say, have you gone crazy? What's wrong with you? You are Gutheil and not Lotte Lehmann. That doesn't suit you. Forget as fast as you can everything that's been drummed into you. You're already 'tamed' and don't need this piece to do that to you."

The reviews were good, of course. In Vienna Lehmann could do no wrong. But one gets the impression, nevertheless, that she was more lovably mischievous than ferociously shrewish.

On the day of the dress rehearsal there was a most unpleasant confrontation. Lotte was summoned to the office of General Director Franz Schneiderhan, informed that she would not receive the raise she had requested, and told that if she wished to leave Vienna no one would prevent her. Those were blunt words, and very hurtful. Almost immediately startling headlines hit the streets:

STATE OPERA DOES WITHOUT LOTTE LEHMANN
FLAT REFUSAL TO MEET HER SALARY DEMANDS

LOTTE LEHMANN WANTS TO
LEAVE THE STATE OPERA
LOTTE LEHMANN TIRED OF STATE OPERA

The Viennese were in a state of shock when they read their newspapers. It was unthinkable. Lehmann was their brightest, most beloved star.

There was pandemonium at the première. Everyone was shouting: "Long live Lehmann! Stay! Don't leave us!" Here is the background. Austria was in a bad economic situation. Furthermore, the state-supported theatres had run up an unusually large deficit. The directors of the Berlin, Dresden, and Vienna opera houses had made a gentleman's agreement not to enter into any new contracts that would pay solo singers more than 1000 marks (1700 Austrian schillings) per performance. Lotte Lehmann's contract was about to expire (at the end of that season). She had asked Schalk for a raise of 300 schillings, to bring her fee up to 2000 schillings. Kiepura, on his still valid contract, was receiving 4000. Jeritza, when she sang in Vienna, got even more. Even 2000 would have been about sixty per cent less than what Lotte was currently earning in Berlin and London. Lotte assumed that her reasonable request for a raise—a matter of professional prestige—would be granted and that the contract only lacked the necessary signatures. It was a great shock to her to be told by Schneiderhan that her demands had been rejected and that her services were no longer indispensable to the Vienna Opera. The implication, or so it seemed to her, was that she was not, in effect, worth as much to the opera house as certain singers who were receiving much higher fees. Schneiderhan wanted, of course, to take a stand, as a warning to all the other artists (many of whom were also dissatisfied with their pay), by making an example out of his most prominent and important star.

Deeply offended, Lotte announced to the press her decision to leave Vienna. There was consternation everywhere, as she certainly knew there would be. Eventually, with the help of her husband, a mutually acceptable compromise was worked out so that neither party would be forced to lose face. Instead of the usual eight months' commitment to Vienna, she agreed to six. That meant fewer guaranteed performances, therefore a financial saving for the theatre, but at the fee she had requested. Lotte now would have two more months for guest engagements elsewhere.

And she was in demand everywhere. A second Paris season (in 1929) brought even more adulation. She sang Elsa in German while the rest of the cast addressed her in French. Then she gave a lieder recital at the *Opéra*. It created a sensation:

> ...*This admirable priestess of* bel canto *is perfection itself....*
>
> ...*What power, what articulation in the singing, and what inner flame!.... A rare mastery.*

The *New York Herald Tribune* (February 2, 1929) was no less enthusiastic in its report:

> ...*The recital given by Mme. Lotte Lehmann at the Opéra on Thursday was not merely a success, but a veritable triumph. It must be said that the art of the great Viennese singer has attained such a point of perfection that...singing becomes, or rather seems to become, so easy that everybody could practise it. But what is Mme. Lehmann's very own is the simplicity of her art. No aiming at effect.... It is by vocal flexion alone that she obtains the desired intensity.... Such a soirée is a festival for musicians; it is also a lesson.*

Lotte, like all theatre people, had her pet superstitions. Before singing she always went through the ritual of kissing photos of her mother, her father, her husband, her grandmother, and her brother. Although she was not a Catholic, she had learned in Vienna also to cross herself. In an interview she tells about a missing good-luck charm:

> *I am very superstitious! Always, since the very beginning of my stage career, I carry a little chimney sweep around with me. The head is broken, one leg no less, but—it is my talisman. This spring, while I was here in Paris, I missed that little doll. My maid tearfully confessed that she had forgotten to pack it! When she noticed her error, she ran all over the city to find a similar one, hoping through an amputation or two to make it look like the old one.... She couldn't find one.... But somehow I had luck anyway. Quite a lot, in fact!*

Even the chimney sweep could not always help. A singer is not a machine. There are better days and bad days. No other type of performer is so handicapped by a cold. Lotte was never one to pamper herself. She believed like many Germans that the best way to prevent illness was to toughen oneself up through, as she put it, "familiarity with wind and rain and weather." She loved to swim, no matter how cold the water. Sometimes, in her youth, she was the only bather at the seaside resort. Years later, in California, she would go swimming in the Pacific all year round. But even so, be the outer body tough or not, there is no way to toughen those delicate membranes upon which the art (not to mention the bank account) of a singer depends. During Lotte's earlier years in Vienna a very tiny nodule, smaller than a pinhead, was discovered on one of her vocal cords. Her doctor wanted to remove it; but her parents were against any operation that might alter the unique sound of her voice. It was left alone and in a few years there was no more trace of it. During one of those examinations, while the doctor was spraying Lotte's throat, she accidentally swallowed the spray-nozzle. After it had passed through her safely, she gave it back to him. He wore it proudly as a watch-fob, boasting to everyone of its journey through Lotte Lehmann.

No one is immune to the demands of the body. During a particularly dramatic moment in a Lehmann performance of *Madame Butterfly*, the child who played her baby suddenly broke up the whole performance by loudly announcing: "Frau Butterfly, I have to go pee-pee."

That was not Lotte's only worry in that opera. After the scene in which she learns that Pinkerton has left her for another wife, she could not help crying, really crying; and that made it almost impossible for her to sing the very emotional, very demanding aria of farewell to her child, just before she commits ritual suicide. Schalk scolded her. "You forget that you are an actress and a singer; you need more self-discipline!" Lotte explained that she was always so carried away at that point that she simply forgot. "I'll remind you the next time, just before we get to that passage," he promised her. At the next performance, she noticed, subliminally, that he was making all sorts of peculiar signals in her direction and wondered what kind of frightful musical mistake she must be making. Before she had time to remember the reason, however, she had as usual started to cry. That last aria always came out choked with tears.

Her fear of a conductor's wrath led her to turn down a very special offer. *La Scala* had invited her to sing Eva in *Die Meistersinger*, in Italian, at the special request of Arturo Toscanini, who would be conducting. She had heard harrowing tales of his fanatical obsession with precision. Since her conscience was never totally spotless where musical accuracy was concerned, she was afraid of becoming a target for his tempestuous temper. Later she regretted immensely the missed opportunity. It was many years before she had another chance to sing with him; and, when she finally did, their collaboration became one of the incomparable artistic highlights of her life.

Meanwhile, Lotte was making musical history at Salzburg. Her name will be forever associated with the Salzburg Festivals of the 1920's and 30's. Her first appearance there, in 1926, was as Ariadne, for just one performance (the first of three that season; the other two were sung by Claire Born). Clemens Krauss was the conductor. The following year she returned for four Fidelios, under Schalk, with the Vienna cast. In 1928 there were three more Fidelios. Then, in 1929, besides Fidelio, she sang the Marschallin. From then on, those two roles were rarely missing from her Salzburg repertoire (Fidelio only in 1933, the Marschallin only in 1936). Strangely enough she never sang any of her Mozart roles in the Mozart City. Her homage to Salzburg's greatest native son was expressed through her passion for the famous *Mozartkugel*, a local chocolate specialty. Her whole life was a constant struggle between a desire, as a conscientious actress, to look her part, and a dangerous fondness for the sort of delicacy that practically precluded a delicate figure.

In that she was not alone. Plenty of glamorous prima donnas kept her company. Nevertheless, she was offered the part of Helen of Troy (and turned it down). Strauss and Hofmannsthal both knew that Maria Jeritza would be the ideal Helen for the première (in 1928) of their opera, *Die Aegyptische Helena* (literally, the Egyptian Helen). She had the seductive charisma, the physical magnetism that the part obviously called for. But, although she cabled her willingness to sing the première, either in Dresden or Vienna, her fee as a Metropolitan super-star had become exorbitant. Lotte was the obvious choice, after Jeritza. She had created leading roles in the last three Strauss premières (*Ariadne, Frau ohne Schatten,* and *Intermezzo*). She was at that time Strauss's favorite singer. He had already declared her Marschallin to be the finest of all. But Lotte was immersed in another project, dear to her heart: she was learning Isolde, much to Strauss's chagrin, as is clear from the following correspondence between him and Ludwig Karpath, the Viennese critic and one of his friends. First, Karpath to Strauss, October 17, 1928:

> Strictly confidentially I have to tell you that Lotte does not want to learn Helena. She has taken it into her head to sing Isolde and wants to work on that part. I told her quite frankly that she is heading toward her ruin, but nothing can take her away from Isolde....

Then, from Strauss to Karpath:

> It is a pity that poor Lehmann is so blind! Too bad for that beautiful talent and that rare and precious voice! But there is nothing we can do about it!....

Leo Slezak and Lauritz Melchior both urgently advised Lotte not to attempt Isolde, her dream role. On the other hand, both Franz Schalk and Bruno Walter were willing to risk it with her, promising to hold down the orchestra and to cast as her partner one of the more lyrical Tristans. Caution eventually won out. But she never lost a sense of regret that that dream remained a dream.

Her consolation was the chance to sing the *Liebestod* in concerts and on a recording, and the satisfaction of being acclaimed as supreme in so many other roles. Every year she could count on a rapturous reception from her fans in London. In 1925 for Eva, "the Eva of our dreams;" the Marschallin again; and Elsa, "perfect in phrasing and diction, and...inimitable in its tenderness, poignancy and charm."

In 1926, in London, it was the Countess (in German), Donna Elvira and Desdemona (in Italian), a Sieglinde, and another Eva.

> ...Lotte Lehmann was a perfect Desdemona, in fact the best I can recall—Albani, Eames, Melba, I have heard them repeatedly in that role, but I place Lehmann first.

> ...Frau Lotte Lehmann was a surpassingly fair Sieglinde, singing with rare beauty and acting with still rarer charm. One of the thrills

of the evening was her great cry of exultation when Brünnhilde announced to her the future coming of Siegfried.

Jeritza, incidentally, shared with Lotte the role of Sieglinde in London that year and was torn apart for having vamped Siegmund *à la Thaïs.*

That same season Lotte gave two recitals at the enormous Royal Albert Hall, with Bruno Walter at the piano as her accompanist. Besides two arias by Weber, she sang lieder by Brahms and by Strauss in the first recital; in the second, *Dich, teure Halle,* the *Wesendonck Lieder,* and, of all things, according to an excellent review in her scrapbook, the final scene from *Salome.* The following, however, refers to her first program:

> *...A performance that can be described as the perfection of singing. She is a complete mistress of the almost neglected art of phrasing....*
> (J.A.F.)

At one of those recitals Lotte met royalty in a rather disconcerting way:

> *I was giving a recital with Bruno Walter, and in the interval a very nice-looking young man, whose face was vaguely familiar to me, although I had no idea who he was, came into the greenroom. I went on looking through my music and paid no attention to him. With one ear I heard Walter calling him "Your Majesty," but I thought it must be a nickname, because this "Majesty" spoke with all the enthusiasm of a devotee addressing his idol.... He also paid some charming compliments which I acknowledged with an absent-minded nod. It was only when he took his leave and I saw Walter's ceremonial bow and noticed the manager's deference that it began to dawn on me that I had behaved in an unbecoming manner....*
>
> *"Who was that?" I asked in astonishment.*
>
> *"That was King Manoel II of Portugal—and you treated him as if he had been a student from the top gallery...."*

Later the ex-king accompanied her on the organ at his castle.

In 1927 she opened Covent Garden season with her Marschallin, rarely absent from her seasons in London, and again sang a Sieglinde:

> *...Her performances last year and again last week led us to expect great things. But, however well prepared, one does not come in contact with such most admirable art without feeling the thrill and the*

wonder as of a perfect thing. She sang not a phrase that was not as perfect as a good voice and an unerring taste could make it, and she spoke not a word that was not pronounced so as to carry the full weight and significance it was meant to carry. And how well her histrionic genius filled in those long silences....

After their first collaboration in London, Bruno Walter had of course invited Lotte Lehmann to sing in Berlin at the *Städtische Oper,* Charlottenburg, which was now under his musical direction. There, in 1925, she performed with him Eva, Elsa, and Lisa in *Pique Dame* by Tchaikovsky, returning regularly in subsequent seasons to sing most of her major roles there. Working with Bruno Walter was always a special learning experience for Lotte. If she was nervous he knew exactly how to put her at her ease and guide her to the perfect artistic results. As Eva, for instance, she was always understandably nervous before the great quintet, one of the truly sublime moments in the opera. The singing is exposed; the phrases are long and very sustained; the beginning, sung by Eva alone, calls for a dreamy, ethereal *pianissimo;* the last seven bars—which seem to last forever—are one long, powerful *crescendo* in a mercilessly high *tessitura,* capped with a climactic B flat. Furthermore, to give the singer plenty of time to get nervous, there is a very long, very slow, very soft orchestral introduction during which absolutely nothing happens on stage. The way in which Bruno Walter helped her through that interlude was such a revelation to her, that she later passed it on to all her students; for the same approach he used in that particular scene can be applied, with a little bit of imagination, to any number of situations on the stage. He took her mind off her nervousness by focussing her thoughts as Eva:

> *Just be Eva, think as Eva, and forget all about Lotte Lehmann. Just think this way: "Hans Sachs wants me to make a speech. I don't quite know what I'm expected to do, I've never had to say anything quite so important in a formal context, and I wonder how I'm going to find the right words; but on the other hand, why should it be so hard? After all, I'm among friends. There is Sachs, whom I respect so highly. There is Walter von Stolzing, to whom my heart belongs. It ought to be easy to express such deep happiness...."*

And those thoughts led her serenely into the opening words.

The critics singled out that dreaded quintet for special praise. All
in all it had been a magnificent performance under Bruno
Walter's inspired direction. But Lotte got the best reviews:

> ...The most perfect interpretation of Wagner's conception. And her
> precious voice is the consummate expressive medium for every im-
> pulse—its bloom, its melting loveliness, the model phrasing, all culmi-
> nate in the quintet. The soul-filled tone, the full splendor of the fresh,
> floating sound, rise here to a climax, elevating the extraordinary to
> the level of the unique.

> ...Lotte Lehmann, the one and only, caught the style, unerringly,
> with the instinct of genius. This Evchen was the crown of the per-
> formance, attractive and lovely to look at, dignified and genuine in
> every gesture. And what a treat, that glorious voice! A radiation of
> most golden splendor not only in the quintet; even in the slightest in-
> terjections, like those in the second act from the linden bower, every
> tone "sat," every syllable was clearly understandable.

Die Meistersinger was an especially brilliant opening for the season. But Lotte's other roles were as warmly admired in Berlin.

> ...Lotte Lehmann's Elsa can be called absolutely perfect, lifted far
> above the standards of any usual evening at the opera.

> ...The incomparable Lotte Lehmann [was] Lisa [in Pique
> Dame].... Her great scene by the river is one of the most glorious op-
> eratic moments one has ever heard. The music is radiant in her, she
> lifts it far above its niveau, she colors it in a personal way, so that it
> becomes triumphant in itself, apart from any drama on the stage, so
> that in that moment it seems to become a real experience, not a per-
> formance but reality itself.

That was one of Lotte's special attributes: each of her roles became a living reality, each of her songs a glimpse into a life.

Chapter Eleven

WILD INDIANS AND OTHER DANGERS

THE NEW DECADE began auspiciously. Who, at that time, would have guessed that it would end in war and disaster? On January 1, 1930, Lotte Lehmann sang Fidelio at the Vienna Opera in a performance conducted by Richard Strauss. It was noted that his *tempi* were unusually fast; but the dungeon scene built to an exceptionally gripping climax:

> ... There one felt the dramatic fire of the composer of Elektra. The tragic storm exploded in lightning and thunder; one felt shivers down the spine. But this scene was brought to a climax also by the magnificent voice of Lotte Lehmann. One experienced something extraordinary. The warmth of this so tenderly human Leonore was transformed into heroic power. The moment became monumental. With every performance the Leonore of Lotte Lehmann becomes more remarkable, more gripping.... (E. B.)

Later that month there was a revival of *Intermezzo*. Lotte, of course, sang Christine. Her personal maid took another girl to hear the performance. The girl was horrified. "You mustn't work for such a devil of a woman!" she said, "I'll get you a different job." The reaction would no doubt have been different had she seen her friend's *Gnädige* (mistress) as the saintly Elisabeth, the lovable "Lotte" in *Werther*, Marguerite, Manon, Maddalena in *Andrea Chenier*, or Ariadne, the other roles that Lehmann was singing in Vienna at that time.

There were also lieder recitals in Vienna, Paris, and London. Lotte had, of course, been singing lieder since she first began to sing in public; and from the earliest days her audiences had responded with great enthusiasm. Critics had praised her lovely voice, her simplicity, her naturalness, her warmth of feeling. But, looking back later as a mistress of the form, Lehmann felt that her development as a lieder singer had been a long, gradual process that only reached full maturity as she was beginning to retire from the operatic stage.

Lotte wrote the following remarks as part of the preface to a book by her brother about German lieder:

> Many years ago, at a time when the world of opera was my very own—and lieder a rather foreign territory for me, I sang my lieder recitals in blessed innocence. I remember that one day I said to my brother, Fritz Lehmann, "Singing lieder doesn't make me very happy. They are melodies and any instrument will do them better justice than the human voice." He answered that in his opinion each Lied has its own story, is created out of a very personal experience. That remark opened a door for me. Slowly I grew into the perception that a Lied, in a subtle way, is born from an experience, from a "story."

After coming to Vienna, Lotte first had as her accompanist Professor Ferdinand Foll, who had been a friend of Hugo Wolf's, as already noted. In an unpublished article about her various accompanists she wrote of him:

> Artistically, my choice of programs—songs mixed with arias—must have caused him pain; but he was a shy man—and the only objection that he ever expressed came at the end of one of those recitals that were always so successful with the audience. He said: "You could be a really good lieder singer if you would only concentrate. But you always do everything much too quickly. You learn too hastily, you don't take lieder seriously enough." I was astonished! I found myself a very good lieder singer—wasn't the audience shouting for joy? I did not stop to think that they loved me because of my work on the stage, and that it was only my voice that helped me to have such an easy victory....

In *Midway in My Song* Lotte Lehmann has more to say about Ferdinand Foll:

> [Foll] gave me my first real idea of lieder-style. I still sang too robustly, not intimately enough. With all his benevolence and sensitive understanding, he was only once satisfied with me—when I sang Schumann's Frauenliebe und Leben with him in Vienna. Perhaps it was very near to his way of thinking, for while we were going from the platform of the Musikvereinssaal back to the greenroom he said in his quiet way: "That was an experience for me. It was most beautiful...."

Certainly in the 1920's most people thought of Lotte Lehmann as an opera singer, one of the very greatest. Her recitals were sold out, they were occasions. Her audiences were ecstatic, jubilant, delirious. But generally it was the odd aria on the program that carried them away. A typical program from that period of her career would include an aria from *Oberon* or *Der Freischütz; Dich, teure Halle* from *Tannhäuser* or Ariadne's Monologue; *Vissi d'arte* from *Tosca* (in German, of course) or Maddalena's aria from *Andrea Chenier;* the brilliant *Nun, eilt herbei* from *Die lustigen Weiber von Windsor* (one of her most irresistible recordings) or Katharina's solo scene from *Der Widerspenstigen Zähmung.* The lieder were generally familiar chestnuts. Even the most jaded critics had to admit, however, that she brought every one of them to new and exciting life. Still, it was years before she began to venture into the less-traveled regions of the *Lied.* It was often noted that she sang certain songs considered to be more suitable for a man than for a woman. Since that refrain reappears in reviews throughout her career, it may be well to consider the subject here.

The trouser role is an old tradition in opera. Mozart's Cherubino, Verdi's Oscar, Strauss's Octavian were all written for the female voice. If a woman can pretend to be a man on the stage, why not in a song? Women have long been accepted in such roles as Orpheus, Romeo, even Julius Caesar. Sarah Bernhardt and—not very long ago—Dame Judith Anderson played Hamlet. Quite apart from the customs of the stage, however, is the simple fact that most of the poems that were set to music by the great composers were written by men and express the point of view of a male poet as interpreted in music by a male composer. If one were to be pedantically consistent, logic would deprive a woman singer of the great majority of all the songs ever written, including some of the most charming and feminine. How poor the repertoire would be, for instance, if every serenade were denied to the female voice because the serenader is presumably a male. It would be a great loss if women were limited to lullabies and Schumann's *Frauenliebe und Leben.* If a woman can feel the same emotions as a man, why should she not express them in a song? Imagination is the key.

Here are some reactions to Lotte's recitals; first from Vienna:

... Then, strangely, from the profusion of available songs by Schubert
and Schumann, she chose several which were composed for the male
voice, the Doppelgänger, the Erlkönig, Ich grolle nicht, and Früh-
lingsnacht, probably more out of vocal considerations than because
of the content to be expressed, which would justify sharper accents in
these very songs. [It is interesting to note that Lehmann was later
criticized for over-dramatizing some of those same lieder.] But
this is just what is so special in Lotte Lehmann's art: the noble har-
mony, the lovely evenness of moods, the comforting warmth, which
are a part of her temperament and which her singing communicates
to the listener in such a lovable way.... (E. B., February 10, 1930)

At least three other critics also objected to her choice of
Männerlieder in that program. Another review conveys an impression of honeyed blandness that is almost inconceivable to
those who heard Lehmann sing lieder in later years, and—in that
respect—utterly incompatible with many vivid memories:

... An evening of lieder by Lotte Lehmann is the loveliest, most pre-
cious treat for the ear. Mellifluous sweetness floods over the hearer
and one does not grow tired of admiring the divine gift of this voice.
Every tone is sent forth in its acoustic perfection with an additional
spin from the heart, a sort of soul-vibrato. In such a way, every song
becomes a tasty delicacy for the ear, which in turn wants nothing to
disturb such egotistical enjoyment. Not even through the fact that
any just demand for spiritual [as distinct from sensual], truly lieder-
like interpretation of the individual songs is as good as totally un-
fulfilled. Meanwhile, the Lehmann voice is an exceptional case, and
that must satisfy us. Even then, when everything that is actually
characteristic and significant has been taken away from the fever-
visions of "The Erlking" or the ghostly apparition of the Doppel-
gänger,.... such honeyed euphony, such cozy singing is welcome, even
when, apparently quite inorganically, it is supposed to be coming from
the spheres of the uncanny and the demonic.... (Heinrich Kralik,
February 10, 1930)

At least one reviewer found nothing to criticize at all:

... The voice of Lotte Lehmann is of such beauty that one should
erect altars to it. That voice alone, even without the natural charm
of her personality and a singing technique sublimated to the last de-
gree of purity, would have to lead her to the highest summit of inter-
national fame. Brilliance emanates from her.... Such mastery is

*hard to reach, harder still to maintain. But in one sense, Lotte Leh-
mann has it easy: she has only to sing a "Lehmann tone," a
"Lehmann phrase" in an old Italian aria or a German Lied, to let
loose a storm....* (from an unidentified clipping on the same page
of Lehmann's scrapbook)

Here are some of the reactions of London reviewers to her recital in Queen's Hall, February 25, 1930:

*... Seldom, if ever, do we hear a more glorious voice than Lotte Leh-
mann's.... Unfortunately her operatic trick of clipping her words
short, though it can be dramatic enough when accompanied with a
gesture on the stage, ill befits the singing of lieder. Perhaps she is
aware of this, for she sang Ich Grolle Nicht badly in this respect, and
then in response to the undiscriminating applause, sang it well again.
But I wonder why she sang it at all....*

Reading through reviews of Lehmann recitals over the years,
one is struck by the frequency with which her interpretation of
Ich grolle nicht seems to arouse either very positive or very negative reponses in her listeners. Audiences as a whole were
thrilled by her way with that song. It very often had to be repeated. She delivered it with enormous emotional intensity, building
to a shattering climax on the word *elend* in the phrase, *"Ich sah,
mein Lieb, wie sehr du elend bist,"* achieved technically through an
immense *crescendo* (starting *after* the high notes), combined with
a devastatingly effective, almost physically dangerous glottal attack on *elend* and a daringly, controversially broad *ritardando.*

A contrasting view of the same song, among others, at the
same recital:

*... Even such a song as Schumann's Ich grolle nicht—essentially a
man's song—was a perfect thing, for the quality of tone and expression levelled all differences.... Every song revealed such complete
mastery that it might have been mistaken for ease, and it is significant that in an age which prides itself on its cool, practical attitude towards all that stirred most deeply the conscience of the last
generation, a simple, sentimental song like Beethoven's Wonne der
Wehmut should rouse an audience to enthusiasm. In different ways,
every song bore evidence not only of Mme. Lehmann's vocal art
and gifts, but also to her genius as an interpreter....* (F. B.)

The Parisians were treated to two concerts and a song recital in March. Only praise flowed from the critical pen:

> ...It is always a pure joy, an intoxication, to listen to her! At first one is amazed at the instrumental beauty of her singing. There is not a mediocre note from top to bottom. And what nobility of phrasing!...What caresses in the poems of Wagner! We have, alas! all too few singers in France to place opposite this lady from Vienna. Where has technique disappeared to, here?...Can't someone send a mission to Austria to recover the principles...?

Two days after her Paris recital, Lotte sang Sieglinde in a new staging of *Die Walküre* in Vienna. Then back across the continent two days later for an Elsa in Antwerp, followed soon by Eva in *Die Meistersinger* for the opening of the Covent Garden season (Elisabeth Schumann shared the role with her that year). The novelty, for Lotte as well as for London, was a production, in German, of *Die Fledermaus* by Johann Strauss. The idea of an operetta at the Royal Opera House, especially sandwiched between a *Siegfried* and a *Parsifal*, was somewhat startling. A typical headline was "*FRIVOLITY AT COVENT GARDEN*." King George V and Queen Mary lent the luster of royalty to one of the "Fledermice," the first time "in many years" (presumably since the war) that they had attended a performance of anything in German. An Austrian reporter sent the following description of their majesties back to Vienna: "The king is friendly and human, as always.... The queen, tall as a giantess, tightly corseted, with a diadem of diamonds in her hair, looks unapproachably regal, like the royalty of pre-war days. She smiles, but her smile has iron in it." (Two years later, incidentally, the royal couple again attended a Lotte Lehmann performance, this time *Tannhäuser*, dining during the interval in the retiring room at the back of the royal box; the linen, cutlery, and table decorations, as well as the food, had all been brought over from Buckingham Palace.)

The Londoners loved *Fledermaus* and they found Lehmann's Rosalinde "delicious." Just before one of the later performances Lotte lost her voice. At 5 p.m. she could not sing a note. A famous laryngologist, Sir Milsom Rees, was urgently summoned. At 6 the leading lady was still voiceless. No one else could be found to sing the part. Wild consternation. At 7 the audience began to fill the auditorium. Too late for a change of program. At 7:30 Sir Milson's ministrations seemed to be reviving the recalcitrant larynx. Lotte agreed to risk it. It was decided to cut the *Czardas*, but otherwise she sang the whole role—"superbly," according to the press. The headline was "*A 'MIRACLE!'*"

Neither Lotte nor Elisabeth Schumann, the Adele, was able to match her London success when, at the end of May, *Fledermaus* was presented at the Vienna Opera. The style was too "German" for the Viennese. They considered themselves, with good reason, the last authority where operetta was concerned, and found most of the singers (not just Lotte and Elisabeth) too heavily operatic. They missed *das Wienerische*. It did not take Lotte long, however, to capture that style, too, to their complete satisfaction. A few months later she was starred at the *Staatsoper* in another Viennese operetta, *The Opera Ball*, by Heuberger. Angèle was a part she had sung sixteen years earlier in Hamburg, when the public wanted a little escapism during dark days of the first world war.

June brought "her Grace, the Marschallin," to Graz:

> ... She portrayed with moving poetry the last glow of a noble woman's heart. Rococo magic blossomed around her figure. Every gesture, every tone testified to a wonderful mellowness and wisdom.... It is not too much to say that through Lotte Lehmann art becomes ennobled.

Der Rosenkavalier was repeated at the Salzburg Festival, and Lotte sang one performance, the first of three. The role of the Marschallin was then taken over by Viorica Ursuleac, who was the mistress, later the wife, of the conductor, Clemens Krauss, since September 1929 the new director of the Vienna Opera. Lotte's relationship with Krauss was—and remained—extremely strained. She strongly suspected that he was trying to ease her out of her well-established position as star of the Vienna Opera, in favor of the lady he loved. Ursuleac joined the roster of the Vienna Opera immediately after her Salzburg appearances. Lehmann's international prestige and her popularity with the Viennese public were unassailable; but except for the first nights of *Arabella* in 1933 and *Eugen Onegin* in 1934 (the latter at the spe-

cial wish of Bruno Walter), there were few Lehmann premières
in Vienna during the régime of Clemens Krauss.

Meanwhile, Lotte's single Marschallin and her two Fidelios
were undisputed highlights of the Salzburg Festival that year.
First, *Rosenkavalier*:

> ... *Glorious, unforgettable, transfigured in every respect is Frau Lotte
> Lehmann as the Marschallin. Highest effectiveness, noblest art.*

> ... *With Lehmann the ending of the first act becomes one of the pur-
> est, most precious impressions which any opera stage can offer today.*

Then *Fidelio*:

> ... *Leonore's tremendous destiny can not be embodied more gloriously;
> her simple nobility, womanly dignity and active faithfulness cannot be
> interpreted more tenderly. And the triumphant radiance of her
> voice—truly "it penetrates into the depths of one's heart"* [a quotation
> from the dialogue of the dungeon scene].

> ... *The Fidelio of Lotte Lehmann, a perfection, a probably unsurpass-
> able accomplishment, uplifting and deeply stirring...filled with truly
> Beethovenesque transfiguration.*

Wherever she sang, Lotte Lehmann seemed to inspire the
critics to soaring flights of poetic fancy, such as one seldom reads
anywhere else in the newspapers of our prosaic century. Back in
Vienna, in October, after a *Tannhäuser*, they might have been
minnesingers competing for the hand of her Elisabeth in a Contest of Song:

> ... *Her singing was a living miracle, more beautiful than in the leg-
> end, "The Rose-Miracle of Saint Elisabeth." The extraordinary, the
> unique thing about this vision of an artist, her incomparable voice
> and her genius for acting, can scarcely be put into words. The exper-
> ience of hearing her and seeing her, as on this Tannhäuser-Sunday,
> reveals mysterious secrets of eternal beauty, which will remain in
> memory, unextinguishable, indescribable....* (D.)

> ... *In every respect a perfect accomplishment. The gentle radiance
> of the wondrously moving voice glows like a halo around her appear-
> ance.... The Elisabeth of Lotte Lehmann is a saint with a strong
> feminine nature, earthly and heavenly at the same time.... She gives
> poetry to the expression of the words, there is poetry in every gesture,
> down to the graceful play of her hands.*

... The Elisabeth of Lotte Lehmann is now the best Elisabeth of all the opera stages on earth.... (R. K.)

Her Manon, four days later, was less rapturously received. It had been one of Lotte's most popular parts. But now there was some talk that after her many Fidelios and other heavy roles her voice had become too dramatic for the light, charmingly frivolous character of Manon.

Lotte was about to make her first trip to North America. She had a contract with the Chicago Opera. She had long hoped to hear from the Metropolitan, but as long as Maria Jeritza was there, there was little hope that Lotte Lehmann would be invited. The Met was not big enough to hold both of them, as far as Jeritza was concerned. Now the Viennese were afraid that America, which had monopolized Maria, would keep their *geliebte* Lotte, too.

The trip to America meant another separation from Mama. That was as painful to Lotte as it was to her mother, who again worried about all the wild Indians and other new-world dangers. But this time, of course, Otto would be there to protect Lotte from those Chicago gangsters one had read about. There was a "farewell" recital in Paris, all lieder, before the sailing of the *Europa* on October 17 from Cherbourg.

For two days the ship was tossed about by a truly Wagnerian storm. Everybody was horribly sick. But when the sea was smooth again, Lotte loved the adventure of shipboard life, now that she had Otto beside her, as well as many favorite colleagues who were also headed for Chicago. She especially loved the big swimming pool, glamorously illuminated at night with blue lights under the water.

The first sight of the New York skyline was very impressive. Later she and Otto went to the top of the Empire State Building to marvel at the lights of the city spread out so magically before them down below. But first they had to pass through customs. Fidelio's boots were searched for booze. The officials rummaged for rum in the nun's habit that Elisabeth wears in the third act of *Tannhäuser*. This was Prohibition! An old friend, Mia Hecht, a loyal fan from earliest Hamburg days, met the ship and joined Lotte and Otto again in Chicago. She was now living in Atlanta.

Her daughter, named Mia-Lotte, was Lotte's godchild.

There was a little time for sight-seeing; then onto the sleeper for Chicago.

America's over-heated hotel rooms are always something of a shock to European singers. The dried-out air is dangerous to vocal cords. On the other hand, when Lotte rushed to open the windows, she was met by a blast of polar cold. The U.S. seemed to be a land of extremes.

Lotte's North American debut took place on October 28, 1930. She sang Sieglinde in *Die Walküre*. It was called "one of the most significant American debuts in the history of Chicago opera." Elsa came next, on November 9, and Elisabeth six days later. Altogether there were nine performances. The reviewers knew that this was something special:

> ... Her Sieglinde is perfection itself—perfection of voice and action.... (Musical Courier)

> ... She has one of the loveliest voices ever heard on the Civic Opera stage. It is of a freedom and purity seldom discovered in American singers and employed with an eloquence and artistry that moved the audience to a great demonstration.... (Musical America)

> ... In musical perception, in vocal beauty, in histrionic intelligence, Mme. Lehmann was at once a lesson and a reproach to most of her colleagues who specialize in the Bayreuth master's works.

> ... Mme. Lehmann was the ideal Elisabeth. Here is one of the great artists of the century.

Such reviews make it hard to understand how Lehmann could have felt that her American debut had been merely "a good average success—nothing more," which is how she described it in her autobiography.

Nevertheless, her manager, Francis Coppicus, was disappointed. He had hoped for the kind of sensation that would help him to "sell" her—Lotte hated that American expression—to many other cities at high fees. As it was, only Minneapolis seemed to take an interest. Her only recital in America that season took place there and was very warmly received. But Coppicus decided to wait with Lotte's first New York recital until her next visit, a little over one year later. Lotte managed a trip to Atlanta to see

her godchild. She surprised and delighted her fellow-guests by
singing at a party while she was there. Otto had had to return to
Europe for business reasons before Lotte's Minneapolis recital.
She told the press that he had instructed her friend, Mia Hecht,
to spank her if she cried too much. The interviewers were
charmed by her accent and the quaint syntax of what Lotte—
meaning to be politely apologetic—naively called her "English-
English, not American-English."

On December 5 Lotte boarded the S.S. *Europa* to return to Europe. On her way back to Vienna she sang a recital in Paris. She
also sang a Sieglinde at the *Opéra* in German, while the rest of
the cast sang in French. Reunion in Vienna was celebrated with
another *Tannhäuser* Elisabeth, just before a Christmas with her
loved ones.

The new year brought a concert in Bucharest, attended by
Queen Marie, and a new production of *Die Frau ohne Schatten*. In
February and March there were concerts and recitals in Vienna (a
radio broadcast), Paris, and Monte Carlo, as well as Fidelio and
Elisabeth in Antwerp. The critics were completely under her
spell, as usual:

> ...A singer? More than that! A soul that sings! [Une Âme qui
> chante] Song incarnate!...The infinite variety of her singing!...
> (Paris)

Fidelio returned to Vienna for April but the Marschallin was
needed to open the London season with her special glamour be-
fore the end of the month, to the applause of the Duke and
Duchess of York (the future George VI and Queen Elizabeth).
Elsa, Sieglinde, and Rosalinde were also welcomed back. It was
Bruno Walter's last season of opera in London.

After some more performances in Vienna, Lotte spent her vacation on Sylt, riding and swimming with Otto and storing up
strength for the season ahead.

At Salzburg, besides two Marschallins (the first performance
was sung by Ursuleac), Lotte sang two Fidelios, both operas
with Krauss as conductor. "Her Fidelio represents the zenith of
German opera." "An absolute summit of the music drama." Such
were the critical comments.

An *Ariadne* in Vienna in June turned out to be the last performance that Lotte sang with her beloved Franz Schalk, who was failing fast ever since he lost the directorship of the Vienna Opera. He died on September 3, 1931, and Lotte walked behind his coffin to the cemetery. That evening, at the opera house, Clemens Krauss conducted Siegfried's Funeral March before a memorial performance of *Die Meistersinger*. Lotte was the Eva. She recalls how deeply she was moved, in *Midway in my Song*:

> In the last act the chorus, "Awake!" [*Wach' auf!*], recalled to my mind the familiar figure at the desk.... I closed my eyes, and it was as if he were there again—surrendered to the waves of music.... An uncontrollable fit of weeping shook me, and my colleagues quickly formed a protecting wall round me so that no one might see my tears....

On December 8, 1931, there was a special concert in memory of Franz Schalk. Two great orchestras, the chorus of the Vienna Opera, and many leading soloists were involved. Bruno Walter conducted and Lotte sang Mahler's magnificent song about Christ in the Garden of Gethsemane, *Um Mitternacht*. The stirring words addressed to the "Lord over Life and Death" climaxed a deeply moving experience for the performers as well as for the audience.

The fall of 1931 brought a new role into the Lehmann repertoire, Georgette (Giorgetta) in *Der Mantel*, the German version of *Il tabarro*, the first of the three one-act operas that make up Puccini's *Trittico*. The restless, sensual young wife of the captain of a barge on the Seine, who finds the corpse of her lover, a dockworker, murdered by her husband, under the "cloak" of the title, is a world away from the gentle nun, Sister Angelica, in the second piece. Lotte sang both roles on the same evening, an interesting study in contrasts.

There were recitals in Paris, Vienna, Prague, Brussels, and Athens (where she was accompanied by Dimitri Mitropoulos by candlelight, after a power failure). Paris heard her also as Elsa, Sieglinde, and Elisabeth, all performances sold out, and in two more orchestral concerts. As usual, the reviews were especially fantastic in Paris. "This famous singer is, all by herself, an entire School of Singing."

The time had come to attempt again the conquest of America.

Chapter Twelve

ONE DOES SEE THE GARDEN

JANUARY 7, 1932, was a major new landmark in Lotte Lehmann's career. It was the date of her first New York recital, at Town Hall, and the beginning of a long series of such recitals, a series that made musical history. Success in New York is essential to success in America, at least for a singer. Lotte knew that, and she was understandably nervous. Unfortunately, Otto had not been able to accompany her on this crucial trip. She thought of a young lady whom she had always seen in the front row at her recitals in Paris, a young lady whose lovely, receptive expression had put her at ease and inspired her to give of her best. Now, if ever, she needed the encouragement of that familiar face.

> Shaken with nerves and only half-conscious, I stepped from the threshold of the artists' room onto the platform of the Town Hall.
> I was greeted, quite unexpectedly, by welcoming applause that lasted for several minutes.
> Lots of the people in the hall must know me, many must love me and be glad to see me in New York! And I had thought I was going to appear before an audience that expected "someone new."...And there—in the front row—was the lovely face of my unknown friend! Suddenly I was no longer alone....The storm of applause had delivered me from the bonds of fear, and I sang the whole evening through as if I were drunk with happiness, ecstasy and jubilant triumph! Oh, and it was a triumph! I have no intention of bragging about my successes in this book, but this first New York recital was tremendously important for my whole career in America, and I simply can't pass over it in two words. The audience became as ecstatic as myself—there was a constant give and take—and it was only after many recalls and encores that I had at last to make an end....

The unknown friend, whose name was Viola Westervelt,

soon became a part of Lehmann's inner circle, the nucleus for the ever-growing group that was soon to be known as the "Lehmaniacs." Another new friendship was also made that night. Geraldine Farrar, Caruso's most popular partner during their years together at the Met and, earlier, Lotte's great idol in Berlin, was there in the audience, applauding enthusiastically. Later, when Lotte sang Tosca at the Metropolitan, Farrar gave her the spectacular spray of flowers that she herself had carried onto the stage as Tosca, at her first entrance, to decorate the statue of the Madonna.

Here is a condensation of the review by Olin Downes, then the leading music critic of *The New York Times*:

> ...*The audience that gathered in Town Hall last night to hear Lotte Lehmann's first song recital in this city was not only impressed but thrilled. It has been a good many years—more years, at least, than the writer has spent in this city—since any local song recital has offered such excitements and distinctions. Singing songs by Brahms, Schubert, Schumann, Mme. Lehmann swept her listeners from their feet. She has a voice of magnificent range and color. Above all, it is an intensely communicative voice, one that stirs with feeling and that immediately affects those who hear it. She herself is a woman of superb temperament and capacity for the expression of great and varied emotions. The moment that the first song, Von ewiger Liebe, had ended, the audience knew that a great artist was present .... This first impression was not lessened but intensified as the concert proceeded. To claim that every song was perfectly sung would be exaggeration. That is a thing which never happens. But in sum the vocal and interpretive gifts of the singer surpassed the highest expectations....There were moments last night when Mme. Lehmann was operatic, and when, as an interpreter of song, her temperament got the better of her and she stepped from the frame. But even when she did...as in the final measures of Schumann's Ich grolle nicht, she was so puissant, noble, and impassioned in her style, supplementing interpretation with such vocal resource and such a wealth of nuance, tone-color, and all-conquering sincerity, that if she had sung the song backward it would have been hard to keep cool and refuse to be moved by what she did.... She sang songs which have become household words in such a way as to resurrect every wonderful thing which familiarity had caused us to take for granted or to accept as a*

*matter of course. At her height she displayed interpretive genius—
nothing less....*

Incidentally, Downes told her two years later that after the recital every leading critic in New York had received an anony-
mous letter stating that Lotte Lehmann was a morphine addict,
that everyone in Vienna knew that, that only morphine had made
her sing so well that evening, and that her voice would soon
show signs of deterioration because of her addiction. "Lovely
world, isn't it?" was Lotte's comment to her friend, Mia Hecht.

Kurt Ruhrseitz was her accompanist at that first Town Hall recital. Besides the German lieder (including a Strauss group, not
mentioned above), her program offered a group of French songs,
by Hahn, Chausson, and Fauré.

The conquest of America seemed to be off to a very promising
start.

Chicago came next, Lotte's second season there. She sang
two roles this time, Elsa and Eva, and the engagement included
performances by the Chicago Opera in Boston. The critics noted
right away that Lotte was 20 pounds slimmer than the season
before. She had learned a little about American tastes that time
and wanted to look her best for New York. Later Europe, too,
took grateful note of her new svelteness—while it lasted. But
Lotte felt that the weight-loss was responsible for what seemed
to her to be an edge on her voice. It wasn't very long before she
let her waistline lapse again.

Two clippings from Chicago:

*...Mme. Lehmann challenges all other sopranos, German, Italian,
American or what you will, by the utter purity of her tone, the superb
distinction of her style, the genuine musical and spiritual beauty of
her interpretation.*

*...She is slimmer [than last season], but her crystal and silver voice
has gained in beauty—if that were possible.*

And one from Boston:

*...Her Elsa was at once the most moving and most convincing one
ever has heard.*

Just before Lotte's ship was to sail for Europe, literally *just* before, she gave a second New York recital. It was Sunday after-

noon, February 7, and she offered Schumann's *Frauenliebe und Leben*, among other lieder....

> *...The early part was sung with indescribable tenderness, innocence, and happiness, and in this she had the expression of a girl of seventeen; but as the mood changed she seemed actually to grow older before one's eyes, and the last three songs of the cycle had a depth of passion and grief that was overwhelming....* (Doris Madden, February 12, 1932)

The concert began at 3 p.m.; the ship was sailing at 6. Lotte sang the program with many a glance at the clock between numbers.

> *Encore after encore prolonged the recital interminably, and at last I had to say to my audience: "I should like to sing you lots more songs, but my boat won't wait...."*

Lotte went on board "with a contract for a long concert tour" in her pocket. After her sensational New York success, Coppicus, her manager, would surely have no trouble "selling" her to plenty of cities.

Her only worry was that her mother would suffer from too long a separation. At every new parting there were many tears on both sides. Fritz had lost his first wife to cancer the summer before, after ten years of marriage. He spent as much time as he could with Mama, but he was now very busy teaching opera dramatics at the New Vienna Conservatory, and had even set up a little stage in his town house so that he could teach privately at home as well. As for Lotte's own private life, she had found a most understanding mate in Otto. She respected him and relied upon him for advice and emotional support. She wrote about their relationship, if somewhat indirectly, in *Midway in My Song*:

> *After many obstacles and great struggles, I was able to unite myself officially to the man who has become my best and most understanding life's companion, Otto Krause. It is not easy to be the husband of an artist. It is a life that, with its constant ups and downs without rest or peace, its ambitions and torments of depression alternating with ecstatic joys, demands, even more than an equable bourgeois disposition, a great deal of patient forbearance from one's life partner.... It indeed demands of him a great deal of self-denial, consider-*

ation, understanding and forgiveness. And the artist who can say: "This was and is the right husband for me," has more reason to be grateful to her fate than the majority of women.... I know it only too well.

To an interviewer in Fort Wayne, Indiana, Lotte said of Otto:

> To me he is like a rock to which I can cling and be safe from drowning in the turbulent, tempestuous seas that swirl around almost every international prima donna.

After a brief reunion with Mama, Lotte's career called her again to foreign climes. First, in March, to Marseilles, a new destination. There were many empty seats; but those who had stayed away could learn the next day from the papers what they had missed:

> ... For the sake of all those who have not yet had the good luck to hear her, let me say that the recital of the celebrated singer Lotte Lehmann was a prodigious revelation. And those who were absent...missed an artistic satisfaction of the first order.... She truly touches the highest summits of her art, and her program was one long, continual rapture [ravissement]....

But the same reviewer expressed regret that Lehmann sang only three French songs—especially since he found her French "very correct"—and that the rest of her program was in German, a language neither liked nor understood in Marseilles:

> ...If we found a very real joy in listening to the eight songs of L'amour et la vie d'une femme in their original language, it was because our comprehension was aided by that veritable mirror of the soul which is Lotte Lehmann's face.... (Jacques Dordet)

Another critic had no reservations whatsoever, despite linguistic chauvinism:

> ...It seems as if for her, uniquely for her, the art of bel canto, deserting the balmy skies of Italy, has consented to cross the Rhine. Certainly the German language, above all to French ears, does not naturally lend itself to that sweetness of accent which seems to be a privilege confined to the Latin tongues. Nevertheless, Lotte Lehmann has achieved the miracle of usurping that privilege; and, perhaps for the first time, we have enjoyed the charm of a German song in its origi-

*nal text, so well has this admirable singer been able to soften its
harshness with the caress of her heavenly voice....* (Ch. Varigny)

Paris, more cosmopolitan than Marseilles, was happy to hear
Frauenliebe und Leben in any language.

Next stop was Italy, her very first visit. There she sang four
concerts in ten days, three in Rome and one in Florence. In between, to fill a few empty hours, she visited Naples and Venice.

The first recital, on April 1 in Rome, was "an absolutely sensational success.... The audience applauded through the entire intermission." The program consisted entirely of German lieder.
One critic wrote:

> ... *Eighteen German lieder, all sung in the original German. Mon-
> otonous recital? Not on your life! Signora Lotte Lehmann is such a
> brilliant, versatile interpreter that she easily holds the attention of the
> audience.... Although expressing herself in a language that, in Italy,
> is familiar to very few people, she was able to make herself under-
> stood—at least in a general sort of way. Even those who knew noth-
> ing of German were listening with lively interest and obvious
> joy.... It was an authentic success, one hundred per cent....* (Alberto
> Gaseo, April 26, 1932)

Two of the three concerts in Rome were at the *Augusteo* by the
glorious *ara pacis* of the Emperor Augustus. There she first sang
the *Fidelio* aria, three Strauss songs (with orchestra) and the *Liebestod* from *Tristan und Isolde*, with *Träume* as an encore, to "*un delirio
d'applausi.*" The concert was so successful that she was asked to
add another at the *Augusteo*, this time singing arias from *Oberon*
and *Tannhäuser* and Wagner's *Wesendonck Lieder*. No one would
leave at the end. She sang "Elsa's Dream" and *Morgen* by Strauss
as encores. Still no one left. Lehmann explained that no other
music had been rehearsed with the orchestra and no other parts
were available even for sight-reading. A lady from the audience
came up with a vocal score of *The Marriage of Figaro*. The accompanist of Lotte's earlier recital happened to be in the hall. A piano
was wheeled into place, and Lotte endeared herself to everyone
by graciously singing the first aria of the Countess, *Porgi amor*.

The Florence recital was in the Pitti Palace. Lotte's program of
twenty lieder, with many repeats and many encores, was accompanied by composer Mario Castelnuovo-Tedesco.

In Venice Lotte was particularly impressed with the Palazzo Vendramin, where Wagner died, and the *Casa di Desdemona*. It was fun to have flocks of San Marco pigeons eating out of her hands.

April had her hopping back and forth across the map: from Venice to Vienna (Marschallin and Fidelio), then to Paris for a recital (*Le Figaro* reported that nearly every number had to be repeated), then a recital in Hamburg, an orchestral concert in Dresden, and back to Vienna for an Elisabeth and a birthday concert for Josef Marx.

Hamburg was more critical than usual. There were mild complaints about "too many *Männerlieder*." She was scolded for too much rhythmic freedom and advised to check her intonation in the upper register. Someone felt she was depending more upon the text for inspiration than upon the music.

Dresden was another story. Besides the aria from Oberon, she sang a group of Strauss lieder and, as an encore, Wagner's *Träume*. The critic who signed himself "H. Ch." wrote: "She showed herself to be a magnificent lieder singer, one of the finest interpreters of the *Lied* that we possess today."

Her Elisabeth in Vienna inspired the usual hymns:

> ... A peak of incomparable artistic enjoyment.... The ideal type of Elisabeth.... She draws out of this noble role all its magnificent depths, which she fills with the breath of the spirit and the drama of the soul. Lotte Lehmann stands at the zenith of world fame, the Vienna State Opera can be proud.... The entrance aria was a powerfully thrilling experience; the prayer floated, a deeply inner, blessed revelation, into the most blissful regions of infinite art.... (A. M. P.)

A few days later she was in the cast of a rather unusual performance of *Otello*. There were two Iagos. The first one, Karl Hammes, was too sick to continue after the first act. Alfred Jerger, who had the reputation of being able to do anything, was quickly summoned. He did not know the role, but that hardly mattered. Several copies of the score were placed on stage at strategic points, hidden among various theatre props, such as a pile of musty books on Otello's desk. Jerger, a resourceful actor,

simply sight-read the part as he moved about the stage from
score to score.

Lotte's Desdemona aroused new raptures:

>...Her every appearance upon the stage is like a sunrise.

>...Her acting and her singing have been refined to a point of simple,
classical greatness and most ideal perfection. Her Desdemona, like
her Elisabeth, can be designated as a most faithful re-creation, the
highest achievement that the art of the stage can offer....(A. M.
Pirchan)

Jeritza was back in town.

>...Lehmann is a genius of feeling, as Jeritza is a genius of demonic
theatricality [Theaterteufelei].

May meant London again, this time with Sir Thomas Beecham instead of Bruno Walter. Lotte had so much trouble following Beecham's beat that she smuggled another "maestro," Robert Heger, into the wings to conduct her. (Later, Kirsten Flagstad, too, was baffled by that notorious beat, claiming that Beecham had conducted an entire performance of *Tristan und Isolde*
with nothing but horizontal strokes of the baton.)

Die Meistersinger opened the season, with Friedrich Schorr as
Sachs and Lotte as Eva. The newspapers noted that "four gallant
ladies" had waited twenty-four hours in the rain to buy their tickets. One review was particularly amusing:

>...Eva usually goes about in a dream, and Lotte Lehmann—the El-
len Terry of the operatic stage—woke her up.

Two more reviews are worth noting:

>...It was whispered that Sir Thomas Beecham does not like the ope-
ra [Meistersinger], and certainly the way he conducted it suggested
an impatient desire not to dwell on its intricacies.... The adorable
Lotte Lehmann, distinctly slimmer, actually elevated the part of Eva
into something dramatic as well as lovely.

>...The Eva of Mme. Lehmann is familiar, but not her appearance.
Last year she was handicapped by the conventional embonpoint of
the grand operatic heroine. This year she is as slim as a film star and
her lovely voice is, if anything, better than ever.

Lotte sang two Elisabeths and two Sieglindes ("sheer beauty

from first to last"), besides her four Evas. A few hours before one
of the *Meistersinger* performances, she sang at a socially glamorous
Aeolus Concert at the home of Lady Cunard. Vladimir Horowitz
shared the program with Lotte. The Aeolus series was created
"to provide real music lovers with first-rate concerts in private
houses." The guest list of real music lovers read like a digest of
Debrett's Peerage.

June included some particularly memorable Sieglindes, first in
Vienna....

> ...*Lotte Lehmann lent to Sieglinde all loveliness, all poetic mag-
> ic.... An ideal creation, a poem, the essence of romantic grace, cap-
> tured from the world of German fairy-tales and legends. The image
> of the musical idea becomes visible to the eye, held fast in the lovely
> appearance, in the expressive movements of the body....*

Then in Berlin, at the *Staatsoper:*

> ...*The sensation of the evening [was] the world-famous Sieglinde of
> Lotte Lehmann.... Her Sieglinde is a full-blooded woman filled with
> an uninhibited passion that breaks through all the limitations of con-
> ventional operatic acting. Her voice is as radiant, as brilliant, as
> ever. After the first act a hurricane of applause broke loose.*

Leo Blech was the conductor. There was also an Ariadne, with
Maria Ivogün as Zerbinetta.

In August Lotte first sang Elsa in three open-air performances
of *Lohengrin*, spectacularly staged in the forest by Zoppot. Then
came Salzburg, for *Rosenkavalier, Fidelio,* and *Die Frau ohne Schatten,* two of each. The *Fidelio* was conducted by Strauss, the others
by Clemens Krauss.

It was the first time that *Die Frau ohne Schatten* was presented
in Salzburg. In those days the "Big" Festival Theatre had not yet
been built. The theatre now known as the "little" one was really
much too small for the sort of extravagant production that
Strauss's most elaborate opera demands. It took all the ingenuity
of the stage director, Lothar Wallerstein, to suggest the many
magical events in a reasonably convincing manner. At the dress
rehearsal everything went wrong. Everyone was ripe for a nervous breakdown. Just before the first performance, Wallerstein
made the sign of the cross. "I'm a Jew, of course," he explained,

"but I thought it couldn't hurt and it might just possibly help." According to Lotte's account, it did.

The season in Salzburg was followed by Sieglinde and Elsa in Vienna; a concert with Bruno Walter at the Leipzig Gewandhaus; Eva with Wilhelm Furtwängler, the Marschallin with Otto Klemperer, and a recital, all in Berlin; an Elsa in Munich; recitals in Munich, Graz, and Paris.

Winifred Wagner, the widow of Richard Wagner's son and reigning queen of Bayreuth, heard Lotte's Eva and had a talk with her later. In an interview for a Munich paper, Lotte recalls the gist of their conversation:

> She told me it was the personal wish of Toscanini that I should sing Eva and Sieglinde next year in Bayreuth. I don't yet know if I shall; probably I would not be able to participate in the Salzburg Festival if I did.

Klemperer's *Rosenkavalier* was not a success, according to all reports, except when Lehmann was on the stage. Critics missed the Viennese lift in the waltzes, the lightness of touch that other conductors had managed to bring to it. Maurice Abravanel, then a very young man, later a distinguished conductor and—among many other activities—Lotte Lehmann's colleague at the Music Academy of the West, confirms that view, recalling that the performance was heavily Teutonic, musically, except when Lotte sang, and then, each time, "it was as if the sun came out."

Munich had not heard Lehmann since 1926, when she had sung Sieglinde, Eva, and the *Figaro* Countess in their opera festival without creating any overwhelming sensation. Now they were "fascinated" with her:

> ...The voice of this woman alone is like a miracle: one is fascinated by the fullness and clarity of her sound, by the astonishing range both high and low, and by the ineffably noble charm of her timbre. No less enthralling is her phenomenal mastery of that voice, a mastery which seems too natural to have been learned, which seems more likely to have been a gift from heaven.... But in the final analysis the determining factor is neither voice nor technique: Lotte Lehmann's greatest, loveliest gift is rather the art of interpretation. More inspired singing is not even to be dreamed of. The power of passionate feeling and the power of genuine artistic understanding are combined in her in perfect unity. There was not one piece that she did

not bring fully to life, down to the last nuance of expression, preserving at the same time the overall line.... How amazing it is that she
could sing with equal intensity two such totally different pieces, one
right after the other, as "Death and the Maiden" and "To be Sung
on the Water," the one full of deathly fear and darkness, the other
all spring and light. And what she makes of a somewhat over-
familiar piece like Schumann's Ich grolle nicht.... its inner dramatic
vehemence and shattering climax when Lotte Lehmann sings it!
.... (Dr. A. W.)

The Berlin recital was also her first in that city. She had an
enormous success with the public; but the critics were not prepared to capitulate as quickly as their colleagues in Munich (and
practically everywhere else).

...Lotte Lehmann is conquering Berlin; the success of her lieder recital has perhaps even surpassed her operatic triumphs of the last few
weeks. Yet, fundamentally, Frau Lehmann is no lieder-singer. Dramatic song is her natural domain. She is accustomed [on the stage]
to make everything that she sings the expression of definite dramatic
characters. With this intention, she characterizes, she dramatizes.
And in that way she also dramatizes lieder; if she sings Schubert's
"Serenade," then a whole stage setting is there, the garden at night,
the little house, in front of the house the lover—and that is she herself—who sings his song of longing. It is very beautiful, but it is not
quite right; for it is just the difference between lieder and opera that
the Lied is not intended to be the expression of a particular person
.... (V. Z.)

Mme. Lehmann's partisans would answer Herr V. Z. that just
that is the miracle of her lieder singing: that one does see the garden, feel the scent of flowers on the evening air, and experience
all of the lover's longing in that living moment! Is that not great
art? And she accomplishes that miracle without resorting to any
stage effects, without any operatic gesture, without leaving her
place in the curve of the piano. She does it with the power of her
imagination, with her heart, with her voice, with her expressive
eyes, with a deep inner conviction that communicates itself to
every responsive listener immediately. As she has said, every
poem, every song, was born from an experience. She re-creates
that experience, that inspiration, and shares it with her audience.
The only negative result is that one is spoiled, having experienced Lehmann; the other school of lieder singing, however

tastefully and musically phrased, however well-pronounced the
words, will always seem rather boring in comparison; one can
admire the craftsman-like detail, but how seldom one is truly carried away.

The day after her first Berlin recital Lotte sailed for New York
on the *Bremen.* According to an interview she gave in Leipzig,
thirty-five concerts had been scheduled for her. With Otto—on
leave from his position as vice-president of the Vienna Phoenix
Insurance Company—and Ernö Balogh, her accompanist in
America during the next few years, Lotte raced all over the
U.S.A. and Canada in a more strenuous concert tour than any she
had known in Europe.

> *Two things one must never say in America, "I am tired," and "I
> don't feel well."...It is a hard business learning that cruel, but at the
> same time, incredibly self-disciplining expression: "Keep smil-
> ing."...People often ask me what the American audience is like—to
> which I cannot possibly give a comprehensive answer. It is absolutely
> different [in different places] and always unexpected: often in
> smaller towns one comes across an astonishing degree of appreciation
> of the German Lied, often one has the depressing feeling of singing
> to bare, dead walls.... Then it is always a battle: I vow obstinately to
> myself that I will conquer them—that I will trap them in the net of
> lieder I will cast over them.... Sometimes I don't succeed. Then I
> am as exhausted as if I had been through the hardest physical la-
> bor.... In many parts of America it is pioneer work, awakening the
> appreciation of the Lied.... Of course I am only speaking of one
> part of the audience. There are towns with a European apprecia-
> tion of music, not to mention New York which is, of course, entirely
> cosmopolitan, very spoiled, and tremendously critical.... Meanwhile
> [on tour] it was hard enough to say with a smile that I felt fresh as a
> daisy when I stepped out of the train dead tired, and was met by a
> delegation of clubwomen or managers at the station.... It was
> difficult after a recital to have to sign hundreds of autographs pa-
> tiently, hurry off to the station in my concert gown, frequently with
> almost nothing to eat but a sandwich in a drugstore.*

That was written for publication; the following immediate impressions were shared with her new friend, Viola Westervelt, in
a letter:

> *I was a driven workhorse, not a human being any more. I sold my*

voice for dollars, lived in a train or on the concert platform; and the only beautiful time—California—was spoiled by the flu, which made me very miserable and nervous. If my husband hadn't been with me, I could not have borne any of it at all. Of course, there were individual lovely and artistic highlights: orchestral concerts with Bruno Walter, lieder recitals in New York, Boston, etc. Also Oberlin was nice [where Viola had been married]. An enchanting little city. On its friendly streets I began to realize that there is still some nature left in the world, and not just gasoline stations, neon signs, and movie houses....

Except for that bad case of the flu, California had at least three lovely things to offer: a new friend in Lili Petschnikoff (herself a violinist and the wife of the violinist, Alexandre Petschnikoff); Santa Barbara (Lotte's future home); and what became known, and was frequently quoted, as "the perfect notice."

Madame Petschnikoff, who quickly became a very dear friend, was later instrumental in providing a number of distinguished refugees from the Nazi terror with opportunities to find worthy employment in the U.S.A. (not an easy task during the depression and the war), to the great enrichment of America's cultural life. Lili Petschnikoff gave Lotte a uniquely appropriate gift: a gold pendant with two cameos that had belonged to the original Elisabeth in *Tannhäuser*, Johanna Wagner, Wagner's niece.

As for Santa Barbara, where the Krauses spent Christmas, Lotte fell in love with that very special spot, and tried to persuade Otto that they should retire there when her career was over. He, however, could not imagine that any place but Vienna could ever seem like home to him.

And here are excerpts from that "perfect notice," which was written by Redfern Mason for the *San Francisco Examiner*, December 20, 1932:

MME. LEHMANN RECOGNIZED AS GREAT ARTIST....

...It is said that every woman often thinks she is in love. But when it really happens, she doesn't think; she knows. It is the same with the dear public and artists. They often credit greatness to inferior talent; but, when the real thing comes along, they know beyond the possibility of doubt.

By the time Lotte Lehmann had sung Von ewiger Liebe last night [the first number on the program] the audience gathered in the Opera House recognized not merely a singer of unusual merit, but one of the succession of great artists.... Nobody, in my experience, has ever sung the Erlkönig with such mastery of characterization .... This was magnificent singing and the audience, guided by the infallible instinct of the crowd, was fully aware of it.... That heavenly Ständchen [Schubert's]...had a beauty that left folks not far from tears.

And it is not an aloof, distant talent, that of this young German lieder singer: she is not a goddess condescending to humanity; she is a priestess who raises men and women to heaven's gate....

Lehmann plays on all the stops of human emotion with a victorious sincerity. She can make her voice swell out in ecstatic triumph; yet the tone is never harsh; and always, between her and the audience, there is the feeling of a subtle sympathy, as if the artist were singing, not merely her own emotions, but the emotions crying out for expression in your heart and mine.

Which means that Lotte Lehmann is a great artist, one of the uncrowned queens of humanity, uncrowned because her art is nobler than any merely physical crown could be....

Lotte's American tour included three New York recitals, one in Carnegie Hall (a benefit for the Women's Trade Union League; Eleanor Roosevelt gave an introductory speech), as well as concerts with the New York Philharmonic and Bruno Walter.

A major success in New York. Outstanding reviews in Chicago, Boston, San Francisco. Nevertheless, away from those great centers it seemed as if no one had ever heard of Lotte Lehmann. Her accompanist urged her to hire a publicist. America is such an enormous country. Good notices in New York papers are not necessarily read in Detroit or New Orleans or Kansas City. Lotte was horrified at the thought of paying to get her name into circulation. How unworthy of the dignity of an artist! In Europe that had never been necessary. She was famous because of the excellence of her art. Publicity of the American type is still practically unknown in European musical circles. Lotte was adamantly against any such thing. So Otto and Ernö Balogh, the accompanist, decided that a bit of subterfuge was called for. Behind her back, they hired Constance Hope, a brilliantly clever publicist who had recently opened her own business and—partly thanks to her success with Lehmann—soon had most of the great names in the classical music field as clients. The next time that Lotte returned to America she was astonished to find her name everywhere. Sometimes she was not exactly thrilled with what was written about her. Often the Lotte Lehmann of the articles was unrecognizable as herself. She might read about "Lotte Lehmann's favorite recipe for 'brown Betty'" (definitely not a typical Lehmann specialty); her advice on child rearing (she was actually terrified of children); almost anything that would present her to the American people as folksy, lovable, and down-to-earth. But the name Lotte Lehmann, like the name of a toothpaste or an automobile, was beginning to get reader recognition. Lotte was told that her manager had arranged for the publicity, and that it was he who had hired the charming Miss Hope, who soon made herself indispensable to Lotte, performing all sorts of helpful services not generally included in a publicity contract. By the time Lotte found out the truth—that Constance was on her own payroll—they were fast friends and the advantages of the relationship were totally obvious.

Lotte had never lost her love of writing. As a schoolgirl she had submitted poems to all the Berlin papers. She sent many of them to her elocution teacher for criticism and advice. Later, in Vienna, she published a little book called *Verse in Prosa*, dedicated to her parents. She was the author of numerous newspaper articles about her travels in various countries. Now she was writing her autobiography. Some fairly extensive excerpts were printed in the *New York Herald Tribune*. The first part was published by Breitkopf and Härtel in Leipzig, in 1933 (the expanded form appeared in German in 1937, in English in 1938).

Back in Europe, Lotte returned to Rome and Marseilles for recitals, sang eight of her well-loved roles and several concerts in Vienna, opened the London season with *Rosenkavalier* again, and performed the Marschallin and Sieglinde in Paris.

A particularly memorable event in Vienna was a joint recital with Alfred Piccaver at the end of May. "Sensational Concert" was the headline of the following review:

> …How Vienna celebrates her favorites and how the Viennese hold art above everything else! That could be experienced anew in this unique concert. Two of the most beautiful voices of our time were

> *united in a joint recital and were frenetically applauded by the en-*
> *thusiastic crowd that filled the auditorium of the Concert House up to*
> *the ceiling. The greatest of all miracles is the singing soul, and that is*
> *what our Lehmann possesses; whether she sings lieder or opera arias,*
> *the listener always forgets the world around him, for this enchantress*
> *ensnares him completely with her great art....*

Besides lieder and arias they sang duets from *Faust* and *Tosca.*
It was a comeback for Piccaver. The fans—and that means most
of Vienna—were thrilled.

Lotte was understandably in need of a real vacation. She and
Otto went to Fritz's 160-year old Frisian house, with its pictur-
esque, moss-covered, thatched roof and its tiled inside walls, on
the island of Sylt. They went riding every morning. Lotte loved
the austere beauty of the rather barren landscape beneath a grey
sky. She described her mood in one of her articles. "How wonderful that was for me: far from any ambition, far from any
battles to be fought, to lie in the grassy dunes, with a quiet heartbeat and a deep awareness of happiness, and to look up at the
sky...."

Something new was introduced into the Salzburg Festival,
something so successful that it became a regular feature of every
festival there for the next four years as well. Lotte Lehmann
sang a lieder recital at the Mozarteum, accompanied by Bruno
Walter. The two of them, an unbeatable team, made a sensational impression. Their recitals together were considered highlights
of the Salzburg Festivals until the *Anschluss* put an ugly end to
their participation. Lotte wrote to Viola Westervelt: "It was
wonderful to make music with him. What marvelous things he
told me about those songs! A rehearsal with him is always an experience for me."

Lehmann sang only one other performance that season in
Salzburg, a Marschallin in the last of three *Rosenkavaliers*. She had
turned down an offer from Bayreuth, and canceled the other
Salzburg appearances that had been planned for her, because she
felt that she really needed a complete rest that summer. Elisabeth
Rethberg sang the only Fidelio that year; Rose Pauly took over
the Dyer's Wife; and Ursuleac did the other two Marschallins. All
sorts of rumors were circulating, of course. That Lotte was fatally

ill. That she had lost her voice. But she came back from Sylt healthier than she had felt in ages.

Immediately after Salzburg, in September, the famous, heavily abridged recording of *Der Rosenkavalier* was made in Vienna. Robert Heger conducted the Vienna Philharmonic Orchestra (the regular orchestra of the Vienna State Opera). The recording, long the only one available at all, preserved at least part of three world-famous interpretations: Lehmann's Marschallin, Mayr's Baron Ochs, and Schumann's Sophie. Maria Olszewska, the Octavian, was particularly admired for her Wagner roles; some find the sound of her voice a trifle too mature for the 17-year-old Quinquin.

Incidentally, the voice that sings the Marschallin's very last line, the famous "*ja, ja,*" is not Lotte's at all. After the trio, absent-mindedly forgetting that there was that one more phrase to sing, she simply left the studio. No one knew where to find her and time was running out. So Elisabeth Schumann, the Sophie, sang the Marschallin's last words. She had sung opposite Lotte so many times that she felt confident that she could catch the special Lehmann inflection. It was some time before anyone noticed.

That recording helped to make Lehmann's Marschallin familiar to music lovers all over the world. The music critic of *The New Yorker* (February 17, 1934) wrote: "Mme. Lehmann runs away with the album. Her Marschallin is the finest performance of any role that I ever have heard on records, a masterpiece of expressive restraint."

Strauss had asked Lotte to create the title role in his new opera, *Arabella,* at the world première in Dresden. It took place on July 1, 1933, without her. According to her statement at the time, "the Austro-German border troubles" made it impossible for her to keep that engagement. Strangely enough, Lehmann, who was never very certain about dates and had little awareness, then, of the complicated political tensions involved, seems to have completely forgotten the reason by the time she wrote her book about the Strauss operas.

"Mephisto's Musings," a humor-and-gossip column that used to appear regularly in *Musical America,* offered the following version—which may or may not contain an element of truth—in October 1934:

> ...I wonder how many American music lovers noticed in June 1933 that the much admired Lotte Lehmann did not sing in the première of Strauss's new opera, Arabella, in Dresden, for which she had been engaged?... Fact is that she was engaged for it by Fritz Busch, when he was at Dresden. But with his removal from the scene by Adolf the First [Hitler], Clemens Krauss was called from Vienna to conduct the première.... Rumor had it that Krauss insisted that Viorica Ursuleac sing the title role, in fact, he made it a stipulation of his conducting the work. I never printed this, although I had it at the time from an unimpeachable source. [Fritz Busch was not Jewish; he chose to leave Germany in protest against the Nazi régime.]

Lotte, however, was asked to sing the first Vienna performance of *Arabella*, in October. She was enchanted with the part and looked forward eagerly to the Vienna première. Her enthusiasm for Arabella, during the period of study, is alive in a letter to Viola Westervelt:

> I am learning Arabella as if possessed. The part is glorious, extraordinarily singable and simple in the vocal line, as well as dramatically enchanting. I don't know how I'll learn it in time.... My whole day is filled with singing and studying! My recreation is an hour in the morning when I ride through the Prater under a shower of floating chestnut blossoms. Then I think: Oh, there is that too—divinely beautiful nature! My work keeps me far from her, and yet near through my longing for her.

That was written in April; in September she had more about Arabella to tell Viola:

> You'll like "Arabella" very much. I am delighted. It is an enchanting role, full of charm and vivacity [Schwung]. I am completely under the spell of this very graceful music.

Later, her feeling for the part was soured; subconsciously perhaps, it became inextricably associated with the heart-wrenching circumstances of the première. Lotte's mother died on October 20, 1933, the day between the dress rehearsal and the first performance.

> Clemens Krauss...called at once to say that everyone understood

what this death meant to me and that therefore he scarcely dared to ask if I would consider going on just the same. However, I should bear in mind that critics from everywhere had come to Vienna especially for this performance, that of course it had been sold out long before that; as there could be no possible substitution for a Strauss première, the house for the first time in history would have to be closed if I refused. Viorica Ursuleac was due to sing Arabella that same night in Berlin and therefore could not take my place.

Crushed as I was by the burden of my loss, by the death of the person who was to me the best mother in the world, I could react only with a lethargic assent: "I'll go on."

It was an experience I shall never forget. No power in the world is greater than that of music. For two brief hours it enabled me to forget my deep personal grief, to be Arabella rather than my own tormented, pain-racked, and mourning self. This, in my opinion, is the highest kind of satisfaction our work has to offer, the magic ability to transform and transcend one's self, to escape from the grey routine of everyday life into a different and far more fascinating world. Blessed work, after all; and how grateful I was for that première.

Strauss, profoundly touched by my consent to go ahead and sing, wanted to take me out with him to the footlights at the end of the performance, but I had to refuse. I had done all I could, but I certainly did not want to be applauded for having, by the grace of God, passed a test.

Thus Strauss himself stepped out instead and announced that he would accept the thanks of the audience on behalf of Lotte Lehmann.

Toscanini attended this performance and heard me for the first time. Later on he told me how very moved he had been.

There is a touching letter to Viola:

The day before yesterday I buried my good, old mother, who was released from great pain through a gentle death. It was a lived-out, fully completed life; she was eighty-three years old. But I loved her above everything else, and I am infinitely sad that she is not here any more. She died on the 20th; on the 21st I had to sing the Arabella première, to save the performance. That I was able to, yes, that I was only "Arabella" on the stage, and not the grieving daughter, that is the miracle through which an artist is given grace. I am happy that today I begin a strenuous concert tour; only work is the best helper and comforter....

Chapter Thirteen

THE LIONESS WAS LESS DANGEROUS

WHAT SINGER HAS NOT dreamed of a Metropolitan Opera contract, the confirmation of operatic success? There are a few great singers who made a name in opera during the past hundred years without ever having appeared at the Met. But they are the exceptions. No other opera company has consistently presented so many international stars. Yet Lotte Lehmann, by 1934 the most famous, most admired leading lady in European opera, had apparently been ignored by America's leading opera company for a strangely long time:

> It is curious, how long it was before the Metropolitan Opera engaged me.... I had already been an internationally well-known singer for some time; but it was only after my successful recital at New York's Town Hall that I received the contract I had longed for for years.
>
> The Metropolitan, like the Vienna State Opera, is the dream of all opera singers. So it was with high expectations that I began my engagement in New York. But the actuality was a sort of anticlimax. All my colleagues there were long-familiar friends from festival performances all over Europe. And I saw right from the beginning that there would be nothing especially different here.... My debut was as Sieglinde with the one-and-only, the incomparable Siegmund: Lauritz Melchior...[Giulio] Gatti-Casazza, the general manager, came to my dressing room afterwards with many flattering compliments. I would have liked to answer: "You could have had all that a lot sooner...."

The Metropolitan was not immune to the Great Depression. Many of its backers had suffered financial ruin in the crash of 1929. The income of the opera company began to drop by a million dollars a year. In 1932 the management asked the leading singers to accept a substantial cut in their fees. Two of the brightest stars, Maria Jeritza and Beniamino Gigli, promptly left the Met. With Jeritza gone, the way was clear for Lehmann. Her Town Hall recital, in January of 1932, had created an enormous stir in New York musical circles. Many well-to-do Americans had heard her Fidelio and her Marschallin in Salzburg. It was perfectly clear that Lehmann belonged at the Met.

She was almost forty-six when she made her Metropolitan debut as Sieglinde on Thursday evening, January 11, 1934, ten years after Covent Garden, eight years after Salzburg, six years after Paris, three after Chicago. It was high time. Besides Melchior, the cast included Gertrude Kappel as Brünnhilde, Ludwig Hofmann as Wotan, and Karin Branzell as Fricka. Artur Bodanzky was the conductor. The debut was a triumph for Lehmann:

> ...Never before in the history of the Metropolitan Opera House has there been such a scene as that at the close of the first act of Die Walküre last night.... The instant the curtain fell the applause rang out spontaneously; then when Lotte Lehmann came before the footlights it rose in volume, and as her confreres left her alone—something rare on the first curtain call—the whole audience broke into cheering which lasted a full ten minutes.
>
> Lehmann is the very essence of grace and beauty. We knew she could sing, for she gave us a recital last season; but we didn't know what the great love scene at the end of the first act was like until she showed us, and, rising fully to the occasion, Melchior played up to her and sang up to her as he never has before. She was an inspiration. What a glorious voice she has.... (Charles Pike Sawyer, The New York Evening Post, January 12,1934)

> ...To those familiar with her lieder singing her finished phrasing, precise in definition yet always plastic, and her crystalline diction were no surprise. Yet even her admirers in the recital field were not altogether prepared for the other qualities she brought to her superb impersonation: the dramatic fire, the capacity to endow the vocal line with a breadth befitting Wagner's immense canvas yet to retain always the purely musical finish she might have bequeathed to a phrase of Hugo Wolf; her telling restraint and sureness as an actress. At the end of the first act a cheering audience recalled her seven times.... But if the first act was of a sort to startle the critical faculty into sharp attention and admiration, her performance in the second had an electrifying quality that swept that faculty away for once and made even the guarded listener a breathless participant in the emo-

tions of the anguished Sieglinde.... (H. H. [Hubbard Hutchinson],
The New York Times)

...There has not been such a vital and thrilling first act of Die
Walküre at the Metropolitan in years.... (W. J. Henderson, The
New York Sun)

Time had this to say in the January 22 issue:

...If the singer had been an Italian tenor who had spent his last
nickel on the claque, the ovation could not have been bigger.... [Before the performance] Lehmann was nervous. Her husband knew it. The battered old doll which she kisses for luck each
time she goes on stage trembled in her hands. But the audience saw
no signs of uncertainty, no lack of confidence....

Lotte went from Buffalo to Cuba and then to Milwaukee,
which was having an unusually severe cold spell. It was quite a
shock to Lotte and her accompanist after the heat of Havana. The
Milwaukee Leader ran the headline:

WARMTH OF LEHMANN'S VOICE
THAWS HER AUDIENCE

...Lotte Lehmann, who sings lieder as a fine actor reads lines, came
to the Pabst Theatre last night. She saw practically the entire mem-
bership of Miss Rice's Music Lovers thaw under the warmth of her
performance, and conquered every cold hand in the throng.... A
glow settled over the audience which mounted into an excited flame
as the singer progressed.... (Harriet Pettibone Clinton, Milwaukee
Leader, January 30, 1934)

The very next night she sang in Cleveland, to an even more
ecstatic audience.

...Somehow this recital revived one's faith in man and his possibili-
ties.... If human beings can create songs such as were presented on
the program last night, and if every so often there comes an artist
such as Lehmann who can recreate their splendor in such matchless
fashion—then this old world is, indeed, a good place to live
in.... (Denoe Leedy, The Cleveland Press, February 1, 1934)

February 11, 1934, was a major date in Lehmann's career. On
that evening she sang for the first time under the baton of Arturo Toscanini. For him, too, it was a first: the first time that he had

participated in a commercial radio broadcast. It was "The Cadillac Hour." Before Beethoven and after Mendelssohn the announcer touted as tastefully as possible the advantages of the Cadillac car. Lotte sang *Dich, teure Halle* and Fidelio's aria. It was a landmark for radio. The response was so favorable that General Motors was moved to sponsor an entire series of classical music broadcasts.

The next day Lotte was back in Town Hall, sharing a program with Myra Hess and others for the Beethoven Society. There was Toscanini in the front row. Lotte was so startled that she nearly forgot to sing her first phrase.

Then, on February 24, she sang her second Metropolitan Opera performance. This time the opera was *Tannhäuser*. Toscanini was in the audience, with Geraldine Farrar. Melchior sang the title role, Maria Olszewska was Venus, Friedrich Schorr the Wolfram, Bodanzky the conductor. Once again Lotte had a remarkable triumph as Elisabeth. Once again the reviews were fantastic.

She soon was on the road again to Washington, D. C. and Montclair, N. J. On March 4, she was back in New York's Town Hall for a recital of Schubert, Brahms, Wolf, Strauss and eight encores. The venerable W. J. Henderson noted in his review that Lotte "held the audience in the hollow of her hand." That audience included once again both Toscanini and Farrar.

> ... *What might be the secret of the spell she wove? Possibly, first of all, the healthiness of her art. Second, perhaps its revelation of a very fine type of womanhood.... When she sings she does so with a conviction you cannot resist. You feel that you are receiving something precious from an exceptional person....* (W. J. Henderson, *The New York Sun*, March 5, 1934)

Without pausing to rest, Lotte moved on to Toledo, Minneapolis, and Reading. In Minneapolis she confided her happy feelings to Viola Westervelt, who had returned to France, in a letter dated March 9, 1934:

> *Up to now everything has been a true triumph for me—I can say that without exaggeration. Never before has a tour been so untroubled, so full of unforgettable impressions, as this year. Everything has*

gone so well and so beautifully that I often think my good mother must be with me…. The Elisabeth was a stunning success—[Lawrence] Gilman wrote that I would have been the fulfillment of Wagner's dreams if, eighty years ago, he could have had the luck to hear me. On the 4th I had a sold-out Town Hall recital; the people simply went <u>mad</u> and I sang exceptionally well—you know how seldom I ever feel that—but I was as if intoxicated and raised above everything terrestrial by that enthusiasm. The charming Farrar and Toscanini were at the recital from the beginning to the end. Toscanini means to me a very special chapter in my life. This man, before whom everyone that sings or plays for him trembles, is so <u>wonderful</u> to me, that I am quite speechless. After the recital he said to me that absolutely no one compares to me ("une artiste sans égale") and that no superlative would be too high to tell me how delighted he is. I am so proud—I almost wept for happiness. The reviews are all glorious, except that the critics all write that I often let myself be carried away too much by my temperament and that I then overdramatize. That may well be. But only a block of ice can remain cold—in such a tumult of enthusiasm…. The Herald Tribune (a third-ranked critic, so I hear [Jerome D. Bohm]) tore me to pieces. I would have been very upset by that if Toscanini had not said such beautiful things to me. He inscribed his picture to me: "alla cara Lotte con affetto, amicizia e grande ammirazione" [to dear Lotte with affection, friendship, and great admiration]…. Dear Viola, the world all around us has gone crazy—caught up in politics and fighting—and yet in me something is singing and ringing. Music is the most beautiful thing after all. Whoever can live in this world of music, and not worry about the other one, is very lucky.

Before very long Lotte too would have to worry about that "other one." In the year since Hitler had become chancellor of Germany, Nazism had spread its tentacles into every stratum of German life. A ruthless persecution of the Jews had begun almost immediately. A national boycott of all Jewish professions and businesses was in effect since April 1933. The Hitler Youth Movement was indoctrinating the younger generation with Nazi ideology, to undermine any counteracting influence from the family or the church.

Bruno Walter was refused entrance to the Leipzig Gewandhaus when he arrived to rehearse for a concert. He left Germany. Austria, however, was still free.

The quintessential Marschallin of *Der Rosenkavalier*: Lotte Lehmann.

Left: Lotte Lehmann
as the Marschallin in
Richard Strauss'
Der Rosenkavalier,
Act I: "Jetzt wird
gefrühstückt—jedes
Ding hat seine Zeit..."

Right: Act I: "Quinquin, es
ist ein Besuch..."

Below: Act I: "Ich hatte diesen Morgen die Migräne..."

Photos on these two
pages are of *Rosenkavalier*
performances in
Salzburg.

Right: Act III:
"Da steht der Bub..."

Below: Act I:
"Warum versteckt er's
nicht vor mir?"

Lotte Lehmann and Arturo
Toscanini, inscribed by Toscanini
to Lehmann with a phrase from
Fidelio's aria, "*Komm', Hoffnung.*"

Toscanini and Lehmann taking bows after Salzburg performance of *Fidelio*.

Bas relief of Toscanini head by
Lotte Lehmann.

Right: Toscanini and Lehmann
on the patio of Orplid in Santa
Barbara.

Toscanini and Lehmann rehearsing *Fidelio* in Salzburg.

Left: Lotte Lehmann
with Richard Strauss after
a performance of *Fidelio*
which he conducted.

Right: Lehmann on 1937
Australian tour cuddles the koalas.

Lehmann tries a duet with a kookaburra in Australia.

Lotte Lehmann as consummate lieder recitalist.

Above: Lehmann rehearsing with Paul Ulanowsky.

Above: Recital with Bruno Walter at the Mozarteum in Salzburg.

Right: The 1951 Farewell Recital at Town Hall, New York City. Below: Just after Lehmann broke into tears at the last line of An die Musik.

In protest against such treatment of Jewish artists, Toscanini refused to conduct in Bayreuth, where he had been the leading attraction, the guarantee of high artistic standards. Wagner's stepdaughter, Daniela Thode, made a special trip to Italy to plead with him to change his mind. Hitler wrote him a personal letter, urging him to return. Toscanini was adamant.

In February 1934 fascists and socialists were battling in the streets of Vienna.

Near the end of 1933, on November 19, Lotte had sung a recital in Geneva, for the first time. She sang in the mammoth Palace of the Reformation, where the sessions of the League of Nations took place, because no theatre or concert hall in the city would have been large enough to accomodate the enormous demand for tickets. Germany had withdrawn from the League of Nations just one month before, so she could hardly avoid political questions in her meetings with the press. One paper printed the following statement from her interview with a reporter who signed himself André de Blonay:

> I hate politics.
>
> I am an artist, nothing but an artist: I have the marvelous privilege of living in a land where there is only beauty.
>
> I like to sing everywhere, in all countries, before all audiences.
>
> I know the miraculous power of art to unite people, to lift them above themselves, to let them forget their shabby disputes.
>
> In the presence of art, there are no enemies, no borders, no political parties; there are human beings who suffer and look for the light.

Lotte sensed the ugliness that was darkening the land of her birth, but it had not yet touched her personally. Her eyes were not yet opened to the full reality. She was not alone in that.

While Hitler was perverting and distorting Wagner's message for his own ends, Lotte was helping to hymn the greatest of Germany's treasures, immortal art, which, as Wagner wrote at the end of Die Meistersinger, will outlast any earthly empire. In My Many Lives Lehmann has this to say on that theme:

> In these days it seems doubly thrilling to recall this speech [of Hans Sachs]. There will always be masters, who will hold high the greatest gift which mankind can offer, wherever it may have been born;

there will always be masters to remind the world that one thing is eternal, that one thing stands supreme above all others: Art.

On March 15, 1934, she sang Eva in that opera, as her third performance at the Metropolitan. Friedrich Schorr, a very great Hans Sachs, was her partner, along with Max Lorenz as Walter. Lotte's Eva was another revelation to New York, for no one before her had ever given that character so much personality and life, either at the Met or anywhere else.

Lotte Lehmann's first season at the Metropolitan Opera was a mere three performances, one each of three roles, which was strangely few, in view of all the acclaim. Most of the subscribers never got to hear her at all and there were many complaints. She sang Sieglinde in one of five *Walküres* (sharing the part with Göta Ljungberg, Grete Stückgold, and Gertrude Kappel); Elisabeth in one out of five *Tannhäusers* (Maria Müller and Elisabeth Rethberg having sung the other performances); and Eva in one out of four *Meistersingers* (versus Rethberg, Müller, and Editha Fleischer). Nevertheless, those few appearances rated as highlights of the season.

Two days later, on March 17, Lotte sang a recital at Columbia University. Toscanini was again in the audience. Something happened between them that night. He never forgot that special date.

One of his biographers, George R. Marek, wrote about the relationship that began with the Cadillac broadcast of February 11 (he misremembered the year as 1935 instead of 1934):

> With this concert began a close friendship. Toscanini was then almost sixty-seven [age corrected], but he fell in love with her with the fervor of a young man…. He used to phone her almost every day wherever she was…and he sent her orchids several times a week. She traveled, he traveled, but there was always the phone, and wherever he might be he thought of her and there were long confidences to be exchanged.

Toscanini and Lehmann were both remarkably successful at keeping their affair a secret, though there were hints in Toscanini's inscriptions on the photos Lotte had framed.

After Toscanini's death a mutual confidante found Lotte's letters to him before his family could do so, and she sent them to Lotte, who burned them. As for his letters to her, Lotte tore them into four to six large pieces each and tossed them into the fireplace. But no fire was burning and she did not strike a match. Lotte had a habit of throwing away letters, and her friend, Frances Holden, with a historian's instinct, had a habit of rescuing them. The Toscanini fragments were retrieved from the fireplace, stuffed into a file, and remained there unread and unnoticed, until the research for this book began. Pieced together and translated from the French in which Toscanini wrote to Lotte, the letters provide a record of a passionate and very private friendship. Their contents illuminate the close emotional bond between two supremely great artists.

Since Lotte did not speak Italian and was not yet fluent in English, Toscanini wrote to her in his own brand of French, seasoned with an occasional dash of Italian spice. He always signed himself "Maestro," which is what nearly everyone called him in those days. Sometimes there was only "Mae..."

In the first of the surviving letters to "cara, divina" Lotte, he began to address her with the formal "vous" but soon shifted to the intimate "tu." He complained of crushing rehearsals without a single day of real rest and longed for an opportunity to be alone with her. "You are like a dream in my spirit," he said. He begged her not to stop writing her beautiful letters "full of love and of enthusiasm." He requested small copies of her portraits to carry around with him, "always," in his pocket.

How Lotte felt can be gleaned from several letters to her confidante, Mia Hecht:

[March 6, 1934, from Toledo, Ohio (on tour)] *I had a wonderful letter.... He wrote that he was suffering* "comme un chien" [like a dog] *and* "je vous aime, oui, oui, je vous aime...." " [I love you, yes, yes, I love you] *well, I am totally out of my mind....*

[later that month, from Reading, Pennsylvania] *Mia, I am half crazy. These ever more intense letters are killing me. I gave him two postcard-sized pictures of me...and he wrote me, quite _madly_, that*

*he keeps them next to his heart at night and kisses them like a mad-
man and is dying of desire for me, etc., and laments that there is no
chance to be alone together! He seems—or so it looks to him—to be
constantly watched. He wrote "quelle vie de chien..." [what a
dog's life.] It is good that we are sailing soon; my nerves are destroying me totally. It also seems that people are talking already. We were
recently at [Olin] Downes' party [then the leading music critic of
The New York Times] and he said: "What is this about you and
Toscanini? I think your husband must take care of you...." It was a
joke—but it's strange nevertheless, isn't it?*

*[March 21, New York] The thing between T. and me has taken on
unforeseen and unwanted dimensions...It is good that I am leaving—I can't take any more, I am at the end of my strength, my
nerves are finished...Otto is sad, he feels everything—he said yesterday that I no longer seem to be living at his side, but rather in some
other world, since I met T.... I could not even deny it.... Now I
don't know what will happen....*

Lotte had to leave New York all too soon, first for a recital in
Boston; then, March 22, on the *Berengaria*, to return to Europe.
Toscanini wrote her an ardent letter on that day, full of his misery
and unhappiness due to her departure. He longed to hear "your
divine voice which so sweetly soothes my soul, my ears, and all
my being!!!"

There was a new role to study on the way to Europe: Tatiana
in *Eugene Onegin* by Tchaikovsky. Bruno Walter had cabled that
she should arrive with the part completely learned. There had
been no time for study during her concert tours....

And so on the trip back to Europe I sat at the piano in the dining
room of the ship, every day after lunch, learning the Tatiana, while
the stewards with much clatter cleared away the tables around me.
It was the only "undisturbed" time to use the piano. But I did it and
knew my role when I arrived in Vienna.

Before returning to Austria she gave a recital in Paris. It was
to have been a joint recital with Heinrich Schlusnus, himself a famous lieder singer; but he was ill and Lotte sang alone.

Back to Vienna. With Mama gone it no longer seemed like
home. "Home is where I hang my pictures," Lotte told an interviewer. Yet she now thought of herself as Viennese. "Yes, I am

Viennese," she had told the reporter in Geneva. "Not by birth—
Franz Schalk used to say that that must have been a mistake—but
in my heart." She and Otto resumed their early-morning rides in
the Prater. There were rehearsals with Bruno Walter for *Eugene
Onegin*. Lotte fell in love with Tatiana; it turned out to be her last
new role. The première took place on April 10, 1934. Six days later, from Budapest, she wrote to Viola Westervelt:

> On the 10th I sang Tatiana in Eugene Onegin in Vienna under
> Bruno Walter. It was for him and for me a colossal success. I was
> given an ovation—minutes long!—on the open stage. Ah, here I am
> being a real "prima donna" again, bragging about her triumphs. I
> can just see you wrinkling your pretty nose.

Every review was a rave. Tatiana turned out to be one of the
perfect "Lehmann roles." It was remarkable how convincingly
Lotte, at forty-six, could play a teen-aged girl.

One week later she and Bruno Walter gave another of their
lieder recitals together. The critics reached for new superlatives:

> ... Working together with Bruno Walter seems to lead the artist even
> beyond herself and to draw her up to unimagined heights. How those
> two up there on the concert platform, music-possessed, make music
> together—that verges on the miraculous.... (H. E. H.)

The very next evening she was singing in Dresden. And
there, finally, politics caught up with her. Heinz Tietjen, then the
general director of all the Prussian state theatres, had already
called her in Vienna to tell her that Hermann Göring, Hitler's
Minister of Education, was personally inviting her to come to
Berlin for a few guest performances at any fee she should care to
name, and that she should cancel her première and come right
away. Lotte answered that such a cancellation would be out of
the question, but that she would be in Germany later, on a recital
tour, and could speak with him then.

On April 19, in the middle of her lieder recital in Dresden,
Göring tried to reach her on the telephone. Lotte tells the whole
fantastic story in her article, "Göring, the Lioness and I." The following excerpts give some idea of her precarious experience and
a hint of the black humor with which she described it.

During my recital, in the middle of a song, I suddenly sensed a curious unrest in the audience. It irritated me immensely, and I attempted, by closing my eyes, to regain my concentration. But the unrest only grew worse. I opened my eyes, and saw, right in front of me, a man, an official of some kind, who was desperately trying to interrupt me in mid-song. Little did he know me! I again closed my eyes, and sang to the end, disregarding the mounting unrest all around me. When I had finished my song, I bent down to the interrupter and whispered: "What's the matter? Why are you interrupting me?"

He looked at me with pleading eyes, and I noticed with astonishment that he was shaking with nerves from head to foot. "His Excellency, the Minister of Education, is on the telephone. He wishes to speak to you."

I laughed in his face. It must have been a tremendous shock for him when I said: "First I shall complete my group of songs. How dare you interrupt me like this?"

I finished the group of songs. No applause. The audience sat paralysed. Only later did I realize why. They must have thought that I had fallen into disfavor, and expected me to be arrested at any moment....

Lotte was informed that Göring was sending his private plane to bring her to Berlin. She was blissfully unaware of any danger.

I have always lived for music. Especially so during the time when the Vienna Opera was my real home, and the whole universe seemed to me merely a backdrop for the stage.... I had never taken any interest in politics, and, unsuspecting, had assumed that the Nazi régime would mean nothing more than an unpleasant temporary change of government in Germany. Not for one moment did I realize that it meant the beginning of a world-shattering struggle between good and evil. I knew next to nothing about Hitler, since I read only those parts of the paper that dealt with music and the arts.... Of course, as I write this I realize that I was behaving like an idiot.... I was saved from making a hasty decision that might have landed me unwittingly in a trap leading straight to my destruction. Of one thing I am certain: had I been foolish enough to stay in Germany I should have ended up in a concentration camp. I can never keep my mouth shut and, once I grasped the whole frightful situation, I should have said things which, during that terrible time, could have meant only my end.

The Director of the Opera was waiting for me at the aerodrome.

He was a changed man. He looked thin, and his face seemed tired and anxious. In the car on the way to Berlin he tried to explain to me that the times had changed drastically. "Above all, do be careful, and please think before saying anything," he whispered, nervously watching the chauffeur who could certainly not hear a word through the dividing glass.

"Why are you whispering? He can't hear a thing."

"Oh, one can't be certain. When we arrive let me do the talking, it would be much better if you said nothing."

"You'd have to kill me to achieve that."

He looked at me in horror. I didn't understand. "Don't joke about such things," he said, and his voice was trembling.

He told her that Göring wanted her not only as a guest artist but as a permanent member of the Berlin Opera.

"You can make whatever demands you like, and they will be granted. Understand me aright: whatever you ask, literally. Name a figure, it is yours. Make any conditions you like, mention any personal wishes, they will all be granted." I didn't understand.

"Has everybody gone mad here?"

..."Yes, perhaps that's what it is. But you can profit from this state of affairs. Only be careful, and don't blurt out everything that is in your mind. His Excellency is very sensitive, you must never make him angry. You understand? Never!"

...We drove to the Ministry of Education. Soldiers everywhere. Swastikas everywhere. The "Heil Hitler" greeting everywhere. It all seemed to me like rather third-rate theatre, and I said as much, which produced a very heavy fit of coughing from the Director of the Opera.... It was Hitler's birthday, and there was a huge parade at which, of course, Göring had to make an appearance. But he had left a message that we should make ourselves at home. Feel at home! Hardly likely, since every time I opened my mouth the Director of the Opera looked at me as if I were about to pronounce my own death sentence....

After exercising his horse, Göring came over to meet Lotte. He carried a riding crop and wore a wide knife in his belt. Soon they were having luncheon with him. He used that knife to cut his food.

Göring came straight to the point. "I read about your success in America," he said, between mouthfuls, "and you caused me a sleepless night. Yes. I thought of your future. You had earned a good deal *of money, and you are likely to pay it into a bank in Vienna, where the Jews will deprive you of it."*

"Nonsense, my money would be perfectly safe. Anyway, I don't need other people to lose my money for me. I spend it fast enough myself...."

...He placed the knife and the riding crop on the table, looked at me smiling, and said, in quite a friendly manner, "Let's forget about Vienna for a moment. Let's talk about your contract!"

"I am not in the habit of discussing contracts between a knife and a whip."

Göring proposed an enormous fee that left Lotte speechless. Then he offered her a villa, a pension for life, and a horse. Did she not have a special wish? Laughing, she asked for a castle on the Rhine. What was meant as an ironic joke was soon the talk of Germany.

Of course Göring also had a few wishes: he expected me, as a matter of course, never to sing outside of Germany again. "You should not go out into the world," he said dramatically, "the world should come to us, if it wants to hear you."

"But an artist belongs to the whole world. Why should I limit myself to one country? Music is an international language, and as one of its messengers I wish to sing everywhere, all over the world."

Blushing furiously Göring looked at me with icy contempt. "First and foremost, you are a German. Or perhaps not?"

Lotte could not seriously believe she would ever be prevented from singing outside of Germany. It seemed, at the moment, that it would be sheer madness to refuse such an incredibly advantageous contract. She tentatively agreed.

Göring said with a curious smile: "And in Berlin you will never get bad notices!"

"Why? I may give a bad performance, and not deserve praise."

"If I myself think you are singing well, no critic will have a different opinion. And if he dares, he will be liquidated."

This sounded so absurd to me that I simply laughed.... He gave the impression of being a perfectly harmless and amiable young man. He even had charm, however strange that may sound.... How could I suspect the horrors that lived beneath that smooth brow?

Enter Göring's pet lioness.

I was standing by the window. The lioness came over to me, and put her paws on the window sill. And she, Göring, and I looked out of the window.... "The fearless German woman" between two wild beasts, of which the lioness was the less dangerous.

Lotte went on to sing a recital in Leipzig. After Leipzig came London, where she again opened the season, with *Fidelio*. That was the famous performance in which Sir Thomas Beecham turned to the noisy audience during the overture and shouted: "Stop talking!" Then came Paris for *Meistersinger* with Furtwängler and a rendezvous with Toscanini.

When she returned to Vienna, she found the Berlin contract waiting for her signature. But it was not at all the same contract that had been discussed with Göring. There was not a trace of the fantastic promises he had made. Lotte wrote a frank letter to Tietjen, the Director of the Opera, expressing her reservations, along with some typically outspoken opinions. The letter was intended for his eyes only; instead it was shown to both Göring and Hitler.

The result of all this was that I was forbidden to sing in Germany. The Führer is supposed to have thrown a fit when he saw my letter, and, as they say that whenever he was in a rage he would throw himself on the floor and chew the carpet through, my remarks may well have cost the German Reich a rug. Göring himself dictated a reply to me. It was a terrible letter, full of insults and low abuse. A real volcano of hate and revenge poured over me.

That was the end of Germany for me. Hitler's Germany! Later, they tried to get me back with promises. Everything would be forgiven and forgotten and I would be welcomed with open arms. But by then I knew better. My eyes had been opened to their crimes, and nothing could have induced me to return.

Viorica Ursuleac, who was not present and whose information must have come from Göring or Tietjen, claimed that Lehmann had demanded exclusive rights to three roles, Chrysothemis, Arabella, and Sieglinde; and that, when she heard that Ursuleac's contract included those parts, she "had a fit of hysteria" and "walked out of his office." The reference to Chrysothemis alone is enough to drastically reduce the credibility of that story, since that was never a role that Lehmann wanted to sing. Nor was Arabella a favorite, after the associations with her mother's death.

In any case, Göring had offered Lehmann a special title, *Nationalsängerin*. And before the year was out he had issued a *Reichsbann*, forbidding her engagement by any German theatre. State Commissioner Hans Hinkel made the following deposition: "Despite the proven German descent of Frau Lotte Lehmann, I must judge her political and national reliability to be zero." A few years later, in April 1940, a German composer, Paul Graemer, criticized Lehmann for having sung music by Erich Wolfgang Korngold (who was Jewish), in order to become "popular." "Now," he continued, "Korngold is finished and so is her popularity; we are once again German and pure."

The Nürnberg Laws were still a year away, those infamous decrees which deprived Jews of German citizenship, prohibited intermarriage, and forced those Jews who left the country to forfeit their property and most of their belongings. Otto's four children were half-Jewish, through their mother, but they seemed to be safe in Vienna. There was as yet no persecution in Austria; nevertheless, disturbances were already starting. On June 10, 1934, a performance of *Die Walküre* at the Vienna State Opera—with Lehmann as Sieglinde—was held up for over an hour because a Nazi threw a tear-gas bomb into the auditorium (most of the Viennese newspapers ignored the story in their reviews, except for one that mentioned an "insignificant incident;" only an English-language report gave the facts).

On July 25 the Austrian Chancellor, Engelbert Dollfuss, was assassinated by a group of Austrian Nazis, disguised in army uniforms, as they seized the Chancellery during the so-called *Putsch* (coup—fortunately an unsuccessful one). The opening of the Salzburg Festival, with Lehmann in *Fidelio*, originally scheduled for July 28, was postponed for a day because of the Dollfuss funeral. In honor of the murdered chancellor, Clemens Krauss conducted the Funeral March from Beethoven's Eroica Symphony before the performance of the opera.

German artists were forbidden to participate in the Salzburg Festival of 1934, partly in retaliation for Toscanini's refusal to conduct again at Bayreuth. His stand against Hitler had led to the banning of his recordings in Germany. Salzburg was presenting

Toscanini for the first time, in two orchestral concerts, one with
Lotte Lehmann.

For the second year in a row, the Nazi government imposed a
border tax to discourage Germans from attending the Salzburg
Festival.

Richard Strauss was to have conducted the opening *Fidelio* but
was forced to withdraw, since he too was forbidden to make any
official appearance in Salzburg. Special honors planned for
Strauss's 70th birthday celebration had to be canceled. He came
anyway, though unofficially, and even went up on stage to congratulate Rose Pauly after her performance as Elektra, something
he could not have done in Nazi Germany, since Pauly was not of
Aryan blood. The Nazi vise was tightening. Artistically the Salzburg season was another great success, thanks particularly to
Lehmann, Bruno Walter, and Toscanini. Lehmann sang Fidelio
and the Marschallin, an all-Wagner concert with Toscanini, and a
lieder recital with Bruno Walter. Walter conducted *Tristan und
Isolde*, *Oberon*, and *Don Giovanni*. There was a Strauss cycle, conducted by Clemens Krauss, who was also in charge of *The Marriage of Figaro*. All the operas were by German and Austrian composers. The audience came from many lands, but not from Nazi
Germany. That had been *verboten*, not just for performers.

The correspondent for *The Musical Courier* sent back a glowing
report of the opening *Fidelio*:

> ...Lotte Lehmann *thrilled the audience in the title role. She was not
> only the loving and suffering wife, but she seemed to symbolize in her
> playing and singing the suffering and deliverance of all man-
> kind....* (Paul A. Pisk, September 15, 1934)

Musical America had this to say of the Lehmann-Toscanini concert:

> ...It was uncanny how high a degree of intimacy and facility of ex-
> pression the singer and the orchestra achieved.... (Dr. Paul Stefan,
> September 1934)

In July, before their reunion in Salzburg, Toscanini had written to her from his "*Isolino*," his little island in Lago Maggiore.
Never had he loved "a woman more intelligent, more childlike,
wilder, sweeter, more adorably woman than you."

On the 28th he was in Trento, undergoing treatment for the
chronic pain in his right arm and shoulder that often made conducting an excruciating ordeal. He wrote to ask Lotte about the
troubles at Salzburg that had followed the assassination of Dollfuss. Because of the crisis, telephone and telegraph connections
with Austria were defective and plagued with frustrating delays.
Toscanini reviled Hitler and Mussolini as the cause of the "spirit
of violence …in the process of submerging old Europe."
    Once again Lotte confided in Mia Hecht:

> [August 31, 1934, Grand Hotel de l'Europe, Salzburg] *I feel rather
> miserable. It is beyond my strength, this waiting that wears me down,
> this living in the same hotel — and yet as if an ocean were between
> us…. I do not understand him at all. He was with me on the 28th,
> after I had written him a letter very full of doubts and sadness. He
> was infinitely tender, kept reassuring me that he loves me, and was
> again like a young man of eighteen…. The next day, he went to the
> Rosenkavalier performance. They tell me he was beside himself with
> delight and constantly repeated that there is just one artist
> [Künstlerin] in the world…. The concert yesterday was marvelous,
> perhaps you heard it on the air. Today he is leaving with his family. I
> wonder if I will be seeing him. I am waiting…. I must tell you that I
> am glad that he is leaving. I cannot bear this any more.*

Toscanini and Lehmann gave an all-Wagner concert in Vienna
on October 10. Besides the *Wesendonck Lieder*, Lotte sang the *Liebestod*, Isolde's "Love-Death," from *Tristan und Isolde*. As usual, in
concert performances, it was preceded by the Prelude. The last
notes of the prelude are very low, in the double bass, and very
soft. The singer's first note, also very soft, seems to come out of
thin air. Lotte was afraid she would not find the pitch.

> *For me too he was one with music—and when I sang Isolde's Lie-
> bestod with him in a concert in Vienna, the waves closed over me—
> and in the words, "Ertrinken, versinken" [from the closing phras-
> es: "To drown, to sink, unconscious, highest bliss!"], I felt nearer
> to him than ever before. To him, the great Maestro, the beloved
> friend, the sorcerer, whom the world will never forget….*
> *But even that unforgettable musical experience had its humorous
> side. After the Prelude the singer of Isolde must enter out of no-
> where. I was afraid of that entrance, where there was nothing to*

help me, and I was sure that in my nervousness I would not find the right pitch. So, in the rehearsal, I whispered to my friends, the dear members of the Philharmonic: "Please, someone give me the tone...." Naturally the Maestro had to hear that. He called me a "stupida," which I accepted without protest. Then he said that he himself would give me the pitch, which was certainly very especially nice of him, the Merciless. But—there is a big "but"—vocal talent was not the Maestro's outstanding gift. Thanks to all his screaming during the rehearsals his voice had turned into a peculiar croaking rasp. And during the concert he kept "singing" my tone, over and over.... He seemed to be more nervous about it than I was. Unfortunately, however, his thoughtful efforts were no help to me at all: I could not hear the tone I was seeking in his hoarse whisper. Thanks to a kindly providence, I found it by myself.... My guardian angel must have put in overtime!*

After the concert, Maestro asked me if he hadn't been a great help to me, inspite of my being such a "stupida." And he was quite offended when I told him he had only confused me. I must admit I was more truthful than tactful....

Lotte's love for the Vienna Philharmonic was totally mutual. In 1933, at the rehearsal for her concert with Felix von Weingartner, the orchestra had presented her with its Ring of Honor. She was the first woman to receive it and felt as happy as a bride.

The morning after the concert with Toscanini, at an official breakfast, Lotte Lehmann was decorated with the State Gold Medal of Honor, First Class, for her services to Austrian music.

There was tension in the air in Vienna. In the musical world it centered around Clemens Krauss. Among other things, it was well known that there were serious differences between the director of the opera and his leading soprano star. When the new chancellor, Kurt von Schuschnigg, ostentatiously presented flowers to Lotte Lehmann on stage at her first *Fidelio* of the season in Vienna, many saw in that a slap at Krauss on the part of the government. When Toscanini declared his intention to conduct *Falstaff* at Salzburg in 1935, the first time that an opera by Verdi would be presented there, Krauss promptly announced a Vienna production, in German, in direct competition. That was interpreted as a challenge to see who would have the upper hand at Salzburg. No director of the Vienna Opera ever had it easy. Baiting him, whoever he may be, is practically the Austrian national sport. Krauss was admired as a musician, but his contract was not renewed. When, in December 1934, Furtwängler resigned as director of the Berlin State Opera, in protest against the Nazis' treatment of Paul Hindemith, a distinguished German composer whose works had been banned as "degenerate," Krauss was glad to leave Vienna for Berlin. Several of his favorite singers went with him.

Lotte sailed to America on the *Ile de France* to start another busy season. There would be, as usual, an extensive concert tour; she would make her debut at the San Francisco Opera; America would meet her Marschallin; *Fidelio* was planned for her at the Met; and—astonishingly—the Chicago Opera had announced a production of *Tristan und Isolde* with Lauritz Melchior and Lotte Lehmann.

She never sang in Germany again.

Chapter Fourteen

LIKE A FLOW OF LAVA

WHEN LOTTE RETURNED to America in the fall of 1934, she brought her brother, Fritz, for she hoped to help him establish himself as a dramatic coach for singers. They arrived November 6 in New York. Constance Hope put his name in all the papers; he was introduced to the musical world at a pair of parties. Lotte did what she could to launch him in style. After two hectic days in New York, she and Otto had to leave for her first engagement at the San Francisco Opera. Fritz was left on his own. But it takes more than two days and two parties to build up a following in New York. It was not easy to adjust to another world, another language, a different way of life. Fritz stuck it out for a couple of months; then, discouraged, he went back to Vienna. When he returned, five years later, he was finally able to establish a foothold in New York (as well as, later, in Santa Barbara) with the help of Theresia, his second wife.

San Francisco presented Lehmann in Puccini. All of her previous operatic appearances in North and South America had been in Wagnerian music dramas. She sang Tosca (on November 16) and Madame Butterfly (on November 21), both for the first time ever in Italian. Tosca, especially, was an unqualified success. All the reviewers ranked her portrayal among the great ones.

>...Her Tosca had not the sculptured beauty of Muzio; she did not wallow as Jeritza did when she sang Vissi d'arte. What she did was to give us a Tosca evolved out of her inner consciousness, and in that scene with Scarpia, she touched a note of beautiful humility which neither Bernhardt nor Muzio ever gave us.... (Redfern Mason, San Francisco Examiner, November 17)

>...Superb actress and glorious songstress is Lotte Lehmann.... The German soprano sang the role of the glamorous Tosca...and nego-

tiated the mellifluous Italian phrases as if to the manner born. However, had she sung in Sanskrit it would have mattered not. For the Lehmann voice and the Lehmann dramatic instinct are bigger than nationality or language.... (Marie Hicks Davidson, San Francisco Call-Bulletin)

Some missed an Oriental touch in her Butterfly. Some—those who looked for a Japanese doll—thought her miscast. Most were deeply moved.

...We have been accustomed to the suicide behind a screen.... After witnessing Lehmann's superb acting, her interpretation seems the logical one. She hugged the child in a frenzy of love and despair, shoved him off stage, and then, wrapping a knife in her kimono, committed the dreadful hara-kiri in full view of the audience.... It was a shuddery last act, and one we shall not soon forget. Aside from the sheer drama of Lehmann's acting, there was a quality of voice that spelled agony and death, a kind of declamatory huskiness in minor key that was heartbreak and the will to die.... (Davidson)

...This Butterfly delighted the emotions by approach through the intelligence.... Cio-Cio-San, strictly speaking, is not a Lehmann role. By her mastery of the stage and by the penetration of her feeling she makes it her own.... (Alexander Fried, San Francisco Chronicle)

The next stop was Philadelphia. On November 30, December 1, and December 4, 1934, America saw and heard the famous Marschallin of Lotte Lehmann for the first time, accompanied by the Philadelphia Orchestra, then considered by many to be the best in the world. Elisabeth Schumann was the Sophie. The *Rosenkavalier* production was fully staged by Herbert Graf and conducted by Fritz Reiner. Graf introduced a controversial innovation (repeated many years later, in Zurich): he used a revolving stage in Act III to show Baron Ochs being chased through the inn and out into the street by the waltzing chorus of waiters, lackeys, musicians, stable boys, and screaming children. The great final trio for the Marschallin, Octavian, and Sophie took place in the moonlit garden of the inn, with the candle-lit windows of Vienna as a backdrop.

Lotte Lehmann's Marschallin created the expected sensation. Several important New York critics made the trip to Philadelphia just to hear her, sending back glowing reports to their papers:

...I had heard Mme. Lehmann sing this enamoring role in Europe, but I had never known her to re-create it with so probing a comprehension, so sensitive and sure a touch, a truth of feeling and of utterance so steeped in the essence of the part.... (Lawrence Gilman, *New York Herald Tribune*, December 1, 1934)

...So subtly projected was this great lady that for once the conventions of the theatre ceased to exist, and one felt oneself swept irresistibly into absolute identification with an alien soul. It would take a book to enumerate the details of this extraordinary impersonation, its inspired gestures, its perfection of movement, its uncanny vocal revelations, its pathos, nobility, and tenderness.... (Samuel Chotzinoff, *New York Evening Post*, December 3, 1934)

While in Philadelphia, Lotte invited Reiner and her *Rosenkavalier* colleagues to a "typically American" Thanksgiving dinner in her private suite at the Ritz Hotel. The following report found its way into the *Philadephia Record*:

Mme. Lehmann didn't take her duties as hostess too formally among old friends. When the festal table was wheeled into the room, bearing a huge turkey, its drumsticks adorned with what Herr [Emanuel] List called "lace pants," Mme. Lehmann greeted it with the swan song from Lohengrin and then, seizing a carving knife, rendered the stabbing scene from Tosca, with the turkey cast in the role of Scarpia.... Both performances were hilariously applauded by the small audience present and Mme. Lehmann was repeatedly called from the adjoining bedroom (whither she made her dramatic exit) to bow her acknowledgments.

Both Otto and Fritz were there, to give the touch of family that a real Thanksgiving needs.

Between the last two Philadephia *Rosenkavaliers*, Lotte rushed to New York for a joint recital with Jascha Heifetz at the Waldorf Astoria Hotel (one of the very social Bagby Morning Musicales). Chicago, which was to have been the scene of her first Isolde, with Melchior as Tristan and Frederick Stock conducting, saw Lotte only once that season, as Elisabeth. Instead of Lehmann, Elsa Alsen sang Isolde. No reason was given to the press. Presumably Lotte had second thoughts about the part. She had already canceled a Chicago Elsa, earlier in the season. Maria Jeritza sang that performance, as well as Salome and Turandot.

A concert with orchestra in Toronto won rapturous reviews:

> ...It was a real Wagnerian voice.... As she sang, she seemed like the
> first Frigga, the original Norse queen of the heavens, who was at
> once so majestic as to rule but so sensitive that she could spin the
> clouds on her loom.... There was only greatness.... Her singing of the
> "Love-Death" from Tristan und Isolde had an ecstasy that was tru-
> ly sublime.... (Pearl McCarthy, The Mail and Empire, Toronto,
> December 12, 1934)

After a Christmas spent at Atlantic City, Lotte sang the first
act of Die Walküre in an all-Wagner concert at Carnegie Hall,
conducted by Bruno Walter. Her second Metropolitan season began with Tannhäuser on New Year's Day, with Melchior, Lawrence Tibbett, and Anny Konetzni as her colleagues. The notices were marvelous, at least for Lotte:

> ...The Elisabeth of Lotte Lehmann is one of the most moving em-
> bodiments to be seen on the contemporary operatic stage.... (Jerome
> D. Bohm, New York Herald Tribune, January 2, 1935)

> ...The electrifying spark which set off everything at white heat was
> the superb performance of Mme. Lehmann as Elisabeth....
> (Henriette Weber, New York Journal)

Three days later, on January 4, Lotte sang her first Metropolitan Marschallin with a bad cold. She had begged for a postpone-
ment; but, because the performance was a sold-out charity
benefit, the date could not be changed.

Emanuel List was Baron Ochs, as in Philadelphia; Maria
Olszewska, as on the recording, sang Octavian; the Sophie was
Editha Fleischer, the conductor was Bodanzky.

Der Rosenkavalier had not been performed at the Met for five
years. One of the most complicated operas in the repertoire, with
a large cast of tricky small parts, it received all of three rehearsals
for this important revival. The orchestra had an off-night. But, to
be fair, the score is not the kind that most musicians can simply
read at sight. By the second performance everything seems to
have gone more smoothly. In any case, cold or no cold, the Lehmann Marschallin was warmly received and soon became one of
the major adornments of the Met.

One sign of her success was manifest to all Americans: she made the cover of *Time* magazine. She was the first woman in opera to be honored in that particular way. She was photographed in color as the Marschallin, while a detective with a loaded automatic stood by to guard the jewelery, on loan from a leading Fifth Avenue firm. The issue of February 18, 1935, made clear to the world that Lotte Lehmann had arrived. Meanwhile, however, a bomb had dropped.

Kirsten Flagstad burst upon the scene in a completely unanticipated, sensational way. She had been almost unknown outside of Sweden and her native Norway. Her two seasons at Bayreuth had passed without notice. Yet suddenly, on February 2, 1934, her debut made history at the Met. It was a radio broadcast of *Die Walküre* and she sang the Sieglinde (without a single rehearsal). Geraldine Farrar, who was then the commentator for the Metropolitan Opera broadcasts, told the radio audience that they had just heard one of the greatest voices of the century. Four days later Flagstad sang Isolde. Hers was a new sound, a vocal phenomenon. The voice was enormous, effortless, majestic. Suddenly Wagner became a bestseller at the Met, not just for Wagnerians. *Tristan und Isolde*, with Flagstad and Melchior as the immortal lovers, became the most popular opera in the repertoire. The Metropolitan could count on a sold-out house whenever Flagstad sang. She sometimes sang as much as four performances a week. It was often said, in retrospect, that she saved the Met from the depression.

New York now had the finest Wagner ensemble in the world. Lauritz Melchior had practically no competition anywhere as leading heldentenor. Friedrich Schorr was generally considered to be the greatest Wotan and Hans Sachs, Ludwig Hofmann, Emanuel List, and, somewhat later, Alexander Kipnis were powerful villains, kings, dragons, or giants. Karin Branzell, Maria Olszewska, and, soon, Kerstin Thorborg were worthy queens of Valhalla. Occasionally, Ernestine Schumann-Heink—who had made her American debut in 1898—came out of retirement to sing an earth-mother Erda. The great soprano parts, however, are the crowning glory of Wagner's creations, and there the

Metropolitan had two special treasures: Kirsten Flagstad, the sensational new Isolde and Brünnhilde, and Lotte Lehmann, the world's greatest Sieglinde and Elisabeth, by common consent, and one of the most admired of Evas and Elsas. Those Lehmann roles were also sung at the Met by Elisabeth Rethberg and, for a time yet, by Göta Ljungberg, Maria Müller, and Gertrude Kappel, among others. Strangely enough, the greatest Brünnhilde and the greatest Sieglinde never sang together at the Metropolitan. They were scheduled to do so on tour in Boston (on April 1, 1935), but Lehmann canceled because of illness and Rethberg took her place. Flagstad and Lehmann sang *Die Walküre* together in San Francisco (November 13 and 22, 1936) and in Milwaukee (December 14, 1937), but never anywhere else. There is an exciting off-the-air recording of most of the second act (all but the very end), with Melchior and Schorr, Reiner conducting, from the first of the two San Francisco performances.

As for the performance in Milwaukee, there is a letter to Constance Hope that records some of Lotte's impressions of that event:

> I missed Lauritz enormously. Laholm [Eyvind Laholm, real name Edwin Johnson, from Eau Claire, Wisconsin] has quite a good voice but he sings so inexpressively [so wurschtig] as to make everyone yawn.... I tell you, it takes a sense of humor to sing such a performance. For example: my dressing room was directly adjoining the men's room, which could not be closed.... But all went well. Flagstad listened to the whole first act. She said she wanted to watch because she is going to sing it soon. So she sat in the wings. Don't you agree that even if she found me horrible she should have said something to me afterwards? To listen to a whole act—to tell me in advance that she would—and then not a word.... That hurt me a bit. Constance, I don't know, am I such an envious, spiteful person that I can't be objective? I found her voice very beautiful, very fresh and flowing, but nothing that special...It fails to touch my heart. It doesn't grip me. Always, when I heard dear [Helene] Wildbrunn sing the glorious phrase: "Zu Wotans Willen sprichst du, sagst zu mir, was du willst; Wer bin ich, wär ich dein Wille nicht?" [you are speaking to Wotan's will when you tell me what you want; who am I, if I am not your will?]...tears came to my eyes. And yesterday there was nothing there—not for a moment the living heartbeat which is

after all the absolutely essential thing in art—for what else is "art"? Only artfully technical singing? ...But the people who make up the audience and whose opinion is decisive think differently: they applaud wildly and see in her the greatest artist.

Flagstad, in turn, had her own particular reaction to Lehmann's Sieglinde. She said in a BBC interview that she was as embarrassed by such emotional abandon as if the singer were undressing in public. Temperamentally they were poles apart.

All in all, the advent of Flagstad was a damaging blow to the Lehmann career. One year after Lotte's arrival at the Met, she was partially eclipsed, at least for a part of the public, by the sudden, overnight sensation of Kirsten Flagstad. During that spring of 1935 Flagstad sang two Sieglindes (Lehmann sang none), two Elisabeths and an Elsa (Lehmann sang one of each), along with her Isoldes, Brünnhildes, and three Metropolitan concerts. True, the critics almost all preferred Lehmann in the roles she shared with Flagstad; but Flagstad was the new attraction and the general public wanted to hear her in anything she was willing to sing. *Fidelio*, originally announced for Lehmann, was eventually given to Flagstad. The Met version replaced the spoken dialogue with recitatives Bodanzky had arranged from Beethoven themes. America never heard Lotte Lehmann in the role that many considered her greatest and noblest achievement.

Elisabeth Rethberg, Lotte's other leading rival at the Met, had a very lovely voice; as an actress she was rather conventional and unimaginative. She was versatile, the Met's most valuable Aïda, but she lacked theatrical magic. There was never the slightest friction between her and Lotte; they were, in fact, very friendly.

Lotte sang her first Metropolitan Elsa on February 14, with excellent reviews, followed by two more Marschallins, and an Eva, her second at the Met. Then, instead of the *Fidelio* that had been expected, she was given a revival of *Tosca*, which had last been heard with Jeritza.

At the ninth hour, Richard Crooks, who was to have sung Cavaradossi, was stricken with appendicitis. Giovanni Martinelli was rushed on stage to replace him, without a rehearsal. Lawrence Tibbett was trying out his first Scarpia. He shocked several critics with some unaccustomed realism in the seduction scene.

Vincenzo Bellezza, the conductor, had more troubles with the orchestra than usual. There seemed to be little coordination in the
staging. Many of the reviews were excellent for Lotte, if not
quite as rapturous as those in San Francisco a few months before. But Lotte was deeply depressed because two critics, whose
opinions she valued, wrote negative notices. Frances Holden,
whom she had not yet met, had heard through friends at the
Constance Hope agency about Lotte's distress and wrote to reassure her, and to reproach her for taking those reviews so seriously. Lotte's reply expressed her feelings in a most revealing way.
Her English was not yet as fluent as it later became:

> Your lovely letter has given me much joy. You must understand me
> and not blame me, that I hear too much what everybody is talking...
> I am always afraid to be an arrogant "prima donna," who thinks
> that everything is well done...I know artist friends, who are very in-
> telligent, but without any objectivity for themselves. I want to be criti-
> cal with myself. I know that often I spoil my life, but it is my nature,
> I can nothing do against it....
>
> The Tosca performance was so bad, it was like under a bad luck.
> But I myself have given all my heart, have soon forgotten that I was
> fighting already against a overworked weakness of my voice. When
> I saw next day the critics of Downes and Chotzinoff, I was so de-
> pressed, because I have said to myself: "I have _felt_ the Tosca, I _was_
> the Tosca. And they have not felt it with me. Therefore perhaps I
> was bad. I have not had the artistic power to _show_ what I was feel-
> ing." Always I search the fault in myself—that is perhaps the
> fault....
>
> Oh, I was feeling _miserable_. And then came the trouble with my
> voice and that the Director in Metropolitan has not believed my ill-
> ness [Lehmann had been forced to cancel a Tosca in New York
> and two performances, Walküre and Lohengrin, in Boston]. He
> thought I have a caprice.... And my doctor has not protected me....
> I never will forget those awful two days.... But now I am recover-
> ing, and my voice seems all right again. And I will find myself, my
> believing in myself—in lovely holidays on the French Riviera.

These are the reviews that caused Lotte such distress:

> ...Mme. Lehmann sang brilliantly, at times in a pseudo-
> melodramatic way. She was a German Tosca, rather heavy, lacking
> the mobility and the quick and light play that Italian or French sing-

ers can give the part.... (Olin Downes, *The New York Times*, March 22, 1935)

> ... Miss Lehmann, laboring under the disadvantage of some ill-fitting costumes, gave a vivid portrayal of the chaste Roman opera singer, and sang with her usual fervor. Yet, somehow, her Tosca did not achieve the reality of her Eva, her Marschallin, and her Elisabeth. It was a stagey facsimile of a hectic lady, melodramatic and rather self-conscious.... (Samuel Chotzinoff, *New York Evening Post*)

Other critics, on the other hand, had nothing but praise:

> ... Mme. Lehmann, looking very beautiful and dashing, reminded us from her first entrance that she is a versatile and imaginative singing actress and can turn from Eva to Floria Tosca as easily as most of us can turn from sherry to champagne.... (Lawrence Gilman, *New York Herald Tribune*)

There had been considerable talk, before the season started, of combining the Metropolitan with the New York Philharmonic. That plan fell through, for a number of reasons, but Lotte had asked Toscanini if he would be willing to conduct her in *Fidelio* at the Met. He had replied that he could only consider conducting that opera for her at Salzburg; the Metropolitan Opera orchestra in those days did not meet his exacting standards.

During this time, her affair with Toscanini, which was to ignite again in the blaze of their collaboration at Salzburg that next summer, was causing Lotte considerable distress, as she confessed to Mia Hecht:

> [March 4, 1935, Indianapolis] T. was with me once in New York. The flame is extinguished, I cannot deceive myself any more. He is different. And even if he is overcome by the moment—it is nevertheless the passion of the <u>moment</u>, not of the heart.... I can see it very clearly and gradually come to terms with that. But something <u>incomparably precious</u> has been broken for me.... He has taken the whole affair as an impetuous adventure, above all he has represented it as such to me, and is surprised—and not even pleasantly surprised—that I can't get over him. He kept saying: "Mais tu es une folle! Pourquoi m'aimes-tu encore? J'avais oublié toutes les femmes—pourquoi m'as-tu éveillé? Soi bonne——oublies-moi..." [But you are crazy! Why do you still love me? I've forgotten all the women—why have you aroused me? Be good—forget me.] He was

sweet and enchanting—but a world away from me.... I can also not understand that he never mentions my singing in his concerts any more.... And yet he certainly loves me more as an artist than as a woman. Oh, much more!! He came to my recital and was very enthusiastic and very moved....

Otto is on his way to America right now.... When I arrive in New York he will be there. Thank God. He is really the only one, the best one. Oh, how foolish I would have been to leave him last summer, when I was so close to doing so....

Looking back at the opera season past, *Esquire* had this to say:

...Gatti-Casazza's final season at the Metropolitan Opera House will probably be remembered chiefly for the rise of Kirsten Flagstad and the recognition of Lotte Lehmann. Through the magic of the first of these two singers, Wagner's Tristan und Isolde actually became the most popular opera of the year, breaking all box-office records for the old building; and Mme. Lehmann succeeded not only in establishing the Strauss Rosenkavalier as the masterpiece that it is, but in bringing new life to several other operas that had all but succumbed to the spell of perfunctory routine.... ("The Listening Post," *Esquire*, June 1935)

Altogether Lotte sang seven performances at the Met that season. Flagstad, who started a month later, sang thirteen, Rethberg fourteen, Müller twelve. But Lotte was singing recitals and concerts everywhere: Greenwich, Wellesley, Washington, Princeton, Kansas City, Ann Arbor, St. Louis, Detroit, Saginaw, Brooklyn, Philadelphia, Chicago, Omaha, Indianapolis, Charleston, Pittsburgh, Scranton; two Town Hall recitals; the General Motors broadcast with Bruno Walter as conductor and accompanist, and "The Ford Sunday Evening Hour."

The radio concert with Walter inspired a lyrical review:

...Lotte Lehmann's Isolde [she sang the Liebestod] contained everything that Wagner wrote into the music; and for the creation of such an Isolde there must be not only a great singer but a great woman.... She did [lieder] in such a way that made us wonder whether all music might not be great music if it only had a Lotte Lehmann to sing it.... (Aaron Stein, *New York Evening Post*, January 15, 1935)

While dashing about the country, Lotte was irritated to read a

"Profile" in *The New Yorker*, by Marcia Davenport, which, to Lotte's way of thinking, seemed to portray her as a singing housewife, rather than as an artist.

> Lehmann is a woman of simple German sentiment. She is gentle and jolly, of medium height, and plump.... Her speaking voice is intimate and a bit throaty. She has rather heavy eyebrows, unusually mobile and expressive, and her eyes are characteristically humorous. When she sits on a camp stool in the wings during a rehearsal at the Metropolitan, she looks rather like the schoolmistress her father wanted her to be. Five minutes later, in an old blue dress, with a round comb skinning her hair back, she walks on the stage and complete dramatic illusion walks on with her....
>
> Singers like Lehmann are a problem for opera managements in that they take a performance out of the rut of easy-to-cast mediocrity; only a first-class cast can meet the challenge of excellence .... Temperament, as found in Lehmann, seems to mean that if the other singers are hams, they will be a thousand times more ham in their inadequacy, and that if they are competent, they will rise with Lehmann to genuine inspiration. Lauritz Melchior demonstrates this latter case every time he sings with Lehmann, and says so....
>
> Other singers are fascinated by her and she by them. Rosa Ponselle met her for the first time in a crowded greenroom and without any words rushed into her arms. Last year, after hearing Ponselle's Donna Anna, Lehmann was moved to tears and was having a little cry on the staircase when an admirer rushed up and started to gush about her singing the week before. Lehmann stopped her brusquely. "How can you say such things to me," she scolded, "when you have just heard Ponselle sing like that?" ...
>
> Last year some friends gave Lehmann a birthday party, with a huge cake iced and decorated with inscriptions.... She said she must take the whole thing back to Vienna with her. They told her the filling would get stale. "Very well, then," she said, "but I must have the top of it with all the beautiful Glückwünsche on it." So she took a knife and sliced off the whole top of the cake and handed it to Kahti [Otto's nickname] to put in a trunk. He got it in somewhere....

The author of the offending article was actually one of Lotte's most devoted fans. In fact, the heroine of Davenport's novel, *Of Lena Geyer*, about an opera singer, was a composite of her own mother (the well-loved soprano Alma Gluck), Nellie Melba, Geraldine Farrar, and Lotte Lehmann. Later she and Lotte became

good friends and laughed away any lingering pique about that
"Profile."

On the way to Omaha, Lotte wrote her own self-portrait.

*You wanted to hear from me, myself, what I am like, which puts me
in a rather embarrassing situation. I feel myself sitting before a mirror and looking at myself with strict objectivity, and I am afraid I
will see myself in a more favorable light than I deserve.*

*What I see at the first glance: a fantastic enthusiasm for my pro-
fession, which I consider as a mission. To devote myself to it is my
only urge, desire, and even more—an imperative command which I
happily obey.*

*The next thing I love in life is freedom. I could not sing in a
country where they would prescribe what I sing, how to sing, with
whom, and in whose composition.*

*I like to travel, to sing to new audiences, which don't know me
yet, and I find a compensating satisfaction if my singing creates a
bridge between me and my public, if art brings us together in a happy mood.*

*I love the German lieder of the romantic period, as I love every-
thing romantic and mystic in life.*

*I love parts and figures on the stage which have strong personali-
ties and whose fates are of a gripping nature.*

*If I am nervous I am likely to be unpleasant (mostly before open-
ing nights, or sometimes before concerts). Then I can also be unrea-
sonable, which I regret almost immediately.*

*Around the household I am useless—no talent at all for it. People
think I am not vain, but I am vain enough to feel hurt if I am too
much criticized....*

*But I had better stop now. It is horrifying to see oneself through
X-rays. It's better not to know too much, especially for my public,
which should like me for myself.*

Lotte was exhausted and ill when she sailed from New York
on the *Paris*. She longed for a little rest. After three days in Paris,
she reveled in Riviera sunshine for a week. Then one disappointing rainy day in Venice and back to work in Vienna. A lieder
recital with Bruno Walter. Tosca and Elsa. A lady in the audience
turned to the correspondent for a New York paper and asked: "Is
it possible that they have criticized Lotte Lehmann's Tosca in
America?" Such blasphemy seemed unthinkable to the Viennese.
London for Elsa and Sieglinde. A concert in Milan with Mitro-

poulos. Then back to Vienna for *Otello*, with Victor de Sabata, and, on June 20, 21, and 22, a remarkable recording: Act I of *Die Walküre* and the Siegmund-Sieglinde scenes from Act II, with Melchior and List under the inspired direction of Bruno Walter. Act I was released in due course, and made history. It has often been reissued and never been surpassed.

Act II has a strange story. As finally released, it features two conductors, two orchestras, two Wotans, and two Brünnhildes. Apparently the singers who had contracts for the Wotan, Brünnhilde, and Fricka were denied permission to leave Germany to come to Austria because of the political situation in 1935. Since September of 1934, Lotte Lehmann was forbidden to sing in Germany. The theatres and the agents had all been notified that her presence was *unerwünscht* (undesirable). Bruno Walter, a Jew, could not conduct in Germany. There were two halves of a cast, both under contract, on opposite sides of an uncrossable border. Rather than scrap a magnificent start, it was decided to engage Alfred Jerger and Ella Flesch to sing the Wotan and Brünnhilde, respectively, in the last few pages of the act (twenty bars for him, only five for her), so that all of Sieglinde's scenes, at least, would be complete while Lehmann was available and in her prime. The rest of Act II was recorded more than three years later, in September 1938, in Berlin, with Hans Hotter, who was on his way to becoming the greatest Wotan of his generation, Margarete Klose, a magnificent Fricka, and Marta Fuchs as Brünnhilde. The orchestra of the Berlin State Opera was conducted by Bruno Seidler-Winkler.

Bruno Walter had wanted Lotte for the title role in Gluck's *Iphigenia in Aulis* at Salzburg, which had already been announced. But Lotte wanted to save all her concentration and strength for *Fidelio*, her first opera with Toscanini. She begged off. Walter reluctantly canceled the production.

Toscanini's letters, a year later, are just as ardent as they were when he and Lotte started their affair. Above all, she made him feel young again. As in her singing, she gave her whole being generously, unreservedly, to the expression of her love. Her passion replenished his creative springs and revitalized his aging energies.

Evidently, Lotte had reproached him for not writing more often. He attempted to convince her that her place in his heart was secure. But it seems that he, too, craved some reassurance. He was afraid that perhaps her amorous letters might be insincere, meant only to make him happy for the moment. Toscanini was sensitive about the difference in their ages. Lotte still felt insecure. Again and again he tried to reassure her that his love was not a passing infatuation. Giving her the name of his hotel, he told her he would be arriving in Salzburg alone. He left it to her to try to find a place where they could meet privately.

Again a so-called cure for his troublesome arm had failed to relieve the pain. He felt that Lotte had made the right decision when she canceled *Iphigenia,* although he could sympathize with Bruno Walter for losing his star. Toscanini had heard reports that Richard Mayr was dying. The loss of such an artist seemed to him a tragedy. That last, lingering illness of Lotte's beloved colleague and friend cast a shadow over an otherwise brilliant season at Salzburg.

One of Lotte's summer projects seems to have fallen through: she had planned to make a movie. It was to be the story of an opera star who tries in vain to give up her career for the sake of home and family. It would be filmed in Austria. The English version of the title was *Farewell to Fame.* It was never produced.

At Salzburg the sensation once again was Toscanini. This summer, for the first time, he conducted opera there. For him, "conducting" meant staging as well. He acted out all the roles, showed the singers their gestures and facial expressions. Everything came out of the music, as it must in an ideal performance. The stage directors seem not to have resented this invasion of their territory, as the results were so spectacularly successful that everyone involved could bask in reflected glory.

First came *Falstaff,* hailed as a revelation by the musical world. The whole production was considered to be about as near to perfection as mortals can aspire.

Then *Fidelio.* Toscanini and Lehmann set Salzburg on fire. Lotte's Fidelio had already come to seem as much a part of Salzburg as the cathedral or the castle. She had sung the role there every summer but one since 1927, under Schalk, Krauss, and

Strauss. But with Toscanini everything seemed to be reborn.
Here, from *My Many Lives*, is Lotte's recollection:

> *Toscanini? He made Fidelio flame through his own fire. There was*
> *thunder and lightning in his conducting—his glowing temperament,*
> *like a flow of lava, tore everything with it in its surging flood. I shall*
> *never forget the wave of intoxicated enthusiasm which broke from*
> *the Salzburg audience after the third Leonore Overture [played be-*
> *tween the dungeon scene and the finale]. There was something*
> *almost frightening in the storm—but the maestro let it break over him*
> *with his characteristic look of helplessness. It was as if he were saying:*
> *"You should honor not me but Beethoven."*
>
> *I was always exhausted after the terrific strain of the prison scene*
> *and at first paid no attention to the music, but just sat waiting in the*
> *wings, grateful for a moment of rest after such drama. But the fire*
> *which flamed from the conductor's stand out to the remotest corners*
> *of the house always tore me out of my exhaustion. Even behind the*
> *scenes we all joined in shouting enthusiastic "bravos."*

Vincent Sheean, among others, has left us some eloquent eyewitness testimony:

> *...Toscanini...was swayed not by her fame as Leonore but by his*
> *own ardent admiration, which on one occasion, I was told, led him*
> *to declare at the end of a difficult passage in rehearsal: "You are the*
> *greatest artist in the world."*
>
> *...There was an element in this Fidelio at Salzburg which defies*
> *technical definition. It was not perfect—not as, for example, Falstaff*
> *was perfect or nearly so—because in this Fidelio there were singers*
> *who were not physically able to reach the exalted mood in which Leh-*
> *mann and Toscanini performed. The incandescence of the conduc-*
> *tor and the soprano produced the very curious effect of making one*
> *pass over these imperfections almost without noticing them....*
>
> *Lehmann was not a sylph in 1935, but her appearance in that*
> *ungrateful costume was more convincing than any other I remem-*
> *ber, and every note of her voice conveyed the meaning of the*
> *part.... Blaze is the word that comes to mind most often in thinking*
> *of this collaboration between Lehmann and Toscanini. They seemed*
> *to take fire from each other; the resulting conflagration warmed all*
> *of us for as long as memory can last....*

By this time, Lotte was finding the highest notes harder to
reach. For her sake, Toscanini transposed the aria. A shockwave

coursed through the musical world. Toscanini, the stickler for exactitude, for utter faithfulness to the composer's conception, *Maestro Come Scritto* in person, allowed a transposition. The purists were scandalized, horrified, everything but speechless. Actually, as anyone can hear who follows Toscanini's recording of *La traviata* (for instance) with a score, the maestro often departed from the printed page. It was utter faithfulness to the composer's *intention*, rather than to the i-dots and fly-specks, that mattered to him so intensely. It is interesting to note that the great recitative, *Abscheulicher! wo eilst du hin?* began in the original key; Toscanini wanted to keep the phrase about the rainbow in C major. The transposition started in the phrase, *"der spiegelt alte Zeiten wieder,"* the singer's F sharp becoming F natural, at which point the accompaniment simply dropped a half-tone (the harmony of the preceding bar was changed from E minor to C minor for a smoother transition). That was not the only surprise. At the very end of the aria, Lotte startled everyone with a mini-*cadenza* that no one ever remembered having heard before. After what was now the high B flat, Toscanini had asked her to sing the little notes, marked *ad libitum* in the score, that take the voice up to a second fermata on A (flat). It was authentic, and—as Lehmann sang it—very effective; but absolutely untraditional.

There exists a recording, taken off the air from a short-wave broadcast of the Toscanini-Lehmann Salzburg performance of *Fidelio*. It runs from the beginning of the overture to the end of her aria. The sound quality is full of static and interference, but the atmosphere of an exciting performance penetrates the thick curtain of extraneous noise. Lehmann's spoken dialogue, where it can be heard, is fully as fascinating as her singing.

During the rehearsal period, Toscanini wrote out for Lotte a description (in French) of how Maria Malibran had played the opening scene a century before:

> For Fidelio...
> According to the report of contemporaries, Malibran made out of Leonore's first entrance something profoundly moving. She admirably gave the impression of a being morally and physically broken by sorrow and waiting.
> Her face ravaged, she appeared at the door of the prison, crushed

by the weight of the chains and the provisions, out of breath, support-
ing herself against the wall, mute, answering Rocco's questions with
effort; and when, afterwards, her voice entered into the canon-
quartet, it was less a song than a succession of sighs, as if there were
no more in life for her than suffering....

Besides four *Fidelios* with Toscanini, Lotte sang the Marschallin
in three *Rosenkavaliers*, conducted by Josef Krips, opposite three
different Octavians. The *Sänger* was a young American, Charles
Kullmann, who had a fine success at Salzburg, also in *Così fan tutte*
and *Die Entführung aus dem Serail*, and later joined Lotte at the
Met. There was again a lieder recital with Bruno Walter. After
Salzburg came Vienna and Prague.

On October 9, 1935, Lotte sailed on the *Ile de France* with a
larger entourage than usual. Two maids, Resi and Marie, and a
dog, Mohrle II. Marie and Mohrle had been inherited from her
mother. Lotte had decided to make a new home in New York.

Her season started with a recording session, her first in America, for Victor, a recital of lieder by Mozart, Schubert, Schumann,
Brahms, and Wolf, accompanied by Ernö Balogh.

Following a recital in Toronto and a concert with the Boston
Symphony, Lotte was scheduled for two performances of *Rosenkavalier* with the Cleveland Orchestra. The demand for tickets
was so great that a third performance had to be added. After
Cleveland, there were four more Marschallins and a pair of Elsas
in Chicago. Once again Chicago announcements promised unde-
livered sensations: Lehmann and Jeritza were to sing together
in *Rosenkavalier*. One—or both—of the divas decided against that.
Grete Stückgold was the Octavian of the actual performances.

While in Chicago, Lotte acquired a new dog, a Pomeranian
like her Mohrle. Since he was an "American," and from Chicago,
she named him "Jimmy the Gangster." He later made his debut at
the Chicago Civic Opera House, carried on stage by the Animal
Vendor in the *levée* scene from Act I of *Der Rosenkavalier*. After a
while his American name was saved for formal occasions and the
German nickname "Mausi" took its place.

Back in 1932, at Lotte's very first New York recital, she had
been relieved to see a familiar face, that of Viola Westervelt, in
the front row. Two rows behind Viola there was an unknown

young woman who would later play a leading role in Lotte's life.
Dr. Frances Holden, Assistant Professor of Psychology at New
York University, was deeply enthralled, though less ostentatiously so than Viola, whose ecstatic gesticulations during Lehmann's
singing distracted and disturbed those who were sitting behind
her. Dr. Holden was at work on a scholarly study of the psychology of genius. There before her, it seemed to her, stood the living
embodiment of genius. From that day on, she made every effort
to arrange her teaching schedule so that she could attend every
possible Lehmann performance, in opera as in recital, in New
York or out of town.

Lehmann gave her something precious she had never known
before. In her gratitude, she sent welcoming flowers, without a
card, to nearly every concert. But it was more than two years before she wrote to Lotte, to ask for information about her autobiography. It was still incomplete, but excerpts from the early part
had already been printed in the *New York Herald Tribune*. She did
not try to meet Lotte. She wanted to study Lehmann the artist,
not Lotte the woman.

The artist, however, was not so easily separated from the
woman. Lotte was always curious to meet her especially devoted
fans. Her first letter to Frances was to thank her for flowers;
then, in the letter quoted earlier in this chapter, for kind words
about her *Tosca* at the Met. A third letter brought them closer together, though they had not yet met. Lotte had heard, through
another fan, that Frances had lost her mother. Here are her touching words of condolence (originally in German):

> Dear Miss Holden—to my sincere thanks for the welcoming greeting
> of your lovely flowers I must add today the expression of my heartfelt
> sympathy.... Please believe me that I sincerely and warmly share
> what you are feeling. Just two years ago today I lost my beloved
> mother—I know how hard that is, and how infinitely sad you must
> be now.
>
> In our lives we go through many dark hours—and one of the most
> painful and fateful is when we have to bury our mother. That is no
> empty figure of speech! With her death I lost the feeling of "home."
> And even if time heals _all_ wounds, _that_ scar will never stop hurt-
> ing....

Finally, Lotte decided to invite Frances to Thanksgiving dinner. It was a rather Austrian version of Thanksgiving. The turkey was served already cut in little slices, swimming in some exotic sauce. The table conversation was in German, too fast to follow. Lotte found Frances a bore. Frances was appalled that a high priestess of song could laugh at an off-color joke. The occasion was no overwhelming success. But from such an inauspicious beginning a unique and beautiful friendship was born.

Just before Christmas, Lotte went to Detroit to sing on the General Motors radio hour. She was met at the station by a welcoming committee in Austrian *dimdls* and a life-sized gingerbread Santa. For the return trip she booked him an upper berth. Back in New York, Lotte gave a Christmas party of her own. Every guest received a gift. There were two critics present. One got a pot of honey and a pen, the other a pair of rose-colored glasses.

There was a new general manager at the Metropolitan Opera. Edward Johnson gave up his position as one of the leading tenors of the company to take over the directorship when Herbert Witherspoon, the designated successor to Giulio Gatti-Casazza, died suddenly before his first season had started. New contracts had to be negotiated. The Big Four, as Ponselle, Pons, Lehmann, and Tibbett were called by the press, were hold-outs at first; Johnson, roundly scolded for risking the loss of such important artists, soon charmed them back into the fold.

Lotte's new season with the Met started out of town, with *Tosca* in Philadelphia. There were only four performances in New York, one each of Elsa and Tosca, two of Elisabeth, with one more on tour in Boston. *Der Rosenkavalier*, such a success the previous season, was not given at all. Flagstad sang Fidelio. Kappel and Rethberg shared Sieglinde; Rethberg and Fleisher sang Eva. As usual, there were a number of concerts and recitals, some as far away as Seattle and Los Angeles.

Lotte, Otto, Resi, Marie, Mohrle, and Jimmy sailed to Europe on the S.S. *Paris*, with many trunks and bags and some liquid gifts from Constance Hope, with whom Lotte shared the following glimpse into life on board in the Lehmann cabin:

> Once again you spoil us with the wonderful drinks which we enjoyed for dinner.... Otherwise the trip is miserable.... Resi and Marie are both laid low, but Otto is a sea hero.... It's all the same for Mohrle;

he goes brightly for his morning walk and looks in vain for his beloved squirrels. Jimmy is so afraid that he has practically stopped eating.... At the moment both dogs are on my bed, surrounded with miscellaneous toys, a lamb bone, and a piece of cheese; and surrounding the prima donna. When the ship rocks too much, Mohrle gets up and growls, which doesn't help a bit.

Lotte was busily writing a novel. She named it *Orplid mein Land*, after part of the opening line of *Gesang Weylas*, Hugo Wolf's setting of a poem by Eduard Mörike. It began as the story of a pair of twin sisters, one a world-famous dancer, the other a small-town gym teacher. It is set in all the glamorous places Lotte knew so well. She describes to Constance work in progress:

My novel is coming along very well. I have rewritten all of the first part and I think it is pretty good. I myself am curious to see how the ending will work out.... I find that my plot is taking a completely different turn from what I'd planned. It is going to be quite long—about 28,000 words—and I still don't see the end in sight. I have just given birth to a dollar-millionaire and to a completely mad opera singer. What am I to do with the whole crazy cast of characters? There is plenty of love in this novel. There is one lone virgin in it, but I must in the end make up for this sad state of affairs. I am at the moment hunting for a suitable betrayer....

For the first time since 1924, Lotte missed a Covent Garden season.

In Vienna a gang of Nazi rowdies threw stink-pots around at a performance of *Tristan und Isolde* conducted by Bruno Walter at the opera house. He refused to give them the satisfaction of having disrupted the performance, and kept on conducting. The singers became hoarse from inhaling the fumes, but gallantly carried on to the end. Although that disturbance was part of an organized demonstration at all the theatres in Vienna, and not meant for Walter specifically, he received several death-threats before a Philharmonic concert he was scheduled to conduct. He still looked upon Salzburg as a last refuge for the finest in German culture.

Besides *Fidelio* and *Falstaff*, Toscanini was to conduct *Die Meist-*

ersinger, with Lotte as Eva, in the Salzburg Festival of 1936.
Something about the way the festival was run must have upset
him enough for him to threaten to withdraw. Bruno Walter
wrote him an urgent letter:

> I can no longer imagine Salzburg without you. Salzburg needs you,
> we all need you.... Salzburg is perhaps the last non-political place
> where art still has a roof over its head. Do not leave this place....

Toscanini relented.

Troubles started soon enough, however. The Maestro and
Friedrich Schorr, the world's most admired Hans Sachs, had in-
compatible interpretations. Schorr, of course, would have to go.
It was announced that he was "ill." Jerger was suggested, but
Toscanini found him lacking in *"bonhommie."* A genius of diploma-
cy managed to wangle permission out of Nazi Germany for Hans
Hermann Nissen to come from Munich and save the day. Then
Lotte became ill (without quotation marks). She wrote to Con-
stance on August 6:

> I have a fearful cold, and had to cancel Fidelio yesterday [Anny
> Konetzni sang instead], so that I would be sure to be able to do the
> Meistersinger opening on Friday [August 8], so eagerly awaited.
> I'm still feeling pretty miserable, and we are having rehearsals till I
> almost lose consciousness. The Maestro has been very kind to me.

There were problems, too, as well as troubles. The stage was
so small and so shallow. Yet the second act calls for a street in
sixteenth-century Nürnberg, with the entire cast and chorus on
stage near the end, in the famous *Prügelszene* (cudgel-riot). Furthermore, Toscanini had insisted upon a particularly big chorus.
Herbert Graf, the stage director, literally "rose" to the challenge;
since there was neither depth nor breadth available, he used,
with great ingenuity, many levels in the vertical dimension.

As usual, Toscanini demanded—and got—unlimited rehearsal
time. Lotte tells what that was like:

> I will never forget the nerve-shattering rehearsals which brought us
> all to a point of desperation, for the much-feared maestro was never
> really satisfied with anything.... Instead of venting his displeasure
> through one of his well-known tempests, before which everyone trem-
> bled, and which we awaited with a horrible inner tenseness, he

wrapped himself in an icy silence and just looked at us sadly and scornfully. If we hadn't been good this certainly didn't make us better.... We began to stumble over the simplest phrases, exchanged glances of despair, and would have welcomed any display of temper.... Finally I mustered up my courage and approached the fuming lion. "Maestro," I said, "won't you please tell us what crime we have committed? We want to do everything you want, but won't you please tell us what you want?"

He looked up at me with the eyes of a dying faun and said: "There is no fire...."

Deep breath.... Fire.... All right...let us forget that it is the much-feared maestro before whom we are singing. Let us forget that we must be exact to the finest detail.... Let us forget that any and every mistake is a deadly sin. Let us just be normal human beings, who are not without faults, like this genius—then the fire will blaze which had been dampened through our fear.... Then Toscanini showed us his wonderful smile.... And whoever in that ensemble had no real fire was actually kindled through his glowing flame.... I remember the dress rehearsal of Meistersinger—that very special rehearsal, for I don't believe that there was in the actual performance the frenzied intoxication of this unique rehearsal....

I myself was quite delirious.... I rushed into the maestro's room without knocking and found him scantily dressed—or rather undressed—and wasn't the least disturbed, much to the horror of Emilio, his chauffeur and general factotum.... I embraced him in tears and could only stammer: "Thank you, Maestro...."

The Austrian and German governments had planned an exchange of broadcasts: Salzburg to Germany, Bayreuth to Austria. But Bruno Walter's performances were not to be included in the deal, since the Nazis would not profane their Aryan air with any Jewish music-making. When Toscanini heard that, he threatened to leave Salzburg if even a single performance were broadcast to Germany.

The *Meistersinger* performances were a magnificent success. Toscanini, Graf, and Lehmann won the major laurels.

In 1936 the first Mrs. Otto Krause died. Lotte suddenly inherited four grown-up stepchildren, aged 17 to 21. There were three boys and a girl. Lotte called them "her four-leafed clover."

She prepared to play the role of a mother.

Chapter Fifteen

ABOVE ALL, A WOMAN

FOR THE MOMENT, Lotte's new family presented no problems. Their mother had left them well-provided for, and there was a well-to-do uncle. The three athletic young men were Ludwig (always called "Pucki"), 21; Hans, 18; and Peter, 17. Manon, named for one of her father's favorite Lehmann roles, was 20. Lotte hoped to be a good friend to them. When Peter, the youngest, began to call her mother, she was proud and very pleased. He loved poetry and music. He soon became her pet.

Lotte always gave herself wholeheartedly to whatever she did. Had she had children of her own, she would have been all mother. Some opera stars have managed successfully to combine motherhood with the demands of a career. But full acceptance of responsibility for the emotional and physical needs of little children would have precluded the kind of career that Lotte had, constantly singing, sometimes every other night, constantly away from home—in London, Paris, Vienna, New York, or on tour.

Now she had a family of young adults, without having to go through the tribulations of parenthood—or so it seemed.

Lotte, who liked a funny story, was never afraid to tell one on herself. She claimed to be a coward when faced with physical pain. Her doctor once told her, so she said, that he was glad she never planned to have a baby. Pregnancy would surely have meant nine months under total anaesthesia.

She was always a bit afraid of children. When, in her movie, *Big City*, one of the scenes called for her to hold a baby in her arms, she was nervous and uncomfortable. What if she dropped the baby? What if it bawled its head off in those unaccustomed arms? When the filming was finished, she was relieved that all had gone smoothly. But friends who knew her well had a little chuckle: she had patted and stroked the baby in just exactly the way she would have held and petted one of her favorite dogs.

Lotte had another "family," even before she became a stepmother. Wherever she went, there was a close-knit group of fans who adored her. It had been like that in Hamburg and in Vienna. Now it was the same story in New York. Most of those fans, like Mia Hecht from Hamburg days and Hertha Schuch (née Stodolowsky) or Friedl Hoefert from Vienna, remained faithful for life. Constance Hope and several of the young people who worked for her were dedicated "Lehmaniacs." So was Marcia Davenport. These were not the usual groupies who follow after stars; these were mature young women. There were men of all ages as well. But the most eccentric admirer was a white-haired English woman, considerably older than Lotte, who followed her wherever she went. She was adept at worming Lotte's whereabouts out of managers. Then she would book the adjoining room at whichever hotel that happened to be, claiming to be one of Mme. Lehmann's most intimate friends. Welcome or not, she never ceased to follow her star. That seemed to give her life a meaning.

Most of the people in a Lehmann audience fell in love with her, at least temporarily. She cast a spell. She radiated love. Each person felt personally addressed. It is no wonder that to many young people, hungry for something beautiful in life, she represented an ideal. They wanted to bask in that beauty. They were prepared to give her in return almost unlimited devotion.

Those in the inner circle would run every sort of errand. They would find her an apartment or a house to rent. They were dedicated to serving her in whatever way they could.

Two became especially close to her. Viola Westervelt was very beautiful—she looked a bit like Marlene Dietrich—but emotionally unstable. Frances Holden was intelligent, deep, and dependable. She could do almost anything and do it well. Once, a neighbor who had locked herself out asked Lotte if she could use her phone to call a locksmith. "That's not necessary," Lotte told her, "Frahnces will get your door open." And, of course, "Frahnces" did, scaling a wall and scrambling through a little window.

To serve a diva in mid-career one needs the patience of a saint, the tact of a diplomat, the nerves of a surgeon, and the endurance of an athlete. "Lotte is like the sun," said Frances. "If you come too close you get burned; but without her you feel wretched."

The Salzburg Festival of 1936 (the first since 1928 without a *Rosenkavalier*) was followed for Lotte by some Toscas and Tatianas, another lieder recital with Bruno Walter, and a *Fidelio* with Toscanini, all in Vienna. Then she sailed with Otto on the *Ile de France*, arriving in New York on October 6. Her schedule called for forty-eight appearances in the next five-and-a-half months, in recital, concert, opera, or on the air. One of them was somewhat less exalted than the others. She was the happy guest of Bing Crosby on the Kraft Hour, a radio program sponsored by the makers of Kraft cheese. Besides her fee in dollars she received a generous bonus paid in cheese. Later, another of her radio sponsors, the Ford Motor Company, gave her a seven-passenger Lincoln as a token of esteem. She looked forward to Salzburg.

The dogs went west with Lotte, Otto, and the maid; three adults and two animals shared a drawing room on the train.

However well planned, no tour was ever free of problems, delays, drafts, missed connections, missed rehearsals. An unfamiliar partner at the piano could spoil a recital:

> The accompanist at the concert was a fool, and had luke warm milk in his veins instead of blood. I missed Ernö [Balogh], and dragged this one along with me through the songs, whether he liked it or not. He got even with me, however, in all the musical interludes. It was frightful....

There were also consolations. Once again she was enchanted with her favorite spot in California:

> When I have made my first million dollars, I will buy myself a house here in Santa Barbara. It is heavenly...like a fairy tale. /

On her way back east she caught a cold. The critics in Denver were reproachful; they misunderstood her caution and assumed that she considered Colorado provincial and not worth the effort of giving more voice and emotion. Holding back was utterly foreign to her nature, both as woman and as artist; but her schedule was strenuous and she was forced to be careful. A disappointed

was strenuous and she was forced to be careful. A disappointed
audience rarely makes allowances for the difficulty of singing
with a cold. As it turned out, she had to cancel two *Toscas* in Cincinnati (Göta Ljungberg sang instead).

The San Francisco season had included the two *Walküres* with
Flagstad, mentioned in the last chapter, and a *Tosca*.

Lotte's Metropolitan season started with a Sieglinde on January 16, a Saturday matinee broadcast. It was only the second time
in New York for the role of her successful debut, two years before. Lotte found herself a "re-discovered star," as she remarked
with a trace of ironic bitterness in a letter to Mrs. Bruno Walter.
Flagstad continued to be the superstar—though that expression
had not yet been coined. Her popularity put every other singer in
the shade. Lotte marveled at Flagstad's phenomenal endurance:
on three successive days, for instance, she sang the
Götterdämmerung Brünnhilde, Elsa, and Isolde. The score that
season at the Met: Flagstad 26, Lehmann 6 (two each of Sieglinde, Elisabeth, and Eva—her last Evas ever).

To make matters worse, Flagstad was angry at Lehmann.
Someone named John Hastings wrote a letter to *The New York
Times*, printed January 24, 1937, praising Lehmann at Flagstad's
expense. Flagstad jumped to the conclusion that Lotte had personally instigated an intrigue against her. That ended cordial relations between them, at least for a while. It is a fact that Lotte
had nothing to do with the letter. It did her more harm than
good. In any case, here are some extracts:

> At long last the critics have paid adequate, long overdue homage to
> one of the few genuinely great artists of the age, Mme. Lotte Leh-
> mann....
>
> The epidemic of idolatry for Mme. Flagstad as the greatest of
> modern Wagnerians, if not, in fact, for a vast percentage of opera-
> goers the only Wagnerian, is preposterous and entirely out of
> proportion to her artistic and histrionic, as exclusive of her vocal, en-
> dowment.... It seems, at least to this one finite music-lover, that Flag-
> stad's pre-eminence begins and ends with one bewilderingly simple
> thing, and that is a great voice perfectly produced and miraculously
> inexhaustible.
>
> Her acting is straightforward and of refreshingly natural simplici-

ty, which modern opera can well use, but it assuredly exhibits none of
the many soaring, mystical qualities of sheer inspired creation which
are so frequently attributed to her....

With Lehmann one does not think of such terms as simplicity,
naturalness, vocal perfection, or any of the other merits for which
one might justly praise Mme. Flagstad, because somehow her vastly
inspirational and deeply intuitive art does not lend itself easily to such
facile clichés. One might, indeed, almost say of Lehmann that mere
vocal perfection is beneath her. [That line stirred another storm!]
The absorption in a mood that is exclusively her province is so complete that faultlessness of production ceases to be a criterion....

Her voice is one of ineffable warmth, lustrous and filled with endless variety of shimmering nuances and colors, a voice which, even
though not always flawlessly employed, succeeds in conveying un-
dreamt-of revelations and beauties in the music that she sings. Her
movements about the stage bear the authentic mark of spontaneity
and actual experience of every implication of a role. Who, then, that
has seen and heard what Mme. Lehmann can do...can doubt that
here is the greatest singing actress of our time?

It is more than possible that the infrequency with which we are
permitted to hear her at the Metropolitan has had much to do with
the critical unappreciativeness of Mme. Lehmann, at least in ratio
to the critical adoration of Mme. Flagstad....

Needless to say, the partisans of Flagstad soon took up the
cudgels to retaliate in print. Less prejudiced heads and hearts still
found it possible to admire both of those great artists and to be
thankful that the world of opera was all the richer for having both
of them.

Olin Downes, the critic of The New York Times, had this to say
on January 17, 1937, about the "rediscovered" Sieglinde:

... As for this writer, who has been privileged to hear some great Sieglindes at the Metropolitan, and that within no distant date, he
would sacrifice them all, great and small, high and low, for the glory,
the sweep and the transfiguring emotion of Mme. Lehmann's interpretation...one of the warmest, most womanly and beautiful enact-
ments of the Sieglinde part we have seen...one sustained sweep of
line and surge of feeling....

The same critic, on February 13, lauded her Eva:

...Mme. Lehmann graced the role of Eva, and she draws the portrait of Pogner's daughter with a girlish impulsiveness and warmth of feeling which represent the most exceptional understanding. The voice itself becomes that of Pogner's daughter....

Lawrence Gilman was equally enthusiastic in the *New York Herald Tribune:*

...And there was Lotte Lehmann's unmatched Eva, which gives us the spiritual essence of a role that is often slighted....

Yet Lotte had read the report of Carleton Smith, writing of her Salzburg Eva for the *New York Herald Tribune* of August 30, 1936:

...The advantage of having a Walther [Charles Kullmann] who was young and exuberant was offset by the disadvantage of his being matched with an Eva [Lotte Lehmann] who looked old enough to be his mother....

No doubt Lotte was hurt; but she wisely took the hint to heart. She had learned with the Marschallin to accept the inroads of time with a tear in her eye but a smile on her lips. She decided not to sing Eva again and accepted, at the special request of Bruno Walter, the role of the Countess in *Le nozze di Figaro,* to be performed in Italian at Salzburg. The Italian version (the original one) was new to her. She planned to learn it during her tour of Australia.

Looking back at the season past and forward to Salzburg, Lotte wrote the following lines to Else Walter, Bruno Walter's wife, on February 22:

Above all I must tell you that I am looking forward enormously to singing the Countess with Bruno this summer. The second aria, which I was always so afraid of, gives me no trouble at all in Italian. I can see now it was only an idée fixe. In another language the aria seems completely new to me; that proves that my problem with it was purely psychological. I believe I have overcome that now and hope that the Countess will take her place as a worthy companion to my Marschallin, for the part naturally lies well for me (if only through the blueness of my blood!!!).

That I shall no longer sing Eva in Salzburg doesn't bother me at all. I really do think that a younger singer should be cast in that part and I shall never sing it again. I was recently forced to sing it at the

Metropolitan and I had a colossal success with it, but I shall not let that success lead me astray. I still have to sing Eva here one more time. Then no more. There are still several glorious roles in my repertoire which I can sing without hesitation. Why should I act like a bad prima donna who sits on her roles as if she owned them, afraid to let younger singers take them away from her.... I am, thank God, a bit too intelligent for that.

My novel has really had a big success in Vienna. I asked the publishers to send you a copy and I hope you have found the time to read it. If you don't like it, don't tell me that too clearly. That happens to be my Achilles' heel; I'd rather that you find I sing the Countess horribly than that I write badly.... On the other hand I don't want you to think that I flatter myself that Goethe was a dog compared to me. I know that my novel is Kitsch, but it's nice Kitsch....

At the moment I'm writing my memoirs like mad. The book is supposed to come out in time for Salzburg. It is only too bad that I can't be as frank as I would like to be.... Naturally, dear Else, if you're hoping for an interesting exposition of my love-life, I have to disappoint you in this book. Since I would not want it to be confiscated by the censor, I have to leave out that charming chapter!! The latest era in my life would in any case be a desert.... I can just hear you saying: "Isn't Lotte embarrassed to be dictating this letter to her secretary?"

No, not at all. She is smiling a very understanding smile.

Her novel soon appeared in Italy, France, and Holland. The English translation came out, in the fall of 1938, as Eternal Flight.

Lotte decided to limit her performances in Vienna to the month of September. That would free her for more lucrative recitals. She needed the money. In spite of his job—mostly honorary—with the insurance company, Otto had next to nothing of his own, and his children were accustomed to a certain degree of luxury. He and Lotte were two generous and expansive natures. They spent their money—which means her money—very freely. Concert managers negotiated fees and booked the dates and hotels; the artists themselves had to pay for everything, accompanist, travel with entourage (including pets), publicity, advertising, photographs, taxes, and agents' percentages. In those days opera stars were expected to provide their own costumes and accessocessories. In America, especially, concert gowns had to be spectacular, and could never be worn twice in the same area. A famous prima donna had to stay at prestige hotels. Her wardrobe would be photographed, and discussed in the local papers. In Lotte's case, she rarely traveled alone; whenever possible Otto was with her, often Constance Hope as well, usually a maid, and almost always the accompanist (except perhaps for orchestral concerts). Even with many concomitant expenses, recitals paid better than opera.

For the record, Lotte's contract with the Metropolitan Opera Association for the season 1934-1935 (her second) guaranteed four performances at a fee of $700 each and called for her to place at their disposal the following repertoire: Fidelio, Elsa, Eva, Elisabeth, Sieglinde, and the Marschallin in German; Tosca, Butterfly, and Mimi in Italian; and Rachel in La Juïve in French. Her average fee for recitals during the same period was $1,350. In 1940 the San Francisco Opera paid Lehmann $4000 for three Marschallins (not for each of three, but altogether); in 1943, $675 for each of several. During the war years, concert fees were considerably lower and bookings far fewer.

In March 1937 Lotte wrote to Bruno Walter that she was now "a concert singer who sometimes sings opera, and surely not much longer." She promised to have the Countess learned "faultlessly" by her arrival in Salzburg. She urged him to agree to the Dichterliebe, (A Poet's Love), a cycle of sixteen songs by Schumann, for their Salzburg recital. She had sung the cycle for the first time, and very successfully, in America. Since it was obviously meant to be performed by a man, she hoped for his support in her decision—sure to be criticized—to attempt it in Salzburg. In her letter to his wife above, she had broached the now-delicate subject of a group of songs by Richard Strauss. Walter had reasons, personal and political, for refusing to play anything by Strauss. But he nobly agreed, and Strauss songs were included in each of their two Salzburg lieder recitals that summer.

First, however, came a trip around the world, via Hollywood, Hawaii, Samoa, Fiji, New Zealand, Australia, Ceylon, Cairo, and Genoa. For the first time in her adult life, Lotte decided to keep a diary. It overflows with fascinating descriptions of exotic scenery, strange new animals, and curious customs of other cultures, not excluding that of Hollywood. She had set her heart on meeting Greta Garbo, her favorite star. Some mutual friends had arranged to introduce her at a tea. At the last moment Garbo sent her regrets. She had a cold. She was out of town. Lotte, who, in her own words, had been "as excited as a schoolgirl," was dreadfully disappointed. That little ambition was never achieved. Instead, she met lovely Jeanette MacDonald, then the "Queen of M-G-M." Later Miss MacDonald became a Lehmann pupil.

Ernö Balogh could not come to Australia. He was about to get married. Lotte engaged Paul Ulanowsky as her accompanist for the Australian tour and the concerts on the way. It soon became clear that here was the ideal accompanist for her. She felt totally free with him. She could follow a sudden inspiration during a performance, fully confident that he would be with her. She could ask for a last-minute transposition as she was making her entrance, and know that he would carry it off without a flaw. She thought of Bruno Walter as her teacher and was forever grateful for the insights he shared with her; her recitals with him were among the artistic highlights of her career. But she felt more herself with Ulanowsky.

Furthermore, she found Ulanowsky charming as a traveling companion and very witty. He knew how to make her laugh. Sometimes, before a concert, she would be near hysteria with nerves. Everything seemed to be going wrong. A quiet, humorous remark from "Paulchen," and the sun would come out again.

At first she missed the warmth—the *Herzenswärme*—of Balogh. Ulanowsky was still new to her, and as yet understandably reserved. She wrote to Constance Hope, on May 2, that she would not dream of making Ulanowsky her regular accompanist, much as she loved singing with him; she felt too strongly the bond of friendship with Balogh to allow herself to hurt him, personally or professionally. Nevertheless, by June 19 it was obvious to Lotte that she would have to make the change, however painful. Her decision and the struggle it cost her are clear in this letter to Frances Holden:

> I found in Ulanowsky an _absolutely_ _ideal_ _accompanist_.... I am determined to try to free myself [from Balogh]. You know that that will

*not be easy for me. It is cruel, from the human point of view. I must
find a way to make myself free without hurting him, and without doing damage to his career. But I see now with Ulanowsky how much
easier and more wonderful my recitals will be when I have him at
my side. Toscanini was right when he said to me that there is no
friendship and no considerateness in the realm of art. But it is very
hard for me to do something like that.*

For Balogh it was surely a very bitter loss. A world career is
rarely made without giving injury somewhere. Relationships are
sacrificed along the way, inevitably. But the break was as painful
to Lotte as it must have been to him. She tells about the switch
in an article—as yet unpublished—about her accompanists:

> *In 1937 I received a contract with the Australian Broadcasting
> Commission. Now Balogh had just got married and would have
> faced a separation from his wife only with a heavy heart. I was
> somewhat at a loss. Naturally, if I had insisted that Ernö come with
> me to Australia, he would probably have done so. But I did not par-
> ticularly want to take a love-sick Romeo along.... So, with Ernö's
> blessing and fervent prayers, I searched for another accompanist for
> Australia—and found him!*
>
> *Paul Ulanowsky. I stole him, I behaved very unethically: he was
> accompanying Enid Szantho, the excellent mezzo-soprano, in a lied-
> er recital that I happened to hear. After five minutes I whispered to
> my husband: "He's the one, I want to have him!"*
>
> *When I asked him if he wanted to come with us to Australia, he
> was equally unethical and immediately agreed, leaving Szantho, who
> had every right to be incensed.*
>
> *Blissful and free from any twinges of conscience, however appro-
> priate, I left for Australia with my prey. I must have a very flexible
> conscience, for I have never regretted my sin....*

Lotte, Otto, and Ulanowsky started their South Sea adventure
on March 31, 1937. The dogs, by the way, had to stay behind with
Marie: quarantine regulations. Lotte had the best intentions to
study the Countess's Italian recitatives every day, for Salzburg
and Bruno Walter. But her brain went "on strike," as she put it in
her diary (with two exclamation points). First she felt entitled to
a little holiday. Then it was too hot. Then the doors to the salon,
where the only piano was, could not be closed. "Against regulations." Then, in Australia, she was too busy. Result: she can-

celed the Countess. Walter was "furious" with her, and his wife
even more so. Later, just before her first recital with him in Salzburg, Lotte wrote to Constance Hope:

> Bruno Walter is frightfully angry with me. He wrote me a terrible
> letter in which he told me, among other things, that he was no longer
> my friend.
>
> I have a lieder recital with him on Sunday and I hope that I can
> manage a reconciliation by then, for it would be horrible to have to
> sing with him in disharmony. Whether I can ever bring Else
> around, and move her to forgive me my sins, is very doubtful.

The tempo in Australia seemed, if anything, even more fre-
netic than in America. Interviews one after the other, newsreels,
radio talks, speeches galore (with Lehmann in a new role as public speaker), publicity, parties, receptions, all the things she generally hated. This time, through some antipodean magic, she reveled in it all, relatively speaking.

She confided the following to Constance:

> You can not imagine how my day is filled up. You may kill me if I
> ever again complain that your lust for publicity borders on the un-
> bearable. It is nothing, compared to what they ask for here. I'm sur-
> prised they haven't tried to take my picture in the loo.
>
> I recently said reproachfully to the secretary of the Broadcast
> Commission: "I haven't seen my picture in the 'funny papers' yet."
> She thought I was serious, looked quite crestfallen, and stammered:
> "Shall I call for a caricaturist?"

Not only Constance; Coppicus (Lotte's manager) and all the local impresarios of America were upset that Lotte declined to accept social invitations. She had the quaint idea that her only obligation was to give her very best on the stage or the concert platform. But an artist is also expected to go to a reception and shake
hands with all the sponsors and their spouses after even the most
exhausting concert. And that Lotte would almost never do, except in Australia.

> I don't dare tell you what I'm doing here socially. You wouldn't rec-
> ognize me. The people here are enchantingly nice. I have the feeling
> that they really try with all their hearts to make my life here as pleas-
> ant as possible. It would be even more marvelous if they'd leave me
> alone now and then. But their love for me doesn't extend quite that
> far, and I am constantly being invited.

> *It must be because the ocean voyage did me so much good: I
> "smile" and go out.... I can just see your astonished faces. I hear
> your cry of indignation: "Why doesn't she do that here in America?"
> I'll tell you why: I am only here for a very short time. If I started
> all that in America you could bury me at the end of one season.*

The Australian interviewers refused to be satisfied with su-
perficial answers to conventional questions. Lotte was rather clever at dodging the traps.

> *Interviews here are more exhausting than in other countries. Here
> they want to know more...not just the names of my dogs, my diet, or
> my hobbies. Instead they give me a thorough musical examination,
> probing down to the bones, so to speak.... The last one said: "You al-
> ways say you like everything...German songs, but also French songs,
> English, but also Italian.... There must be some kind of serious music
> that you don't care for. It is just not possible that an artist of your in-
> telligence finds everything beautiful...."*
>
> *I was dead tired and it was not easy to squirm out of that with di-
> plomacy. But I found, thank God, the Ariadne thread I needed to
> escape from that labyrinth. I answered: "Every kind of serious music
> has its value. If I do not happen to like a certain type of worthwhile
> music, that is just a sign that I do not understand it. I have not
> come to Australia, however, to show my failings; I should rather ac-
> quaint you with my virtues."*

Watching the comings and goings of the Lehmann entourage
soon became a popular spectator-sport. People would stand outside her hotel and gape in astonishment as a stuffed giant kanga-
roo, two koala bears, a kookaburra, armfuls of flowers, and mass-
es of luggage were carried by.

Lotte loved flowers almost as passionately as she loved animals. She was shocked to see that florists had thrust wires right
through the calyces. After a recital she took the time to free every
single flower from its "instrument of torture." Otto smiled indul-
gently. Someone asked him what marriage to an opera star was
like. "Eleven years in a madhouse" was his answer.

A Miss Clarke was assigned to be Lotte's guide and assistant.
The woman was quite overwhelmed in the presence of such a
celebrity, and terrified of doing or saying something wrong.

> *Why is she afraid of me? She has eyes like a frightened rabbit looking
> straight into the barrel of a rifle...When she has to tell me "bad*

news"—and she knows that every invitation is my idea of bad news—she looks at me with ghastly expectancy. I am very calm around her—at least I try to be. I would not want her to see me in anger.

But Lotte had to explode when she received the bill for her Australian income tax, the highest she had ever encountered.

I wanted to cancel everything and leave. Miss Clarke stood there, pale and horrified to see the hypocritical angel's mask fall from my face.... But I soon recovered myself—and she said she had never seen anyone so quick to laugh again after so much fury.

There was another problem. It was winter down under. Some of the concert halls were unbelievably cold. There was often no central heating at all, only a few inadequate portable electric heaters. Lotte sang in her fur coat. She could see her breath in front of her at every phrase. Inhaling such icy air while singing was murderous for sensitive vocal cords.

The day after the first and worst of such concerts, she dashed off an angry letter to the Australian Broadcasting Commission, the sponsors of her tour. They should not expect her to sing in an icebox. If anything happened to her voice, they would have to take the consequences.

The boat trip to Tasmania was so frigid that even Otto, an inveterate night-owl, had to turn in early, his teeth chattering, to seek a little warmth in his bunk. Lotte's diary listed that as "a historical moment in his life."

The trains, too, were freezing. Hotels were noisy. Lotte became so accustomed to the constant racket that when she rented a quiet, secluded villa in Adelaide the deep nocturnal silence almost kept her awake. Ulanowsky offered to hire a couple of workmen to hammer all night outside her window, so that she could sleep again.

In spite of all discomforts, Lotte loved Australia and its people. Her concerts were sold out. She had to sing many extra recitals to accomodate the demand. Her voice was broadcast all over the country and everyone seemed to have heard her and to know who she was. She sang at hospitals and for the handicapped. Everywhere she was warmly welcomed. What pleased her the most was that she was asked to sing only the sort of lieder programs she loved best. They specifically vetoed any second-rate songs in English, of the kind she had so often been asked to sing in America. That made a great impression on her, and she spread the word among her colleagues that audiences in Australia were very discriminating in their musical tastes. The Australians were gratified to hear that. Dame Nellie Melba is said to have told Dame Clara Butt, when asked what to sing in Australia, "Give 'em muck; that's all they understand." They found that very hard to forgive.

It was easy to guess that Lotte would fall in love with the famous, cuddly looking koala bears. The first ones she had tried to hold had been very wild and frightened, and had scratched her as they struggled to get free. But at the zoo in Adelaide the koalas were much tamer. They even fell asleep in her arms. She was blissful.

The Australians are famed for their love of sports. One of the gentlemen of the broadcasting commission taught Lotte to box. He recklessly showed her some knock-out techniques. The next thing he knew he was spitting out bits of tooth. Lotte, who did nothing by halves, had underestimated the power in her punch. He threatened to hang a sign on her door: "Keep out! Dangerous woman!"

Before leaving Australia, Lotte signed a contract to come back in 1939.

From the cold of Tasmania to the tropical heat of Ceylon! From Port Said and Cairo to the *Schnürlregen* (drizzle) of Salzburg —the contrasts in climate were too much for Otto. Back in his beloved Austria he became feverish and very ill. Heavy smoking was hardly a help. He developed a persistent cough, and lost a lot of weight. His lungs were infected. His heart was not in order. Lotte was terribly alarmed; he had always seemed so robust, so athletic. By September it had become clear that he could not accompany her abroad, at least not for a while. The doctors demanded that he stay in bed; and when she had to leave for America, he was to go to a sanatorium in the mountains.

In a letter to Frances Holden, Lotte expressed her worries about Otto, and her dread of having to cope alone with all the strains of her American tour—including the confrontation with

Balogh—deprived of Otto's "calming influence." She saw the children, though, as a positive factor. "With them," she wrote, "a new world has come into my life, and it is lovely to have so much carefree youth all around me."

Professional matters were going quite well. The memoirs, *Anfang und Aufstieg*, had a great success and a second German edition was due in September. Movie rights for the novel were under negotiation. There was talk that Marlene Dietrich should play the double role of the dancing twins, and that Lotte herself would portray the opera singer. She was looking forward to that. A producer wanted her also for a film with Richard Tauber.

Although she did not know it then, the Salzburg Festival of 1937 was Lotte's last. She sang two Marschallins, under Hans Knappertsbusch, and two Fidelios with Toscanini. She managed a reconciliation with Bruno Walter. Their first recital was so "colossally" successful that a second was added. Aulikki Rautawaara, the Finnish soprano who had done the part in Glyndebourne, sang the Countess in Walter's *Figaro*. Maria Reining was Toscanini's new Eva. He had asked Lotte to sing Elisabeth in *Tannhäuser* with him in 1938. She was uncertain whether to accept. On the one hand, she longed to slow down, to have an easy summer to look forward to. On the other, she suspected that people might be saying, because of Reining's Eva, that Toscanini was no longer interested in working with Lehmann. She wrote Constance that "Toscanini is very sweet to me, but I hardly see him." There was a big reception in her honor after the last *Fidelio*, at which Lotte was decorated with the cross of an Officer of the French Legion of Honor. She remarked to Constance that her previous title, *Chevalier*, sounded much more romantic.

In September Lotte opened the Vienna season in *Der Rosenkavalier*. She also sang Tatiana, Elsa, Sieglinde, and Elisabeth, before leaving for America on the *Europa*. Otto, of course, had to stay behind, at the Semmering Sanatorium. Lotte hoped he would be well enough by Christmas to join her in New York. His daughter, Manon, would accompany him and stay for a visit, her first in America.

This year Lotte made an effort to sing more "consciously." For years there had been a tug-of-war between technique and the spontaneous gush of feeling. She had noticed lately that if she gave her heart and soul as an actress to the expression of Leonore's overwhelming emotions in the great *Fidelio* aria, the high B (now demoted to B flat) would often suffer. On the other hand, if she kept her emotions on a short leash and concentrated on smooth singing, there would be impeccable high notes and lots of applause—but she would feel that she had somehow cheated the audience, Beethoven, and herself. She was determined to find a solution to that problem, a way of using conscious technique without a sacrifice of spontaneity. Furthermore, a temporary weakness had been detected in her vocal cords. She *had* to be more careful.

She wrote to Constance from Cleveland, Ohio:

> You know, I sang *very* well—very artistically. But it makes me sick, this *conscious* singing…I was totally depressed after the concert. It used to be so wonderful, when I could give myself fully to my singing—and I didn't care a rap whether it was perfect stylistically or not. What I am now doing, *anyone* can do, with a good technique, and better than I—for I, in my old age, so to speak, am a "beginner" where good technical singing is concerned…. Will it always have to be like this?? Always having to sing with "temperament under control?" You are a virgin (silly!) [this was a running joke through their correspondence that year; Constance was in love and engaged to be married] so you won't understand when I compare the way I am singing now to a night of love between two convalescents, during which one keeps saying to the other: "Don't get too excited, it could give you a relapse." Even a virgin can imagine that *that* sort of rapture is *too* modified…. And that's the way it is with my singing at the moment. When will I again experience a *beautiful* night of love in my singing???

Eleven days later she was more optimistic. She had just sung *Die Walküre* with the Chicago Opera in Milwaukee. She described her relief in a letter to Frances Holden:

> Yesterday I sang a very good Sieglinde. I have won back my self-confidence. I sing more "consciously" than before, but am still able to let my feelings flow out through that more conscious singing, which is probably the really right way. Sieglinde, with her strong dramatic accents, was a hard test. And I am happy that she did me no harm.

Rosenkavalier returned to the Met. It was the second evening of the new season, after an opening *Tristan* for Flagstad and Melchior. This time Kerstin Thorborg played Octavian to Lotte's Marschallin. The following review, by Oscar Thompson for the *Sun*, is typical:

> ...Lotte Lehmann's Marschallin is a famous one, and not without reason. But when it was first disclosed at the Metropolitan three seasons ago it fell short of its full effectiveness, as experienced by those who had sat in the spell of her characterization in Vienna, Salzburg, or elsewhere abroad. As had been true earlier of the Baron Ochs of the lamented Richard Mayr, its detail did not entirely register in the extensive reaches of the house [the old Metropolitan, like the new, was almost twice as big as many leading European opera houses]. Last night Mme. Lehmann's first act Marschallin [the reviewer had to miss the last act to meet his deadline] was altogether charming for those seated fairly close to the stage. How it was further back is for someone else than this reviewer to say. The soprano was continent in the use of her voice and the music benefited thereby. The monologue was fashioned with just the right note of wistfulness. Elsewhere were phrases of haunting loveliness, as in the snatch of Lied, "Du bist mein Bub, du bist mein Schatz," [You are my boy, you are my treasure] soon after the parting of the curtain; and in the high-arched phrase, "Da drin ist die silberne Ros'n" [The silver rose is inside], at the end of the act. This Marschallin was an aristocrat, a philosopher, and above all, a woman, which is precisely what the role requires....

That season, 1937-1938, Lehmann sang seven performances at the Metropolitan, and one on tour in Boston. Her roles were the Marschallin, six times, and Elisabeth, twice. Flagstad sang thirty-two performances that season at the Met, not counting the tour. Rethberg did her usual eleven.

On March 13, 1938, came the *Anschluss*. Nazi Germany annexed Austria. Toscanini had seen it coming. One month earlier he had already canceled his participation in the Salzburg Festival of 1938. For the second time, Lotte had lost a homeland. First Germany, then Austria.

Otto, who had apparently recovered enough to risk the trip, had come over with Manon in time to spend Christmas with

Lotte. Now he had to return immediately to try to settle the affairs of his children. They were half-Jewish, through their mother, and in very real danger, although no one realized yet the full enormity of what might lie ahead. Manon had to go with her father to Vienna, for legal reasons, before they could return to America as immigrants.

After fulfilling her American contracts, Lotte sailed for London, where she was engaged again, after two years, for the season at Covent Garden. The crossing was a rough one. Nature added an unwelcome contribution to the human cause for despair.

Meanwhile, Lotte pulled every string she could to find a way to get Otto's children out of Austria. She did the same for as many as possible of her Jewish friends and colleagues. She begged her American friends to help by sending affidavits obligating them to accept financial responsibility for the new immigrants.

Otto's condition worsened. He was sent to a sanatorium in Davos, Switzerland. Lotte, naturally, was desperately worried about him, about Austria, about her stepchildren and so many dear friends who were in mortal danger. She arrived in London in a horrifying state of nerves.

At the gala opening performance of May 4, 1938, on stage at Covent Garden, in the middle of the first act of *Der Rosenkavalier*, Lotte collapsed.

Chapter Sixteen

NOTHING BUT AN EARTHQUAKE

SOBBING DIVA FAINTS ON STAGE
DIVA STRICKEN WHILE SINGING
LOTTE SEASICK, COLLAPSES ON STAGE
HYSTERICAL, SHE STOPS OPERA
DIVA FLEES STAGE, NEAR COLLAPSE

Such were the headlines that appeared May 5, 1938, in Philadelphia, in Huntington, West Virginia, in Pittsburgh, Newark, and Detroit. The news had sped around the world: to Austria, to Australia, to every place where opera was known.

It was the opening performance of the Covent Garden season. Erich Kleiber was conducting. The opera was being broadcast. Lehmann had just started the monologue. She sang the first six bars of the vocal part, then suddenly stopped, just before the phrase, *"als müsst's so sein"* (as if it had to be so). She cried out in English: "I can't! I can't!" Then she raised her hands to her head, ran into the wings, and fainted.

The distinguished opening-night audience sat there stunned. The orchestra stopped playing, the curtain came down. Then a member of the management came before the curtain and appealed from the stage to Mme. Hilde Konetzni, who was known to be in the house, to save the performance. According to Walter Legge's account, a costume was improvised for her by pinning together the elegant evening wraps of several kind ladies from the audience. Lotte's costume was too small for the even more ample figure of Mme. Konetzni. In only twenty minutes the performance continued, with the new Marschallin, at exactly the point where it had been interrupted. Mme. Konetzni received an ovation for her gallantry and spunk, as well as for her

195

fine performance under trying circumstances, without a rehearsal
or any clue as to the staging. One man asked for his money back,
and got it.

Meanwhile, Lotte found herself on a stool in the wings,
trembling and crying uncontrollably. Miss Constance Parrish,
who had been watching the performance from out front, hurried
backstage. She sent an eyewitness account to Viola and Frances:

> The troupe were all around her. She was in floods of tears and said
> she could not continue, that her voice would not function. We took
> her up to her dressing room and a doctor appeared from the audi-
> ence and said it was a nervous collapse. [A throat specialist] exam-
> ined her throat and said there was redness between the vocal cords
> but nothing on them, and he offered to touch her up to carry on. But
> her nerves were in no condition to do so.

Lotte's letter to Frances fills in further details:

> On the day of the Rosenkavalier I felt very miserable and was in
> very bad voice. But the vocal cords did not look bad at all, a little
> flabby perhaps, but heaven knows that I have sung with them in
> much worse shape!!! And now comes a strange thing that I can't
> explain to myself: I felt totally hoarse—so hoarse that I was sure eve-
> ryone in the audience was whispering about me...Yet everyone—but
> everyone—tells me that I did not sound hoarse at all. So I must be
> crazy. I can't explain it any other way. In any case, I suddenly
> could not go on singing. And I don't remember anything else until I
> was backstage and Parrish was holding me in her arms....

The first story to reach the press was that Lehmann was
suffering from chills caused by sea-sickness during a stormy Atlantic crossing. All sorts of rumors began to circulate, of course.
That there were hostile Nazis in the cast. That Lotte's jewels
were being smuggled out of Austria. Lotte had almost no jewelry and none at all in Austria.

The next day she consulted several doctors. One diagnosed a
state of nervous exhaustion and ordered two days of total rest.
The other, sent by Elisabeth Schumann, "put her right in two
treatments."

She was much better by Monday the 9th, although she was
still desperately worried about Otto. The doctors in Davos reported that he had tuberculosis and that the treatment he had re-

ceived in Austria had been completely wrong for him. That news, on top of the troubles of his children and the financial crash in Vienna, was devastating to Otto, and, of course, to Lotte too.

When she was well enough to do so, Covent Garden asked her to receive the press, so as to allay any fear that she might not sing other scheduled performances.

Lehmann's statement to the press, as reported in the *Daily Herald* of May 10, was as follows:

> It was worry, and not my cold, that made me stop singing....I was so ashamed the next day that I wanted to leave London at once.
>
> Now nothing but an earthquake will stop me from singing at Covent Garden on Thursday night.
>
> I have been through hell these last few weeks. The cold only came as a last straw on top of all my personal troubles.
>
> I have often sung before with worse colds. I even sang in a première in Vienna the day after my mother died.
>
> But this time the worries were too great.
>
> If my husband had been with me...I might have been strong enough to go on.
>
> I do not know what happened to me or what I said. I saw black shadows before my eyes....

A special secretary had to be hired to handle the thousands of letters of concern that poured in from all over the world.

The day after the press conference, on the very day the reports appeared in print, Covent Garden had another crisis, and this time Lotte Lehmann was the heroine who saved the performance. Richard Tauber, who was to have sung Belmonte in *The Abduction from the Seraglio* by Mozart, developed throat trouble only hours before the opening curtain. There was no understudy. *Rosenkavalier* was given instead, with the fervent hope that the people who came to hear Mozart and Tauber would not demand their money back when faced with Strauss and Lehmann.

It was one of the great Lehmann nights in London. Some thought it was the finest Marschallin she had ever sung there— and she had sung that role in six of her twelve seasons at Covent Garden. Lehmann herself was very happy to have proved that her voice was still intact.

Here is an excerpt from Richard Capell's review in the *Daily
Telegraph* of May 11:

> ...*A supremely beautiful and affecting performance* [was] *given by
> Lotte Lehmann as the Marschallin. As if to make up for last week's
> disaster, it seemed, she gave a finer subtlety and deeper tenderness
> than ever to a part which London operagoers of the last fifteen years
> must feel to be peculiarly and even exclusively hers. Word after fa-
> miliar word in* Rosenkavalier *will be associated, while memory lasts,
> with Lotte Lehmann's characteristic enunciation, to say nothing of
> the charming woman and true princess she represents in her ap-
> pearance.*

Two days later, on the 12th, she sang another performance,
this time for an audience that had come to hear *her*. The next day
the *Daily Mail* wrote that Lotte Lehmann "made the greatest personal conquest of Covent Garden since Dame Nellie Melba...."

On the day between those two performances Lotte found herself weeping convulsively, over and over. After the second *Rosenkavalier* she had had a late supper with Bruno Walter, who was in
London for only a very few hours. He described to her the horrible ordeal his own family was suffering. The news had reached
Walter and his wife, during the intermission of a concert he was
conducting in Amsterdam, that one of their daughters had been
arrested by S.S. men, together with her friends, while they were
playing bridge one evening. They were thrown into a prison cell,
seven men and women all together, with only one bed, one
mattress, and an open privy in the center. The food they were
offered was so disgusting that they could only eat the bread. After almost two weeks of frantic efforts by the Walters' powerful
connections in Vienna, the daughter was finally set free. Getting
her out of the country was another matter. The borders had been
closed immediately after the *Anschluss*. Walter was told that he
could go back into the country, but might never be able to get
out again. After many incredible difficulties, which Walter describes in his book, *Theme and Variations*, the entire family was reunited in Switzerland.

Walter also told Lotte about Austrian Chancellor Schuschnigg's ordeal, which Walter had heard from him via telephone.

Schuschnigg had been ushered into a room at Berchtesgaden, Hitler's mountaintop retreat, and shown a large map with the plan of the German invasion of Austria. Then he was taken in to Hitler, who shouted at him for an hour, treating him as his prisoner. He returned to Austria a broken man. During the actual invasion, he was forced to listen to Hitler's speech and the ovations it aroused. When he smashed the loudspeaker in bitterness and desperation, another one was attached to the ceiling, where he could not reach it.

Lotte was more afraid for her stepchildren than ever. The letter from Miss Parrish describes the state of her nerves:

> The next morning [after the second Rosenkavalier], when I called for her, she told me about [Bruno Walter's] visit and his terrible account of his daughter's imprisonment and Schuschnigg's ordeals. Then all her own troubles loomed before her and she broke down completely. I said and did all I could to buoy her up and so did the doctor, where we went afterwards....
>
> The next evening before Rosenkavalier she told me it was going to be her last performance, that the doctor was going to give her injections to get her through this performance....In the first act I saw how she was fighting with herself. For one awful moment, just before Ochs's entry, she faltered, but gallantly conquered herself. What worried me most of all, however, was the fact that she was having to force her voice, and I trembled for fear she would have a Bluterguss [a hemorrhage] and no Meyer Hermann [her New York doctor] to look after her. After the first act she asked to be released from her three remaining engagements....

Besides another *Rosenkavalier*, for which Lotte recommended Mme. Konetzni, there were to have been *Die Walküre* with Furtwängler and *Fidelio* with Beecham. Lotte was obviously in no condition to cope with such strenuous roles. Miss Parrish continues her report:

> Mme. Schumann came in [to Lotte's dressing room] during the Second Act and at first wanted her to carry on; but when we told her about the strychnine injections she too realized the danger and thought it better to cave in.
>
> At any rate, Lotte proved to the London public that there is noth-

*ing the matter with her voice and that she is still supreme. She has
gone away in a blaze of glory. Her high notes were more beautiful
than ever. In the trio one got the impression she could soar up to any
heights. To give her confidence, Mme. Schumann stood in the wings
and sang the trio with her, though, as Lotte said to me afterwards, it
did not prove necessary....*

*Then, the next morning, the curtain lifted and it was like a fairy
story. Manon and Co. had escaped and were safe in Paris and
Lotte would be with them there the next evening. When she rang
me up she was so excited she could hardly get the words out quickly
enough—and the joy in her face when I saw her that afternoon! She
looked ten years younger and laughed and smiled...*

*I do not yet know the details of their flight, except I understand
that that wonderful Manon told the lawyer that they did not mean
to spend the rest of their lives in Vienna and that the ransom of one
million schillings was going to be paid. She thereupon packed all their
trunks and they all made off with their passports and emigration vi-
sas. The only thing they did not have was the permit to leave, but
apparently the dolt at the frontier let them through without it. I sup-
pose he thought they looked young and innocent and did not bother!*

The train was the Orient Express, made famous by so many
mystery stories and movies. It was a grand gamble, and they
won. To leave Austria one needed two things (besides a passport): official proof that all taxes had been paid, and evidence of
professional necessity to travel abroad. Otto's children had neither. The taxes due on their mother's estate were still in dispute.
Perhaps that is what Manon meant by the million-schilling ransom. They bluffed it out at the border with a great show of the
casual confidence they could not have been feeling.

Lotte's letter to Frances tells the sequel:

*Did you ever hear of such cleverness??? I was overjoyed — at least
one worry, the greatest one, was out of the way. I met the children
in Paris, though not so cheerful as I had expected them to be. They
were all a bit shaken by what they had gone through. Even Manon
had become very quiet. I knew now that Otto would be very much
relieved, and that was a great relief to me. We all went together to
Davos [Switzerland]. There is something strangely uncanny in the
air there! It is not the altitude alone; there are supposed to be certain
"earth-currents" there which make the area so favorable for those*

with lung diseases. I do not think, though, that it is good for Otto, and I don't believe he will stay. He is always very hoarse, looks tanned but miserable, so peaked and angular. I am terribly worried about him.... He was treated like a dog by the famous head doctor of the sanatorium, who is known to be a brutal fellow (unfortunately we found that out too late). He said to Otto: "You have tuberculosis, and if you want to save your life, then you belong in bed for six months; you're not an old auntie, so I can tell you the truth." Otto had a horrible shock—that's not the way to talk to him. He doesn't want to be in a sanatorium any more, he doesn't want to go to any more doctors. It cost me a great effort to wring from him the promise that he will consult a specialist in New York....I myself cannot take the air in Davos. It made me quite feverish. I was coughing, had a strange kind of cold, felt utterly shattered, and couldn't sleep. I was freezing the whole time—there was deep snow up there....

The family went to Cap Martin on the French Riviera for some overdue rest.

Lotte needed money. Otto's position with the Viennese insurance company had been a rather vague one, an insubstantial title with little or no salary behind it, so that he would have an occupation on his passport, and an identity other than that of "Mr. Lehmann," the opera singer's husband. Now, in any case, even that shadow of a job was gone. For some time now, Lotte had been sending money regularly to his sister in Germany and other relatives. Now she asked her manager to arrange some concerts for her in America. It was a shock to her when he could only come up with two dates. It seemed better to see what could be done in Europe.

Meanwhile, Otto's condition was getting critical again. Since he refused to go back to Davos, Lotte sent him with Manon to America in June, where he checked into a sanatorium at Lake Saranac, New York. Manon was instructed not to leave him alone. Lotte stayed behind, with her three stepsons. She sang some recitals in France and Holland and tried to get some desperately needed rest at Deauville.

On August 3 Lotte sailed with Pucki, Hans, and Peter from Le Havre. Their arrival in New York was covered by all the papers and there were many photos of Lotte and her three athletic-looking escorts. The whole family, Lotte included, announced their intention of applying immediately for American citizenship. The first necessity was to find temporary housing for the children, since the apartment that had been rented for Lotte in New York was too small. They were farmed out among the fans. Frances generously took two of them. Then Lotte helped to find them jobs; through her connections and thanks to some influential admirers, Pucki was able to work for NBC and Peter for Agfa. Hans had always wanted to be a pilot. Lotte arranged for him to have flying lessons on the West Coast, and he was guaranteed a position after three months' training. She even made the down payments on cars for two of the young men. Manon eventually went to Hollywood and got married.

Lotte was informed that her home in Austria was now occupied by Nazi officers. She thought with aching nostalgia of her rose garden, where every bush represented a particular performance she had sung. Friends in Paris, London, Berlin, and New York, who knew about her garden, had sent her rose plants instead of cut flowers, as souvenirs of her recitals. But Lotte tried always to look ahead and not behind. She resolved to start a new rose garden as soon as she found a new home. She poured out her feelings in a long letter to Else Walter:

> That I lost a second homeland—that is now the common lot of so many that one individual has no right to complain any more.... As old as I am, I have never stopped picturing new goals. Now I have to make a new home—and why should I not feel at home in America? I love very much this country that I first saw in the gorgeous colors of fall. You simply can't imagine these fairy-tale forests, as if on fire with gold and red, a most glowing red...I was as if intoxicated, although at the moment I have little enough occasion to be drunk with joy....
>
> Heaven knows it was not easy to find jobs for the children, you can believe me. America is not in a rosy condition, economically, as you well know....
>
> Being a mother is exhausting me. Singing is child's play compared to that. How one underestimates it, when one has not experienced it! Worry over the children has nearly finished me. But now I am relieved that they are taken care of for the present.
>
> I waited until the end to tell you about Otto...Oh, Else, he is so frightfully sick. The doctors say he will get better. I can hardly believe that, when I look at him. He is the shadow of himself, so enervated,

wretched, and weak. He has been lying in bed for <u>eighteen</u> weeks al-
ready. He still has to stay in bed for <u>months</u>. Imagine that. He is piti-
fully thin, there is always some fever, even though the terrible spitting
of blood has stopped.... He never wanted to believe he was sick. He
was always vain about his health, proud of being a dashing, good-
looking man.... Both of his lungs are infected, though he does not
know that yet.... It is very hard for both of us that I can only be
with him so seldom. I love him so much—never was I nearer to him
than now, when he is so miserable. I mull over in my mind what I
might be able to do to make him happier. But how can I help him?

Between concert engagements, Lotte tried to be with Otto as
much as possible, but she had to earn money to cover their enormous expenses. She worried about him constantly, and tried to
make sure that there was always someone with him who spoke
German, to keep him company, for Otto still spoke scarcely a
word of English and was frightfully homesick for his lost father-
land. Lotte sent Marie, her maid, to Saranac to cook for him, because he longed for Austrian food.

Coppicus, still her manager, had managed to find a few off-
season singing dates after all: she sang in the Hollywood Bowl,
in Colorado Springs, Santa Barbara, and Milwaukee. The regular
recital season started for Lotte at Town Hall on October 18, and
continued with a series of joint recitals with Lauritz Melchior.
Each sang a group of songs; then they joined forces for three
Schumann duets (which they later recorded); more solos were
followed by the love scene from *Die Walküre*. As an encore they
sang *O namenlose Freude*, the rapturous reunion of husband and
wife from *Fidelio*.

Lotte's new season with the Metropolitan started with a happy discovery: in Risë Stevens she found her favorite Octavian.
Their first *Rosenkavalier* together, the first of many, happened to
be Miss Stevens' debut with the company. It took place on November 22, 1938, not in New York but in Philadelphia, where the
Met often performed on Tuesday evenings. It was the beginning of a delightful friendship, as well as of an artistic collaboration that was deeply satisfying to both of them and unforgettable
to their delighted audiences.

There were glowing reviews:

...The Metropolitan launched its season here last night at a new

highwater mark with dazzling brilliance on both sides of the foot-lights.... The performance of Der Rosenkavalier came near mak-ing operatic history...nothing short of superb...an evening of delight from the first page of the score to the last. Of course Lotte Lehmann was the Marschallin.... There would have been no perfection with-out her presence in a role to which she is as Flagstad to Isolde—namely the greatest of our time. In excellent voice, Mme. Lehmann gave her usual heart-warming impersonation....

But a stage debutante whom last night's audience took especially to its heart was a young American mezzo, Risë Stevens.... She is, vo-cally and dramatically, one of the best—perhaps the best—"Octavian" seen here in many years, possessed of a fine vocal equipment intelli-gently used and of a stage presence and acting ability far above the usual "operatic" standards. Strauss should have been present though. For last night's performance was undoubtedly the kind that every good composer will hear of his own music in Elysium when he puts down his pen.... (Edwin H. Schloss, Philadelphia Record, Novem-ber 23, 1938)

Miss Stevens had studied Octavian with one of the great ones, Marie Gutheil-Schoder, in 1937, at the Mozarteum in Salz-burg. That summer she took advantage of every chance to hear Lotte Lehmann at the festival. Recently, during an interview in New York, she reminisced about those early impressions, and about the unique inspiration she found in singing with Lotte Lehmann:

I shall never forget her Evchen, her Fidelio with Toscanini. There was not anything with her that I missed. But Rosenkavalier was nat-urally the thing I was most excited about; that was, after all, my rea-son for being in Salzburg. As a student, I was allowed to watch re-hearsals of the festival performances. It became a dream of mine one day to sing Octavian opposite Lehmann's Marschallin!

After that summer, in Prague and elsewhere, I sang many per-formances of Der Rosenkavalier with many partners.... But none of them fully existed for me; until I was able to sing with Lotte Leh-mann I had not yet sung with the Marschallin herself.

When I finally had the chance to sing with Lotte, I was like a sponge! I wanted to soak up that interpretation, to feel her reactions, to watch her mold a scene. I learned from her, I learned so much! As a colleague she was wonderful to me. She was a mentor. She handled me almost as if I were her own child. I had that feeling

Above: Lotte Lehmann with her parents, Carl
and Marie Lehmann, and her brother, Fritz.

Above: Baron
Konrad zu Putlitz,
Lehmann's
benefactor.

Right: Lotte
Lehmann's wedding
day, April 28, 1926,
with husband Otto
Krause and Mama
Lehmann.

Oil painting of her brother, Fritz Lehmann, by Lotte Lehmann.

Portrait of Viola Westerwelt Douglas by Lotte Lehmann.

Lotte Lehmann with husband Otto Krause on the *Bremen*.

Otto Krause, an excellent horseman, puts a Lippizaner through its paces.

Left: An unfinished portrait of
Frances Holden painted by Lotte
Lehmann in 1941. Above Right:
Lehmann and Holden by outdoor
fireplace at Orplid. Below: Holden
(left) and Lehmann (right) at Orplid
in Santa Barbara, early 1940's
before the trees grew tall.

Top: Visitors at the mountain lodge in 1940, (l-r seated), Thomas Mann, Lehmann, Bruno and Elsa Walter, (standing), Klaus and Erica Mann. Above Left: Fritzi has a singing lesson. Above Right: Frances Holden gives the painter a few pointers.

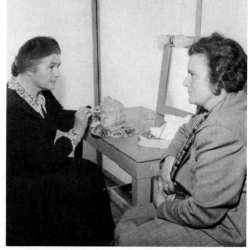

Above Left: Fritzi poses in the Marschallin's finery. Above Right: During a break in filming of Big City, Lehmann, in costume, sculpts a head of Frances Holden.

Above Left: Lehmann with Lauritz
Melchior and wife "Kleinchen."

Above Right: Lehmann
with Risë Stevens and
Bruno Walter on the
steps of Orplid in
Santa Barbara.

Left: Lehmann with Fritzi,
Rose Bampton, and
accompanist Brooks Smith

Left: Befurred Lotte
Lehmann and Frances
Holden with
accompanist Betty
Alexander (hidden),
General Warren Fales
in the driver's seat and
Dick Pleasant in rear.
Lehmann sang an
outdoor recital for the
troops at Camp
Roberts in California
in 1944.

Left: Lotte Lehmann at the reopening of the Vienna State Opera, 1955, with two colleagues from the golden years, Alfred Piccaver and Hans Duhan.

Right: Master classes at the Music Academy of the West, with Lotte Lehmann demonstrating the interpretation of a song, Gwendolyn Koldovsky at the piano.

Below: Accompanist Beaumont Glass (left), Lotte Lehmann and students of the Music Academy of the West.

Right: Lehmann demonstrates some vigorous action during an opera class at Music Academy of the West. Below: Photo inscribed to Beaumont Glass, 1959.

Above: Lehmann during a master class at the Music Academy of the West, 1961.

Left: Lotte Lehmann in her studio works with Grace Bumbry, with Beaumont Glass at the piano.

Lotte Lehmann as photographed by Lotte Meitner-Graf, London.

when I was on the stage with her, and even in our curtain calls.

As a singer, as a person, as a performer, Lotte had a tremendous effect on my life. She had a kind of charisma that very few people possess. You don't see that kind of magnetism any more, it doesn't seem to exist today. I had such an awe of her that I almost felt—in a way—inhibited by that huge personality. But every time I stood on the stage with her I learned something new. There was such a total involvement in whatever she sang! I found myself so mesmerized that I almost tried to sound like her. I used to copy tones and inflections. Our voices blended so well that when she would finish a cue I would try to take the same tone and go on from there; and she would do the same. It was a wonderful give and take. With our acting it was the same. We would bounce reactions back and forth.

I loved the special sound of her voice, I really loved it. No one else had that heart-tugging quality, nor such intensity.

I shall never forget Lotte's farewell performance, the last we did together at the Metropolitan. I wept so much that I could hardly control myself.

And her recitals! I tried never to miss a concert that she sang, particularly in Town Hall, because there was an intimacy there. I would sit close and really observe her very carefully. She lived, really lived those songs. I learned so much from her. Her whole being was involved in singing, not just her voice. I'm not talking about big gestures. But what she did with that body and those hands! To watch her hands alone was really to learn a lesson. Her hands had expression, they said something. Teachers today are teaching their students not to be so intense, to give a relaxed feeling in singing, so that from the throat on down nothing is saying anything. Hands just dangle at their sides. Isn't that weird?!

When Lotte walked on or off a stage you were fascinated. She mesmerized her audience. There wasn't a moment when I took my eyes off her, because it was always a fabulous learning process for me.

On November 26, 1938, Lotte sang her last Elsa, ever. Three roles remained: Elisabeth, Sieglinde, and the Marschallin. That season at the Met she sang an Elisabeth and two more Marschallins, the last on January 7, a broadcast performance, with Risë Stevens, that has been preserved on records.

Then death stalked back into her life. Otto died on January 22, 1939. Lotte was on tour when it happened. She was in Spokane when she heard the news that he had contracted pneumonia.

Lotte immediately canceled her remaining concerts and tried to charter a plane. That was impossible, flying conditions were bad. There was a blizzard in the East. She took a train. Desperately she hoped to reach his side in time. At Fargo, North Dakota, she was able to persuade officials of the Great Northern Railway to delay the train for fifteen minutes while she telephoned the sanatorium at Saranac.

The doctors called for Otto's friends to be near him. Viola went first. Robin Douglas, her new husband, followed with Frances and Pucki. The roads were covered with ice. Robin could not drive her car, so Frances had to do all the driving during a long, exhausting night. First to Saranac, which they reached at 4 a.m., then to Syracuse, to meet Lotte's train. Viola and Pucki stayed with Otto. Driving conditions were indescribably harrowing. Giant billboards were blown from their moorings and flapped this way and that across the icy roads. From Syracuse Frances called Saranac; Viola told her that Otto was dead. Lotte, who had called from Toledo, had already heard the heart-breaking news. Callous photographers had actually tried to photograph her weeping. When her train reached Syracuse she cried out: "Peter!" He ran into the train to join her, and suddenly it left the station with both of them on board. Frances and Robin headed back to Saranac through ice and snow. For those who went through it, that was a night they would never forget.

Before he died, Otto had told Lotte that of all their friends the one she could best depend upon would be Frances Holden. Otto had always liked her especially. He knew she would be able to take care of Lotte without making any emotional demands upon her. Lotte needed someone to lean on, to be there for her. She hoped that Frances could be that person. But Frances was reluctant to come so close to the woman Lotte Lehmann, much as she revered Lotte Lehmann the artist. Viola was out of the question. She was married again and there were problems with her marriage. There was friction with Otto's children, except with Peter; and they needed now to lead their own lives.

Lotte's brother Fritz was still in Austria when Otto died. Lotte urged him to emigrate too. In February he arrived in America with Theresia, his second wife.

Lotte needed someone to turn to.

First, however, she had professional obligations to fulfill. She had canceled all remaining performances at the Metropolitan for the rest of that season. But there were recitals and concerts. She needed the income. And she needed to lose herself again in singing, the only real cure for her distress.

Then there was a second tour of Australia. Lotte and Paul Ulanowsky, now her permanent accompanist, sailed from Los Angeles on March 1. First stop: Honolulu, for a recital. Then on to the Antipodes. It was a very different sort of trip this time.

Lotte and Otto had been very close to each other on the previous tour. It had seemed like an exotic vacation; Lotte had been more relaxed about her singing than usual, happy at her overwhelming success, exhilarated with the conquest of a new continent. She returned a widow, depressed and disoriented.

The Australians felt the difference immediately. Her first recital struck them as strangely somber and subdued. Lotte seemed to have changed. She sensed their disappointment, perhaps, and interrupted the program to tell the audience that she had lost her husband just a few weeks before. Her listeners were moved, the ice was broken. Gradually she recovered her usual warmth and vivacity. By the second concert she was almost herself again.

As before, the Australian press gave exceptional coverage to everything that Lotte Lehmann said or did. The papers were full of her. Of the stray dog whose owner she had found. Of her dim view of Australian blue laws and "gloomy Sundays." Of her visit with the blind children, who called her the "Pussy Lady," because she had let them stroke her fur coat.

. A chance remark about her admiration for Bing Crosby, her host on the Kraft Hour, stirred up a typhoon. The controversy over crooning raged for days.

Lotte had prepared completely new programs for her second visit to Australia; but there were many requests for a repeat of Schumann's touching cycle about a woman's life and love, *Frauenliebe und Leben*. Eight weeks after Otto's death, it was a severe test of her self-control as an artist to sing that last song, about the loss of a beloved husband. Her voice never faltered; but tears streamed down her cheeks during the heart-breaking nostalgia of the long piano postlude. Most of the audience cried with her.

Back from Australia, Lotte invited Fritz and Theresia to join her in Santa Barbara, where she spent the summer. Brother and sister loved each other deeply; but their two powerful personalities could no longer live together under one roof.

When they returned to the East, Lotte rented a house in Riverdale, a suburb of New York where Toscanini and Elisabeth Rethberg had also made their homes.

Viola was having a nervous breakdown. She was under the spell of Schubert's cycle, *Die schöne Müllerin* (The Miller's Beautiful Daughter), in which several of the songs have as their theme the color green. Suddenly everything and everybody began to look green to her. One day in late September, when she was acting rather strangely, Frances was asked to drive her to Lotte's house. For a while Viola seemed to be quietly resting. Then, without warning, her emotions became more violent. She struck Frances. Lotte was terrified and ran out into the street in her bathing suit, with a Pomeranian under each arm, shouting at every passing car: "Help! Someone here is going crazy!" The people seemed to think that person must be she, and stepped on the gas. Finally Fritz remembered that there was a sanitarium across the street. A frantic telephone call brought over a doctor. Viola followed him meekly. She thought he was Jesus.

That night Lotte was afraid to sleep alone. She asked Frances to stay with her. Little by little, Frances found herself inextricably entangled in Lotte's life. Lotte needed her strength and came to depend upon her more and more. Frances had taken a sabbatical year from her professorship at New York University and had then asked for an extension. In the end she gave up her own career entirely to devote herself to Lotte Lehmann. It is doubtful whether Lotte could have continued singing as long as she did if Frances had not been there to keep her going.

For one thing, Lotte had developed an obsession about her age. At fifty-one, she was convinced that she was finished as a singer, in spite of the protestations of her friends, the adulation of her fans, and the reassurance of her doctors. She had lost her zest for life.

Frances sensed that Lotte needed to find a new and stimulating creative outlet. She had the inspired idea to get her started
painting. Lotte's very first effort in oils, a snowstorm in Riverdale, turned out remarkably well. She graphically captured the
force of the elements in paint on canvas. Her energy began to
flow again. She hurled herself into her new hobby with the same
sort of intensity she had lavished on Sieglinde or Fidelio.

At the end of a performance Lotte was almost always much
too excited to think of going to sleep. Now she found painting
the perfect way to wind down. After a particularly stimulating *Rosenkavalier*, she would set up her easel and get out her paints—all
energy. Frances—an early-to-bed, early-to-rise type—would have
to pose. If she so much as yawned, Lotte would pretend to be angry: "*I* do all the work and *you're* the one who's tired!!!"

The Metropolitan Opera season of 1939-1940 was Lehmann's
busiest ever, with eight performances in the New York house
and another six on tour. Her roles were the Marschallin, Sieglinde, and Elisabeth. Frances went with her on the tour. Baltimore, Boston, Dallas, New Orleans, Atlanta. They drove around
the country in an open car, Lotte often singing on the way. They
would stop for picnics under the shade of a tent. Then they drove
right on to Santa Barbara and bought a house high up on a mountain. The way there was so precarious, that several times Lotte
begged the driver to turn around; but the road was too winding
and narrow for any such maneuver and the real estate agent was
sure the eventual view would be worth the nerve-wracking
ascent. It was. Lotte fell in love with the place. They moved right
in.

Five weeks later it burned down.

Chapter Seventeen

THE MOUNTAINS WERE ON FIRE

I T WAS NOT JUST THE GLORIOUS VIEW from 3,000 feet above Santa Barbara. The house itself, made of redwood and stone, was something special. An eccentric millionaire, who loved to do the impossible and had the cash to do it, built the place; Frances bought it for a song. The deal included a house organ fit for a cathedral, a waterfall that could be illuminated with colored lights, and 160 acres of what Southern Californians call a forest.

There was also an artist's studio, to Lotte's delight; she immediately began to decorate the house with her paintings. Otto Klemperer came up for a visit. He played on the organ and judged it magnificent. He was less enthusiastic over Lotte's latest masterpieces. "Tell me," he said, "do you really think you have any talent?" Klemperer's manners had changed remarkably little since Hamburg days.

When all was ready, or nearly so, Lotte and Frances gave a house-warming party. Among the guests were Bruno Walter, Thomas Mann, and their respective families. Gazing out at the fantastic view, Mann said he felt as if he were standing on the moon. Later, when Lotte had moved a few thousand feet lower, he disparaged her former eyrie. Lotte, slightly offended, reminded him how enthusiastically he had compared her mountain scenery to a moonscape. "Who would want to live on the moon?" was his unromantic reply.

In one of her flushes of creativity, Lotte had painted a Mexican peon, asleep under his sombrero, on the seat of a chair. Unfortunately, the paint had not yet dried when Klaus Mann, the distinguished author's son, sat on that chair in a pair of brand new white trousers. When he stood up, Lotte's Mexican was neatly transferred to the seat of his pants. All but he were in hysterics.

The nights were hot up there, when the notorious Santa Ana wind was blowing, too hot for sleeping indoors. Lotte and Frances moved their beds out onto the terrace and slept under the stars. Fortunately Lotte had not noticed the pair of tarantulas that were sharing the house with them. Frances surprised them one day in a love scene on the stairway, but she wisely kept her mouth shut. For all her love of animals, it is not certain that Lotte would have welcomed a tarantula as a bedfellow.

One day, not long after the house-warming, Frances saw a cloud of smoke in the distance. The mountains were on fire. The blaze became more and more spectacular, but still seemed too far away to give cause for immediate alarm. Lotte was at her easel, on the terrace, painting Mia Hecht, her house guest. Frances noticed that the wind was blowing the sheets of flame in their direction. She began to pace about nervously, and that bothered Lotte at her work. From time to time flecks of ash would drop onto the wet paint of the embryonic portrait, another impediment to artistic concentration.

Lotte wrote about the fire in an unpublished piece called "The Mountains Are Burning":

> We did not realize the danger in a California forest fire and calmly watched the spark-spewing clouds of smoke, swirling up from the horizon.... Suddenly some men came running up and ordered us to vacate the house.... The danger seemed exaggerated, the flames were far, far away from us, and would surely soon be brought under control. Frances asked me to drive down to town with Mia, the maid, and the chauffeur. She, however, wanted to stay there and defend our home. I was determined to stay with her—but not out of any foolhardy spirit of adventure or self-sacrifice for the sake of a comrade: it was simply a case of unenlightened ignorance.
>
> Besides, I wanted to finish my painting....
>
> The fire crept nearer, like a gigantic snake slithering across the ridges of the mountains.... Slowly I too became anxious. Suddenly, without any noticeable warning, the nearest peak broke out in flashing, crackling flames. Frances and the chauffeur rushed to get the car and the jeep, and we squeezed ourselves in with the two dogs and a few hastily gathered essentials. As I was about to get into the car, I saw the maid with my concert gowns piled over her

> arm…. *Incorrigible optimist that I am, I found that to be a superfluous precaution and told her to take them back to the house. Even if the fire did come nearer, it seemed impossible to me that our property could be a prey to the flames. What do we have a fire department for?!*
>
> *Instead of quickly joining me in the car, my friend Mia was admiring the conflagration in a sort of ecstasy and kept gasping: "How glorious! Just like Götterdämmerung!" until Frances unceremoniously shoved her into the jeep.*
>
> *Our "Adagio," a beautiful cocker spaniel, was our maid's special darling. I don't believe that her husband, the chauffeur, can have been especially delighted to hear her sobbing, as she hugged the dog, "If only you will be saved, only you, my Adagio." For by then the danger was clear to everyone….*

They started down the winding road to Santa Barbara, past precipitous drops already filling with dark strata of smoke. They discovered that the usual road was closed. They were forced to make a long and perilous detour along the mountain ridges, 3,000 feet high. Finally they reached the Samarkand Hotel. When Frances found out that the precious concert gowns were not in the car, she quickly made up her mind to go back and get them, despite the enormous risk. She arrived at the house just in time for the rescue. A little while later the place was an inferno. The house burned down in a matter of minutes. Lotte concluded the story like this:

> Bruno Walter made a lovely comparison between the mountain house and our present home at Hope Ranch: "The mountain place was an enchanting lover, fascinating, but not the sort you want to marry. The house you live in now is like a good, solid spouse, with whom you will live to the end of your days."
>
> All very well! But I was always for adventure—and the short time on that uninhabitable crag lives in my memory like an alluring dream.

Lotte needed a place where she could recover from the shattering after-effects of paradise lost. Frances rented a house that was touted to be the very abode of tranquillity. The day after they moved in, an ear-splitting hammering began. The owners of the land next door had decided to start building a house. Right next to theirs. Another move was necessary.

An idyllic spot in the section of Santa Barbara called Hope Ranch was up for auction. Frances had already looked at it before buying the mountain house, but she was only willing to buy it if the two lower acres would be included. Now they were available, making six acres, sequestered from the world, with a glorious view of the Pacific. The competitors stopped bidding at ten thousand. Frances got it for eleven. Today it is part of one of the most exclusive areas of Santa Barbara.

She soon turned it into a Garden of Eden. It was paradise regained. She named it Orplid, after the dream-island in *Gesang Weylas* by Hugo Wolf. Lotte at last had found her home. It soon became a sort of private zoo, full of dogs and exotic birds. Their mutual love of nature and of animals was one of the strongest bonds between Lotte and Frances. It was very clear to Lotte that she had chosen the perfect companion. Frances did everything possible to make Lotte comfortable, to keep her active with new interests, to find new channels for her inexhaustible creativity.

They painted together. When Lotte was on tour she would sketch everyone in sight on the train. Then came ceramic tiles. Orplid is studded with them: operatic characters, Michelangelo-faces from the Sistine Chapel ceiling, portraits of friends, every subject imaginable. Lotte could turn out a dozen in half an hour. She could never understand why it should take two hours to fire them. Energetic as she is, even Frances could never keep up with such prolific productivity.

Then Lotte became fascinated with a new medium, glass mosaics. She would break up colored glass into small bits, and arrange them to form translucent pictures. It was a little like painting with colored light. The stained-glass effect gave a luminous beauty to religious themes.

Among her most colorful creations are pictures made of bits of colored felt. All of the *Rosenkavalier* characters have their portraits in felt. In the telephone alcove there is a jungle scene with a tall felt giraffe and a little felt monkey, both with telephones held to their ears. A feast-day in a German country village, a Tahitian beauty *à la* Gauguin, the Nativity, and an extravagantly gorgeous Christmas tree—all of those, in colored felt, help to give Orplid still today an atmosphere of charm and fantasy.

The house began to grow, a process that never ended. For each new activity another space was created, studios for painting and singing, workshops, a kiln. Frances was always adding something: aviaries for the talking Mynah birds, a swimming pool, fountains and fishponds, terraces and winding walks through delectable gardens and groves, with a surprise at every turning.

For exercise Lotte and Frances would go horseback riding and gallop through the surf, up and down the beach. Hardy souls, they went swimming even in winter.

Here is a verbal portrait of Frances Holden by Lotte Lehmann:

> She comes from a family totally dissimilar to mine: she is a regular Yankee, through and through; her family belongs to one of those that came over on the Mayflower. For twelve years she was a professor of psychology at New York University. With an unquenchable thirst for knowledge, she lives in the world of books. We are so different that all my friends—and hers too—predicted that we would part as bitter enemies after two weeks at the most.
>
> They all guessed wrong: since the death of my husband in 1939 we have lived together in the most beautiful harmony.
>
> Perhaps it is true that opposites attract. But in our case it is more than that often-cited theory. For we do have much in common: a great love of nature and of animals. A certain creative urge that seeks to explore and to conquer new areas of art. And best of all, we try to season life with a dash of wit and to overcome our troubles with humor....
>
> Through the illness of a very dear mutual friend it happened that Frances came to stay with me "for a while"—and that extended till today. She is quite a wonderful person. Her character is almost faultless, I would say. It is not always easy to live with somebody so perfect. Or better said: it was not always easy. Now, after all these years, I am accustomed to it. I know that when we have an argument about the right or wrong of something, her decision is generally right....
>
> Our life together is based on understanding of each other, and may God grant that it will continue that way.
>
> Amen.

At first, of course, Santa Barbara was just for vacations, between the seasons of singing opera in the East and recitals everywhere.

In October, 1940, Lotte rejoined the San Francisco Opera, after a three-year absence, for three highly acclaimed *Rosenkavaliers* with Risë Stevens, the third in Los Angeles. That engagement led indirectly to a movie contract for Miss Stevens. Various officials of M-G-M caught her performance and ordered a screen test. The following summer she made a film with Nelson Eddy, *The Chocolate Soldier*. Lotte came to visit her on the M-G-M set.

While in California making movies, Miss Stevens was a fairly frequent guest at Hope Ranch. Once Lotte even painted her portrait. Another time she was invited with Bruno Walter for a day of stimulating conversations, to which the talking Mynah birds made their edifying contributions, no doubt. One of them, whose name was Jocko, used to say: "I will only accept a contract from M — M." For some reason, he always left out the G. Later, when Mme. Lehmann was teaching, it was quite disconcerting to visiting pupils to hear Jocko reminding them: "Sorry, time to go!" The birds had an uncanny knack for imitating the voices of Lotte and "Frahnces" to perfection. When Frances heard "Frahnces!" she could never be quite sure whether Lotte or Jocko was calling her.

There were seventeen Lehmann concert and recital bookings for the season 1940-1941, including two at Town Hall, one of which was a landmark occasion: on February 2, 1941, Lotte sang the complete *Winterreise* (The Winter Journey) by Schubert for the first time in her career. Among the lofty peaks of lieder, that cycle is the Everest. The twenty-four songs are steeped in winter colors, twenty-four shades of icy grey. It is a severe challenge to the artistry of a singer to keep the unwavering interest of an audience through so many songs of darkness, heartbreak, and despair, unrelieved by any happiness or humor. Lotte Lehmann held them spellbound. She found a thousand subtle variations of feeling in those haunting, wonderful songs. This review is typical:

> [Die Winterreise] *Although in the abstract ideal these songs are more suited to a man's voice than to a woman's, we can think of no man appearing before the public today who could have made them*

*more his own than did Mme. Lehmann on this occasion.... Each
song came fresh and spontaneously to the audience. The shades of
melancholy, nostalgia, anguish, bitterness, and resignation passed in
review and the listeners were drawn with the singer through the ga-
mut of a poet's emotions.... It was very near perfection.... (K., Musical America, February 25, 1941)*

As usual, there was incessant travel, from Vancouver to Albu-
querque, from Boston to New Orleans. Now always with that
sketch pad.

There were recording sessions in February, this time for Columbia instead of Victor. The songs from the *Winterreise* that had
not been included in the Victor album were now recorded by Columbia. Combining the two albums, it is possible to hear a complete performance of the cycle. *Die junge Nonne* (The Young Nun)
and *Der Doppelgänger* (The Phantom Double), by Schubert, as well
as a recital of songs by Brahms, date from the sessions in March.
There were more in June and July, and in August the *Dichterliebe*
cycle with Bruno Walter.

Lotte's season with the Metropolitan Opera consisted of five
Marschallins (one of them in Philadelphia) and two Elisabeths
(one in New York, one in Boston). Already the season before,
Helen Traubel had begun to sing some of Lotte's repertoire, en
route to the Brünnhildes and Isoldes for which she was indispensable to the Met after Flagstad's departure at the end of the
season. A new and important arrival was Eleanor Steber, who
made her debut as Sophie in *Rosenkavalier*. As it happens, Lotte
had had to cancel that performance; but they often sang together
subsequently. Later Miss Steber studied some of her repertoire
with her.

Lotte rented another house in Riverdale, on Waldo Avenue,
to be her home in the East. One day Toscanini decided to walk
over in the snow to see her. He got lost on the way and never
arrived. Picturing him with snow and ice in his windblown hair,
wandering about and lost in the blizzard, Lotte could only think
of the *Leiermann* from the last song of the *Winterreise* (the poor
demented organ-grinder with the frozen fingers—or was it a
phantom in the snow?). The *Leiermann* became his name, for a
while at least.

On the other side of the world, Hitler was in charge. Between March of 1938 and June of 1940, he had swallowed up most of Europe. Austria, of course; then Czechoslovakia, Poland, Denmark, Norway, Holland, Belgium, and France.

Shortly after the beginning of the war in Europe, Britain broadcast a specially recorded speech of Lotte's to Germany. She was told that three-quarters of the German people would be secretly listening to that forbidden broadcast. She took that as a hopeful sign of growing dissatisfaction there. "I find that today it is a question of *character* whether someone voluntarily lives in Germany or not," she wrote her friend, Mia Hecht; "I would have no sympathy with anyone who chose to go back to that band of criminals and murderers."

On August 23, 1941, a spectacular collection of talent was assembled at the Beverly Wilshire Hotel in Beverly Hills, California, to give a benefit concert for British War Relief and the Royal Air Force Benevolent Fund. Jascha Heifetz and Artur Rubinstein played together and individually; Lotte Lehmann and Bruno Walter offered lieder by Brahms, Schubert, and Strauss. Later there was dancing, accompanied by the orchestras of Kay Kyser, Ray Noble, and Rudolf Friml Jr.

At the end of the Metropolitan season of 1940-1941, Kirsten Flagstad decided to return to her native Norway, which had been occupied by Germany since April 9, 1940. Understandably, if unwisely, she wanted to be at the side of her husband during that dark and dangerous time.

Fidelio had been revived for her, with Bruno Walter as conductor. Her departure left the role of Leonore open for its most logical occupant. Three performances were arranged for December, 1941, the first of them in Philadelphia, then two in New York. It was announced in the newspapers that Lotte Lehmann would at last sing one of her greatest roles at the Metropolitan Opera, under the baton of Bruno Walter.

Lotte, wisely, decided not to sing the part. It was now too late in her career. That decision must have cost her an agonizing struggle. For ten years, from 1927 to 1937, she had been hailed as the greatest Leonore in the world. Yet America had never heard her in her most glorious role. When she could still have sung it,

was in fact singing it with enormous success in Salzburg, the
Metropolitan gave it exclusively to Flagstad. That had left a scar
on her heart. Should she risk it now, when the top notes were
starting to give her more trouble? She would still be incomparable in the part; but there would be more effort than before as she
struggled with the high *tessitura* of the dungeon scene and the
finale. Better to leave untarnished a major contribution to the
performance history of *Fidelio*.

What that renunciation must have meant to her can be
gleaned from a letter she wrote to Walter ten years later, on
March 10, 1951, after hearing his *Fidelio* broadcast:

> *Dear and so very honored Bruno—I don't really know what to say.
> You were beautiful beyond description today in Fidelio—Oh, how
> that sounded!!! Not to mention the Leonore Overture, which was a
> great experience for me,—but the whole thing!!! I could clearly see
> you, standing at your desk, and I was consumed with envy and with
> the glowing desire to be two decades younger, just for a little while,
> and to sing all other Leonores off the stage...That's easy to say!
> "Everything has its time" [Jedes Ding hat seine Zeit, a quotation
> from the Marschallin's part in Rosenkavalier].... But then there
> comes this music, breaking over me, stirring up all my memories, and
> leaving me breathless. I sat in our blooming, exuberantly colorful gar-
> den...on a typically radiant, truly Californian day...with little white
> feather-clouds...everything concentrated beauty. And I would have
> sold my soul, to be able once more to sing Leonore, to sing Leonore
> with you....*
>
> *A thousand thanks for that painful joy today.*

Die Walküre and *Der Rosenkavalier* were substituted for *Fidelio* in
Lotte's Metropolitan schedule for 1941-1942. On December 6
she was to sing Sieglinde in a Saturday afternoon broadcast performance. At the last moment she had to cancel. Astrid Varnay,
who was only twenty-three and had never stood upon an opera
stage before, saved the performance with all the assurance and
skill of a veteran. The American musical world was astounded by
the feat of a very great artist at the very beginning of her career.
One week later, even more amazingly, Miss Varnay jumped in
for Helen Traubel and sang her first Brünnhilde.

Her surprise debut would have been front-page news on any

other day. But on Sunday morning, December 7, 1941, the Japanese attacked Pearl Harbor. On December 11 Hitler declared war on the United States and the European nightmare became a world conflagration.

It is surprising that most Americans have forgotten—or were never aware—that Japanese submarines shelled the coast of California, near Santa Barbara, on February 23, 1942. Frances was with Lotte on tour at the time. Just before a recital at Dartmouth College on February 24, Paul Ulanowsky read in a newspaper that Santa Barbara had been bombed the night before. He kept the news from Lotte, of course, but told Frances, who was naturally frantic with worry. She could not help wondering whether their home would still be there when they returned. When she intercepted a telegram from Mia Hecht to Lotte with the message, "Deepest sympathy," she naturally assumed the worst. The main thing, however, was not to upset Lotte before the recital. Frances and "Paulchen" were able to persuade the hotel to remove all newspapers from the lobby whenever Lotte was expected to pass through on her way to and from both her rehearsal and the recital. Lotte was at her most radiant. She had a superb success. But she could not help wondering why poor Frances—who was struggling to hide her anxiety—looked so blank and distracted afterwards. That annoyed Lotte. For all the adulation she received, she had surprisingly little self-confidence. One sour face, and she suspected a flop. She reproached Frances for her lack of enthusiasm. "What I can't understand about you is that you're never excited about anything." Then Frances exploded. The next day brought the reassuring news that Santa Barbara was still intact, despite the shelling.

Although she had applied for U.S. citizenship in 1939, Lotte found herself in the legal position of an enemy alien. A short-wave radio receiver was confiscated. There were severe travel restrictions. For every concert, she had to apply for special permission to leave her home. Sometimes that was arbitrarily denied by this or that ignorant official. Once Frances, in despair, telephoned the officer in Sacramento who was in charge of alien affairs and asked him what he would do in Lotte Lehmann's place with a contract for a concert and no permit to travel to the concert hall. "I would just pack my toothbrush and leave," was the honest, encouraging hint.

A worse problem for Lotte was a sudden, sharp falling-off in her recital dates. The season 1941-1942 was, of course, already set before the war began. It included twenty recitals, eight of them with Melchior, as well as orchestra concerts in Pittsburgh (*Rosenkavalier* excerpts with Reiner) and Indianapolis (with Fabien Sevitzky). Then there was the Met, seven performances (two of them in Boston, her last Met tour), and San Francisco (two *Rosenkavaliers*, one of them in Los Angeles). Of those twenty recitals, five were in New York City.

The next season was dismal: only five recitals in all (two of them at her own expense), one each in San Francisco, Buffalo, and Boston, two in New York. The rest of the country was apparently not eager to hear German lieder that year. Moreover, travel conditions were chaotic during wartime. And Lotte, as an enemy alien, was deprived of her former freedom of movement. For Lotte and Frances that season was a financial disaster.

At the Met, besides three Marschallins, Lotte sang her last Elisabeth on February 1, 1943 (it was noted that she omitted the high B in the entrance aria), and her last Sieglinde (except for excerpts) on February 16. Rose Bampton and Astrid Varnay were now also singing many of her former roles. A letter to Mia Hecht tells how Lotte felt about that final Sieglinde:

> ...It is simply too tiring for me now. I am too old, I have lost some of my strength, and I cannot risk endangering my voice with such extravagances. Therefore I have canceled the performance announced for the 27th and will <u>never</u> sing Sieglinde again. She has disappeared from my repertoire, which now consists only of the Marschallin and Elisabeth.... The first act was perfect, I was in glorious voice and was emphatically applauded by the audience. The second act nearly killed me; and in the last act I drowned in the ocean of orchestral sound, struggling along with the last remnants of my voice.... My vocal technique is so adapted now to the more delicate requirements of lieder that it is a crime even to attempt anything so dramatic....

Her Elisabeth, however, could still inspire critical superlatives:

...Mme. Lehmann seemed to forget she had ever sung any other part, even that she was Lotte Lehmann. For three acts she was Elisabeth, ailing and pleading for her hell-bent Minnesinger. Such acting is rare, whether in opera or theatre, and the more brilliant because bound by musical pace. In awkward waits between sequences Mme. Lehmann went on living Elisabeth in thought and gesture, not just priming for the next cue. It was a tender and womanly portrait....(Louis Biancolli, New York World-Telegram, February 2, 1941)

Lotte gave up the house in Riverdale. From then on, Santa Barbara was her home, and she tried to keep her seasons in the East short and concentrated, so as to minimize the expense of living in hotels.

She began to teach. At first it was her colleagues who came to her for coaching. Among them were such distinguished, well-established artists as Rose Bampton, Eleanor Steber, and—briefly, for lieder—Risë Stevens. Dorothy Maynor—a colleague in the concert sphere if not in opera—also studied with Lotte, as did Anne Brown, the original Bess in George Gershwin's only opera, *Porgy and Bess*.

Rose Bampton offered these memories of Lotte Lehmann in an interview in January 1986:

When I was asked to sing Elisabeth in Tannhäuser for the first time, I remembered Lotte in that role and longed to study it with her.... So I took along a flower and went to her hotel. She was so wonderful! Speaking with her about the role made everything so much clearer to me.

Buenos Aires...asked me to do more German roles. I just knew I'd first have to go out to California and work with Lehmann for about a month before my next South American season. I had not yet performed those parts and I needed her guidance, especially after I had felt the results of our talk about Tannhäuser.

I stayed in a little hotel in Santa Barbara and spent most of the day with Lotte. Every night, when I went back to my room after a lesson, I would write down everything I could remember that she had said. The next day I would come back to her full of enthusiasm—and then realize how much I had missed. That night: back to the writing desk! Soon I had reams of notes. I carried them with me for years, wherever I went to sing those roles. I kept going back to those papers, and each time it was like being with her again…and having her talk to me. I studied Sieglinde, Elsa, and Eva with her that time.

While I was in Buenos Aires I was asked to sing the Marschallin. Jarmila Novotna, a great Octavian, was there too. But I said: "No, I can't do it this year."

"Why not?" they wanted to know. "We'd give you all the coaching, and you would have a wonderful director."

"Because I haven't worked with Lotte Lehmann yet. Until I've worked with her on that role of all roles, I won't feel I know it."

So I didn't do Rosenkavalier that year. In a sense that made me sad, for I would have loved to do it with Novotna. But I had seen Lehmann in the part; and that had been such an unforgettable experience that I knew I would have to study it with her.

When I was acting out the end of the first act for Lotte, I did what I had always seen her do in that touching postlude, when she lets the mirror slip out of her hand. That was a famous moment in her interpretation. But she stopped me. "No," she said, "you may not copy me! It's very nice; but you must never copy anything I do. It must come from within you. You must find a way to do it that is from you."

Nevertheless, that gesture seemed so natural and so right, that I confess to using it after all, when I performed the Marschallin. I couldn't help feeling it had to be like that.

Sieglinde was another problem. I was very straight-laced; I was brought up that way. One day she was absolutely furious with me. "Oh, you're too much the lady! That has nothing to do with what you're singing! I don't think you know the least thing about love!"

"Well, whatever I know about love is my private business."

"Oh, that's where you make a great mistake!" she told me. "Everything that you know about life—all your experience of life—has to come out in the part you're doing; and if you are in love with Siegmund, you have to show that love!"

For some people, that approach might be too personal; but she had to work that way with me, because I had too much restraint.

I also studied lieder with her, when I was preparing a Town Hall recital. What an insight she had into the poetry! I had previously studied with Elena Gerhardt, another great lieder singer, who was of course completely different, much more restrained in expressing her emotions. When I came to Lehmann it was just a whole new world! With Gerhardt the musical line was everything; with Lotte there was first the poem.

Her approach has naturally influenced me in my own teaching.

> *You know how so many of the youngsters just stand there doing*
> *nothing until it's time to open their mouths. I have to remind them*
> *that the song begins with the first notes of the accompanist and ends*
> *with the last notes of the postlude.*

Jeanette MacDonald was another famous star who studied with Lotte Lehmann. She had sung scenes from *Roméo et Juliette, Tosca, La traviata,* and *Faust* in such immensely popular moving pictures as *Rose Marie,* with Nelson Eddy, and *San Francisco,* with Clark Gable; but she had not yet sung an opera on the stage. It was Constance Hope who suggested to Miss MacDonald that she study with Lotte Lehmann, to "put the cherry on top of the sundae," as she phrased it.

Lotte and Jeanette MacDonald began working together in the summer of 1944 to prepare the role of Marguerite in *Faust* for some performances with the Chicago Opera. After their first two-hour session, Miss MacDonald telephoned Constance and told her that the lesson with Lehmann had been a revelation, "as if I had been in a dark room and suddenly a window was opened and sunshine flooded all around me.

The next summer Jeanette MacDonald returned to study lieder. Lotte was surprised at her aptitude for an art-form so far removed from her usual repertoire.

After the lean harvest of 1942-1943, Lotte changed managers. Coppicus, of Columbia Concerts Corporation, ascribed his failure to secure more Lehmann bookings to her standing refusal to attend social functions after her recitals. He claimed to have received many complaints over the years from disgruntled local concert promoters. That may well have been true. But Lotte had already suspected for several years that he was really not doing everything he could to get her dates. She transferred her allegiance to Marks Levine of the National Concert and Artists Corporation (N.C.A.C.). It was he who conceived the idea that she should sing an annual series of three Town Hall recitals, each featuring a different composer, or a different segment of the lieder repertoire. Those recitals became an institution. More than anything else, they helped to consolidate Lotte Lehmann's reputation for supremacy among the lieder singers of her era.

Levine made an immediate difference. In the first season under his management, 1943-1944, Lotte had thirty bookings, the most in years. Possibly America was suddenly less paranoid about Schubert, Schumann, and Strauss. There were seven recitals in New York City alone, five (the new series of three, plus two extras) in Town Hall, one each at Columbia University and Hunter College. New York, it seems, could scarcely get enough of Lotte Lehmann. At least in recital. Strangely, she sang no performances at the Met that season.

There was a new accompanist for Lotte's West Coast recitals after 1943: Gwendolyn Williams, now very well known as Gwendolyn Koldofsky, her married name. Paul Ulanowsky was so much in demand in the East, that it was more and more difficult for him to free himself for transcontinental tours, especially in wartime, when travel was unpredictable and complicated.

Once, for instance, Lotte's plane from Toronto could not land in New York and had to return to Toronto. There seemed to be no way to get to New York for her concert. Frances, who was with her, managed to get space for them both on a troop train. They arrived just in time.

For the rest of her singing career, Lotte continued to engage Mrs. Koldofsky as her accompanist for recitals in the western states. Superb musicianship and an impeccable sense of musical style were combined in her with an elegant appearance and a sweet nature. For many years she has been a highly respected, well-loved teacher at the University of Southern California and at the Music Academy of the West in Santa Barbara, where she also accompanied the Lehmann master classes in lieder while Lotte was teaching there.

Lotte sang for the armed forces on a number of occasions. Whether at Town Hall or an army base, her warm personality, along with her voice, quickly won the hearts of her audiences. In July 1944 she also sang at the Hollywood Canteen, where famous movie stars used to entertain the troops.

On October 15, 1944, Lotte's first art show opened at the Santa Barbara Museum of Art. One of the paintings was stolen. Lotte was thrilled. She took that as a compliment.

Later she had another show in New York. It featured her imaginative visual interpretations of each of the songs in the *Winter-*

reise and *Dichterliebe* cycles. (She has also made a complete set for *Die schöne Müllerin*.) She succeeded, often very movingly, in capturing the mood of the individual songs in striking images.

The season 1944-1945 offered twenty-one recitals, starting in November with Tucson, Arizona, and Salt Lake City. There were eight recitals in New York, counting one in Brooklyn.

After an all-Brahms recital at Town Hall, Louis Biancolli wrote eloquently of Lehmann's special magic as a lieder singer, in the *New York World-Telegram* of January 22, 1945:

> ...Lotte Lehmann's heart went into each number. You could feel it beat in every phrase, almost as if she had either written the song herself or lived the poem. The personal note was that strong.... There was no sense of illusion here. It sounded too real and went too deep.... Of course, Mme. Lehmann has a knack of breathing life into song that few can equal and none surpass.... The real Brahms, the poet of passion and pathos, writer of noble, stirring songs, is a special treat. So special, only the finest seasoned style is equal to it. And every one of these songs was warmed over in the heart, mind, and vocal cords of a great personality....

On February 17, 1945, a few days before her 57th birthday, Lotte Lehmann took leave of the Metropolitan Opera as the Marschallin. It was her only performance there that season, and the first in exactly two years. For the audience, who gave her an endless ovation, and for her colleagues, who were in tears, it was a profoundly moving occasion.

It was not her last Marschallin, however. She sang two more performances in San Francisco that fall, and again in 1946. Her Baron Ochs was Lorenzo Alvary. Risë Stevens was Octavian in 1945, Jarmila Novotna in 1946. The Sophies were Eleanor Steber and Nadine Conner.

The pathos of the final exit in Act III, of that series of final exits, is almost palpable in Lotte's own words, here quoted from *My Many Lives*:

> Each time when, leaving Octavian and Sophie alone together in the third act, I close the door behind me, it is as if with a smiling farewell I were closing the door upon an experience of my own.
>
> And isn't this really so? Isn't each time a farewell, now that I so rarely return to the opera? I am now only a guest. I no longer feel

that I belong to the colorful world of the stage. Waiting in the wings for my last entrance in the third act, I feel as a stranger to whom this fantastic world is something new.

Then I realize again with a kind of melancholy that this was once my whole life—the theatre and all that went with it. And the Vienna Opera rises before me in all its old splendor....

There is an off-the-air recording of the last act of the October 18, 1945, San Francisco *Rosenkavalier*. By that time Lehmann was leaving out the high notes in the trio. The high B natural at the end, meant to be sung first by Sophie and then by the Marschallin, without a break, had been sung by Sophie alone, for its full duration, during recent years. But now the B flat in the opening phrase was also out of reach. The orchestra played the melody while Lotte sustained a lower tone. The record is nevertheless a very touching souvenir.

The Metropolitan Opera heard her voice one more time. When Lauritz Melchior celebrated his twentieth season there with a special Gala Concert, Sunday evening, February 17, 1946, Lotte joined him in the closing scene of the first act of *Die Walküre*. The program also included excerpts from Act II of *Tristan*, with Astrid Varnay, and from Act III of *Lohengrin*. Fritz Busch opened with the *Meistersinger* prelude. Melchior and Lehmann had each made their Covent Garden debuts in the season of 1924, Melchior as Siegmund. He went on to become the greatest heldentenor in the world. Lotte was his favorite Sieglinde. They had sung the twin lovers together in many great opera houses.

Lotte's final farewell to opera was a very last Marschallin, sung in Los Angeles, on tour with the San Francisco company, on November 1, 1946. When she gave that wonderful last look to Octavian she said goodbye to a part of her life.

Chapter Eighteen

A LOOK INTO THE MIRROR

ON MAY 9, 1945, Germany surrendered, unconditionally; on August 14, 1945, V-J Day, World War II was over. The devastation in much of Europe was indescribable. Block after block of what had been Berlin was nothing but piles of rubble, and roofless, windowless walls, full of gaping shell-holes. Many other once-proud cities were hideous, burned-out shells, nauseating, mind-numbing spectacles of desolation and despair.

Americans can be proud of the philosophy that gave birth to the Marshall Plan. How rarely, in the history of warfare, the victor helps the vanquished to rebuild. Whether inspired by altruism or enlightened self-interest or both, such aid to former enemies was unprecedented in its scale, and in the genuine spirit of good will with which most Americans accepted and applauded that nobly humanitarian policy.

Lotte had a one-woman Marshall Plan of her own. As soon as the war was over, she began the work of establishing contact with old friends and colleagues. No sooner had she tracked down an address, than she sent off a package of food and clothing. Long before CARE had been organized, Frances was wrapping bundles and lugging them to the post office. Then, later, a large part of Lotte's concert earnings went into CARE packages. Hers were the first to reach Vienna, according to the testimony of many grateful recipients.

Lotte was deeply moved by the heart-wrenching tales of personal loss and deprivation that poured into her mailbox. But one letter cheered her immensely. Alfred Muzzarelli, an old friend and colleague from Vienna Opera days, had finally found the head-tones he had been searching for during all the years they were singing together. The opera house was gutted. St. Stephen's Cathedral, the symbol of Vienna, had been bombed. The old world was in ruins. But Muzzarelli had found heaven at last. Those elusive high notes were finally his.

Other letters were less gratifying. Some old colleagues seemed to have learned all too little from the lessons of the war. Although professionally Lotte had left them far behind on the road to a career, she had never forgotten Magda Lohse and Annemarie Birkenström, her fellow page boys in so many performances in Hamburg, back in 1910. Annemarie had emigrated to America, Magda had stayed behind. Lotte was overjoyed to reestablish contact with Magda after the war; but she was evidently not very reassured by something her old friend had said, and reproached her in the following words:

> Dear, good Magda, I <u>know</u> that you were fervently anti-Nazi; I remember the foolhardy letters in which you always used to ridicule the régime, to the point where I was sometimes afraid that if they would read your letters carefully you might land in a concentration camp...so I know that you personally can never have approved of the atrocities that were committed "in the name of Germany." But how is it possible that you can speak as though the German people were persecuted innocents? If I had lived in Germany during that time, I should know that no punishment could be hard enough after such inhumanities...Sometimes I thought: "Oh, it couldn't be as bad as they say, everything is being painted blacker for propaganda purposes...." But the [Nürnberg] trials have proved that it was all true. Things have come out that could make one want to shoot oneself rather than live in an age in which such things are possible.... This eternal arrogant sense that "we are better than the others"—that has brought on everything...Oh, open your eyes! I am far removed from any politics—but I have lived in many lands, and I know what it means to be able to breathe in a free country....
>
> I was born and bred a German. But I do not like to think that I come from a country where such cruelties were possible. I want to be a free American always. Amen.

Three months later, the subject came up for discussion again:

> Everything you tell me about Germany naturally interests me very much; and I have to believe you, for I know that you always tell the truth. I cannot understand that people who lived in the vicinity of the concentration camps should not have heard or seen anything

and spread the news about that reign of terror. It is all so inconceivable, that one really cannot understand the world any more.

Lotte was deeply depressed by conditions in the land of her birth and in Austria, her home for so many wonderful years. That depression naturally took its toll in physical terms. Her nerves were frayed; there were frequent hemorrhages of the vocal cords.

Nevertheless, she continued to force herself into concert trim; her art as a lieder singer was deepening every year, and her repertoire was constantly expanding. Now that she had closed the door on her opera career, she gave herself completely to the *Lied*. Lotte found joy in new discoveries. Her explorations along the byways turned up many unfamiliar masterpieces, which then enriched her programs. If she had earlier been mildly reproached for singing too many chestnuts, now her managers had to remind her to throw in a few, at least as encores. They asked for more sugar in her programs, to please the general public; the connoisseurs, however, were jubilant. She began to educate her audiences, who were becoming more and more sophisticated and knowing, thanks in part to her pioneering, to the interest she herself had helped to awaken.

Thanks also to her new book. That remarkable treatise on the interpretation of lieder, *More Than Singing*, was published in 1945 and soon ran to several printings. Although her views were not uncontroversial, that book helped to spread an awareness of the wonders one can find in a *Lied*. It opened a door to deeper understanding. It showed that there is infinitely more in a song by Schubert or Wolf than a pleasing melody with words, and that the singer needs more than a voice: that the eyes, for instance, are indispensable tools of expression.

Lotte describes how an interpretation can be built up, based upon a thorough inner understanding of the story or picture that gave birth to the song, and suggests ways in which that interpretation can be communicated to the listeners. She analyzes eighty-one individual songs and five cycles from the point of view of expression. She demonstrates possible ways of *externalizing inner feelings*, so that they can be projected to the audience. Her

interpretation is not imposed from the outside in, so to speak;
the singer is urged to develop an interpretation from the inside
out, through awareness of the hidden meanings and the possibil-
ities for expressing them.

Here, as an example, is part of her interpretation of Schubert's
wonderful song, *Im Abendrot* (At Sunset):

> This Lied is for me one of the most beautiful treasures of our whole
> musical literature. The deep emotion that flows through it like a
> stream of warm gold, is overwhelming in its extreme simplicity. Sing
> it simply, sing it as you would a prayer....
>
> Imagine that you are weary of life and wounded perhaps by a bit-
> ter disappointment. You are sitting by a window, your head buried in
> your hands. Looking up from out of a deep melancholy you suddenly
> see before you the beauty of the sunset and you awaken to its over-
> whelming loveliness.
>
> This is the atmosphere of the prelude. As it begins raise your head
> which has been slightly bowed. Your eyes open. With an exquisite joy
> you realize that all your sorrows have been meaningless and insig-
> nificant. The glow of the setting sun is like a gateway opening upon
> heaven—and peace and eternal beauty flood your heart. You feel
> that God is very near you—so near, that you speak to Him, calling
> Him simply "Father"....

Frances remembers that often at Orplid, when late-afternoon
sunlight was gilding the trees, Lotte would sit at a window,
looking out at all the beauty, and softly sing that song.

Most of *More Than Singing* was written in trains while Lotte
was on tour. Every day a progress report went back to Hope
Ranch.

> Dear Frances, this is a terrible train; it jiggles like crazy, I feel abso-
> lutely as if I am a medicine bottle....

Frances made the translation, no easy task. Lotte had a weakness for adjectives, especially for strings of them. Naturally, every
one of them added its own nuance to what she wanted to say.
Those clusters may have sounded normal enough to German
ears, accustomed to *Schlangenworte* (snakewords), constructed by
joining any number of words together to form a new concept; to
Frances, however, it seemed less than stylistic to write in Eng-

lish a phrase like this: "in a tender, breathless, silvery, floating *pia-nissimo....*"

One day Frances forgot to pack the little book of words that Lotte had up until then always held in her hands for security. (She used to change the cover to match her concert gown.) Now, suddenly without it, she realized how expressive her hands could be, freed of that booklet. So much could be conveyed through the way she would hold them, whether lightly or tightly clasped, whether relaxed or tense, whether nearer to her breast or reaching forward. She never made a gesture, in the theatrical sense. Her fingers remained entwined. But she found infinitely subtle variations. She never used a booklet again.

In the first season after the war Lotte sang twenty-seven recitals, six of them in New York City. The next season there was a falling-off. As the care packages flew eastward and more and more pathetic letters made their way to Santa Barbara, she found herself suffering vicariously with her friends in Europe.

It was a while before Lotte could even consider going back for a visit. She dreaded having to face the reality of so much destruction in places that once had been dear to her. Tears came so easily now. Besides, she would be expected to sing. Would her former fans overlook the ravages of time in a voice that was still beautiful and haunting but had lost some of its splendor at the top?

Lotte had developed a complex about her age. "It is easy to be wise on the stage as the Marschallin," she said, "but in real life I feel rebellion, not wisdom."

Bruno Walter asked her to sing in the Edinburgh Festival of 1947 and offered to be her accompanist on a European tour. After some soul-searching, she agreed and programs were discussed. Would the *Winterreise* be too gloomy for a festive occasion? No sooner were the contracts signed than panic took hold. As the summer drew nearer Lotte became more and more nervous. In April she wrote Walter that she must have been "an idiot" to accept a European engagement.

It soon became clear that her health was in jeopardy. Her nerves would not survive the strain. On the advice of her doctor, she canceled.

Her self-confidence was at its lowest ebb. Then, out of the blue, came an offer from M-G-M to make a motion picture. That was just what Lotte needed, a new interest, a new challenge. She had always dreamed of the chance to be an actress without having to worry about her voice. Little by little her old vitality began to return.

When Walter heard the news that Lotte had signed a contract to make a movie during the time they would have been performing together, he was shocked and hurt. He jumped to the conclusion that she had turned down Edinburgh for Hollywood.

Lotte was too upset at first to reply. Frances wrote to confirm her precarious condition. Finally Lotte was able to speak for herself:

> Dear and honored Bruno—I was so unhappy about your letter and so near the verge of a nervous breakdown that I couldn't answer you right away and Frances wrote for me.... You must believe me that I did not give up that tour frivolously. I had been very ill for months.... I know that you are a better, nobler human being than I am; but please do not believe that I bear lightly the burden of this very unhappy matter. On the contrary, I have been simply crushed by a chain of circumstances that has trapped me in a spiderweb.... I know that I am losing Europe right now. Although I feel at home in America, it hurts me, nevertheless, to have to give up my old homeland, perhaps never again to return there as a singer. But what can I do?

A few months later, after having made the movie, Lotte wrote him again:

> I have heard from several sides that you aren't angry with me any more for my European cancellation. I can't tell you how glad I am that I canceled: I could not have survived the emotions.... To see horrible deprivation, constantly to meet old acquaintances and hear about their terrible experiences and not to be able to help!!! It would have been frightful....

Bruno Walter's answer was charming:

> Dear Lotte,
> Many thanks for your lovely letter. Of course I'm not angry with you. How could anyone be? In spite of all my talent for resentment

*and my inclination toward anger, you will always keep your place in
the Californian Zone of my inner climate.*

*I am very eager to get to know you in your new capacity as a mo-
vie actress. I scarcely expect that you will reach the deep effectiveness
of my speaking scene in the Carnegie Hall film, during which the
cameraman was so moved that he dropped his equipment. But, seriously, I have full confidence in you and find it admirable and very
gratifying that you could channel your overflowing talent in this new
direction....*

> *Your old friend*
> *Bruno*

The title of the film was Big City. Lotte played a character part
opposite Margaret O'Brien, the famous child-star. Danny Thomas, the popular comedian, was given a straight dramatic role as
Lotte's son. George Murphy and Robert Preston also starred.
Now and then the film shows up on late-night television.

Several opportunities to sing had been written into the script
for Lotte, and the songs were later released in a record album.
There was the Brahms "Lullaby" and a vocal version of Schumann's piano piece, *Träumerei* (about as close to lieder as Hollywood was likely to come in those days), also "The Kerry Dance,"
and, in a grand finale that was later partly cut, "God Bless America," which Lotte sang with all her famous fervor.

Gwendolyn Koldofsky recalls having seen Big City in a Los Angeles movie theatre. She was astonished and delighted that the
audience broke into applause after each of Lotte's numbers.

Lotte described to Bruno Walter how she felt about her new
experience:

> *A real acting role, without music, has always, always been my
> dream. I wanted to test myself, to see whether I am a true "actress"
> or whether I can only act when I am borne along by the music. All
> singers have failed—you remember that as an actress even Gutheil
> [Marie Gutheil-Schoder] was good only in opera. So the chance to
> play a real character role in the film was a temptation I couldn't re-
> sist. The part was actually written for Ethel Barrymore—the singing
> was only added after Pasternak decided to give the part to a singer.
> I must say, I enjoyed the whole thing immensely. Every profession
> has its shadow side. The eternal waiting around is naturally dread-*

> ful—and the purely mechanical process of being photographed from
> various angles is not very enjoyable. But all the preliminary work
> with the director [Norman Taurog] was very satisfying artistically.
> He allowed me complete freedom. It is curious: not for a moment did
> I feel at all strange in front of the camera. And if the movie public
> will like me as well as the people at M-G-M seem to do, then I may
> have a career in front of me.... Not bad for a woman of sixty.

After seeing herself on the screen, Lotte was decidedly less
enthusiastic:

> I saw "my" film and found myself ghastly. I look so absolutely con-
> vincing as an old grandmother that I get nauseated when I see my-
> self. Funny, that a woman finds it so hard to let go.... If I ever have
> to look at more movies of me (though I have every intention never to
> admire myself again), I will have to learn the art of resignation....

Among the children of her literary imagination, Lotte's personal favorite, *Heaven, Hell, and Hollywood*, never found a publisher. It is a fantasy combining movieland satire and affectionate
caricatures of famous colleagues with mystical speculation about
the afterlife.

She also wrote an article, "My Hollywood Adventure," part of
a loose collection of memoirs to which she made additions from
time to time. Here are some excerpts:

> I had always heard that in Hollywood there was money lying on
> the streets and all one had to do was simply sweep it up. It was my
> bad luck to come along just at the time the movie industry was begin-
> ning to tighten its belt. But they told me there were great possibilities
> in my role and a big dramatic scene for me at the end.
>
> Like a little beginner, I had to go to a "coach" to study the dia-
> logue....
>
> Margaret O'Brien was such a sweet child that I sometimes won-
> dered whether she was really so naïve, after having made so many
> films, or just acting as if she were....
>
> She could cry on command. In one scene I heard her ask the di-
> rector, in that bright child-voice of hers..."Mr. Taurog, shall I be cry-
> ing already when the scene begins, or shall I gradually start to cry?"
>
> "You're crying already."
>
> "Just a moment, please."
>
> She swallowed a couple of times and then two big tears rolled
> down her thin little cheeks and Taurog called out: "Camera!"

My special friend was Jack, the make-up man. I also had a tear-
ful scene to play and was scared to death of it. But he comforted me
and said he would be standing by with a tear-inducer; I would only
have to sniff it to start the tears flowing. I found that a swindle, and
decided that if that little Margaret could do it I could too. And I did!
Everyone showered me with praise. Mr. [Louis B.] Mayer, then
still the president of Metro-Goldwyn-Mayer, said I was the greatest
screen mother in the world. Everyone prophesied a future for me in
films that would make my entire singing career crawl off into a cor-
ner, ashamed. I must confess that it all went a bit to my head. For
the first time in my life I had fits of megalomania. No wonder, when
one is constantly hearing murmurs of deep admiration at every little
insignificant scene....

Lotte bought a house near Hollywood, on a steep hill, 2,000
feet above the city, and began to make plans for other movies.
Several scripts were discussed. One would co-star Kathryn Gray-
son. Another would be filmed in Tahiti. (That one was later reborn as an Esther Williams swimming extravaganza—without
Lehmann.)

Naturally I thought I had Hollywood in my pocket, and was quite astonished when my contract was not renewed. The film was not a
success. Therefore it was soon forgotten that I was "the greatest
screen mother in the world."

For years movies had been one of Lotte's favorite forms of relaxation. In the 1930's, like almost everyone else, she had been
fascinated by Garbo. Now Bette Davis was the screen star who
impressed her most deeply. On tour in Denver she happened to
see Davis in Deception, and wrote her impressions to Frances:

You have to see it. Davis is wonderful. I have to add her to my
manuscript, at the place where I talk about the expressive face of
Katharine Cornell. There I would like to say: "And among movie
actresses I most admire Bette Davis for her vivid expressiveness. Her
face, which can be breathtakingly beautiful, is often quite contorted
with emotion but always full of life and fierce temperament." Something like that.

Lotte was working on a new book at that time. More Than
Singing had been devoted to the interpretation of lieder; My Many
Lives now dealt with her understanding of the characters she had

portrayed in opera. There are chapters on each of her favorite roles, interspersed with diverting digressions, anecdotes, reminiscenses, advice. Her insights are illuminating, uncanny. It is as if she really had lived those lives. Lehmann gives us the thoughts and feelings, the psychology of the characters, explored in depth, seen from the inside out. What other singer has done that so eloquently? Her description, for instance, of Elisabeths's reactions to the Contest of Song, a scene in which she has not a note to sing, is a lesson, not just for potential Elisabeths but for any actor—singing or otherwise. Here is her interpretation of Elisabeth's defense of *Tannhäuser* at the end of Act II:

> [Her] collapse should not be an indication of any inner weakness: a world falls in ruins before her, the world of her happiness, the world of her faith in him whom she loves and whom she has supposed to be pure and noble. In this moment she must seem to age years: she has learned the meaning of sin. Sin, which until now had been nothing more than a word, now stares at her from the eyes of her beloved. At the same time a torturing fear rises within her: she knows the harsh laws of her country.... With this realization Elisabeth awakens: with an effort she rises, fighting her weakness with superhuman strength. She must save him.... Consumed by anxiety she watches the action of the knights.... She plunges between their drawn swords and Tannhäuser, protecting him at the risk of her own life.
>
> One must consider what it meant in this period for a woman, a virgin, to take the part of a sinful man so fearlessly. She, the child of a duke, defends an outcast.... The knights, unable to understand her, yield in horror.
>
> It now must be another Elisabeth, an altered Elisabeth, who struggles to save Tannhäuser. She has lost all her shyness, her reticence is transformed into glowing action, her dreaminess into passionate challenge. Filled with the realization that it is not God's will to punish in the way in which the world punishes, knowing that God has chosen her to speak for him, to plead for him, she bares her heart before these men, confessing her love. A love which is magnanimous enough to forgive, a love which rises above earthly grief, a love which has become an intercessor, a love which will not cease to hope and to believe.... Until the end of her plea Elisabeth seems apart from reality: she is love transfigured as prayer, she is sacrifice and passionate renunciation.

The historical Elisabeth was a saint. Wagner has captured the essence of her being in two resonant phrases: "*Der Mut des Glau-bens*"—The courage of faith—and "*Mein Leben sei Gebet!*"—may prayer become my life!

The season of 1947-1948 offered twenty recitals, with five each in Chicago and New York. In 1948-1949 there were only ten. This time the reason lay in Lotte. More and more she preferred the calm beauty of Orplid to the racket and the slush of big Eastern cities during the concert season. Now that Lotte was a "movie star," there were also some unexpected problems.

Movie fans were less reticent than their opera-loving counterparts. Lotte describes to Frances a frightening example:

> *Thank heavens the first recital [Town Hall, February 20, 1949] is over and quite satisfactory.... I was in very good voice in spite of a totally sleepless night: two days before someone called me in the evening and asked if "fans of mine who had seen me in Big City" could visit me. You can imagine my answer. Next day—the day before the concert—at six o'clock in the evening the doorbell rang. I had double-locked the door, Marie [the maid] was not here. I went to the door and asked who it was. First silence. I repeated the question and a man said: "We are great fans of yours, we saw you in Big City and we would like to see you now."*
>
> *I said: "Write to me and I will send you autographs."*
>
> *But he said very urgently: "Oh no, please, we want to see you personally."*
>
> *"No, that is out of the question," I said; "Please go away."*
>
> *I trembled like a leaf, as you can imagine, and went over to the telephone. Suddenly they tried to get in. They turned the doorknob violently and pushed against the door. I called for help through the telephone. I said that someone was trying to break in and they should send up somebody.*
>
> *In the meantime, Marie came and tried the door.... The boys— three young men—said to her: "We only wanted an autograph"—but they ran away; and when the man from downstairs came (very quickly, I must say) they had disappeared. I was half fainting. I trembled so that I could scarcely stand on my feet. That sort of thing <u>can</u> be harmless; but then it may not be harmless at all.*
>
> *Now Marie sleeps in the living room, on the sofa. I am too frightened to sleep alone. It may be very harmless—the young people nowadays have no consideration; and being "movie fans," they are even fresher than generally.*

A few days later, on February 24, after a recital in Boston, Lotte was feeling discouraged. Certain songs she had always loved to sing would have to be dropped from her repertoire. It was a hard goodbye.

I have to replace Cäcilie with Zueignung, [both by Strauss]. Cäcilie is surprisingly tiring. I really am too old now. My programs are only good when the songs are floating and soft. But one cannot make programs interesting with soft songs only.... I am a finished story. Never, never shall I be able to sing the Marschallin. I know that....

Europe was trying to tempt her back for some performances of *Der Rosenkavalier* in 1949. For a while she had even toyed with the idea. But she knew herself too well.

For some months her voice had not felt quite right to her. Her laryngologist assured her that she had the vocal cords of a young woman. But she sensed a veil over her voice. Frances (who, as usual now, had stayed behind in Santa Barbara to look after the animals) ascribed the trouble to a too strict reducing diet of grapefruit juice and cottage cheese.

Before her second Town Hall recital, Lotte did her best to keep calm. She was relieved to find herself less nervous alone than she had expected to be, and stronger.

I sang well and without the veil today. I am quite unhysterical.

March 1 brought a new accomplishment into Lotte's life. She felt quite triumphant. For the first time she had balanced her checkbook. She sat there with tears of frustration running down her cheeks. She was happy to feel that little bit more capable, that little bit less dependent upon Frances.

The March 3 recital at Town Hall made her very happy:

The public went wilder than ever.... They absolutely shrieked. For the first time in my life I have seen Elisabeth [Schumann] excited. She said that she admires me boundlessly....

Before the tour, Lotte had dreaded having to cope with the strains of travel and the nervous excitement of recitals without the moral support of Frances at her side. She was encouraged and reassured to realize that she was doing very well alone. She wanted also to reassure Frances:

I would be much happier if you were with me here in the East. But it makes me feel better to think that I have not lost my indepen-dence.... I sometimes felt that I was losing my personality, of which the foremost characteristic has always been: independence, freedom. I always give in to what you say, I always do what you think is right to do. Generally you are right, without any question. But that is not the point. The point is that I had lost the ability to judge. And now I have it back. Don't be afraid that I shall start being "difficult." There is no reason for that, and I shall be quite the same. You have lost nothing, I have lost nothing; I have only gained an inner confidence.

Lotte was a bit afraid that Frances might be hurt, thinking she was perhaps less needed than before. But Frances's answer shows exceptional understanding:

That you should be delighted to find that you can get along by your-self is very understandable. That fact delights me too. It has worried me increasingly how little you arranged for yourself, and I have been terrified as to what would happen if anything happened to me. That you should think you couldn't make your own judgments without me is of course nonsense, though you are so easily influenced sometimes that I have been concerned as to what might happen if you fell into wrong hands. I don't want to influence you ever. I want only to show you how I see things and then have you make up your own mind. Often your judgment is better than mine. I think it has been very good for you to be alone, for many reasons. You misunderstood me as much as I you in thinking I could ever be unhappy because you were happy. Let us now rejoice in that new-found independ-ence.

After the third Town Hall recital, Lotte went to visit Toscanini.

Dearest Frances—that man is a miracle. I have no other word. How is it humanly possible that a man of eighty-three had more sex appeal than anybody I know? First, when I came in, he looked rath-er frail, a little stooped, and somehow so touchingly old in his red house jacket.... But then his eyes, looking at my face, slowly lost the kind and almost absent-minded expression, grew darker, and full of fire—and suddenly the touching old man is a rather dangerous-looking person who makes you feel: this is like old times, this is like Salzburg and Paris and Vienna.... Quite the same old devil, whis-

pering to me: "For heaven's sake, if only we could be alone...." Can
you imagine??? eighty-three!!!! I can't get over this!!! On the whole:
he is an adorable man and he really and honestly loves me.... He
said to me softly again and again: "I love you and I shall love you al-
ways, always, as long as I live." I feel rather silly....

Maestro said to me just now on the telephone that I am very
beautiful. What a pity that he cannot see quite clearly—or better:
what a blessing!!!

The reaction of another old friend was less flattering; Lotte
wrote Frances that Viola had reproached her with being cold. She
was always hurt and surprised when people thought that of her.
They were always looking for the same outpouring of love that
they felt in her singing. But that side of Lotte belonged to her art.
Here is what Frances wrote in reply:

Your letter about Viola distressed me in so far as you say that it
makes you feel horrible to think that people think you are cold. In the
first place that is nonsense. There is no person on earth who exudes
warmth and radiance as you do. That is why everyone who once
feels your personality loves you. When Viola or I or Lili
[Petschnikoff] or anyone else says you are cold, we mean simply that
you are rather impersonal in your reactions to other people. Person-
ally I think that is wonderful, on the whole, even though in a weak
moment I may once in a while have a twinge of regret. But those
moments are few and far between; and I know that it is only be-
cause you are what you are, that companionship with you has be-
come a constantly increasing joy for almost ten years. When one is
"warm" as Viola and Lili mean it, there is something unhealthy
which weakens one's affection as time goes on. I am quite sure that
Lili, Viola, and some others set themselves up as patterns of warmth.
Yet you and I know that at bottom they are not warm but only inse-
cure....

You always like to have your cake and eat it too. Sometimes the
cake can be divided and part eaten, part kept. But some cakes
aren't divisible, and one can't be a great and a petty person at the
same time. You are a great person in the real sense of the word, and
you shouldn't waste a moment of regret on the fact that you can't be
little like the rest of us.

On March 9, 1949, Lehmann made her last commercial recordings. Since 1947 she had been back with Victor. On the last

records were four French *mélodies*, her first in that language to be commercially released, and three songs by Richard Strauss. Paul Ulanowsky was again her accompanist. Although some discographies give different dates, Lotte's letter of March 10 to Frances makes it clear that all seven songs were recorded at that one session. She had planned to do even more, but felt too tired.

There was again little touring in 1949-1950: Pasadena and Berkeley in October; in January and February five recitals in New York (including her 50th at Town Hall), one each in Boston and Chicago. A novelty in New York was Lotte's exhibition of her ceramic tiles. Those of *Der Rosenkavalier* sold very well. She took in over a thousand dollars, before deducting expenses.

While in New York, Lotte went to see a matinée of *South Pacific*, the enormously successful Rogers and Hammerstein musical. She had been curious to see her former colleague, Ezio Pinza, on Broadway. (They had once sung together in *Tannhäuser* at the Met.) Unfortunately, Pinza canceled that performance of *South Pacific*; but Lotte found Mary Martin "absolutely wonderful; such humor, such charm, so natural, so full of temperament!"

Lotte Lehmann's last recital tour started on January 28, 1951, with the first of her usual series of programs at New York's Town Hall, followed four days later with a recital in Washington, D. C. As usual, Lotte sent Frances the reviews. One of those from Washington had upset her. Frances wrote the following reaction:

> It is certainly typical of you that out of three reviews—two of which are ecstatic and rave about you—you only notice the one which was slightly carping. Considering that that one was written by Mr. Gunn, who many years ago said you should be hissed from the stage, or something to that effect, I think he was almost won over. He always loathed anything remotely connected with Germany. That he thought Hahn the only adequate music on the program was enough to make you think him an idiot even if you had forgotten your earlier experience with him. Perhaps his approach to a mild enthusiasm made you think it wasn't the same man. It was.

After Washington came Hollins College, Virginia. There was a *Winterreise* for the New Friends of Music at Town Hall on February 11. Frances sent a telegram:

WITH YOU IN SPIRIT IF CONFIDENCE IN LEHMANN
IMPOSSIBLE TRUST AT LEAST IN GOD AND
SCHUBERT

The dogs used to send telegrams also, to cheer her up.

Then, on February 16, 1951, Lehmann sang her famous Farewell Recital, her last concert in New York; although there were still a handful of other recitals to be sung on the West Coast during the months immediately following (and two in Wisconsin on her way back home), the last Town Hall recital was in effect her farewell to her career as a singer.

When Richard Pleasant, a friend and fan, got wind of Lotte's decision, he persuaded her to let him record the recital. It is a deeply moving document of a landmark event in the Lehmann career.

There was no advance publicity. Only a very small circle of close friends had suspected that this recital might be the last. Even Frances did not know.

The program started with five Schumann songs. The second group included Mendelssohn, Cornelius, and Wagner. At the end of the first half, just after Wagner's *Träume*, Lotte held up her hand to speak. There was a moment of breathless suspense. This is what she said:

> *I didn't announce it before because I don't like to celebrate my own funeral: but this is my farewell recital in New York.*

A roar of "No, no!" rumbled through the hall.

> *Thank you. I hoped you would protest. But please don't argue. You see, I started to sing in public in 1910 and after forty-one years of hard work, of anxiety and nervous strain, I think I deserve to take it easy and to relax. I think you know that the Marschallin in Rosenkavalier has always been one of my favorite parts. This Marschallin is a very wise woman. She looks into the mirror, and she says: "It is time!" So I as a singer look into the mirror and I say: "It is time!"*

There was again an uproar in the audience. Someone shouted: "Oh no!"

> *"Oh yes!" said Lotte...*
> *I have made up my mind. These have been very, very happy*

years which I have sung for you. The Town Hall has always been a
kind of home to me, a home which I now reluctantly and sadly have
to abandon. My managers have been very nice. Everything they did
for me was for my good. They have been my friends and I hope they
will remain my friends....

At this point, she thanked Marks Levine, Constance Hope,
and Richard Pleasant. Then she turned to her accompanist...

And Paulchen, don't think I would forget you!
[enthusiastic applause]
Paul Ulanowsky has been the ideal accompanist for me....
[prolonged applause]
We understood each other musically in perfect harmony, and always when I sang with him it was as if the hands of an angel have
supported me—now don't you get conceited!
[laughter from the audience]
I only mean, you know, you were an angel when you played.
Otherwise you were not so angelic.
[laughter again]
He has a very keen sense of humor, and you can believe me that
that is a great asset on concert tours where many incidents happen,
and where one gets hysterical and upset. But he smoothed out everything and always made me laugh and turned every tragedy into a
joke—really he's quite a wonderful guy!
I hope that my successors who will sing with him in future will be
as happy as I have been with him musically and personally. Thank
you, Paulchen.
Last but not least I come to you to thank you, my public; and
there I am a little at a loss what to say. The colors on my palette are
not glowing enough to paint you a picture, even if I flatter myself to
be definitely a painter. You have always given to me more than I
gave you....
[another roar, "No-o-o-o!"]
Let me explain what I mean. When I came home after a recital,
I had always a feeling of deep dissatisfaction. I know so much better
what perfection means, perfection which always was a goal for me
and never attained. There were always so many limitations, vocal
limitations, limitations in my technique, in my expressive power. So I
have sometimes failed you. But you as a public have been perfect.
You were kind and understanding. You gave me your enthusiasm,
you gave me everything, and you gave me your heart.

Now I really think you like me as a person, too, don't you?
[an enthusiastic murmur of confirmation]
*So when I say goodbye to you I say goodbye not to a public but I
say goodbye as though to a very beloved person, and I will cherish the
memory as long as I live. You have given me much inspiration, you
were the wings on which I soared, and if sometimes it was possible for
me to take you with me on my flight into beauty and into a better
world, then perhaps I have achieved a fraction of what I wanted to
give you.*

After the intermission, Lotte sang five songs by Robert
Franz. Her last group was six of the songs from Schubert's
Schöne Müllerin cycle. The audience, of course, demanded an encore. Lotte said: "I will try to sing *An die Musik.*" It is Schubert's
heartfelt hymn of gratitude to the art of music that saw him
through so many grey hours by lifting him into a lovelier world.
At the last words, "*Du holde Kunst, ich danke dir!*" (Beloved art, I
thank thee!), Lotte choked up with emotion and could not sing.
She covered her face with her hands as Ulanowsky played the
final bars alone. Most of the audience were crying with her.

Louis Biancolli's report appeared the next day in the *New York
World-Telegram & Sun:*

...*Then began a wild stampede backstage to bid Miss Lehmann
farewell. At least two-thirds of the audience joined in the rush that
soon jammed the entire stage.... As she entered her car, the vast
crowd surged after her, cramming sidewalk and street till all forms of
traffic were blocked.... As the car moved slowly toward Broadway,
[the crowd] watched silently and wept....*

Irving Kolodin had this to say in *The Saturday Review:*

...*Lotte Lehmann taught us something about the singer's art almost
every time she sang. In the latest and unfortunately the last appearance she taught us how a great artist says goodbye to a career.... As
she approached the climax of [Schubert's] hymn to the power of music...neither words nor tone would come.... If anything, these last
seconds drew an exquisite line to underscore the joy Lehmann conveyed with her singing by revealing the agony it was for her to re-
nounce it. Artists come and go; the memory of such a human being
will remain.*

Lotte expressed her own feelings about her farewell in a letter to Bruno Walter, written on February 22:

I kept my word. I never wanted to take my leave when people are saying: "It is high time." I myself wanted to be the one to decide that time. I wanted to go when they would feel regret and not relief. And therefore I feel that what I did was right and good. All my friends were horrified that I had the intention of making this my last season. Frances also did not quite believe it—said, however, that the main thing would be what I wanted myself. They all warned me not to burn my bridges behind me; so I kept silent during the days before the recital, and informed no one that I would make an official farewell. That is why the announcement came as a surprise to almost everyone.

Believe me: it was a wonderful and unforgettable highlight of my life. One of those highlights which make one feel it was worthwhile to have lived. To feel the love of the audience—really love*—was deeply moving.*

On February 19 and 21 there were concerts in Madison, Wisconsin. On April 10 in Los Angeles. On June 28 and July 5 in Berkeley. On August 7, in Santa Barbara. (A private recording has recently been made available, issued in 1977 by Aquitaine of Ontario, Canada; the record jacket carries the erroneous claim that this was "the last lieder recital of her long and distinguished career.")

On November 11, 1951, at the Pasadena Community Playhouse, Gwendolyn Williams Koldofsky accompanied the recital that was actually Lotte Lehmann's very last.

Chapter Nineteen

SHE MADE THE MOON RISE

FOR SOME TIME LOTTE HAD DREAMED of founding an American Salzburg. Santa Barbara, with its natural beauty, far enough—but not too far—from metropolitan centers, seemed a perfect location. Many distinguished musicians of the first rank had made their home in Southern California. While she was still active in her concert career, Lotte had talked to several of them about her idea, and had stimulated considerable enthusiasm. First there would be a school, like Salzburg's Mozarteum, where the great traditions could be passed on by acknowledged masters. That school would be the nucleus for an annual summer festival. Out of those discussions, which Lotte had instigated, the Music Academy of the West was born in 1947; it found its first home at the Cate School in Carpinteria, a few miles down the coast from Santa Barbara. At one time Jascha Heifetz, Artur Rubinstein, and Gregor Piatigorsky were all interested in participating. The right moment seemed at hand when Miraflores, a magnificent estate in Montecito (an elegant section of Santa Barbara), was donated to the Music Academy of the West in 1951. The first director of the academy at its new home was the popular American baritone, John Charles Thomas, who also taught voice there that first year. Lotte Lehmann, who had just decided to retire from recitals, was invited to teach interpretation.

She accepted a fee of $3,000 for the summer session. Heifetz, Rubinstein, and Piatigorsky, however, asked for considerably more. While she was in the East, Lotte tried to raise the money. She applied to all the foundations for funding; but, since the Music Academy of the West had as yet no national recognition, no one would listen. The engagement of that glamorous constellation fell through.

246

When she returned to Santa Barbara, Lotte inspected the new home of the Music Academy. The amazing story of its acquisition was relayed to Bruno Walter in her letter of March 8, 1951.

> Yesterday I had a look at the fantastic house that someone gave to the Music Academy of the West. Such a thing could only happen in America: some madly rich people named Jefferson left their house and eighteen acres to their niece, and an enormous bequest to a secretary who had been with the family for thirty-six years. That bequest was so large that the secretary said: "It is wicked to keep it all...." So she bought the house with the eighteen acres from the niece and gave it to the academy—as a memorial to the Jeffersons. It is in Montecito, near the Biltmore Hotel. Unbelievably beautiful.... Naturally there is one hitch: the Academy has not a cent and has to go begging for the means to maintain it. Do you happen to know any maharajah with 100,000 dollars too many who doesn't know what to do with them? We can help him out.

Among the original godparents of the Music Academy of the West there were—besides Lotte Lehmann—Yehudi Menuhin, Pierre Monteux, Bruno Walter, Ronald Colman, Jeanette Mac-Donald, Lawrence Tibbett, Doris Kenyon, Walter Pidgeon, Nelson Eddy, Richard Bonelli, Ernest Bloch, and Richard Lert, an amazing array of stars. Along with her efforts to interest influential musicians and potential sponsors, Lotte helped to launch the Academy with a benefit concert on July 8, 1947. She started her master classes in the summer of 1951.

Some time before, when Lotte had been teaching younger colleagues in New York, Frances had noticed that the same principles were constantly being repeated, the same problems were constantly cropping up. It seemed sensible to teach interpretation in classes, so that Lotte's demonstrations would be observed by all the students at once, so that they could each learn from the mistakes of others as she corrected them. It would save Lotte's energy, and classes would cost the students less than private lessons. Frances Holden originated the idea behind the Lehmann Master Classes. They were the first of their kind in America. Lotte made the concept famous.

Teaching a class, of course, was not new. But Lotte's classes were an innovation in that there was an audience. That provided an extra stimulation for Lotte and inspired her to give her very best; and for the students there was the excitement, the challenge of a performance. The songs (later opera scenes as well) were first thoroughly prepared with the help of experienced coaches, before the students sang a note for "Madame Lehmann," as she was always called. Lotte added the finishing touches, the final polish. She formulated the precepts and demonstrated the examples in her own unique way. Her comments were seasoned with humor, her corrections—*nearly* always—with tact. Lotte taught interpretation, never vocal technique.

Among the coaches were Jan Popper, Gwendolyn Koldofsky, Fritz Zweig, Irving Beckman, Natalie Limonick, and the writer of this book.

The master class format turned out to be ideal. In the beginning, however, she had not had the remotest idea what such a class would be like. She put her trust in her vast experience, her knowledge of the repertoire, and her instinct as an artist; the rest she left to the inspiration of the moment, to extemporaneous improvisation. Lehmann became a past mistress of the medium in no time. Her classes soon were famous.

The setting also played a part. The excitement of discovering new dimensions of meaning in poetry and music and drama was further magnified by the magnificent view of the Pacific, by the gardens of Miraflores, by the mountain backdrop. For the students, the combination of art and nature was intensely inspiring.

There might be a cellist practicing under a palm tree; the sound of a flute would float over the pond; a singer would be humming the *Dichterliebe* under a cluster of butterflies in a eucalyptus grove.

Many students fell in love there. The atmosphere was seductive, the lieder were romantic, the art of Lotte Lehmann seemed to lift one's awareness to a more poetic plane.

Lotte loved the Music Academy of the West. She was always tremendously loyal to it. She also discovered that she loved teaching. Here, for instance, is part of a letter to Bruno Walter in which she expresses her enthusiasm for two of her pupils, as she was preparing them for a performance:

At the moment I am working like mad at the Academy. We are rehearsing Act II of The Flying Dutchman. The young baritone, Harve Presnell, is absolutely astonishing.... Up until now it was just a very beautiful voice; but I have managed to awaken him to the realization that singing is not the end, but rather only the beginning. He is gradually overcoming his inhibitions, and today he was so good that I am in seventh heaven. And the Senta, Shirley Sproule—so touching and so lovely. I would never have believed it possible that I could live like this through others, that I would enjoy it so. I have always resisted the idea of living "vicariously." But that is probably our destiny as we grow old: that we can find joy in that. To be able to transform quite good singers into artists—that has something creative and deeply satisfying in it.

For our last performance we want to present six scenes from Pelléas et Mélisande. And there I feel unsure of myself, whether I can bring it off. I am afraid that I overestimate myself as a stage director; I am more frightened of the first rehearsals than any of these young people, who naturally think it will be child's play for me.

One month later, Lotte again wrote to Bruno Walter. During her preparation of *Pelléas*, her brother Fritz had suffered a stroke:

Fritz is very much better; he can already move his leg a little.... Progress must be reckoned in months, not in weeks. Fritz knows that, and is patient. Theres' is as always his angel. It is simply touching how she does not think of herself at all, but only of him.... Oh, it is really heart-rending to see someone you love so helpless.

After that shock her work came as a blessing.

I thought at first I would not be able to do Pelléas. I underestimated the power of losing oneself. Pelléas is my salvation. I forget everything when I work. What an opera! What a drama! And what happiness it is to create living beings—for it is almost that! Inside excellent singing machines I awaken human feelings. Does that sound very arrogant? It is really so. There is only one who scarcely needs me, or at least only in so far as every singer needs a stage director: Bonnie Murray, who sings Mélisande. She has everything within her—it is there, one has only to call it forth. To "call" it out of the others, I sometimes seem to need a trumpet.... But then to see how everything is working out, and how something wonderful is emerging—Ah, what a joy! I do not know if it is crazy to say so, but it is almost more beautiful than singing oneself.

*Our performance is on the 25th—and even if everything is en
miniature on our little stage—I forget the tiny horizon of my present
occupation and have the feeling that a whole world is there at my
disposal....*

Frances devised and built the essential parts of the scenery.
Mélisande's tower is still in the garage at Orplid. The fountain
has disappeared.

After the success in Santa Barbara, Lotte was in demand all
over. She gave master classes in Pasadena; at Mills College; at
Northwestern University in Evanston, Illinois; later also in Kansas City and in Boston; eventually in Canada, in England, in Austria. Last but not least in New York.

In 1953 she put together a program called *An Evening With
Lotte Lehmann*, in which she talked about her life and some of her
students sang arias or scenes that evoked key moments in the
Lehmann career. The stage was arranged to suggest a living
room in Lotte's home, and she told anecdotes, chatted with the
audience in her inimitable way, and introduced the young singers as if they and the audience were her guests. The show was
taken on tour to many cities and towns in California.

Some of those audiences were hard to play to. Often there
were half-empty houses. Lotte had to marshall all her vivacity and
charm to create a little atmosphere. Probably never before had
that been so much work for her. She also discovered that projecting the speaking voice all evening could be even more taxing
than singing. It was hard to be funny to a lot of empty rows.

The master classes themselves were more interesting, more
fascinating, more entertaining, and far more successful than the
programs. There were never any empty seats.

There were two kinds of classes: those for art song and those
for opera. Generally, in the earlier years, Mme. Lehmann sat in a
special chair at the front of the center aisle, so that she could observe her students from the public's point of view. Later, when
her arthritis made it hard for her to climb the steps, she would sit
on the side of the stage. Frequently she would get up to demonstrate a point; those were the moments that everyone looked
forward to most. Her total absorption in what she was doing

made her forget the pain in her hip and in her knees. In an operatic scene she moved with the grace and energy of the character she was portraying. When she was in her 70s she played Sophie, Evchen, or Micaëla like a young girl. She taught her twenty-year-old pupils how to give a more convincing impression of youth. She could transform herself into any character, instantaneously.

She was both stage director and partner in the opera scenes. To watch her at work was to participate in the creative process, to learn how the character *thinks*. And to learn how a great *artist* thinks, to follow her fantasy as she is developing her role. Even the most thrilling performance in an opera house can hardly give us *that*. Fortunately, Mme. Lehmann had the gift of eloquence in speech as well as in song. She could articulate her thoughts. A thousand nuances that one might easily miss in an evening at the opera were brought to light.

One expected, of course, that her re-creation of the Marschallin and Fidelio would be definitive; more surprising was her flair for parts she had never played upon the stage. Salome, for instance. It made no difference whether the character was a man or a woman. Otello, Don José, Rhadamès. Her Baron Ochs was irresistible. The Supper Scene can never have been funnier!

It was fascinating to watch the young singers gradually overcome their inhibitions under her guidance. One young woman, now a famous star, was rigid with self-consciousness in her first attempt at a scene from *Aïda*. She could barely raise her arm, when Mme. Lehmann called for an imperious gesture. "You'll learn to cross that stage with confidence," said Lotte, "if we have to stay here all night!" Today that singer can chew the scenery with the best of them.

Every now and then there might be a singer who failed to get the point. One young man with more voice than understanding was asked to escort the soprano to a couch in a love scene. "Excuse me, Madame," he asked, "but isn't this my aria? Do you mean I have to *act* in my aria?!"

Reaction was just as important as action. The thoughts of the silent character were often more revealing than those of the one singing. Everyone on stage had to live his or her role every moment. If necessary, one's back had to project the emotion.

Besides the classes in opera, there were performances. At first at the Academy, then at the Lobero Theatre in town. Once the Valkyries, armed with spears and shields, sang their battle cries under the oak trees of a Montecito estate.

Over the years the Academy received gifts from some very distinguished donors. Ganna Walska and Jeanette MacDonald contributed their lavishly beautiful opera costumes. Anna Russell gave some concert gowns. One of them became Rosalinde's ball dress in *Die Fledermaus*. Dame Judith Anderson loaned her *Medea* costume to Grace Bumbry for her first recital. It was later copied in gold lamé for another important concert. She looked like a goddess in it.

During her years at the Academy, Lehmann staged, among other operas, *Ariadne auf Naxos*, *Arabella*, Puccini's *Trittico*, *Fidelio*, and *Der Rosenkavalier*. The last was an enormous challenge for a student orchestra and came off brilliantly, thanks to the wizardry of Maurice Abravanel, who was for many years the Musical Director of the Academy. It is astonishing what he could accomplish during the brief summer session every year, and always with most of the orchestra new. Bruno Walter's very wise recommendation had brought him to the Music Academy of the West.

It was Maestro Abravanel, by the way, and not Mme. Lehmann, as one sometimes sees in print, who made the necessary cuts in a very long opera; he was determined to reduce the playing time to three hours without destroying continuity or effectiveness.

It was a thoroughly successful production of a wonderful, difficult opera. Lois Townsend (known in Italy as Lois Alba) and Kay McCracken Duke alternated as the Marschallin, Mrs. Duke wearing Mme. Lehmann's own costumes. Enid Clement was Octavian; Patricia Jennings, Sophie; James Standard, Baron Ochs.

There is quite possibly not an opera house in the world today without at least one former Lehmann student on its roster of singers. Among the more famous are (alphabetically) Jeannine Altmeyer, Judith Beckmann, Grace Bumbry, William Cochran, Kay Griffel, Marilyn Horne, Lotfi Mansouri, Norman Mittelman, Carol Neblett, Maralin Niska, William Olvis, and Benita Valente.

Some of them have already received the *Kammersänger/Kammersängerin* title. At the very beginning of their careers, Dame Janet Baker, Raimund Herincx, and Alberto Remedios were members of the class when Lotte taught at Wigmore Hall in London in 1957.

Although, perhaps, less well-known than some of those already mentioned, the following have also made—or are making—respectable careers in opera: Lincoln Clark, Jean Cook, Grace de la Cruz, Archie Drake, Ronald Holgate, Raymond Manton, Evangeline Noël, Mary Beth Piel, Harve Presnell, Marcella Reale, Luba Tcheresky, Dorothy Sandlin, and Joan Winden. There are many hundreds more. No doubt there are some other well-known singers whose status as former Lehmann students was unknown to the author.

The lieder classes were just as exciting as the opera scenes. A song was born from an experience; the task of the interpreter is to bring it to life. In the course of a recital, the singer plays many parts, with many imaginary changes of setting and mood. Mme. Lehmann created very vivid images for every song. Nothing was perfunctory or commonplace. Poetry and music express the exceptional; everyday routine would never inspire a song.

"You're not walking down Hollywood Boulevard. This is an enchanted forest!" With those words Mme. Lehmann interrupted a pupil in the middle of a song. The young singer repeated the phrases, and the miracle took place. What before had seemed to come from empty space was now filled with life and fantasy. The singer saw the forest; and *because* she saw it, we were able to see it too. Mme. Lehmann had put her finger on the missing element with accuracy and humor.

Lotte never "walked down Hollywood Boulevard." At least, never in a song. There was always an enchanted landscape, something special. Every single song existed in a world of its own; and with her voice, with her eyes, with all the radiance of her personality she invited us to enter into that world with her.

The vision must first be felt inside, of course. But there are ways to project it to an audience. There are tools of expression. Interpretation has its own technique. That is what the students were there to learn.

The pupil could expect interruptions, sometimes even before the first note had been sung. The piano prelude, the interludes, the postlude—those were sometimes the most striking parts of Mme. Lehmann's interpretation. The singer is not to *listen* to the prelude; the singer *is* the prelude. Those are *your* feelings, it is *your* mood that is expressed in that music. You are immersed in that atmosphere, not apart from it. The way you stand at the piano must convey what you are feeling; whether the mood is relaxed or excited, solemn or playful, dreamy or desperate, your eyes, your hands, the tilt of your head, the posture of your body—all of that must express the message of the song. But without theatricality. Everything must remain within the framework of the *Lied*. Even the nod to the accompanist should prepare the coming mood. There must be a constant harmony between what is heard and what is seen.

Sometimes the very meaning of the song is changed by the last notes of the accompaniment. *Auf ein altes Bild* (In an Old Picture), by Hugo Wolf, provides a touching example. The singer describes a painting. In a serene landscape the Christ Child is playing on His mother's lap. In the background a tree is growing that will one day be a cross. The last words are accompanied by an anguished dissonance at the thought that that happy child is destined to suffer such a cruel death. Mme. Lehmann made us feel the stab of pain. But at the very end of the postlude there is a soothing major chord. During the final bars we could see in her face the dawning realization that the agony on the cross was a prelude to the miracle of resurrection. The sorrow in her eyes was slowly transfigured into a shining expression of reverent gratitude. It was the most moving moment in a wonderful song. And it took place in silence.

Another example is the end of *Beau soir* by Debussy. A subtle shadow falls over the harmony at the last words, "*nous au tombeau*" (the river flows to the sea, our lives move on toward the tomb). Mme. Lehmann guided her singers to the thought, "is it really an end? Or do we somehow become one with infinite beauty…?" The last word of the thought was timed to coincide with the serenely major closing chord.

She would talk her pupils through a long prelude. In *Morgen* by

Strauss, for instance, the first words would arise naturally from the sequence of mental images, as if thought suddenly became audible.

There were exalted moments, there were funny moments.

"Don't sing "Träume der Liebe" as if she were dreaming of a cheese sandwich!"

"Singing is giving emotion. You have to be a little hotter! More ardor—you're not talking to your aunt."

After a singer had finished a Debussy song with many delicate verbal nuances, Mme. Lehmann made the comment: "Very lovely, but you forgot to sing."

Some typical precepts and random examples:

"There is a *crescendo* of emotion, not just of loudness."

"Don't make the words more important than the music; the unity of the *Lied* is interrupted. Both words and music are *equally* important."

"*Legato!* Music doesn't walk—it floats! It moves in waves."

"One must do justice to the musical line; the phrase must *go* somewhere. And the words must move on to the important word, must work up to it, and back from it, like a gentle surf."

"Soar up to the climax on the wings of a passionate emotion!"

"Don't talk of different things with the same expression!" In *Les berceaux* by Fauré: "Now you speak of the ships in the harbor, now of the weeping women, now of the adventurous men, the mothers by the cradles, the men longing for home again, the lure of the mysterious horizon…. Those things call for different expressions. The end is the *triumph* of the wives; the husbands want adventure but are drawn back to the women at the cradles."

La chevelure by Debussy: "Very sensuous when you repeat what he told you at 'cette nuit j'ai rêvé' (last night I dreamed)…. That's not *enough!* Your lover didn't dream about his grandmother!"

La vie antérieure (The Previous Life) by Duparc: "Very mysterious…you remember another incarnation…. It is not: 'I used to live in Beverly Hills, now I've moved to Santa Barbara.'"

Der Erlkönig, Schubert: "Don't start too excited. Don't emphasize 'mit SEINEM Kind' (with *his* child) like that; we can assume the child is his…. The father's voice is not just deep; he is trying to *comfort* his son.... The Erlking whispers—it is the wind over the heath. '*Du liebes Kind*' must already sound sinister, demonic, unearthly.... "

Ich kann's nicht fassen, nicht glauben (I cannot grasp it, I can't believe it), from Schumann's cycle, *Frauenliebe und Leben*:"A difficult beginning; one must feel that you come running in from the garden where he has just proposed to you."

Von ewiger Liebe (Of Eternal Love) by Brahms: "We must see in the girl's expression a fanatical will to succeed, feminine but strong! Even in singing a rather slow tempo one can have a feeling of urgency and of moving forward."

"*Aufenthalt* by Schubert loses grandeur if sung too quickly. You are a part of this storm that roars through the woods, you exult in the uproar of the elements."

Ihr Bild (Her Picture), Schubert: "The portrait comes to life! Sing with a sense of awe, of uncanny mystery."

Der Wegweiser (The Signpost) from *Der Winterreise*: "Not loud in the beginning; contemplative—'what is the matter with me?' Very *legato*... don't hack up the words, don't give too much emphasis to individual syllables.... At 'einen Weiser seh' ich stehen' (I see a signpost standing there) open your eyes widely, stare fixedly into your fate. 'Keiner' (no one) must not be sung brutally; you are not really unhappy that you will die. Death is your goal. You should sing that with a kind of dark triumph! There shall be no coming back to all this pain. Feel a great calm at the end, your lips slightly parted, almost as if in a grim sort of smile. The ending must be mysterious, spiritual. It must not be loud!"

Du bist wie eine Blume (You Are Like a Flower) by Schumann: "The main thing in singing is to have imagination. You are talking to a young child you love. You are almost sad that so much innocence and purity may be soiled by the world. To do justice to this masterpiece you must sing it with all your being and all your soul. It sounds quite lovely, but I do not yet see that child before you."

"Beethoven must have a certain dignity which could be destroyed by the sort of physical movement that might be permissible in a song by Strauss, for instance."

For the students and for the audience it was a great privilege to learn from Lotte Lehmann. She passed on to them a glorious tradition: partly as it had been passed on to her by such masters as Richard Strauss, Bruno Walter, and Arturo Toscanini, all links in an unbroken chain going back to Wagner, Mahler, Verdi, and still further into the past; but also—and above all—filled with individuality and life—as it must be by every artist—by her own personal vitality and the radiance of her spirit.

For Lotte teaching was a great satisfaction when she felt some response, a great frustration when that was lacking. Before every new series of master classes, especially those in a new place, she would be extremely nervous. Would the students be too good? Would there be nothing to correct? Or would they be so untalented that the class would be boring? Such thoughts tormented her beforehand; but the moment she stepped before an audience her theatre blood began to tingle. The old inspiration always came back. No matter how many times she demonstrated a song, no matter how many times she herself had sung it during a long career, it was always like a first time when she stood there in the bend of the piano and the accompaniment began.

When she demonstrated a song or a scene, she did not actually sing it in any usual sense. She generally marked it an octave lower, in a very quiet voice but with full intensity of expression. Once in a great while she might forget herself for a moment and a beautiful phrase or two would astonish and delight her hearers.

That happened, for instance, during one of her master classes in London. The distinguished actor (and author), Robert Speaight, wrote the following impressions under "Critics' Columns" in the *Tablet* of October 12, 1957:

> ...I was lucky enough to hear her in the first act of the Rosenkavalier — the two duets between the Marschallin and Octavian, and the great monologue. This last she went through for us in full, hardly singing but acting it all with such perfect expression that it was easy, from memory, to fill in the contour and the color of the voice. And it was wonderful to see how it was done, and why. At the end of the afternoon, there came one of the most electrifying moments I have ever experienced in theatre or concert-hall. She was demonstrating the ironic gaiety with which the Marschallin should bid Octavian goodbye [presumably just before the arrival of Baron

Ochs]. *Suddenly, from the rather dingy stage of the Wigmore Hall, a sound went up which did not come from either of the very promising pupils of the Opera School. In a second we realized what had happened: Mme. Lehmann had forgotten that she had no voice! The applause went on for about a minute while she brushed aside the moment of oblivion with a good-humored wave of the hand....*

Those master classes at Wigmore Hall in London—the first series was in 1957—were among her happiest memories. She was overwhelmed by the enthusiasm of the audiences, by the phenomenal attention of the press. Those classes were hailed as the artistic event of the season.

She wrote back to Frances:

The public was simply tremendous yesterday.... I had a wonderful reception; but then, after I had started to teach, the audience went mad. I am very relieved and my nervousness has vanished."

Four days later:

"The concert class went beautifully and the audience was quite as wild as in the opera class. All the participants are very responsive, quite surprisingly so."

At sixty-nine the Marschallin, off-stage, seems to have lost little of her charm. A susceptible Quinquin longed to come into her life. (Quinquin was Octavian's nickname.)

I can't understand it—especially since I am very cold to him and always tell him that he is a crazy fool. It flatters me—naturally.... It would be nice to find some pleasure in flirting with such a handsome boy, but I only think it ridiculous....

Ivor Newton, who accompanied many of the greatest artists of his day, played for the classes in London. He wrote about that experience in his book, *At the Piano—Ivor Newton:*

She was kindness itself to the students who, though naturally nervous at singing to her, soon loved her as the audience did. The greatest achievement of Lehmann's classes was the way in which the young singers were persuaded to have confidence in themselves.... She always said: "Don't copy me; don't become a carbon copy of any other artist. When I make a suggestion, think it over and develop it along your own lines."

The master classes made many headlines. To Lotte's acute distress, several made her three years too old. An error in an old reference work had been copied over and over by others. She had her original Perleberg birth certificate and threatened to wear it around her neck on a chain.

AT 72, A MAGNIFICENT SHOW

... Merely to see the way—as the Marschallin—she chucks Sophie under the chin with her fan is worth going to see. She scattered her wit and instruction over a two-hour class, asked the young artists to regard her as a colleague and not "as someone who stands on a pedestal...." (Percy Cater, *Daily Mail*, September 24, 1957)

LOTTE LEHMANN, 72, SHOWS "LOVERS" HOW TO KISS...

Two young singers pallidly embraced each other on the Wigmore Hall stage last night. And a kindly, grey-haired woman watching them shook her head sadly and said: "I have never yet seen young singers play a love scene right. I—an old woman—have to show them even how to kiss!" Lotte Lehmann did just that, with the emotion and fire of somebody fifty years her junior.... (Noel Goodwin, *Daily Express*)

The *Sunday Times* had this to say on November 3:

... She made the moon rise, I swear it, in the middle of Wigmore Hall, at the end of La Bohème, Act I, with a piano and two young singers without costume, lights, or scenery.

She turned, for a quicksilver moment, into an adorably guttersnipe Musetta, when a few seconds earlier she had been demonstrating the right, the only way to burst into tears because your lover is tired and jealous and your lungs are in a shocking condition.

Perhaps there will be no more Lotte Lehmanns, enchanting, witty, tender ladies, high-romantic yet spiced with irony, elegant yet never artificial, supremely graceful and intelligent, and leaving one in no doubt that they are above all things women.... (Siriol Hugh Jones)

Chapter Twenty

EXACTLY LIKE A QUEEN

THE LAST TWENTY YEARS of Lehmann's long life were active, varied, and laden with honors. One of the happiest events was the reopening of the Vienna Opera House on November 5, 1955. She was invited to the celebrations as an honored guest.

In one of the last months of World War II, on the night of March 12, 1945, "Black Monday" to the Viennese, four or five high-explosive bombs and a large number of incendiary bombs struck the roof of the opera house, destroying the stage and the fire-curtain. A frantic effort was made to save the beautiful old auditorium, but there was no pressure in the water outlets. The building burned for twenty-four hours. The majestic façade facing the *Ringstrasse*—the broad chain of avenues that encircles the inner city—remained standing; the main vestibule, grand staircase, foyer, and richly frescoed loggia were preserved. The rest of the interior was gutted down to the ground.

That was a night of heartbreak for the people of Vienna. Nowhere else in the world was a building so important to so many —even to those who had never been inside it and never hoped to be. Since the collapse of the Austro-Hungarian empire, its relative value in glory had only increased. It was the symbol of Vienna's greatest contribution to the world: her music. Proportionately more tax money was spent on the opera in Austria than anywhere else on earth.

The rebuilding of the Opera House was a remarkable achievement. The old appearance was preserved on the outside, and is as magnificent as ever. The auditorium is all new, but traditional in its atmosphere. The reopening was a joyful, sentimental occasion for every Austrian, and Lotte was thrilled to be a part of it.

It was her first return to Europe since 1938.

Frances, as chatelaine of Orplid, stayed behind to care for their large estate and its menagerie. Betty Mont, a friend who had been a great help and support to Fritz at the time of his stroke, was Lotte's traveling companion that year. The trip began in late September with two weeks of master classes at Northwestern University in Evanston, Illinois. There Lotte heard for the first time a young singer who soon became her protégée: Grace Bumbry, then nineteen years old and singing mezzo-soprano. "She is *outstanding*," Lotte wrote to Frances, "she has to come to Santa Barbara next summer."

The next stop was New York. Lotte had lunch with Toscanini on October 16. The next day she wrote to Frances:

> *Maestro has aged very much. He is really very frail, almost blind. He was pathetically happy to see me and was very flattering: "More beautiful than ever and very slender...." So he saw that!!! I am so glad that I saw him. He moved me very much.*

Then came Paris, Rome, Florence, Venice. Lotte had looked forward to seeing again those places of beautiful memory. The reality was melancholy to her. The excitement was gone, perhaps irretrievably. Those places had not lost their beauty; the change was in Lotte. It saddened her to think that she might be too old to recapture the exhilaration of her gypsy days. She found herself standing before great works of art and architecture strangely numb, unmoved. Only one painting stirred her deeply: *Cristo morto*, by Bronzino, in the Uffizi Gallery, Florence. It had moved her many years before. When she looked at it this time she burst into tears. But nothing else seemed to speak to her. She began to wonder if Vienna would be another disappointment.

Lotte had decided to make the trip only with great misgivings. "Never go back," she had often been told. She knew that the older people would remember her. But for the younger generation she was only a name.

> *It would have been a painful experience to walk through the streets of Vienna without being recognized. I prepared myself. "Don't be a silly prima donna," I said to myself. "You are entirely unimportant in Vienna. Don't forget that."*

She steeled herself and drove across the border into Austria.

Then the fairytale began, and she found out that she was the princess.

On her return, she told the story in a talk presented by the Opera Guild of Southern California on January 19, 1956, at the Beverly Hills Hotel:

> We spent the first night in Villach, a small town near the border. And there I had my first taste of things to come, things which overwhelmed me and made me more happy than I can say. I was scarcely in my room when there was a knock at the door. In came the innkeeper, literally trembling with excitement, clutching a bunch of flowers which he may have taken from one of the dining room tables. He almost couldn't talk for excitement. The fact that I was there, spending the night in his hotel, seemed to be something out of this world for him. Being recognized immediately, being greeted in such an enthusiastic way, moved me so deeply that I broke into tears. It certainly made a comic scene, both of us stammering and tears running down our faces.... I said to my friend: "If this already makes me weep, what will happen in Vienna?" The next morning our car was surrounded by people who had heard I was there and we drove away in a flurry of waving hands and shouts of joy....
>
> We stayed two days at Semmering, a beautiful mountain resort.... An old colleague came for a visit; and before entering Vienna I was informed about all the gossip of eighteen years. How truly Vienna that was! I was told exactly what this person said to that person—and the only thing that was different was that all my old colleagues are too old for romances....

In Semmering, her old friend, Alfred Muzzarelli, the one who had found his head tones during the darkest days of the war, was the first of the old colleagues to pay a visit. She wrote about that to Frances:

> Muzzarelli says that Vienna is going to tear me to pieces, _everybody_ waits for me, talks of me.... We felt it already here: even the woman at the newsstand said: "What? Lotte Lehmann?" At dinner yesterday the musicians played music from every opera I had sung in.... It is really very touching. They certainly have _not_ forgotten me!

Lotte's "official" description continues:

> Then, after Semmering—came Vienna.
> We stayed at the Ambassador Hotel, near the Opera House. I

had the so-called royal suite, the walls covered with red silk, everywhere wonderful chandeliers. I really felt like a queen....

My maids from former years had made inquiries when I would
arrive. And there they were—all of them. They had decorated the
door of the apartment with garlands and a big sign: "Welcome home
to Vienna." I don't know what the hotel manager thought about the
nails in the doorframe. My rooms were so filled with flowers that it
was difficult to put anything down....

Eighteen years ago I had some special fans who followed me everywhere. They were young at the time and they lived, apparently,
only for the pleasure of waiting for me on street corners, shouting
"Hoch Lehmann!" whenever I appeared. [Hoch is the German
equivalent of long live... or hurray for....] They are now middle-
aged, married, have children. But there they were—with shining eyes,
hands full of flowers....

You see, there is a very strong bond between the audience and the
singer here, stronger than in any other country, I believe. Music is so
very much a part of their lives. All the people feel music in their
blood, as necessary for them as the air they breathe. And the artist
who brings this music to them becomes much more than an idol—
more like a part of their lives. Therefore, their adoration is a very
personal one. For instance, and you will understand how deeply this
moves me, in all those years some of my loyal young friends went out
to the cemetery on anniversaries to bring flowers to the grave of my
parents. They did that through all those eighteen years.... When I
visited the grave I found candles burning and flowers covering the
stone. I cannot tell you how humble and grateful I felt.

Also the ties which bind me to my old colleagues are very strong
ones. They gave me a big reception. The old ones wanted to see me
again, the young ones to meet me. And they wanted to thank me
for some help which I had given them after the war in the time of
great need. I was very moved about their appreciation of something
that anyone would have done.

She could express her feelings more freely to Frances, without the fear that boasting might be construed as conceit, in the
following excerpts from several letters combined:

I wish—oh, how I wish it!—you could have been there yesterday at
the reception! It was quite incredible: many of the old colleagues
greeted me with tears, some could scarcely speak, they were so
moved. Reporters from all over the world were there who incessantly

photographed me.... Just now comes a package with two <u>marvelous</u>
hats as a <u>present</u> from my old hat salon. I am quite overwhelmed.
How happy I am to have come here!!!

Then, still to Frances, after the gala reopening and other exciting events:

Ach, it was <u>wonderful</u>. It would have been a <u>crime</u> not to come here.
I am borne as if on wings by an incredible love and adoration. That
is really only possible in Vienna, this kind of loyalty! I love America,
as you know, but this kind of faithful adoration is only possible
<u>here</u>.... The people <u>love</u> <u>me</u> <u>still</u> as they did many years ago. Vienna
appears to me in a glow of affection and wonder.... Everywhere
people who recognize me instantly.... I almost <u>drown</u> in love and ad-
miration! Oh, it is quite unbelievable how people on the street greet
me literally in tears! This trip has made me very happy....

Returning to her talk:

On the fifth of November in the morning was the official act of the
reopening of the Opera. Only invited guests were there and the
house was filled with a very distinguished crowd. I sat in the box of
honor with some other honorary members....

Oh, it was an unforgettable moment when the iron curtain rose;
even now, in memory, it chokes me! This wonderful old house which
has served only beauty, which has given joy and uplift to thousands of
music-loving people, had been mute for so long. Now it will live
again. Now the old times will come back again, I am sure of that. I
am not one of those people who sigh for the past. Nobody is irreplace-
able. Wherever some beauty dies, some new beauty is being born....

When I came downstairs at the hotel [the evening of the open-
ing performance] it felt like old times; I knew I looked well—and
you know how that can give one all the necessary poise and dignity.
The whole square before the hotel was black with people who wanted
to see me and there I went, exactly like a queen, through the cheer-
ing crowd!

Arriving at the Opera...we walked through a battery of cameras
up to the box; and the delight with which my name was said, again
and again, awakened in me a delight which certainly matched that
of my old admirers.

The box was decorated with roses; and we were in a crossfire of
popping flashbulbs. There we stood, side by side, Alfred Piccaver and

I, who once had been, and I say this with all humility, favorites of the audience.... He is now old and I am old—but I certainly did not feel it at all at that moment....

The Fidelio performance began. Perhaps you would like to know details about the performance. I am sorry. I was much too excited really to take it in. You see, Fidelio is so very near to my heart. It is difficult for me to go into details.... The important thing was that the Vienna Opera House was alive again. Beauty had awakened out of ruins. The heart of Austria was beating again.... Oh, it is so deeply moving—people began to give money for the rebuilding of the Opera House even before they started to rebuild their own living quarters. And that is a fact! Now all the people were there, standing outside the house like a long wall. Looking at the lighted windows, listening to the radio which brought to them the splendor of Beethoven's music, the lovely voices of the singers who will continue where we had to stop. It was not only a happy day in their lives, it was a holy day, a day of deepest thanksgiving....

I want to tell you something quite interesting: willpower is really all we need when we want to succeed. You see, I have rather bad arthritis in my knee and walking down stairs is very difficult for me. After the performance I had a moment of terrible panic. I had to walk down the stairs which were flanked on both sides with photographers and reporters. I said to myself: "This I cannot do, I cannot show them that I am so handicapped. I just have to walk as if nothing is the matter with me." AND I DID! I just walked down as if going on clouds. I really don't know how I did it. When I reached the ground floor my knee hurt me like the devil. But never mind that....

There were receptions...luncheons...reunions....

At the opera I heard two more performances: Don Giovanni and Die Frau ohne Schatten, which I really heard for the first time from "out front," having always sung the Dyer's Wife myself. The one quite exceptional voice I heard was that of Leonie Rysanek, who sang the Empress....

The trip to Vienna gave an enormous boost to Lotte's morale. From that year on, she went back to Europe for a visit every year. Frances accompanied her only in 1959. Rose Palmai-Tenser and Laura Lee Hammergren filled in as travel companions in the remaining years. In 1956 she invited Marilyn Horne, who had been one of her students, to sit with her in her box at the Vienna Opera. Lotte helped her make important contacts at the very beginning of what turned out to be a brilliant career. She gave her a letter to Herbert von Karajan.

While in Vienna that year, Lotte went to Hinterbrühl, the house in the country she had bought for her parents, where she and Otto had often stayed when they were in Austria. She found it like a "ghost house, terribly run down, dreadfully sad...the walnut tree which Papa planted is a giant now.... It was all very strange and uncanny."

She paid a visit to the grave of Franz Schalk, her fatherly friend and one of the great musical influences in her life. He had died exactly twenty-five years before.

Arthritis was becoming more and more of a problem. Lotte had also just had an operation on her foot. She discovered that the baths at Bad Gastein (in Austria) offered some relief.

While in Gastein she heard about the death of a close personal friend, Noël Sullivan, for years an enthusiastic performer-patron at the Carmel Bach Festival. In a letter to Frances she expressed her fear of losing Toscanini, too.

> I am so deeply sad about Noël. I shall miss him very much. One of the few people I really loved! I think so much about him, and wonder if all his questions are now finding their answers. He wanted to die. He wanted to <u>know</u> if everything would be as he imagined. I hope he found the truth.... I have to be prepared to lose also Maestro very soon—something I dread more than I can say.

In Frankfurt she saw the granddaughter of Baron and Baroness Putlitz, her former benefactors.

> She is a charming young woman, tall and slender and very good looking. She brought me flowers and kissed my hand. I would never have dreamed when I was a little protégée that that could ever happen!!!

During her visits to Europe, some already famous singers, such as Hilde Güden and Rita Streich, came to her for coaching.

In London to arrange the details of her master classes, Lotte happened to see Alec Guinness in *Hotel Paradiso* and went backstage to meet him after the play. She was quite smitten with his "handsomeness, elegance, and gracious manners," she wrote

Frances in one of her daily letters. "A true gentleman!" in person and "wonderful" on the stage.

She loved drama in all its forms: opera, theatre, movies—even television soap operas. She rarely missed *Edge of Night*. Once she had the chance to meet the cast on the set. She was as thrilled as a fan can be. When she found out that John Larkin, who played "Mike," had some of her records, she was doubly delighted. She managed to worm out of the actors all the up-coming twists in the plot. She naturally told them what she thought *ought* to happen.

In 1956, at the suggestion of Dame Judith Anderson, Lotte tried something very new to her: she made her first recording as a reciter of poetry. That maiden voyage, for Caedmon Records, consisted of the poems—without the music—that had inspired the *Winterreise* and *Dichterliebe* cycles and some of the Hugo Wolf settings of Goethe and Mörike, as well as the Marschallin's monologue, entirely spoken instead of sung. Later, in 1961, a second record was released; this time, Lotte attempted poetry that was new to her, by Rainer Maria Rilke. She was thrilled when Paula Wessely, a famous actress of the German-language theatre, called to rave about the Rilke record. "She said she had always known what a great singing actress I had been," Lotte reported to Frances, "but that this record is something which no actress of the legitimate stage could do as beautifully as I have done...." Lotte confessed to Bruno Walter that she hoped to be an actress in the next life; "it is freer...and never mind the rhythm!!!"

On January 16, 1957, Toscanini died at Riverdale. Lotte had dreaded that moment. She wrote a moving tribute:

> It should be a great consolation for all those who loved Arturo Toscanini, to know that he wanted to die! I last saw him at the end of October, a tired, very gentle old man, the fire extinguished in those wonderful dark eyes—eyes which had failed him completely, turning his world into shadows. He complained bitterly about the deterioration of his capacities and said that as he awakened each morning he only regretted that his life had not ended during the night.
>
> Again and again he talked about his loss of memory and I shall never forget the expression of pain in his face when he said: "You see, I just don't remember any more...." He who had been famous

for his fabulous memory could scarcely understand what was hap-
pening to him. I left him with the silent prayer that his wish might be
granted before age should completely conquer his noble spirit.

But heart and mind sometimes speak different languages. I should
only feel gratitude for his release from mortal fetters—and yet a deep
sadness pervades my whole being in realizing that this supreme artist,
this noble and lovable human being has passed away.... But beyond
this personal feeling are memories which death cannot destroy.
Memories of those unforgettable hours of working with him, singing
under his baton, feeling the world vanish and soaring above it on the
wings of music which never sounded more heavenly, more passionate
than under the spell of his fiery command....

Lotte's creative energy seemed inexhaustible. When she was
not working on a new book or writing articles for publication,
she was painting, sketching, sculpturing, or making mosaics.
"There is no hobby that is safe from me," she used to say. Frances
was kept busy cementing Lotte's tiles into fountains, coffee
tables and garden paths, finding room to hang more paintings
and felt appliques around the meandering house and building her
light-filled glass mosaics into the glass-brick walls of a sun room.
Closets and drawers filled up with watercolors, ink drawings,
pencil sketches, caricatures, and copper and plastic etchings. The
walls of Orplid (and cupboards in the garage) were full of oil portraits from earlier years. Lotte's ability to infuse life into a role on
the stage transferred well to portraiture. She painted Toscanini,
Risë Stevens, Strauss, Grace Bumbry, her parents, friends, her
cooks and gardeners, plus innumerable portraits of Frances.

For relaxation there were her romping dogs, talking parrots,
and even—for a brief but disastrous stay—a monkey. Lotte and
Frances shared a great love for animals, and encouraged their
guests to enjoy their four-legged or feathered friends as well.
The first time that Dame Judith Anderson came to call, she was
astonished to see Lotte put bits of teacake on top of her head as
they were sitting on the terrace. The reason appeared soon
enough: a beautiful bluejay (named Oscar) flew down to Lotte
and perched on her head to eat his lunch.

Lotte had an hilarious recording of a chorus of dogs barking
the tune of "Way down upon the Swannee River" almost per-

fectly on pitch, with piano accompaniment. If Lotte played a
record for visiting friends, it was more likely to be those dogs
"singing" than any record of her own.

She once had a rooster named Wotan. One day he went wild
and flew straight into Lotte's face, as if he wanted to peck at her
eyes. Someone had to kill him—behind Lotte's back, of course.
When his remains were served for dinner, even Frances—who
is not the least bit sentimental—lost her appetite.

Lotte loved her life at home in California. Much as she enjoyed
her annual visits to Europe now, she was happy to be a citizen of
the U.S.A. and was glad to do what she could for her adopted
country. She recorded three interviews which were broadcast
abroad for the "Voice of America" in 1958.

In 1961 Lotte retired as Honorary President of the Music
Academy of the West, but she occasionally returned for a series
of lieder classes. She chose *Fidelio* as her farewell production. She
gave a great deal of thought to the problem of the spoken dialogue, difficult enough for our unsentimental era in the original
German, however truncated, with its pathos at least familiar and
hallowed by tradition, but more difficult still when delivered in
English by American singers for American audiences. It was a
question of finding a convincing style, the best balance between
naturalism and heightened expression. She turned to her old
mentor, Bruno Walter, for reassurance that her instincts had
been reliable:

> I have often thought about how to make the dialogue in Fidelio
> "realistic" without robbing it of the tragic line. I find (and hope that I
> am right!) that if Fidelio is made to speak naturalistically, that is, in
> an everyday sort of tone, then the character herself and in fact the
> whole story becomes so improbable that the effect is COMICAL. A
> certain "pathos" belongs to Fidelio. Am I right? The other characters
> can speak without pathos (excepting Florestan—no, Pizarro too must
> have pathos); the others are ordinary, everyday types, Rocco, Marzel-
> line, Jaquino, average human beings. Fidelio's cry, "Two years, you
> say!"—for example—MUST come from another plane, don't you
> agree? I thought of that sentence like this: that Leonore forgets herself
> for a moment; then, when she sees that Rocco and Marzelline are
> looking at her strangely, she catches herself and says with a some-

what exaggerated expression, dictated by her confusion: "Oh, he must be a terrible criminal!!" Am I right? In the dungeon scene, her outcries must of course be considered an inner voice speaking.

Once I had a conversation with [Max] Reinhardt about this question, and he said something quite astonishing: he said that if he would ever stage Fidelio he would have the dialogue done in a sort of "singsong," half sung, so that the idea of reality would absolutely disappear. But how could one achieve deep expression in singsong??????? There is still so much I have to learn. But now there's no time left. Why do we only recognize that when it is actually too late???

She was invited by the Metropolitan Opera to stage a production of *Rosenkavalier* in 1962, with Régine Crespin as the Marschallin. At first she was afraid that Mme. Crespin, who was already well known for the role, might not welcome her suggestions; but John Gutman, assistant general manager of the Met, reassured her that all the artists in the cast had expressed delight at the idea of working with Lotte Lehmann.

Lotte became more and more nervous as the time approached. She had been stage director for many student performances by now; but the Metropolitan Opera? She wrote Rudolf Bing, the general manager of the Met, a desperate letter, begging to be released from her contract. He could say she was sick, anything. Eventually a compromise was reached: she would work with the principals and Ralph Herbert would see to the rest of the staging.

Her letter to Frances after the first rehearsal was full of self-doubt:

Today I just sat there from 11:30 to 3:00. Ralph Herbert is such an excellent overall stage director that I couldn't think of a word to say… I feel embarrassed just to sit and listen. Crespin is very good in the last act; I had precious little to say and felt like a fool. Ach, all this is so horrible….

Her self-confidence was soon regained, however, and with it her usual inspiration. She found plenty to say to the cast, after all.

Régine Crespin was a magnificent Marschallin. Never did I hear the beginning of the trio in the last act sung so divinely, with the most tender of pianissimos, almost unearthly in its silvery beauty. Perhaps my help proved valuable to Régine. In the beginning she seemed rather French, full of charm and grace, perfectly delightful except that the character she was supposed to represent happened to be Viennese…By the time of the première, it was a typical Viennese woman who was singing. To work with that great artist was sheer joy from beginning to end….

According to Lotte, the Octavian, Hertha Töpper, offered resistance to her advice. That was her one disappointment in that short-lived "third career."

The first performance took place on November 19, 1962. During the rehearsal period, there was a curious reunion: Lotte Lehmann and Maria Jeritza, two bitter rivals in the past, sat down at a table together to record an interview with the ever-diplomatic Mr. Gutman. Lotte made a cartoon in colors to commemorate the earth-shaking event. Her picture shows long, bushy cats' tails waving out from under the skirts of the two purring divas.

The Marschallin looked into the mirror and saw the marks of time. But she made up her mind to face the future gallantly. Her monologue concludes with the words, *"Und in dem 'wie,' da liegt der ganze Unterschied"* (And *how* we bear it makes all the difference).

In an otherwise beautiful tribute to Lotte Lehmann that appeared in *New York* magazine on August 15, 1977, the record reviewer surmised that she conceived of the Marschallin "as a genuinely tragic figure, witnessing the end of her romantic life…and terribly sad." Those who actually *saw* her play the role cherish a quite different impression. At the end of Act I, where other Marschallins burst into tears, Lehmann mastered her melancholy with dignity and noblesse. With the last chord she lifted her face, and one could see determination and courage in her eyes. That was the image as the curtain fell. It was not sad. It was positive, a lesson in wisdom.

When she taught that scene to her students, she used to talk them through the postlude, helping them to imagine what the Marschallin's thoughts might be. At the very end, her words were these: "I have made a vow to let go in the right way… lightly…And [raising her eyes, breathing in, slowly, and sitting back in her chair, with the soft hint of a smile]…I will!"

"She really *was* the Marschallin," says Frances Holden. And occasionally the Marschallin allowed herself a backward look. On

August 7, 1961, she shared with Bruno Walter the deep feelings
that flooded over her as she ran across some old reviews.

Dear, beloved Bruno,

*You will understand that this letter was not prompted by idiotic vani-
ty. On the contrary, what I feel is the greatest humility and gratitude.*

*A friend had kept scrapbooks of all my reviews and recently sent
them to me. I had thought they were lost [in the wartime bomb-
ings]. I was looking through them, trying to find the date of a performance.... I cannot tell you how overwhelmed I was at the realization that I had actually forgotten what my career must have
meant, really <u>forgotten</u>!!! That is the honest truth. My tears were
streaming as I read. The past became so alive again, all that I
learned from you, my greatest teacher, all the success that was granted to me—such a different kind of success from the sort one has today: now it is all "sensation," à la Jeritza. I quietly went my own way
as an artist and harvested so much love and recognition. And do
you know what came to my mind most deeply? "Könnt' ich klagen,
könnt ich zagen, irre sein an Dir und mir?" [Could I complain,
could I despair, be confused about Thee and me? from Schubert's
song, Im Abendrot (At Sunset)] No, my rich, wonderful life, which
had so much fulfillment, that is for me the greatest proof of God's existence. I of all people have no right ever to doubt. God will forgive
me for any doubts in the past. He has much to forgive; but my life
would not have been blessed with so much grace if He had rejected
me.*

*I had to tell you all this, because I know that you understand
me....*

Although Lotte occasionally had short-lived "enthusiasms" for
her friends' fervently held beliefs, essentially, according to
Frances, she was never religious in any conventional sense.
"Her personality was always one of shifts and changes. Lotte's
love for nature and her creative spirit were what really sustained
her," she says.

Bruno Walter died on February 17, 1962. Lotte wrote a tribute
which appeared in *Opera News* in March 1962. It ended with:

*What I have tried to give the young singers who have entrusted their
artistic development to me has its source in the wisdom with which
Bruno Walter guided me. He was a great teacher, a noble man, a
beloved friend.*

Fritz Lehmann died on April 26, 1963. Brother and sister had always had a close and loving, but often tumultuous relationship. There had been many storms, many misunderstandings. But their last visit together, at Lotte's home, had been an unusually serene and happy one for both of them. They had shared with each other some charmed memories of the past. Fritz sat beside his wife, Theresia, in the car, ready to be driven home. He told her how much he had enjoyed the rapport with Lotte, how happy he felt. Then he lay his head on her shoulder and stopped living.

During her retirement Lotte produced three more books in addition to numerous articles. *Five Operas and Richard Strauss* (in England: *Singing With Strauss*) appeared in 1964. Because of her authority in singing his works the book is still relevant for singers today, as are most of her other titles, including *More Than Singing*, translated by Frances Holden, which has been recently reissued in paperback by Dover. *Eighteen Song Cycles*, published in 1971, is another fine contribution to the literature of song interpretation.

She enjoyed writing and in addition to prose wrote a significant number of poems in German over the years, which were published in Austria, in 1969, as *Gedichte* (*Poems*).

Many famous artists came to visit Lotte at Hope Ranch. Dietrich Fischer-Dieskau left her a photo with the inscription: *Dem leuchtenden Vorbild in grosser Verehrung*—"To the shining example, in great veneration."

Elisabeth Schwarzkopf, the most famous Marschallin after Lehmann, came to Santa Barbara to talk with Lotte about the role. She graciously gave her predecessor in the part the credit for having called her attention to the crucial importance of the Viennese element in the Marschallin's personality.

After Lehmann's retirement as a recitalist, those two great artists, Fischer-Dieskau and Schwarzkopf, soon rose to preeminence in the realm of the *Lied*. Lotte also admired Hermann Prey for the warmth and spontaneity of his lieder singing.

Another favorite—and dear friend—was Gérard Souzay, the French baritone who was equally at home in the *mélodies* of France and the lieder of Germany. He and his superb accompanist, Dalton Baldwin, were frequent visitors at Orplid. Lotte sent Souzay some suggestions for his program. "I cherish the list," he wrote her. After hearing him in recital in 1955, she wrote out for him detailed comments on his German groups. His photo is inscribed (in French) "To Madame Lotte Lehmann, the most inspired and the most inspiring of the great singers, in homage of fervent and total admiration."

Many years later, when they met again in Europe, Baldwin wrote to Frances a rather perceptive remark about Lotte: "She still glows with that strange force of gravity that attracts but does not allow you to pass a certain barrier." That quality of hers, that several close friends had complained of, is seen there in a special light.

In 1965, in Munich, she heard Souzay sing a "celestially beautiful" recital. His first encore was dedicated to her and the "colossal ovation" she received from the audience thrilled and amazed her, for she had not expected to be so well remembered in Munich.

That same summer there was a reunion with an old colleague in Berlin:

> Frida Leider and I had so many memories it was really wonderful. We drove around with a guide. The Wall is so terrible that <u>words cannot describe it</u>. The destruction all around it you cannot imagine. I was in tears. I really felt <u>sick</u>. I don't recognize anything—it is a foreign city with impressive new buildings, wide spaces of nothing and innumerable ruins of houses. Nonetheless I don't regret having come here: one should know what these poor people have lived through! I do not find Berlin so gay. It is as if they built a fantastic city on a cemetery—such a mixture of horror and progress. I am glad I saw it all—but never again…. [from a letter to Frances]

Other, rather different memories of Berlin must have flooded over Lotte when—after so many years—she met again an old flame from the past, Willi Hilke, her one-time fiancé. He and his wife came to Bad Gastein to visit her.

> The Hilkes were here for dinner. It is disturbing that he <u>stares</u> at me as if I were in a zoo and he were trying to make out what kind of animal I am…. Imagine—I would have married him!!!

Others expressed only admiration in their glances:

> With everyone saying I look younger every year I shall soon be in my teens.

Master classes in Vienna, in 1964, were exhausting and the quality of the students (with two or three exceptions) was disappointing, but the response of the audience was exhilarating. "Perhaps I am mostly a 'showwoman,'" she confided to Frances. "Oh, it is my world: applause, creation.... It exhausts me deeply but it is good for me!"

On April 16, 1966, there was a Gala Farewell performance in the Old Met. That wonderful building on Broadway, between 39th and 40th Streets, where most of the greatest voices of the century had sung, would soon be a victim of the wrecker's ball. A New Met was ready at Lincoln Center. On that last night in the old house, besides the ghosts of the glorious past, most of the former stars who were still alive were assembled, to hear the stars of the present sing their last notes on that stage. "When Lotte Lehmann, proudly erect beneath her years, came forward, everybody stood up."

Lotte was constantly showered with honors. She was awarded honorary doctorates from many institutions, among them the University of Portland; Mills College; University of California, Santa Barbara; and Northwestern University. In 1961 the Austrian government decorated her with the Honor Cross, First Class, for Art and Science. At the same time the soloists of the Vienna State Opera created for her a special Ring of Honor. In May 1963 she received the Ring of Honor of the City of Vienna. In 1969 the University of California in Santa Barbara dedicated a new concert hall, named for her, and established the Lotte Lehmann Archive at the University Library, to preserve her prolific correspondence, her manuscripts and memoirs, her scrapbooks and press books, her photos and recordings, her paintings, ceramics, and mosaics.

In the same year Berndt Wessling brought out a book of tributes to her, in Salzburg, entitled *Mehr als eine Sängerin* (*More Than A Singer*). In addition to biographical material, selections from Lotte's writings, and tributes by many of her colleagues, the book contains one of the first attempts at a discography of this extensively recorded artist.

Many of her recordings were reissued to celebrate first her 75th, then her 80th birthday. Both birthdays were gala occasions.

Paul Ulanowsky and Lauritz Melchior were present in Santa Barbara for the celebration of Lotte's 80th year. Telegrams poured in from all over the world, many of them from heads of state. Some letters found their way to her with no more address than "Lotte Lehmann, Santa Barbara." In 1970, a street in Salzburg was named for her, "Lotte Lehmann Promenade."

> It was really very beautiful. The Promenade is lovely and in the most expensive and beautiful part of Salzburg-Aigen. It was a very happy occasion but I paid for it with pain.... [from a letter to Frances]

Lotte's last years were marked by a long and painful struggle with increasingly crippling arthritis. Nearly every summer she would return to Bad Gastein for the baths, which often seemed to bring her some short-term relief. But traveling was becoming more and more of a strain, and she missed Frances and home and the animals.

"Never again" became an annual refrain. Yet after a few months of peace and harmony in the opulent nature that surrounded Orplid, Lotte would again become restless. Europe met a need that was not fully satisfied in Santa Barbara. People over there remembered her greatness. Everywhere she was met with awe and adulation. That could be a nuisance sometimes, when she was tired and—momentarily—wished for the quiet of anonymity. But something in Lotte needed that recognition and thrived on the stimulation of applause.

During her sojourns in Europe, Lotte wrote to Frances every day. In 1969 there was an especially memorable visit to Vienna:

> I am fine, only so excited I cannot sleep. But the whirl around me is right for me...it is like old times. "_Frau Kammersängerin_"—_I like it!_

A little later, in Bad Gastein, the atmosphere was more peaceful. There was time to read and to reflect.

> Some friends gave me a book about the Vienna Opera. There you can see what Jeritza means to Vienna.... I was and am such a bourgeoise in comparison with her. You have to understand that I always admired her—reluctantly, but I had to. She had that something which made her a prima donna....

> I have heard very interesting things about the past. Oh, I under-

stand now better Strauss's friendship with Krauss and Ursuleac: it was to protect his Jewish daughter-in-law. Krauss and Ursuleac were thick friends with Göring.... Strauss was a very frightened old man and could not have acted otherwise than he did.

Wherever she went, whether in Europe or in America, Lotte was constantly in demand for radio and television interviews, many of which have been preserved on tape and are listed in the discography included in this book. Wit, wisdom, charm, and eloquence were hers as long as she lived. The inevitable physical decline never seemed to touch those qualities of mind and personality when there was the stimulation of an occasion. Privately, though, she could confess to Frances her moments of discouragement:

[May 1970 from Bad Gastein] *Here the people look at me with pity. I am not accustomed to being pitied, I am accustomed to being admired. You will not understand how hard this is for me.... The trip was a great mistake....*

The following year was even more of a trial.

Am trying to get used to crutches....

Few old friends and colleagues were still alive in 1973.

Lotte Klemperer telephoned yesterday. She wanted to prepare me: her father apparently is at last going to die. He had a collapse, as she called it.... It is a kind of shock to me. The last of the great ones! With him dies an era....

In 1974 she made her very last trip to Europe. The baths at Gastein were no more help to her.

I really am only alive to wait for my death. I never want to be a burden to you....

Lotte Lehmann died in her sleep at her home in Santa Barbara, early in the morning of August 26, 1976, at the age of eighty-eight. She had been more than usually exhausted by a visit the evening before. When she did not appear for breakfast in the morning, Frances went to the door of her room, which was always locked. Having a key, Frances entered. Since Lotte appeared to be still asleep, she slipped out again. A little later she returned. Lotte was still asleep. The third time one of the dogs

came into the room with Frances and began to bark. There was
no response. When Frances lifted Lotte's arm it fell back down.

She phoned the doctor, who wanted her to call an ambulance
and take Lotte to the hospital. Frances insisted instead that he
come to the house. When he arrived it was already too late.

It was nine years after Lotte's death before Frances could bear
to play her records. Now, however, Lotte's voice is always there
beside her. There have been few such friendships. In Frances's
own words:

> Our relationship was a very unusual one. Neither of us ever in-
> dulged in any physical expression of affection; but I think we both felt
> a very deep devotion to each other, and a feeling of closeness we had
> never felt with anyone else. Lotte perhaps had this feeling for her
> husband; she certainly felt lost when he died. But he died seventeen
> years after she first met him and we shared our lives for thirty-seven
> years.

After Lotte's death, Frances informed the Vienna Opera that
she would like to return the Ring of Honor, which had been
willed by Lotte to her. She requested that the association of soloists choose the singer who best represented the Lehmann tradition and present her with the ring to wear during her lifetime.
At the death of the singer, the ring would revert to the Vienna
Opera to be conferred anew. The Ring of Honor was presented
to Leonie Rysanek.

The Vienna State Opera arranged for Lotte Lehmann's ashes
to be buried in the Honor Section of the Central Cemetery of
Vienna, the final resting place of so many of the great composers
whose music had been the very substance of her life.

A phrase that Strauss had said of her was carved upon the
stone:

Sie hat gesungen, daß es Sterne rührte.

When she sang, she moved the stars.

Notes

Introduction (pages xiii–xviii)

(Dates of correspondence=month-day-year.)

xiii   Arturo Toscanini, It. cond., b. Parma 1867, d. New York 1957. Conducted the first performances of *Pagliacci* and *Bohème.* Leading It. cond. of his era. La Scala, Milan, intermittently 1896-1908, then 1921-29; Met. Op. 1908-15, N.Y. Philharmonic 1926-36, first non-German to conduct at Bayreuth (1930-31), Salzburg Fest. 1934-37, NBC Orch. 1937-54.

xiii   Bruno Walter, Ger. (later Am.) cond., b. Berlin 1876, d. Beverly Hills, Calif., 1962. Protégé of Gustav Mahler. Vienna Op. 1901-12, Gen. Music Dir. Munich 1913-22, Salzburg Fest. 1922-37, Berlin-Charlottenburg1925-29, Met. Op. 1941-59. One of the best loved of the great conductors.

xiv   Mathilde Mallinger, Aust. dramatic sop., b. Agram, Croatia, 1847, d. Berlin 1920. Deb. Munich 1866 as Norma.

xiv   Franz Schalk, Aust. cond., b. Vienna 1863, d. Edlach, Austria, 1931, studied w. Anton Bruckner. Met. Op. 1898. Vienna Op. 1900-31, musical dir. 1918-29 (in collaboration w. Richard Strauss 1919-24).

xvi   Novel—Lotte Lehmann: *Orplid mein Land*, Herbert Reichner Verlag, Vienna, 1937, tranlated into English (by Elsa Krauch) as *Eternal Flight*, G. P. Putnam 's Sons, New York, 1937.

xvi   Autobiography—Lotte Lehmann: *Anfang und Aufstieg*, Herbert Reichner Verlag, Vienna, 1937; English translation by Margaret Ludwig published in London as *Wings of Song*, Kegan Paul, Trench, Trubner & Co., Ltd., 1938, and in New York as *Midway in My Song*, Bobbs-Merrill, 1938, reprinted Greenwood, Westport, Conn., 1970 (hereafter *MIMS*).

xvi   Books on song interpretation—*Lotte Lehmann: More Than Singing* (translated by Frances Holden), Boosey & Hawkes, New York, 1945, reprinted Greenwood, Westport, Conn., 1975, Dover paperback 1985; and *Eighteen Song Cycles*, Cassell, London, 1971.

xvi   Books on opera roles—*Lotte Lehmann: My Many Lives* (translated by Frances Holden), Boosey & Hawkes, New York, 1948, reprinted Greenwood, Westport, Conn., 1974 (hereafter *MML*); and *Five Operas and Richard Strauss* (translated by Ernst Pawel), Macmillan, New York, 1964, reprinted Da Capo 1982 (hereafter *FO&RS*), published in Great Britain as *Singing with Richard Strauss*, Hamish Hamilton, 1964.

xvi   Poetry—Lotte Lehmann: *Verse in Prosa*, early 1920's, Hugo Heller-Bukum AG, Vienna; and *Gedichte*, Rudolf Reischl OHG, Salzburg, 1969.

xvi   Film—*Big City*, M-G-M, 1947.

xvi   Poetry reading—*Lotte Lehmann Reading German Lyric Poetry*, Caedmon Publishers, New York, 1957; and *Die Weise von Liebe und Tod and Das Marienleben by Rainer Maria Rilke Read by Lotte Lehmann*, Caedmon, New York, 1961..

xvi   "One of her letters makes clear..." Ltr. (1969), in The Lotte Lehmann Archives (hereafter LLA) of the Library of the University of California, Santa Barbara (UCSB), from LL to Natalie Limonick, asking Miss Limonick to tell Tami Asakura that LL has "found a sponsor," but that LL will be teaching her for nothing and does not want her to know it; further, that LL will send an additional $100 a month, as if from the "sponsor."

xvii   Maria Jeritza, Czech sop., b. Brno 1887, d. Orange, N.J., 1982, aged 94. Deb. Olomouc

1909 as Elsa. Vienna Op. 1912-35. Met. Op. 1921-32 (and 1951 for one performance as Rosalinde in *Fledermaus*). Created Ariadne in both versions of *Ariadne auf Naxos* and the Empress in *Die Frau ohne Schatten* by R. Strauss. After the war she returned to Vienna to sing Tosca and Santuzza in 1950, Salome in 1951, and in 1953, shortly before her 66th birthday, Tosca and Minnie in *The Girl of the Golden West.*

xvii Viorica Ursuleac, Romanian sop., b. Czernowitz (Chernovsty) 1894, d. Ehrwald, Austria, 1985. Married conductor Clemens Krauss. Created leading sop. roles in *Arabella, Friedenstag,* and *Capriccio* by R. Strauss.

xvii Elisabeth Schumann, Ger. sop., b. Merseberg 1885, d. New York 1952. Hamburg Mun. Theater 1909-19, Vienna Op. 1919-38. Met. Op. 1914 (one season only). Much admired in New York as a lieder singer. Recital tour of America w. R. Strauss in 1922.

xvii Risë Stevens, Am. mezzo-sop., b. New York 1913. Met. Op. 1938-61. Hollywood films *The Chocolate Soldier* (w. Nelson Eddy), *Going My Way* (w. Bing Crosby). Famous Carmen, Octavian, Dalila, Cherubino.

xvii Elisabeth Rethberg, Ger. sop., b. Schwarzenburg 1894, d. Yorktown Heights, NY, 1976. Met. Op. 1922-42. Created the title role in *Die ägyptische Helena* by Strauss in Dresden in 1928. Distinguished herself at the Met. Op. in both It. and Ger. roles.

xvii Richard Mayr, Aust. bass, b. Henndorf nr. Salzburg 1877, d. Vienna 1935. Vienna Op. 1902-35. Met. Op. 1927-30. Famous Baron Ochs.

xvii Alfred Jerger, Aust. bass-barit., b. Brno 1892, d. Vienna 1976. Vienna Op. 1922-60.

xvii Alfred Piccaver, Eng. ten., b. Long Sutton, Lincs., 1884, d. Vienna 1958. Vienna Op. 1910-37. Sang very seldom outside of Vienna, where he was a great favorite.

xvii Leo Slezak, Aust. ten., b. Schönberg, Moravia, 1873, d. Egern am Tegernsee 1946. Vienna Op. 1901-31. Famous also for his sense of humor and his humorous writings.

xvii Karl Aagard-Oestwig, Norw. heldenten., b. Oslo 1889, d. Oslo 1968. Vienna Op. 1919-26. Created the role of the Emperor in *Die Frau ohne Schatten*, Vienna, 1919.

xvii Lauritz Melchior, Dan./Am. heldenten., b. Copenhagen 1890, d. Santa Monica, Calif., 1973. The leading Wagnerian tenor of his generation. Met. Op. 1926-50.

xviii Mary Garden and Louis Biancolli: *Mary Garden's Story*, Simon and Schuster, New York, 1951. Mary Garden, Scot.-Am. sop., b. Aberdeen, Scot., 1874, d. Inverurie, Scot., 1967. Created Mélisande in Debussy's *Pelléas et Mélisande*, at Opéra Comique, Paris, 1902. Manhattan Op. 1907-10. Her photo as Thaïs in a New York shopwindow stopped traffic. Chicago Op. 1910-1931 ("Directa" for season 1921-22).

xviii Maria Callas, Gr. sop., b. New York 1923, d. Paris 1977, immensely famous for her artistry and for her temperament. Her repertoire extended from Isolde to Lucia.

Chapter I (pages 1-6)

1 "memoirs..." *MIMS* and MSS in LLA. "Letters..." Ltrs. to Baroness Putlitz in LLA; ltrs. to close family members in the possession of Frances Holden, Santa Barbara.

2 Carl Lehmann b. in Prenzlau, Prussia, 1849, d. at Hinterbrühl nr. Vienna, 1928.

2 Mother b. Marie Schuster in Prenzlau, 1850, d. in Vienna, 1933.

5 "school..." *Höhere Tochterschule*, Perleberg.

5 Sophie Arnould, Fr. sop., b. Paris 1740, d. Paris 1802. Deb. Paris Op. 1757. Created title role in Gluck's *Iphigénie en Aulide*, 1774.

Chapter II (pages 7-13)

7 "Go your own way..." *MIMS*, p. 25.

7 "To be able strangely..." Unpublished reminiscences of LL's childhood, MS in LLA.

8 Cockchafers... *Maikäfer*, large European scarab-like beetles.

9 "Royal High School..." *Die königliche akademische Hochschule für Musik*, Berlin-Charlottenburg.

9 Erna Tiedke chose the professional name, Elsa Thiele, before she disappeared from sight.

9   Emmy Destinn, Czech sop., b. Prague 1878, d. Budejovice, Cz., 1930. Deb. Berlin
     1898. Met. Op. 1908-14, 1919-21. Created Minnie in *The Girl of the Golden West* by
     Puccini.
9   Geraldine Farrar, Am. sop. (and silent film star), b. Melrose, Mass., 1882, d. Ridgefield,
     Conn., 1967. Deb. Berlin 1901 (Marguerite in *Faust*). Met. Op. 1906-22. Particularly
     admired as Butterfly, Carmen, Tosca, Zaza, and the Goose Girl in Humperdinck's
     Königskinder.
9   "She loved behaving like a prima donna..." *MIMS*, p. 37-40.
10   "scholarship..." 4-10-07 ("Charlotte Lehmann" accepted for "*eine ganze Freistelle*").
12   Konrad Gans [sic] Edler Herr zu Putlitz-Gross-Pankow, an enthusiastic patron of the
     arts.
12   The title, *Intendant*, is approximately equivalent to Dir. or Gen. Manager.
12   "His brother..." Joachim Freiherr Gans [sic] Edler Herr zu Putlitz.
12   "Countess's second aria..." Generally known as *Dove sono*, its It. title.
12   "Highly praised..." Some reviews quoted in Chapter VI, p. 41.
13   "Once again it had to be the Countess's aria..." Specifically mentioned in her draft,
     dtd. 1-3-09, of a ltr. to Prof. Otto Bake, preserved in an old scrapbook now in the
     possession of Frances Holden.
13   Reinhold ltr. printed in *MIMS*, p. 67-68.

Chapter III (pages 14-18)

14   "*Kammersängerin*..." Feminine form of the title, *Kammersänger*, literally "Chamber
     Singer," a title of honor, originally conferred upon a singer who had been appointed
     to sing for the monarch in his chamber, as a sign of royal (or imperial) esteem, still
     used in Germany and Austria to honor singers of exceptional merit.
14   LL's draft of that ltr. to Mallinger was preserved in one of her early scrapbooks,
     presently in the possession of Frances Holden.
15   "Goodness personified," *MIMS*, p. 82.
16   "Two excerpts from *Lohengrin*..." "Elsa's Dream" and *Du Ärmste kannst wohl nie
     ermessen.*
17   "Here I stood helpless..." *MIMS*, p. 79.
17   "Recommended her to Carl Harder..." Ltr. dtd. 2-3-10, Carl Harder to LL, in
     scrapbook referred to above: "*Sie sind mir von Herrn Regisseur Dahn so
     ausserordentlich empfohlen worden, dass ich Sie bitte, mir morgen Freitag
     Nachmittag zwischen 5 und 1/2 6 Uhr das Vergnügen Ihres Besuches zu schenken,
     um mir etwas vorzusingen.*" [You have been so exceptionally recommended to me by
     Herr Stage Director Dahn that I ask you to give me the pleasure of your visit
     tomorrow (Friday) afternoon between 5 and 5:30 for an audition.]
17   Rudolf Berger, Moravian bar., later ten., b. Brno 1874, d. New York 1915. Met. Op. (as
     ten.) 1914-15. Married Marie Rappold in 1913.
17   Marie Rappold, Am. dramatic sop., b. London 1873, d. Los Angeles 1957. Met. Op.
     1905-20.

Chapter IV (pages 19-30)

19   "I am to sing Gerlinde [sic]..." Ltr. dtd. 8-25-10, LL to Baroness Putlitz, LLA.
19   "This was no seducer..." *MIMS*, p. 92.
20   "He introduced me to the conductor..." Ltr. above to Baroness Putlitz, 8-25-10.
20   Gustav Brecher, Ger.-Bohemian cond. and comp., b. Eichwald 1879, committed
     suicide with his wife, 1940, when his ship was halted by the Germans on the way to
     Lisbon.
20   Otto Klemperer, Ger. cond., b. Breslau 1885, d. Zurich 1973. Ger. Theatre, Prague,
     1907-10, then Hamburg, Strassbourg, Cologne, Wiesbaden, Berlin 1927-33. Forced
     to leave Germany in 1933. Budapest State Op. 1947-50.
20   "I'm getting more and more accustomed..." Ltr. dtd. 9-1-10, LL to Fritz Lehmann,

in scrapbook belonging to Frances Holden (hereafter referred to as FH scrapbk.).

21 Edyth Walker, Am. mezzo-sop. (also sang sop. parts), b. Hopewell, near Rome, N.Y., 1867, d. New York 1950. Met. Op. 1903-06.

21 "Lotte to Fritz," dtd. 9-3-10, FH scrapbk.

21 "Not...as Lehmann remembered it..." *MIMS*, p. 92. Elisabeth Schumann, not Magda Lohse, sang the First Boy on 9-2-10.

22 "Well, yesterday..." Ltr. dtd. 9-3-10, LL to Fritz L., FH scrapbk.

22 Enrico Caruso, It. ten., the most famous of all, b. Naples 1873, d. Naples 1921. Met. Op. 1902-20.

22 "I tell you..." Ltr. dtd. 9-1-10, LL to Fritz L., FH scrapbk.

23 "She counteracted a stupidity..." Ltr. dtd. 9-4-10, LL to Baroness Putlitz LLA.

23 "I'm simply amazed..." Ibid.

24 "Wolfram von Eschenbach..." *MIMS*, p. 97.

24 Arthur Nikisch, Hung. cond., b. Szent Miklos 1855, d. Leipzig 1922. Boston Symph. Orch. 1889-93; Royal Op., Budapest, 1893-95; Leipzig Gewandhaus and Berlin Philharmonic 1895-1922. One of the first to conduct without a score.

25 "I am not at all discouraged..." Ltr. dtd. 9-24-10, LL to Fritz L., FH scrapbk.

25 "That is a wonderful human being..." Ltr. dtd. 9-9-10, LL to Fritz L., FH scrapbk.

25 "I found him enormously interesting..." *MIMS*, p. 92.

25 "This Klemperer..." Ltrs. LL to Fritz L., FH scrapbk. Ltr. dtd. 10-22-10.

26 "I could laugh myself sick..." Ibid., dtd. 10-27-10.

26 "And I have changed..." Ibid., dtd. 11-13-10.

27 "Dear Fritz!..." Ltr. dtd. 11-20-10, Carl Lehmann to Fritz, FH scrapbk.

26 "Finally she was entrusted..." Article by Siegfried Jelenko, Hamburg, clipping in LL's 1929 scrapbk., LLA.

28 "Dear Fritz!..." Ltr. dtd. 11-21-10, LL to Fritz L., FH scrapbk.

29 "At the time, of course..." *MIMS*, p. 99.

29 "When I was just a beginner..." *MML*, p. 172.

Chapter V (pages 31-38)

31 "Bravo, bravo! What a beautiful, magnificent voice! An Italian voice!"

31 "A photograph inscribed..." "To *Mademoiselle* Lotte Lehmann (the charming and lovely Eurydice) very sincerely...."

32 "The next day..." *MIMS*, p. 108.

32 Katharina Fleischer-Edel, Rhenish sop., b. Mülheim 1875, d. Dresden 1928. Deb. Hamburg Mun. Theat. 1898. Met. Op. 1906-07.

32 Felix von Weingartner, Aust. cond. and comp., b. Zara, Dalmatia, 1863, d. Winterthur, Switz., 1942. Lucille Marcel was his third wife (of five).

32 Lucille Marcel, Am. sop., b. New York 1887, d. Vienna 1921. Deb. Vienna Op. 1908 as Elektra.

32 Wilhelm Kienzl, Aust. comp., b. Waizenkirchen 1857, d. Vienna 1941. Of his ten operas, *Der Evangelimann* and *Der Kuhreigen* are best known. LL sang in both of them.

34 "One day Klemperer called me..." *MIMS*, p. 116-117.

35 Alois Pennarini, Aust. heldenten., b. nr. Vienna 1870, d. Usti, Cz., 1927. Hamburg Mun. Theat. 1900-13.

35 Theo Drill-Orridge, Am. contr. who also sang sop. roles, sang as Theodora Orridge at the Met. Op. 1911-12.

35 "Now, I believe, much has been reached..." Ltrs. LL to Baroness Putlitz, LLA. Ltr. dtd. 12-2-12.

37 "After the performance..." Ibid., dtd. 12-31-12.

Chapter VI (pages 39-51)

39 "*Iphigenia in Aulis*..." Sophie Arnould, from whom Lotte, according to Papa, was

descended, had created the title role in *Iphigénie en Aulide* in Paris over 139 years before, on Apr. 19, 1774.

39   Reviews: These, and other unidentified quotations from reviews, are from LL's scrapbooks in the LLA. Generally, the names of the newspapers, the dates, and the names of the critics are missing. In many cases that sort of information is now irretrievably lost, due to wartime bombings. Before his death Carl Lehmann, LL's father, kept the scrapbooks; later they were kept up to date by various fans in Vienna. The Am. press books, now in the LLA, were maintained by Constance Hope Associates, New York.

39   "The next day Norbert Salter..." *MIMS*, p. 120-123.

41   First Sieglinde in *Die Walküre* 1-9-14.

42   First Eva in *Die Meistersinger* 5-29-14.

43   (Sir) Thomas Beecham, Eng. cond., b. St. Helens, Lancs., 1879, d. London 1961. Beecham Op. Co. 1915-20; later artistic dir. and chief cond., Covent Garden. Met. Op. 1942-44. Founded the Royal Philharmonic Orch. 1947.

43   Frieda Hempel, Ger. sop., b. Leipzig 1885, d. Berlin 1955. Met. Op. 1912-19. First Marschallin in *Rosenkavalier* at the Met.

43   Michael Bohnen, Ger. bass, b. Cologne 1887, d. Berlin 1965. Met. Op. 1923-29. *Intendant* of Städtische Oper Berlin 1945-47.

44   Hans Pfitzner, Ger. comp., b. Moscow 1869, d. Salzburg 1949. His most successful opera, *Palestrina*, was first performed in 1917 in Munich.

44   "I would also like to say..." Ltr. dtd. 6-17-14, comp. Hans Pfitzner to LL, LLA. Was dir. of the Mun. Conservatory, Strasbourg, at the time.

44   Richard Tauber, Aust./Brit. ten., b. Linz 1891, d. London 1948. Dresden Op. 1913-26, Vienna Op. 1926-36. Many of Franz Lehár's operettas were written for him.

44   "I have hardly ever seen..." *MIMS*, p. 125-126.

46   "Life for me flows on..." Ltrs. LL to Baroness Putlitz, LLA. Ltr. dtd. 10-18-14.

46   "How the public loves me..." Ibid., dtd. 10-22-14.

47   Wilhelm von Wymetal, stage dir., Vienna Op. 1908-38. Was accused at first of staging the words and ignoring the music.

47   Friedrich Weidemann, Ger. bar., b. Ratzeburg, Holstein, 1871, d. Vienna 1919. Vienna Op. 1903-19.

48   "A man came to my door..." *MIMS*, p. 129-131.

48   William Miller, ten., b. 1880, d. Pittsburgh 1925. Vienna Op. 1910-17. Sang Stolzing at LL's Vienna debut.

48   Alexander Haydter, Aust. bass-barit., b. Vienna 1872, d. Vienna 1919. Vienna Op. 1905-19. Sang Beckmesser at LL's Vienna debut.

49   "I am now looking forward..." Ltr. dtd. 11-29-14, LL to Baroness Putlitz, LLA.

49   Peter Cornelius, Ger. comp., b. Mainz 1824, d. Mainz 1874. Friend and disciple of Liszt and Wagner.

49   Richard Heuberger, Aust. comp. of operas and operettas, b. Graz 1850, d. Vienna 1914. His most popular work is *Der Opernball* (*The Opera Ball*), an operetta premièred in Vienna in 1898.

50   "She was very young..." *MIMS*, p. 133-134.

50   Eugène d'Albert, Fr./Ger. comp., b. Glasgow, Scot., 1864, d. Riga 1932. Composed 20 operas, the most famous being *Tiefland*.

Chapter VII (pages 52-63)

52   "The year 1916..." *FO&RS*, p. 1.

53   "The Vienna Opera was alien territory..." *FO&RS*, p. 2.

54   Marie Gutheil-Schoder, Ger. sop., b. Weimar 1874, d. Bad Ilmenau 1935. Vienna Op. 1900-27.

54   Hans Gregor, German actor, stage dir., and theatre dir., b. Dresden 1866, d. Baden nr. Vienna 1919. Dir. of the Vienna Op. 1911-18. It was he who heard LL in Hamburg and engaged her for Vienna.

55   "Among her loveliest memories..." Quoted in Berndt W. Wessling: *Lotte Lehmann -
     Mehr als eine Sängerin*, Residenz Verlag, Salzburg, 1969, p. 105 (hereafter
     "Wessling").
55   Erik Schmedes, Dan. heldentenor, b. Gjentofte nr. Copenhagen 1866, d. Vienna 1931.
     Vienna Op. 1898-1924. Met. Op. 1908-09.
55   Selma Kurz, Aust. coloratura sop., b. Bielitz 1874 (1875? 1877?), d. Vienna 1933.
     Vienna Op. 1899-1927. Famous for an exceptional trill.
56   Bertha Ehnn, Austro-Hung. mezzo-sop., b. Budapest 1847, d. Aschberg 1932. Vienna
     Op. 1868-85.
56   "Lyon suddenly became very serious..." *MIMS*, p. 145.
57   Lucie Weidt, Bohemian sop., b. Troppau 1879, d. Vienna 1940. Vienna Op. 1902-27.
     Created the role of the Nurse in *Die Frau ohne Schatten*. Met. Op. 1910-11.
57   "It simply hadn't occurred to me..." *MIMS.*, p. 146.
57   "All in all, I felt..." *FO&RS*, p. 2-3.
59   "This curious gentleman..." Wessling, p. 57.
59   Erich Wolfgang Korngold, Aust. comp., b. Brno 1897, d. Hollywood 1957. Child
     prodigy (when he was 11 his ballet, *Der Schneemann*, had a great success in Vienna).
     His most famous opera, *Die tote Stadt*, was composed when he was 20. Went to
     Hollywood in 1934, becoming a leading comp. of film scores.
61   "For years, in Vienna..." *MML*, p. 4.
61   "For example, as the `comp.'..." Ibid., p. 66-67.
62   Aagard-Oestwig: v. note, Introduction.
62   "I was quickly pushed to the front..." *MIMS*, p. 143-144.
63   Plans for tour to Turkey discussed. Ltr. dtd. 5-30-18, LL to Baroness Putlitz.

Chapter VIII (pages 64-76)

65   Julius Bittner, Aust. comp., b. Vienna 1874, d. Vienna 1939. LL also sang the title role
     in his opera *Die Kohlhaymerin*.
66   "He accepted the break-up..." Ltr. dtd. 4-22-19, LL to Baroness Putlitz, LLA.
66   "One day a large package..." *FO&RS*, p. 24-25.
66-69 The letters and telegrams from Strauss are in the LLA.
67   "The crucial figure in the external action": "*Die Trägerin der äusseren Handlung.*"
69   "Strauss just telegraphed..." Ltr. dtd. 7-25-19, Ludwig Karpath to LL, LLA.
71   "Jeritza was quoted..." Jeritza's version of the matter can be found in her book,
     Sunlight and Song, D. Appleton and Co., New York, 1924, p. 81.
72   The première of *Die Frau ohne Schatten*: 10-10-19, Vienna Op.
72-73 "I had been giving some thought..." *FO&RS*, p. 39-40, 43-44.
75   "He was accompanied, as usual..." From LL's unpublished memoirs, chapter entitled
     "Puccini," MS in LLA.
75   Giovacchino Forzano, It. librettist, b. Borgo San Lorenzo 1883, d. Rome 1970. Wrote
     the librettos for Puccini's *Suor Angelica* and *Gianni Schicchi* and staged the
     première of *Turandot*.
75   Rosina Storchio, It. sop., b. Venice 1872, d. Milan 1945. Created Puccini's Butterfly.
76   Puccini died in Brussels, 11-29-24.

Chapter IX (pages 77-89)

80   Helene Wildbrunn, Aust. dramatic sop., b. Vienna 1882, d. Vienna 1972. Vienna Op.
     1924-31.
80   "That inscription, so typical..." Wessling, p. 98.
80   Pietro Mascagni, It. comp., world-famous for his opera *Cavalleria rusticana*, b. Livorno
     1863, d. Rome 1945.
81   "This year's Colón season..." Teatro Colón is the opera house of Buenos Aires (Colón
     is the Spanish form of the name Columbus).
81   "They thought of a singer..." *MIMS*, p. 152.
83   George Szell, Hung./Am. cond., b. Budapest 1897, d. Cleveland 1970. Ger. Op. in

Prague 1929-37, Met. Op. 1942-46. Cleveland Symph. Orch. 1946-70.
84   "Korngold's biographer": Brendan G. Carroll (v. note, Chapter X).
85   Delia Reinhardt, Ger. sop., b. Elberfeld 1892, d. Arlesheim nr. Basel 1974. Munich Op.
     1916-23, Met. Op. 1923-24, Berlin Staatsoper 1924-33.
85   Frida Leider, Ger. sop., b. Berlin 1888, d. Berlin 1975. Leading dramatic sop. of Berlin
     State Op. 1923-40.
85   Maria Ivogün, Hung. coloratura sop., b. Budapest 1891. Created Zerbinetta in second
     version of *Ariadne auf Naxos*. Teacher of Elisabeth Schwarzkopf and Rita Streich.
86   Fritz Busch, Ger. cond., b. Siegen, Westphalia, 1890, d. London 1951. Music dir.
     Dresden 1922-33. Conducted première of Strauss's *Intermezzo*. Dismissed from
     Dresden as anti-Nazi. Helped establish Glyndebourne Fest., 1934. Met. Op. 1945.
87   "Pauline Strauss was incredibly rude..." *FO&RS*, p. 74-75.
87   "A charming production..." *Cuvilliéstheater*, Munich 1960, stage dir. Rudolf
     Hartmann, cond. Joseph Keilberth, set designer Jean-Pierre Ponnelle, w. Hermann
     Prey and Hanny Steffek in the leading roles. Glyndebourne also produced the opera
     successfully, and that production was filmed for television.
87   "An excellent recording": HMV/Electrola, w. Dietrich Fischer-Dieskau and Lucia
     Popp, conducted by Wolfgang Sawallisch.

Chapter X (pages 90-104)

90   "*Eine kleine Liebelei*:" Music by Harry Ralton, text by Rotter-Stransky, recorded
     by LL with "instrumental quartet" in Sept. 1928 (Odeon O-4801).
90   "*Kammersängerin*": v. note, Chapter III.
91   "Honor-Member": "*Ehrenmitglied*."
91   Jean Louis Barthou (1862-1934), former premier, at the time of LL's decoration
     "*Sénateur des Basses Pyrénées*."
91   Barthou quoted in *MIMS*, p. 179.
91   "The King of Sweden...after a performance..." Vienna State Op. on tour.
91   Maria Nemeth, Hung. sop., b. Körmend 1892 (or 1897?), d. Vienna 1967. A famous
     Turandot.
91   "High-dramatic": "*Hochdramatischer Sopran*" is the heaviest female "*Fach*" (vocal
     category, in German), includes, among other roles, Isolde, Brünnhilde, and Elektra.
92   Jerger: v. note, Introduction.
92   Schalk's words quoted in Wessling, p. 125.
92   "After the great Leonore aria..." Ibid., p. 125. Anna Bahr-Mildenburg, Aust. sop., b.
     Vienna 1872, d. Vienna 1947. Vienna Op. 1897-1916, 1919-21.
92   Lilli Lehmann, Ger. sop., b. Würzburg 1848, d. Berlin 1929. Sang in first Bayreuth
     Fest., 1876. Famous for versatility (coloratura to heaviest Wagner heroines). Teacher
     of Geraldine Farrar and Olive Fremstad. Early dir. of Salzburg Fest., founder of
     Salzburg Mozarteum.
93   Slezak: v. note, Introduction.
93   "His autobiography": Leo Slezak: *Mein Lebensmärchen*, R. Piper & Co. Verlag,
     Munich, 1948; Deutscher Taschenbuch Verlag Gmb H & Co. KG, Munich, 1965, p.
     116.
93   Reynaldo Hahn, Fr. comp., b. Caracas, Venezuela, 1875, d. Paris 1947. Wrote operas,
     operetttas, many songs, such as *L'heure exquise* (composed *Si mes vers avaient des
     ailes* at the age of 13).
94   Franco Alfano, It. comp., b. Posillipo 1876, d. San Remo 1954. Besides completing
     Puccini's *Turandot*, he composed several operas, most notably *Risurrezione* (a
     favorite Mary Garden vehicle, in French translation).
94   Jan Kiepura, Polish ten. and popular film star, b. Sosnowiece 1902, d. Harrison, New
     York, 1966. Met. Op. 1938-39, 1942.
95   "Remembered Heliane in a letter..." Undated carbon copy of a ltr. in LLA, LL to
     Brendan G. Carroll, who was planning a biography of Korngold, with Marcel Prawy.

(Brendan G. Carroll: *Erich Wolfgang Korngold 1897-1957, His Life and Works*,
   Wilfion Books, England).
95 Margit Angerer, Hung. sop., b. Budapest 1903. Vienna Op. 1927-36.
96 Hermann Goetz, Ger. comp., b. Königsberg 1840, d. Hottingen, Switz., 1876. *Der
   Widerspenstigen Zähmung* (*The Taming of the Shrew*), his first opera, was
   premièred at Mannheim in 1874.
96 "It was the only role in which I was really bad..." Wessling, p. 105.
100 Claire Born, sop., Dresden Op..
100 Clemens Krauss, Aust. cond., b. Vienna 1893, d. Mexico City 1954. Directed
   Frankfurt Op. 1924-29, Vienna Op. 1929-34. Wrote libretto for Strauss's *Capriccio*.
100 "She cabled her willingsness..." Telegram, Maria Jeritza to Richard Strauss, dtd. 1-
   17-28, from Strauss Archives, displayed in exhibition, *100 Jahre Wiener Oper am
   Ring*, 1969.
101 Karpath and Strauss letters quoted in *Richard Strauss Blätter*, No. 7, edited by
   Günter Brosche, Part 2: 1926-1933, published by The International Richard Strauss
   Society, May 1976.
101 "The Eva of our dreams": Review signed "P. P." in LL's collection of clippings, LLA,
   otherwise unidentified.
102 "I was giving a recital with Bruno Walter..." *MIMS*, p. 170.
102 Manoel II of Portugal, reigned 1908-10. During the republican revolution of 1910 he
   escaped via Gibraltar to England, died 1932 in England.
102-104 Unidentified reviews quoted are from clippings in the LL scrapbooks, LLA.
103 "Just be Eva..." *FO&RS*, p. 40.

Chapter XI (pages 105–116)

105 "You mustn't work for such a devil..." Quoted in *Liberty* magazine, 4-7-34, clipping
   in FH scrapbk.
106 "A book by her brother..." Fritz Lehmann: *Story on the Song Cycle 'Die Schöne
   Müllerin,'* Gill Press, Mobile, 1962
111 Ursuleac: v. note, Introduction.
114 "One of the most significant American debuts..." from Ronald L. Davis: *Opera in
   Chicago*, Appleton Century, New York, 1966.
116 "Both roles on the same evening..." Renata Scotto recently sang all three *Trittico*
   heroines at the Met.
116 Dimitri Mitropoulos, Gr. cond. and comp., b. Athens 1896, d. Milan 1960. New York
   Philharmonic 1950-58. Met. Op. 1954-60.

Chapter XII (pages 117–135)

117 "Shaken with nerves..." *MIMS*, p. 197.
118 Farrar: v. note, Chapter II.
120 "Encore after encore..." *MIMS*, p. 198.
122 Mario Castelnuovo-Tedesco, It./Am. comp., b. Florence 1895, d. Los Angeles 1968.
   Jewish, he left Italy in 1939. Among his operas: *La Mandragola* (1926), *The Merchant
   of Venice* (1961).
123 Josef Marx, Aust. comp., best known for his songs, b. Graz 1882, d. Graz 1964.
123 Karl Hammes, Ger. bar., b. Zell an der Mosel 1896, d. nr. Warsaw 1939 (shot down as
   a flier). Vienna Op. 1929-35.
124 "*Maestro*" can mean anyone who plays the piano in a European opera house.
124 Robert Heger, Ger. cond. and comp., b. Strasbourg 1886, d. Munich 1978. Set some
   of LL's poems to music and conducted her famous *Rosenkavalier* recording.
124 Kirsten Flagstad, Norw. dramatic sop., b. Hamar, Norway, 1895, d. Oslo 1962. Met.
   Op. 1935-41, 1950-52. One of the major Wagnerian voices of the century.
124 "Nothing but horizontal strokes..." Ivor Newton: *At the Piano—Ivor Newton*,
   Hamish Hamilton, London, 1966, p. 280.

124 Friedrich Schorr, Austro-Hung. bass-barit., b. Nagyvárad 1888, d. Farmington, Conn.,
     1953. Famous for his Wotan and Hans Sachs.
124 Ellen Terry, Eng. actress, b. Coventry 1847, d. Small Hythe nr. Tenterden, Kent,
     1928. One of the great Shakespearean actresses.
125 Leo Blech, Ger. cond. and comp., b. Aachen 1871, d. Berlin 1958. Forced to leave
     Germany 1937, being Jewish. Spent war years in Sweden.
125 Ivogün: v. note, Chapter IX.
125 Lothar Wallerstein, Czech/Am. cond. and stage dir., b. Prague 1882, d. New Orleans
     1949.
126 Wilhelm Furtwängler, Ger. cond., b. Berlin 1886, d. Baden-Baden 1954. One of the
     great Wagnerian conductors.
126 Maurice Abravanel, Sephardic-Gr./Am. cond., protégé of Bruno Walter, b. Salonica,
     Greece, 1903. Cond. of the Utah Symph. Orch. 1947-79. Conducted at Berlin State
     Op., Paris Natl. Op., Met. Op., among many others.
128 Ernö Balogh, Hung. pianist and comp., b. Budapest 1897. LL's principal accompanist in
     America 1932-37.
128 "Two things one must never say..." *MIMS*, p. 201-204.
132 Rethberg: v. note, Introduction.
132 Rose Pauly, Hung. sop., b. Eperjes 1894, d. Herzlia, Israel, 1975, especially famous for
     her Elektra. Met. Op. 1938-40.
133 Maria Olszewska, Ger. mezzo-sop., b. Ludwigsschweige bei Wertingen, Bavaria,
     1892, d. Klagenfurt, Austria, 1969. Vienna Op. 1924-30, Chicago Op. 1928-32, Met.
     Op. 1933-35.
133 "Quinquin," 0999pronounced as if French, is the pet name given to Octavian by the
     Marschallin in *Der Rosenkavalier*.
133 "According to her statement..." Quoted in *The Musical Courier*, July 1933.
134 "Clemens Krauss...called at once..." *FO&RS*, p. 91-92.

Chapter XIII (pages 136-154)

136 "It is curious..." From an unpublished MS of LL's reminiscences, LLA.
136 Giulio Gatti-Casazza, b. Udine 1869, d. Ferrara 1940; gen. manager of the Met. Op.
     1908-35.
136 Beniamino Gigli, It. ten., b. Recanati 1890, d. Rome 1957. Met. Op. 1920-32, 1939.
     Gigli and LL sang in Vienna together; he inscribed his photograph "*Kammersängerin
     Lotte Lehmann, bella voce, grande anima* [beautiful voice, great soul], Vienna 1929."
137 Gertrude Kappel, Ger. sop., b. Halle 1884, d. Munich 1971. Met. Op. 1928-36.
137 Ludwig Hofmann, Ger. bass-barit., b. Frankfurt a. M. 1897, d. London 1964. Met. Op.
     1932-38, Vienna Op. 1935-39, 1951-55.
137 Karin Branzell, Sw. contr., b. Stockholm 1891, d. Altadena, Calif., 1974. Met. Op.
     1924-44, 1951.
137 Artur Bodanzky, Aust. cond., b. Vienna 1877, d. New York 1939. Met. Op. 1915-39.
140 Lawrence Gilman: the leading music critic of *The New York Herald Tribune* at that
     time.
142 Max Lorenz, Ger. heldenten., b. Düsseldorf 1901, d. Vienna 1975. Met. Op. 1931-34,
     1947-50, Vienna Op. 1940-62.
142 Göta Ljungberg, Sw. sop., b. Sundsvall 1893, d. Lidingo, nr. Stockholm 1955. Met. Op.
     1932-35.
142 Grete Stückgold, Eng.-Ger./Am. sop., b. London 1895, d. Falls Village, Conn., 1979.
     Met. Op. 1927-35, 1939.
142 Maria Müller, Bohemian sop., b. Leitmeritz 1898, d. Bayreuth, 1958. Met. Op. 1925-
     1935.
142 Editha Fleischer, Ger. sop., b. 1898. Met. Op. 1926-36.
142 "With this concert began..." George Marek: *Toscanini*, Atheneum, New York, 1975,
     p.158.

143 The Toscanini letters to LL, in the possession of Frances Holden, could not be
     published in full as reproduction rights were denied by the Toscanini heirs.
144 "And so on the trip..." *MML*, p. 175.
144 Heinrich Schlusnus, Ger. bar., b. Braubach 1888, d. Frankfurt 1952. Famous for lieder
     as well as for opera.
145 Heinz Tietjen, 1881-1967, *Intendant* of the Civic (*Städtische*) Op., Berlin (1925–
     1930); then *Gerneralintendant* of the Prussian State Theatres (1927–45), Artistic Dir.
     of the Bayreuth Fest. (1931–44).
145 *Göring, the Lioness and I*: Published in *Opera 66*, LL MS edited by Charles Osborne,
     Alan Ross Ltd, London, 1966, p. 187-199. LL misremembered the year of her
     encounter with Göring as 1933; it was definitely in 1934, on Apr. 20, Hitler's
     birthday, since a review of her recital in Dresden the evening before mentions that
     the program had been interrupted by a telephone call from Göring, just as she
     described it (review in scrapbook, LLA).
149 "Viorica Ursuleac...claimed..." In an interview w. Lanfranco Rasponi, quoted in his
     book, *The Last Prima Donnas*, Alfred A. Knopf, New York, 1982, p. 136-137.
150 Hinkel and Graemer quotations printed in Wessling, p. 130.
152 "For me too..." From an unpublished article on Toscanini by LL, LLA.
154 Paul Hindemith, Ger. comp., b. Hanau 1895, d. Frankfurt 1963. His most famous opera
     is *Mathis der Maler*, banned by the Nazis, first performed Zurich 1938.
154 "The Chicago Opera had announced..." Information from *The Chicago Herald-
     Examiner*, 11-11-34, and Lawrence Gilman, *New York Herald Tribune*, 10-28-34.

Chapter XIV (pages 155-176)

155 Claudia Muzio, It. sop., b. Pavia 1889, d. Rome 1936. Met. Op. 1916-22, Chicago Op.
     1922-31.
156 Herbert Graf, Aust./Am. stage dir., b. Vienna 1904, d. Geneva 1973. Met. Op. 1936-60
     (w. occasional later productions as well). Dir. of Zurich and Geneva Operas.
156 Fritz Reiner, Hung. cond., b. Budapest 1888, d. New York 1963. Cincinnati Symph.
     Orch. 1922-31, Pittsburgh Symph. 1938-48. Met. Op. 1948-53. Chicago Symph. 1953-
     62.
157 Emanuel List, Aust./Am. bass, b. Vienna 1891, d. Vienna 1967. Met. Op. 1933-47.
157 Elsa Alsen, Norw.-Fr./Am. mezzo-sop., later sop., b. Obra, Poland, 1880, d. New York
     1975. Deb. Heidelberg 1902 as Azucena, Braunschweig 1912 as sop., U.S. deb.
     Baltimore 1923 as Isolde with the Ger. Op. Co.
158 Lawrence Tibbett, leading Am. bar. of his day, b. Bakersfield, Calif., 1896, d. New
     York 1960. Met. Op. 1923-1950.
158 Anny Konetzni, Aust. sop. (sister of Hilde Konetzni, also sop.), b. Ungarisch-
     Weisskirchen 1902, d. Vienna 1968. Vienna Op. 1933-55. Met. Op. 1934-35.
159 Alexander Kipnis, Russ./Am. bass, b. Zhitomir, Ukraine, 1891, d. Westport, Conn.,
     1978. Career centered in Berlin 1919-34. Chicago 1923-32, Met. Op. 1940-46.
159 Kerstin Thorborg, Sw. mezzo-sop., b. Venjan 1896, d. Falun, Sweden, 1970. Met. Op.
     1936-50.
159 Ernestine Schumann-Heink, Aust./Am. contr., b. Lieben, nr. Prague, 1861, d.
     Hollywood 1936. Last Met appearance, as Erda in *Siegfried*, 3-11-32.
160 Eyvind Laholm (Edwin Johnson), Am. heldenten., b. Eau Claire, Wis., 1894, d. New
     York 1958. He first attracted attention when he sang at a Sunday service on board the
     USS *Arizona* at the time of America's entry into World War I; later he sang in opera
     in Essen, London, Stockholm, Vienna, Munich, Barcelona, and Berlin. Met. Op. 1939-
     40.
161 Richard Crooks, Am. ten., b. Trenton, N.J., 1900, d. Portola Valley, Calif., 1972. Met.
     Op. deb. in Manon, 1933. Retired 1946.
161 Giovanni Martinelli, It. ten., b. Montagnana 1885, d. New York 1969. Met. Op. 1913-
     45. Sang the Emperor in *Turandot* at the age of 81, in Seattle.

162 Vincenzo Bellezza, It. cond., b. Bitonto, Bari, 1888, d. Rome 1964. Met. Op. 1926-35.
165 "Profile..." *The New Yorker*, 2-23-35, reprinted by permission; c 1935, 1963 The
     New Yorker Magazine, Inc.
165 Rosa Ponselle, Am. soprano, b. Meriden, Conn., 1897, d. Baltimore 1981. Made her
     operatic deb. (as Leonora in *La forza del destino*) opp. Caruso at the Met in 1918.
     Retired prematurely in 1937
165 "Davenport's novel..." Marcia Davenport: *Of Lena Geyer*, Charles Scribner's Sons,
     New York, 1936.
167 Victor de Sabata, It. cond., b. Trieste 1892, d. Santa Margherita Ligure 1967. La Scala
     1929-53.
167 Ella Flesch, Hung. sop., b. Budapest 1902, d. New York 1957. Deb. Vienna Op. at 18 as
     Aïda, Met. Op. deb. as Salome 1944.
167 Hans Hotter, Aust. bass-barit. of Ger. birth, b. Offenbach-am-Main 1909. The greatest
     Wotan of his era. Met. Op. 1950-54.
167 Margarete Klose, Ger. mezzo-sop., b. Berlin 1902, d. Berlin 1968. Berlin State Op.
     1931-1961.
167 Martha Fuchs, Ger. mezzo-sop., later dramatic sop., b. Stuttgart 1898, d. Stuttgart
     1974. Leading sop. Dresden (1930-45), Bayreuth.
167 Bruno Seidler-Winkler, Ger. cond., b. Berlin 1880, d. 1960. Berlin Radio Orch. 1925-
     33.
169 "Toscanini? He made *Fidelio* flame..." *MML*, p. 119-120.
169 "Toscanini... was not swayed..." Vincent Sheean: *First and Last Love*, Random
     House, New York, 1956, p. 194-196.
170 Maria Malibran, famous coloratura contr. of Spanish descent, b. Paris 1808, d.
     Manchester, Eng., 1836.
171 Josef Krips, Aust. cond., b. Vienna 1902, d. Geneva 1974. Vienna Op. 1933-38
     (dismissed by Nazis, spent war years in hiding), conducted first post-war opera
     performances in Vienna 1945 and helped to create the "Vienna Mozart style."
171 Charles Kullmann, Am. tenor, b. New Haven, Conn., 1903, d. Bloomington, Indiana,
     1983. Met. Op. 1935-60.
173 Edward Johnson, Canadian ten. and opera administrator, b. Guelph, Ontario, 1878, d.
     Toronto 1959. Met. Op. as ten. 1922-35, as gen. manager 1935-50.
173 Herbert Witherspoon, Am. bass, b. Buffalo, New York, 1873, d. New York 1935. Met.
     Op. 1908-14. In 1935 he was selected to be gen. manager of the Met but died before
     his season began.
174 "Orplid" was Mörike's name for his far-away dream island. (LL and Frances Holden
     named their home in Santa Barbara "Orplid.") The English title of LL's novel is
     Eternal Flight (v. note,Introduction, p. x).
175 "I can no longer imagine Salzburg..." Ltr. dtd. 6-81-36, Bruno Walter to Toscanini,
     quoted in Guglielmo Barblan: *Toscanini e la Scala*, Edizioni della Scala, Milan, 1972, p.
     366.
175 Hans Hermann Nissen, Ger. bass-barit., b. Danzig 1896 (1893?), d. Munich 1980. Deb.
     Berlin Volksoper 1924, Met. Op. 1938.
175 "I will never forget..." *MML*, p. 92-93.

Chapter XV (pages 177-194)

179 "The accompanist... was a fool..." Ltr. dtd. Santa Barbara, 11-25-36, LL to Constance
     Hope, LLA.
179 "When I have made my first million..." Postcard, undated, LL to Constance Hope,
     LLA.
183 *Eternal Flight*: v. note, Introduction.
184 "The now-delicate subject..." Strauss had agreed to conduct a Berlin Philharmonic
     concert for which Walter had been announced. Nazi officials informed the concert
     committee that if Walter conducted "everything in the hall" would be "smashed to
     pieces;" but they refused to forbid the concert, since then the committee would

have been under no obligation to pay the musicians. The Nazis wanted a showdown
(v. Bruno Walter: *Theme and Variations*, Alfred A. Knopf, New York, 1946, p. 298).
185 Paul Ulanowsky, Aust. pianist, b. Vienna 1890, d. New York 1968. LL's regular
accompanist 1937-1951, also accompanied her master classes in New York and
Vienna.
186 Enid Szantho, Hung. contr., b. Budapest 1907. Vienna Op. 1928-39. Met. Op. 1938.
190 (Dame) Nellie Melba, Australian sop., b. Richmond nr. Melbourne 1861, d. Sydney
1931. Covent Garden 1888-1926, Met. Op. 1893-1910.
190 (Dame) Clara Butt, Eng. contr., b. Southwick, Sussex, 1873, d. Oxford 1936. Famous
concert singer. Sang Gluck's Orfeo at Covent Garden 1920.
191 Hans Knappertsbusch, Ger. cond., b. Elberfeld 1888, d. Munich 1965. Bavarian State
Op., Munich, 1922-36, 1954-65. Vienna Op. 1936-50.
191 Aulikki Rautawaara, Finn. sop., b. Helsinki 1906. The Library of Congress lists LL in
error as singing the Countess in the off-the-air recording of Walter's Salzburg
Figaro. It is clear from her letters that LL did *not* sing the Countess in Salzburg.
191 Maria Reining, Aust. sop., b. Vienna 1905 (1903?). Vienna Op. 1931-33, 1937-58.
Salzburg Fest. 1937-53. Chicago Op. 1938, New York City Op. 1949.
191 "'Chevalier'...more romantic..." Letters from LL to Constance Hope, LLA. Ltr. dtd.
8-22-37.
192 "You know, I sang _very_ well..." Ibid, dtd. 12-4-37.

Chapter XVI (pages 195–209)

195 Erich Kleiber, Aust. cond., b. Vienna 1890, d. Zurich 1956. Berlin State Op. 1923-31,
1933-35, Teatro Colón, Buenos Aires, 1939-45, Covent Garden 1950-53. Father of
Carlos Kleiber, distinguished conductor of the present time.
195 Hilde Konetzni, Aust. sop. (sister of Anny Konetzni, v. note, Chapter XIV, p. 158), b.
Vienna 1905, d. Vienna 1980. Deb. 1929, Chemnitz, as Sieglinde to her sister's
Brünnhilde. Deb. Vienna Op. 1936. Continued to sing in Vienna until shortly before
her death.
195 "Walter Legge's account": Elisabeth Schwarzkopf: *On and Off the Record, a
Memoir of Walter Legge*, Scribner, New York, 1982.
198 *Theme and Variations* (v. note to p.184, Chapter XV).
202 "That I lost a second homeland..." Ltr. dtd. 11-7-38, LL to Else (Mrs. Bruno) Walter,
LLA.
204 "I shall never forget her Evchen..." From an interview, recorded on tape, Jan. 1986.
209 "Eight performances in the New York house..." Compare with Flagstad's 29
performances that season.

Chapter XVII (pages 210–226)

216 Helen Traubel, Am. dramatic sop., b. St. Louis 1899, d. Santa Monica 1972. Met. Op.
1937-53. She left the Met when Gen. Manager Rudolf Bing forbade her to continue
singing in nightclubs.
216 Eleanor Steber, Am. sop., b. Wheeling, W. Virginia, 1916. Met. Op. 1940-61, 1966.
Bayreuth Elsa 1953.
218 Astrid Varnay, Sw.-Hung./Am. dramatic sop., b. Stockholm 1918. Met. Op. 1941-56,
1974-76, 1979 (sensational debut, aged 23, as Sieglinde, substituting for LL, first time
on any stage). Bayreuth 1951-67, leading sop. parts. Still active in opera (in 1987), now
in mezzo roles. Vocally and dramatically one of the greatest interpreters of Wagner
and Strauss.
220 Fabian Sevitzky, Russ./Am. cond., b. Vishny Volochok nr. Tver, Russia, 1891, d.
Athens, Greece, 1967. Indianapolis Symph. 1937-55.
220 Rose Bampton, Am. sop. who began her career as a mezzo-sop., b. Cleveland, Ohio,
1908. Met. Op. 1932-50. Covent Garden 1937; deb. Teatro Colón, Buenos Aires, 1942.
Sang Leonore in Toscanini's NBC broadcast and recording of *Fidelio*.
221 Dorothy Maynor, Am. sop., b. Norfolk, Virginia, 1910. Discovered by Serge

Koussevitzky while practicing for her first concert in 1939, she quickly became famous as a concert singer and recitalist.
221 Jarmila Novotná, Czech sop., b. Prague 1907. Deb. in *La traviata* at age 18, in Prague. Vienna Op. 1929, 1933-39. Met. Op. 1940-56. A very beautiful woman, she has appeared in several films and on Broadway as Offenbach's Helen of Troy.
221 Elena Gerhardt, Ger. mezzo-sop., b. Leipzig 1883, d. London 1961, internationally famous as a lieder singer.
224 "Plus two extras..." The last with Bruno Walter as accompanist.
225 Lorenzo Alvary, Hung./Am. bass-barit., b. Debrecen, Hungary, 1909. Deb. Budapest 1933, Met. Op. 1942.
225 Nadine Conner, Am. sop., b. Compton, Calif., 1913. Met. Op. 1941-60.
225 "Each time when..." *MML*, p. 259-260.

Chapter XVIII (p. 227-245)

228 "Dear, good Magda..." Ltrs. from LL to Magda Hansing (née Lohse), LLA. Ltr. dtd. 1-4-47.
228 "Everything you tell me..." Ibid., dtd. 4-22-47.
229 Lotte Lehmann: *More Than Singing*, Boosey & Hawkes, New York, 1945, reprinted by Greenwood, Westport Conn., 1975, Dover paperback 1985.
232 "Dear and honored Bruno..." Correspondence LL-Bruno Walter, LLA. Ltr. dtd. 8-15-47.
232 "I have heard from several sides..." Ibid., ltr. dtd. 12-23-47.
232 "Bruno Walter's answer..." Ltr. dtd. 12-28-47, Bruno Walter to LL, LLA.
233 *Carnegie Hall*, Federal/United Artists 1947.
233 "A real acting role..." Ltr. LL to BW, dtd. 12-23-47, LLA.
233 "Pasternak decided..." Joseph Pasternak, producer.
234 "I saw 'my' film..." Ltr. dtd. 4-16-48, LL to BW, LLA.
234 "*Heaven, Hell, and Hollywood* never found a publisher..." Except that some brief excerpts, with two of her illustrations, were printed in *Opera*, February 1968, p. 97-104.
235 "You have to see it..." Ltr. dtd. 11-20-46, LL to Frances Holden (in possession of Dr. Holden).
235 Lotte Lehmann: *My Many Lives*, Boosey & Hawkes, New York, 1948, reprinted by Greenwood, Westport, Conn., 1974.
237 "Thank heavens..." This and the following excerpts are from ltrs. dtd. betw. Feb. 21 and Mar. 11, 1949, LL to FH, in the possession of FH.
241 Ezio Pinza, It. bass, b. Rome 1892, d. Stamford, Conn., 1957. Met. Op. 1926-1948.
241 "*Tannhäuser* at the Met..." On 3-12-36, one of Pinza's very rare performances in German.
242 "to let him record the recital..." *Lotte Lehmann's Farewell Recital*, a Pembroke Record, New York, 1951, reissued (incomplete) by Pelican Records (P.O. Box 34732, Los Angeles, CA 90034), Pelican LP 2009, 1978...see discography.
245 "A private recording...available..." *Lotte Lehmann in Recital*, Acquitaine MS90420, 1977, missing *A nos morts*, (Acquitaine Records, 1121 Leslie Street, Don Mills, Ontario M3C 2J9)...see discography.

Chapter XIX (pages 246-259)

246 John Charles Thomas, Am. bar., b. Meyersdale, Virginia, 1891, d. Apple Valley, Calif., 1960. Met. Op. 1934-43. Was elected mayor of Apple Valley.
246 "The engagement...fell through..." Although Gregor Piatigorsky did offer occasional master classes in later years and accepted a position as advisor.
247 "Some madly rich people..." Mr. and Mrs. John Percival Jefferson.
247 "Secretary..." Miss Helen Marso.
249 "At the moment..." Ltr. dtd. 7-13-54, LL to BW, LLA.

252 Ganna Walska, Polish sop., b. 1882(?), d. Santa Barbara, Calif., 1984. Famous in the
     1920's and 30's for beauty and wealth —she was married to several very rich men,
     most notably Harold McCormick —and for her frustrated ambition to become a great
     opera singer.
252 Anna Russell, Eng./Canadian concert comedienne, b. London 1911, who has been
     called "the world's funniest woman."
253-256 LL's comments from notes taken by the author during master classes, 1957-59.
258 "She was kindness itself..." At the Piano—Ivor Newton, p. 179-181 (v. note, Chapter
     XII).

Chapter XX (pages 260-278)

261 "It would have been a painful experience..." From My Reunion in Vienna, talk
     delivered by LL in Santa Barbara and Los Angeles, MS in LLA.
265 Leonie Rysanek, Aust. sop., b. Vienna 1926. Deb. Innsbruck 1949, Bayreuth 1951, San
     Francisco 1956; Vienna Op. since 1955, Met. Op. since 1959.
266 "She is a charming young woman..." Ltr. dtd. 10-10-56, LL to Frances Holden.
266 Hilde Güden, Aust. sop., b. Vienna 1917. Deb. Zurich 1938, Salzburg Fest. 1946,
     Vienna Op. 1947; Met. Op. 1951-60.
266 Rita Streich, Ger. sop., b. Barnaul, Siberia, 1920, d. Vienna 1987. Deb. Aussig 1943,
     Berlin State Op. 1946, Vienna Op. 1954, Salzburg Fest. 1954, San Francisco Op.
     1957.
267 "And never mind the rhythm..." Ltr. dtd. 1-5-62, LL to BW, LLA.
267 "It should be a great consolation..." From an unidentified newspaper clipping in LL's
     collection, LLA.
269 "I have often thought...the dialogue in Fidelio...." Ltr. dtd. 8-24-61, LL to BW,
     LLA.
270 Régine Crespin, Fr. sop., b. Marseilles 1927. Deb. Mulhouse 1950, Paris Op. 1950,
     Bayreuth 1958, Met. Op. since 1962.
270 "Régine Crespin... a magnificent..." FO&RS, p. 200-202).
270 Rudolf Bing, Aust./Brit. opera impresario, b. Vienna 1902. Manager of Glyndebourne
     Fest. 1935-39 and 1946-49, helped organize the Edinburgh Fest. in 1947. Gen.
     manager of the Met. Op. 1950-72.
271 Hertha Töpper, Aust. mezzo-sop., b. Graz 1924. Bavarian State Op. deb. 1952, Met.
     Op. 1962-63.
273 "Three more books..." V. notes, Introduction.
273 Dietrich Fischer-Dieskau, phenomenally versatile Ger. bar., b. Berlin 1925. Opera deb.
     Berlin 1948, Salzburg 1956, Bayreuth 1957, Vienna 1957. One of the greatest and
     most-recorded lieder singers.
273 Elisabeth Schwarzkopf, Ger. sop., b. Jarotschin nr. Posen (now Poznán) 1915. Deb.
     Berlin 1938, Vienna Op. 1943, Covent Garden 1947, Met. Op. 1963. One of the
     greatest interpreters of Hugo Wolf lieder, Strauss and Mozart roles.
273 Hermann Prey, Ger. bar., b. Berlin 1929. Deb. Wiesbaden 1952, Hamburg 1953,
     Vienna 1956, Salzburg Fest. 1959, Met. Op. 1960, Bayreuth 1965. Famous lieder
     singer.
273 Gérard Souzay, Fr. bar., b. Angers 1918. Important recital and recording artist. Deb.
     Opéra Comique 1947, New York City Op. 1960, Paris Op. 1962, Met. Op. 1965, La
     Scala 1973.
275 "When LL, proudly erect..." Irving Kolodin: The Metropolitan Opera 1883-1966,
     Alfred A. Knopf, New York, 1966, p. 745.
275 "A book of tributes to her..." Wessling, v. note, Chapter VII, p. 55.

Index

294

Lotte Lehmann
Discography

by
GARY HICKLING

THIS CHRONOLOGICAL DISCOGRAPHY is designed to satisfy the needs of both the serious collector and casual listener. The alphabetical index on page 322 can help locate specific selections. The first section includes commercial recordings made on 78's. The discography's index number is followed by the name of the opera (upper case) or the name of the song. Then the aria, the composer and the recording date are listed. The next data are the matrix, followed by catalogue numbers and the lp releases. The numbers that follow "LP:" refer to the LP REFERENCE catalogue on page 329. When data are incomplete in a listing, look for underlined information in a previous one; this may be the composer, date, accompanying orchestra, conductor or pianist.

A word about original speeds of the 78's recorded before 1931: the well-known discographer William Moran has pointed out the fact that no written record was kept of the speeds used in early recordings. "A deviation in speed of 4 revolutions per minute (rpm) changes the pitch (and thus the key) by one-half tone. Not only is the pitch incorrect...but...the tone and quality of the voice are distorted," writes Mr. Moran in *Nellie Melba, A Contemporary Review*. Only the approximate range of speeds (78's vary from 72-87 rpm) can be offered. The careful listener should compare the recording against the published key. Even the speed of re-released lp's isn't always correct. With a variable-speed turntable, find the key of the selection and adjust with the help of a piano, pitch-pipe or organ to bring the recording to the correct pitch.

The second section contains non-commercial recordings, interviews, master classes, videotapes and films. The listing of these items must be considered limited by the date of this publication because new material constantly appears (much held at the Lotte Lehmann Archive at UCSB.)

This discography is based on that of Floris Juynboll which appeared in the March 1985 *Stimmen die um die Welt gingen* magazine. The Lehmann discography by H. P. Court, updated by Clyde Key, was also helpful. Many thanks to the others who helped: William Moran, who gave me basic instruction and format advice as well as data; R. Peter Munves of CBS; Edwin Matthias of the Library of Congress; Robert Kenselaar of the Rodgers & Hammerstein Archive; Elisa Schokoff of the Museum of Broadcasting; Jerry Minkoff, Alan Kelly, researchers; Joseph Pearce and Harold Huber, private collectors; Manfred Miethe for the German proof reading; Katsuumi Niwa, Frank Manhold, and Paul Glassmann; Dixon Smith, computer aid; and Frances Holden, Dan Jacobson, Martin Silver, and Christian Brun in Santa Barbara.

Unless otherwise stated, all entries are sung in German. In the non-commercial section, speaking is in English. The location of unique items not held by the University of California at Santa Barbara, (if not 78's, then as lp's or tapes), will be evident in the listing. Remember to refer to previously listed underlined composers, dates, conductors or orchestras for these details when they are omitted from a listing.

COMMERCIAL   RECORDINGS

PATHÉ
Two acoustic, single-sided, center-start, etched- label discs made in Berlin in <u>1914</u>, possibly 87 rpm, 11 1/2", entitled "Lotte Lehmann, Stadt-theater Hamburg." No orchestra or conductor is known. The matrix is followed by catalogue numbers and the lp reference.

001 LOHENGRIN: *Einsam in trüben Tagen* (<u>Wagner</u>); 55978; 42048, (14): RA-1110; coupling 5844; LP: 54.
002 LOHENGRIN: *Euch Lüften, die mein Klagen*; 55979; 42048, (14): RA-1008; coupling 5844; LP: 54.

GRAMMOPHON
Approved for registration or issue from December 1916 to early 1921, the individual dating is only approximate. The rpm vary from 78-80. These acoustic recordings also appeared on Polydor and, where noted, Vocalion. Orchestras and conductors aren't known. The matrix is followed by three catalogue numbers: 1) 12" single-sided, which begin with 76, or 12" double-sided, which begin with 72; 2) 10" single-sided, which begin with 74, or 10" double-sided which begin with 70 or 80; and 3) the international catalogue number.

003 TANNHÄUSER: *Dich teure Halle* (<u>Wagner</u>); <u>1916</u>; 1101 m; 76353; 72902; 043294; Voc. B 35045; LP: 54, 66, 74.
004 TANNHÄUSER: *Allmächt'ge Jungfrau*; 1102 m; 76354; 72902; 043295; LP: 54, 65, 66.
005 LOHENGRIN: *Du Ärmste kannst wohl nie ermessen*; 1103 m; 76355; 72903; 043296; LP: 19, 54, 65, 66, 68.
006 (?) CARMEN: *Ich sprach, dass ich furchtlos mich fühle* (Bizet); 1104 m unpublished.
007 (?) DER FREISCHÜTZ: *Wie nahte mir der Schlummer* (Weber); 1105 m unpublished.
008 DER FREISCHÜTZ: *Alles pflegt schon längst der Ruh'* (Weber); 1106 m; 76356; 72904; 043297; LP: 45, 54, 64.
009 DIE MEISTERSINGER: *Guten Abend, Meister* (<u>Wagner</u>); w/Michael Bohnen; 1107 m; 76357; 85305; 044299; LP: 19, 48, 54, 65, 66, 68.
010 DIE MEISTERSINGER: *Doch starb eure Frau* ; 1108 m; 76364; 85305; 044306; w/Bohnen; LP: see 009.
011 FAUST: *Es war ein König in Thule* (Gounod); 1109 m; 76368; 72905; 043309; LP: 54.
012 FAUST: *Er liebt mich* (Gounod); 19037 L; 74607; 70694; 2-43540; LP: 54, 66.
013 FAUST: *Auf eilet* (Trio) (Gounod); 19038 L; 74596; 80079; 3-44159; with Robert Hutt & Bohnen; LP: 49, 54, 66.

014 LA BOHEME: *Man nennt mich jetzt Mimi* (Puccini); <u>1920-1921?</u>; 1220 m; 76402; 72907; 043338; LP: 53.

015 EUGEN ONEGIN: *Ich schrieb' an sie* (Tchaikovsky); 1221 1/2 m; 76369; 72906; 043310; LP: 52, 66.

016 MIGNON: *Kennst du das Land* (Thomas); 1223 m; 76403; 72907; 043339; LP: 53, 74.

017 MADAME BUTTERFLY: *Eines Tages sehen wir* (Puccini); 1224 m; 76411; 72909; 043355; LP: 53, 66.

018 FIGAROS HOCHZEIT: *Heil'ge Quelle* (<u>Mozart</u>); 1225 m; 76414; 72910; 043363; LP: 52, 65, 66.

019 FIGAROS HOCHZEIT: *O säume länger nicht*; 1226 m; 76477; 72910; (043333); B 24072; LP: 52, 66, 65.

020 CARMEN: *Ich sprach, dass ich furchtlos...* (Bizet); 1227 m; 76478; 72914; (043308); B 24073; LP: 52, 65.

021 MIGNON: *Dort bei ihm ist sie jetzt* (Thomas); 1228 m; 76413; 72909; 043362; LP: 53.

022 DER FREISCHÜTZ: *Wie nahte mir der Schlummer* (Weber); 1229 m; 76482; 72904; (043307); B 24088; LP: 45, 54, 64.

023 MADAME BUTTERFLY: *Über das Meer* (Puccini); 19184 L; 74604; 70693; 2-43529; LP: 53, 66.

024 MANON: *Nützet die schönen, jungen Tage* (Massenet); 19185 1/2 L; 74598; 70693; 2-43525; LP: 53, 66.

025 DIE WALKÜRE: *Du bist der Lenz* (Wagner); 19186 L; 74597; 70692; 2-43524; LP: 54.

026 OBERON: *Ozean, du Ungeheuer* (Part 1) (<u>Weber</u>); <u>1922?</u>; 1377 m; 76455; 72913; B 24036; LP: 52, 64, 66.

027 OBERON: *Ozean, du Ungeheuer* (Part 2); 1378 m; 76456; 72913; B 24037; LP: 52, 64, 66.

028 DER WIDERSPENSTIGEN ZÄHMUNG: *Es schweige die Klage* (Götz); 1380 m; 76483; 72914; B 24089; LP: 52, 64, 66.

029 DIE LUSTIGEN WEIBER VON WINDSOR: *Nun eilt herbei* (<u>Nicolai</u>); 1381 m; 76421; 72911; B 24011; LP: 53.

030 DIE LUSTIGEN WEIBER VON WINDSOR: *Ha, er wird mir glauben*; (Part 2); 1382 m; 76422; 72911; B 24012; LP: 53.

031 UNDINE: *So wisse, dass in allen...* (<u>Lortzing</u>); 1383 m; 76484; 72915; B 24090; LP: 52, 64.

032 UNDINE: *Doch kann auf Erden*; (Part 2); 1384 m; 76485; 72915; B 24091; LP: 52, 64.

033 DIE TOTEN AUGEN: *Psyché wandelt...* (D'Albert); 19259 L; 74608; 70692; B 4000; LP: 54, 65.

034 SCHWESTER ANGELICA: *Ohne Mutter* (Puccini); <u>1920?</u>; 150 ap; 76405; 72908; 043346; LP: 52, 64.

035 SCHWESTER ANGELICA: *O Blumen, die ihr Gift* (Puccini); 151 ap; 76406; 72908; 043347; LP: 52, 64.

036 FIGAROS HOCHZEIT: *So lang' hab' ich* (Mozart); 152 ap; 76412; 72933; 044328; with Heinrich Schlusnus; LP: 53, 65, 66

037 DIE ZAUBERFLÖTE: *Bei Männern...* (Mozart); 153 ap; 76415; 72932; 044330; with Schlusnus; LP: 53.

038 MIGNON: *Ihr Schwalben* (Thomas); with Schlusnus; 154 ap; 76409; 72932; 044326; LP: 53, 65.

039 DON GIOVANNI: *Reich' mir die Hand...* (Mozart); with Schlusnus; 155 ap; 76410; 72933; 044327; LP: 53, 65, 66.

040 DIE MEISTERSINGER: *O Sachs, mein Freund* (<u>Wagner</u>); <u>1923?</u>; 416 as; 76486; 72903; B 24092; LP: 54, 65, 66.

041 DIE WALKÜRE: *Der Männer Sippe*; 417 1/2 as; 76487; 72906; B 24093; LP: 54, 66, 74.

042 DER FREISCHÜTZ: *Und ob die Wolke* (Weber); 418 as; 76488; 72916; B 24094; LP: 52, 65, 66.

043 HOFFMANNS ERZÄHLUNGEN: *Sie entfloh'* (Offenbach); <u>1921</u>; 419 as; 76489; 72916; B 24095; LP: 52, 65, 66.

044 *Cäcilie* (R. Strauss); 420 as; 76454; 72912; B 24029; Voc. B 35045; LP: 53, 63.

045 *Morgen* (R. Strauss); 421 as; 76490; 72917; B 24096; LP: 54.

046 *Der Spielmann* (Hildach); 530 as; 76453; 72912; B 24028; LP: 53.

047 DIE JÜDIN: *Er kommt zurück* (Halevy); 531 as; 76464; 72905; B 24045; LP: 52, 66.

048 FIGAROS HOCHZEIT: *Ihr, die ihr Triebe* (Mozart); 1121 ar; 70694; B 4010; LP: 53, 66.

ODEON

Acoustic recordings made from 1924-1925. The matrix is followed by the single-sided, then the double-sided catalogue numbers. The rpm's vary from 72-80.

049 MANON: *Nützet die schönen...*(Massenet); 13 Feb. '24; xxB 6945; Lxx 80934; 0-9510; conductor Dr. Carl Besl; LP: 51.

050 TOSCA: *Nur der Schönheit...*(Puccini); xxB 6946; Lxx 80935; 0-9511; LP: 24, 51.

051 LA BOHEME: *Man nennt mich jetzt Mimi* (Puccini); xxB 6947; Lxx 80933; 0-9502; LP: 51, 64.

052 MANON LESCAUT: *Ach, in diesen kalten...*; xxB 6948; Lxx 80936; 0-9503; LP: 68.

053 MADAME BUTTERFLY: *Eines Tages...* (Puccini); xxB 6949; Lxx 80937; 0-9503; LP: 51.

054 *Wiegenlied* (R. Strauss); date ?; accompaniment ?; xxB 6950 unpublished.

055 *Freundliche Vision* (R. Strauss); date ?; accompaniment ?; xxB 6051 unpublished.

056 MANON: *'s ist für ihn...Leb' wohl...*(Massenet); 18 Feb. '24; xxB 6952; Lxx 80938; 0-9510; conductor: Besl; LP: 19, 51, 68.

057 TANNHÄUSER: *Dich teure Halle* (Wagner); xxB 6953; Lxx 80939; 0-9504; LP: none.

058 DIE WALKÜRE: *Du bist der Lenz;* xxB 6954; Lxx 80940; 0-9504; c. Besl; LP: 64(?), 74.

059 TANNHÄUSER: *Allmächt'ge Jungfrau;* 24 Mar. '24; xxB 6972; Lxx 80947; 0-9509; c. George Szell; LP: 51, 74.

060 OTHELLO: *Sie sass mit Leide...*(Verdi); xxB 6973; Lxx 80955; 0-9511; LP: 51, 64.

061 LOHENGRIN: *Euch Lüften...*(Wagner); xxB 6974; Lxx 80979; 0-9509; c. Szell; LP: 51.

062 DIE TOTE STADT: *Glück, das mir verblieb;* 17 Apr. '24; xxB 6993 (later as electric); Lxx 80944; 0-9507; take 1 also used; c. Szell; with Richard Tauber; many 78 rpm re-issues--see 201; LP: 17, 20, 40, 67.

063 DIE TOTE STADT: *Der Erste, der Lieb'* (Korngold); xxB 6994 (takes 1, 2 & 4 may have been used!); Lxx 80945; 0-9502; c. Szell; w/ high C; LP: 17, 19, 51, 64, 68, 84.

063.1 *Morgen* (R. Strauss); 17 Oct. '25?; accomp. ?; xxB 7432 unpublished.

063.2 *Mit deinen blauen Augen* (R. Strauss); date ?; accomp. ?; xxB 7433 unpublished.

063.3 *Allerseelen* (R. Strauss); date ?; accompaniment ?; xxB 7434 unpublished.

063.4 a)*Zueignung* b)*Cäcilie* (R. Strauss); date ?; accomp. ?; xxB 7435 unpublished.

063.5 *Aufträge* (Schumann); date ?; accomp. ?; xxB 7436 unpublished.

064 DER FREISCHÜTZ: *Wie nahte mir...*(Weber); 17 Oct. '25; xxB 7239; Lxx 81100; 0-9516; c. Hermann Weigert; LP: see 65.

065 DER FREISCHÜTZ: *Alles pflegt schon längst der Ruh'* (Weber); xxB 7240; Lxx 81101 (take 2 also used); 0-9516; LP: 19, 68, 74.

066 DIE MEISTERSINGER: *O Sachs, mein Freund* (Wagner); xxB 7241; 0-9518; LP: 51, 68.

067 LOHENGRIN: *Einsam in trüben Tagen* (Wagner); xxB 7243; 0-9518; LP: 17, 20, 51.

068 DER ROSENKAVALIER: *Kann mich auch* (R. Strauss); xxB 7244; Lxx 81103; 0-9517; LP: 51, 68.

069 MIGNON: *Kennst du das Land* (Thomas); 22 Oct. '25; xxB 7250; Lxx 80997; 0-9515; LP: 51.

070 MADAME BUTTERFLY: *Über das Meer...*(Puccini); with chorus; xxB 7251-2; Lxx 81102 (also take 1); 0-9517; w/high Db at the end; LP: 51.

071 FAUST: *Es war ein König in Thule* (Gounod); xxB 7252; Lxx 80998; 0-9515; LP: 51.

072 *Stille Nacht* (Gruber); 22 Oct. '25; xxB 7253; Rxx 80600; 0-8540 (later); LP: none.

073 *O du Fröhliche* (traditional); 22 Oct. '25; xxB 7254-2; Rxx 80601; 0-8540 (later); LP: none.

074 a)*Da unten im Tale* b)*Gute Nacht* (Brahms); date ?; accomp. ?; xxB 7255 unpublished.

ODEON (Electric)

1926-1933. The first number is the matrix "xxB" for 12" and "Be" for 10", this is followed by the catalogue number. Thereafter: 1) Parlophone (R) 2) American Columbia 3) American Decca 4) French Odeon 5) Austrian Odeon 6) Italian 7) Argentinian 8)Australian (n.b.) Parlophone (AR). If a number, followed by a bracket, does not appear, it means that no release under that label is known. The speed continues to vary from 75 to 80 rpm. The "Berlin State Opera Orchestra" often means members of that group. These ensembles in general often received varying titles.

075 a)*Monatsrose* b) *Wilde Rose* (Eulenburg); 31 Aug. '26; xxB 7477; 0-8703; 3)25800; with Mischa Spoliansky, piano and Dajos Bela, violin; LP: none.

076 *Weisse und rote Rose* (Eulenburg); xxB 7478; 0-8703; 3)25800; p. Spoliansky; LP: none.
077 a) *Rankende Rose* b) *Seerose* (Eulenburg); 31 Aug. '26; xxB 7479; 0-8704; 3)25801; LP: none.
078 *Der Nussbaum* (Schumann); date ?; accomp. ?; xxB 7480 unpublished.
079 No entry.
080 *Heidenröslein* (Werner); xxB 7481; 0-8704; 3)25801; p. Spoliansky, v. Bela; LP: none.
081 TURANDOT: *In diesem Schlosse...*(Puccini); 16 Feb. '27; xxB 7609; 0-9602 (later 0-8720);
    1)RO 20014; 4)123.601; c. Fritz Zweig ; Berlin-Charlottenburg Opera Orchestra; LP: 20.
082 TURANDOT: *Die ersten Tränen*; xxB 7610; other data 081; first version w/high C; LP: 50, 68.
083 OBERON: *Ozean, du Ungeheuer* (Weber); xxB 7611-2; 0-8742; 1)20024; 2)9055 (take 1);
    3)29014; LP: 17, 20, 50, 64.
084 OBERON: *Ozean, du Ungeheuer* (Part 2) (Weber); xxB 7612 other data see 083.
085 ANDREA CHENIER: *Von Blut gerötet...*(Giordano); xxB 7613; not published in Germany;
    1)RO 20025; LP: 68, 70.
086 JOCELYN: *Ach war es nicht... Am stillen* (Godard); 18 Feb. '27; xxB 7618-2; 0-8709; 1)20019;
    c. Zweig; Berlin State Opera Orchestra; LP: 68, 70
087 *O lass dich halten, gold'ne Stunde* (Jensen); xxB 7619; 0-8709; 1)20019; LP: none.
088 *Murmelndes Lüftchen*; xxB 7620-2; not published in Germany; 1)20025; LP: none.
089 *Auf Flügeln des Gesanges* (Mendelssohn); xxB 7621; 0-8713; 1)20013; 2)9059; 3)25806;
    4)123.622; 5)177.056; Odeon E 5136; LP: none.
090 *Von ewiger Liebe* (Brahms); xxB 7622; 0-8713 (later 0-8763); 1)20013; 2)9059; 3)25806;
    4)123.622; 7)177.056; Odeon E 5136; LP: 23.
091 *An die Musik* (Schubert); 6 Dec. '27; xxB 7873; 0-8724 (later 0-8763); 1)20051; 2)9073 (later
    50170); 3)25798; 8)1019; Manfred Gurlitt conducting a chamber orch.; LP: 68.
092 *Ave Maria*; xxB 7874; 0-8719; 1)20050; 3)25797; 7)177.042; 8)1009; LP: none.
093 *Du bist die Ruh'* (first version); xxB 7875; 0-8724; 1)20051 3)25798; 8)1010; LP: none.
094 *Der Tod und das Mädchen*; Be 6397; 0-4800; 1)20061; 3)20281; LP: 50, 68.
095 *Sei mir gegrüsst* ; 8 Dec. '27; xxB 7876; 0-8725; 1)20052; 2)9073 (later 50170); 3)25799; 8)1019;
    LP: 25
096 *Auf dem Wasser zu singen* (Schubert); 8 Dec. '27; xxB 7877; 0-8725; 1)20052; 2)9073; 3)25799;
    8)1010; LP: 25.
097 *Der Lenz* (Hildach); 9 Dec. '27; xxB 7878-2; 0-8727; 2)9054; 3)25802; ch. orch.; c. Gurlitt; LP:—.
098 *Der Spielmann* (Hildach); xxB 7879; 0-8727; 2)9054; 3)25802; ch. orch.; c. Gurlitt.; LP: none.
099 *Ständchen* (Leise flehen...) (Schubert); xxB 7880; 0-8719; 1)20050; 3)25797; 7)177.042; 8)1009;
    LP: 50.
100 *Geheimes* (Schubert); 9 Dec. '27; Be 6400; 0-4800; 1)RO 20061; 3)20281; LP: 25.
101 TOSCA: *Qual' occhio al mondo* (It.) (Puccini); 10 Dec. '27; xxB 7881-2; 0-8743 (also with take 1)
    (later 0-9603); Lxx 9603; 1)20048; 3)29016 (take 1 [black label pressing a dubbing]); 8)1054; with
    Jan Kiepura; Berlin State Opera Orchestra; c. Manfred Gurlitt; LP: 20.
102 TOSCA: *Amaro sol per te* (It.) (Puccini); 10 Dec. '27; xxB 7882-2; other data 101; LP: 68.
103 FIDELIO: *Komm' Hoffnung* (Beethoven); 13 Dec. '27; xxB 7885; 0-8721; 1)20053 (later PXO
    1013), Austrian Parl. BX 601; 3)25803; 4)123.603; 8)1026; LP: 1, 15, 17, 20, 41, 42, 74.
104 FIDELIO: *Komm' Hoffnung* (Part 2); 13 Dec. '27; xxB 7886 all other data see 103.
105 DER ROSENKAVALIER: *O sei ein gut...Die Zeit, die ist..;* (R. Strauss); xxB 7887-1-2; 0-8726;
    1)20054; 8)1022 & (later) PXO 1014 (take 2); 3)25817 (take 1); LP: 16, 46, 68.
106 FIGAROS HOCHZEIT: *Heil'ge Quelle* (Mozart); xxB 7888-1-2; 0-8726; 1)20054; 8)1022 &
    (later) PXO 1014 (take 1); 3)25817 (take 2); LP: 16, 20, 50, 74.
107 DAS WUNDER DER HELIANE: *Ich ging...*(Korngold); 13 Mar. '28; xxB 7997-2; 0-8722;
    3)25805 & 28805; LP: 1, 20.
108 DAS WUNDER DER HELIANE: *Ich ging* (Part 2); xxB 7998-2; all other data see 107.
109 EVA: *So war meine Mutter... Wär es nichts* (Lehar); 28 Aug. '28; recit. & aria; xxB 8150;
    0-8730; 1)20275; o & c see 110; LP: 64
110 *Wenn dein ich denk* (Zauberlied) (Meyer-Helmund); xxB 8151; 0-8730; 1)20275; 2)9082;
    c. Weissmann; Berlin State Opera Orchestra; LP: none.
111 ARIADNE AUF NAXOS: *In den schönen* (Part 2); (R. Strauss); 4 Sep. '28; xxB 8168; 0-8731;
    1)20147; 3)25816; Odeon R 20147; LP: 1, 17, 20 (*Es gibt ein Reich*), 46, 69.
112 ARIADNE AUF NAXOS: *Es gibt ein Reich*;(Part 1); xxB 8169-1-2; 0-8731 (take 1 [*Sie lebt
    hier ganz allein])* 1)20147 & 3)25816 (take 2 [*Sie atmet leich*]); other data see 111.

Recorded 3-7 Sep. '28 with string and piano accompaniment.

113 *Ave Maria* (sung in German) (Bach-Gounod); Be 7174-2; 0-4802; 1)RO 20076; 3)20277; 4)188.651; 6)15005; 8)120; LP: none.

114 XERXES: *Largo* (in German) (Handel); Be 7175-2; 0-4802; 1)R0 20076; 3)20277; 4)188.651; 6)15005(?); 8)120; LP: none.

115 *Eine kleine Liebelei* (Ralton); Be 7176; 0-4801; string quartet; LP: none.

116 *Frühling ist es wieder* (Engel-Berger); Be 7177; 0-4801; string quartet; LP: none.

117 *Der Nussbaum* (Schumann); 7 Sep. '28; Be 7178; 0-4821; 1)RO 20071; 2)4065; 3)20375; with piano; LP: 5, 50, 68.

118 *Mit deinen blauen Augen* (R. Strauss); Be 7189; 0-4846; 1)RO 20081; 3)20339; 8)128; w/piano & violin; LP: none.

119 a)*Aufträge* (Schumann); Be 7184-2; 0-4821; 1)RO20071; 2)4065; 3)20375; with piano; b)*Heimkehr vom Fest* (Blech) recorded on this same matrix? (unpublished); LP: a) 5, 22.

120 *Zur Drossel sprach der Fink* (D'Albert); Be 7185; 0-4823; with chamber orchestra; LP: 50.

121 *Ach, wer das doch könnte* (Berger); Be 7186-2; 0-4823; 1)RO 20263; ch. orch.; LP:none.

122 *O du Fröhliche* (trad.); Be 7187; 0-4810; 1)RO 20098; 3)23052; ch. orch.; LP:none.

123 *Stille Nacht, heilige Nacht* (Gruber); Be 7188; 0-4810; 1)RO 20098; 3)23052; ch. orch.; LP:none.

124 *Morgen* (R. Strauss); with piano & violin; Be 7183; 0-4846; 1)RO 20081; 3)20339; 8)128; LP: 68.

125 *Seit ich ihn geseh'n* (Schumann); 13 Nov. '28; Be 7601; 0-4806; 1)RO 20090; 2)4070; 3)20411; 4)188.785; 6)15013; 7)196.274; 8)143; 125-131 are Frauenliebe und Leben w/strings and piano led by Frieder Weissmann; LP: 5.

126 *Er, der Herrlichste von Allen* (Schumann); Be 7602; 0-4806; other data see 125.

127 *Ich kann's nicht fassen*; Be 7603; 0-4807; 1)RO 20091; 2)4071; 3)20412; 4)188.786; 6)15014; 7)196.275; 8)144; other data see 125.

128 *Du Ring an meinem Finger* (Schumann); 13 Nov. '28; Be 7604; other data see 127.

129 *Helft mir, ihr Schwestern*; Be 7605; 0-4808; 1)RO 20092; 2)4072; 3)20413; 4)188.787; 6)15015; 7)196.276; 8)145; other data see 125.

130 *Süsser Freund* (Schumann); 13 Nov. '28; Be 7606; other data see 129.

131 *An meinem Herzen* (Schumann); 13 Nov. '28; Be 7607; 0-4809; 1)RO 20093; 2)4073; 3)20414; 4)188.788; 6)15016; 7)196.277; 8)146; other data see 125.

132 *Nun hast du mir den ersten Schmerz...* (Schumann); Be 7608; other data see 131.

133 *Halleluja* (Hummel); 4 Dec. '28; xxB 8220; 0-8733; 1)20265; with organ; LP: none.

134 *Wo du hingehst* (from Trauungsgesang) (Rössel); xxB 8221-2; 0-8733; 1)20265; w/organ; LP:—.

135 DIE FLEDERMAUS: *Herr Chevalier...* (Joh. Strauss); 15 Dec. '28; take 2 on 26 Feb. '29; xxB 8266-1-2; 0-8734 (both takes); 1)20085 (take 2) later PXO 1032; 2)9078, Am. Odeon 3268 & 3)29015 (all take 1); 4) 123. 018 (take 2); 7)177.217; 8)1029; with Richard Tauber, Karin Branzell, Grete Merrem-Nikisch, Waldemar Stägemann; c. Frieder Weissmann; unknown orch.; LP: 16, 17, 41.

136 DIE FLEDERMAUS: *Genug damit...* (Part 2); (Joh. Strauss); 26 Feb. '29; xxB 8267-2; 0-8734; other data see 135.

137 DER ZIGEUNERBARON: *Ein Fürstenkind* ; 15 Dec. '28; take 2 on 26 Feb. '29; xxB 8268-2; 0-8735; 1)20104 (later PXO 1034); 2)9079; 3)29013; 8)1035; o & c, cast as 135 plus Hans Lange; LP: none.

138 DER ZIGEUNERBARON: *Er ist Baron*; 15 Dec. '28; xxB 8269-1; other data see 137.

139 *O Haupt voll Blut und Wunden* (Bach); 28 Feb. '29; Be 8038; 0-4811; 1)RO 20215; 3)20336; 8)220; organ; LP: none.

140 *Christi Mutter stand in Schmerzen* (trad.); Be 8039; 0-4811; all other data see 139.

141 *Geleitet durch die Welle* (Marienlied); Be 8040; 0-4803; 1)RO 20205; 3)20337; w/organ; LP: —.

142 *Es blüht der Blumen eine*; Be 8041; 0-4803; 1)RO 20205; 3)20337; with organ; LP: none.

143 DER FREISCHÜTZ: *Wie nahte mir...* (Weber); 26 Feb. '29; xxB 8305; 0-8741; 1)20087 (later PXO 1016); 2)9060; 3)29007; 0-6950, 0-3286; Am. Odeon 3286; Berlin State Opera Orchestra; c. Manfred Gurlitt; xxB 8564-0 (Leise, leise.. only); LP: 1, 16, 20, 74.

144 DER FREISCHÜTZ: *Alles pflegt schon...* (Weber); xxB 8306; other data see 143.

145 *Es gibt eine Frau...* (Cowler); Be 8143; 0-4805; Berlin State Opera Orch.; c. Gurlitt; LP: none.

146 *Der Duft, der eine schöne Frau...* (May); Be 8144; 0-4804; LP: none.

147 *Wenn du einmal dein Herz...* (Rosen); 26 Mar. '29; Be 8145; 0-4804; 4)188.728; LP: none.

148 DIE LUSTIGE WITWE: *Ich hol' dir...* (Lehar); Be 8146; 0-4805; LP: none.

149 TOSCA: *Nur der Schönheit* (Puccini); 16 Apr. '29; xxB 8321-3; 0-8736; 1)20095; 3)25804; Berlin State Opera Orchestra; c. Weissmann; LP: 20, 26, 68, 70.

150 LA BOHEME: *Man nennt mich jetzt Mimi* (Puccini); xxB 8322-2; 0-8736; 1)20095; 3)25804; LP: 19, 50, 68.

151 *Schmerzen* (Wagner); 21 Jun. '29; Be 8299-2; 0-4812; 1)RO 20100; 2)4059; 3)20284; 8)130; LP: 20, 70.

152 *Träume;* o & c see 149; Be 8300-2; 0-4812; 1)RO 20100; 3)20284; 8)130; LP: 20, 70.

153 *Widmung* (Schumann); 22 Jun. '29; Be 8301-2; 0-4824; 1) 20102; 2)4059; 3)20376; 8)132; LP: 5.

154 *Du bist wie eine Blume;* Be 8302; 0-4824; 1)RO 20102; 3)20376; 8)132; LP: 5

155 *Traum durch die Dämmerung* (R. Strauss); Be 8303; 0-4820; 1)RO 20096; 3)20340; 8)129; o & c see 149; LP: none.

156 *Ständchen;* Be 8304; 0-4820; 1)RO 20096; 3)20340; 8)129; o & c see 149; LP: none.

157 *O heil'ger Geist...* (Bach); 8 Mar. '30; Be 8590; 0-4814; 1)RO 20320; 2)4062; 3)20334; Mania, organ; LP: none.

158 *Aus tiefer Not* (Bach); 8 Mar. '30; Be 8591; 0-4815; 1)RO 20309; 2)4057; 3)20333; LP: none.

159 *Ach, bleib' mit deiner Gnade;* Be 8592; 0-4815; 1)RO 20309; 2)4062; 3)20333; LP: none.

160 *Jesus, meine Zuversicht* (Bach); Be 8593; 0-4816; 2)4057; Mania, organ; LP: none.

161 *Wir glauben all' an einen Gott* (Bach); Be 8594; 0-4816; 1)RO 20320; 3)20335; LP: none.

162 *Bist du bei mir* (Bach, now attr. Stölzel); Be 8595-2; 0-4814; 1)RO 20292; 2)4062; 3)20334; Mania, organ; LP: none.

163 *Andachtsstunde* (Ketelby); 21 Feb. '30; Be 8876-2; 0-4818; 3)23058; o & c 149; chorus; organ, Römer; LP: none.

164 *Heiligtum des Herzens;* Be 8877-2; 0-4818; 1)RO 20166; 3)23058; other data see 163.

165 *Es ritten drei Reiter* (trad. folksong); Be 8878; 0-4817; 1)RO 20166; 3)20278; c. Weissmann; Berlin State Opera Orchestra; chorus; LP: none.

166 *Der rote Sarafan* (Russian folksong arr. Römer); Be 8879; 0-4822; male chorus; LP: none.

167 *Es stiess ein Jäger* (folksong arr. Römer); 21 Feb. '30; Be 8880; 0-4817; 3)20278; chorus; LP: —.

168 *Es waren zwei Königskinder* (folksong-Römer); Be 8881; 0-4822; chorus; LP: none.

169 TANNHÄUSER: *Dich teure Halle* (Wagner); 21 Feb. '30; Be 8882; 0-4813; 1)RO 20139 (later PO 156); 2)4063; 3)20283; 5)B 502; LP: 17, 15, 20, 42, 70, 74 & LV 10.

170 TANNHÄUSER: *Allmächt'ge Jungfrau;* Be 8883 other data see 169; LP: 15, 68, 74.

171 LOHENGRIN: *Euch Lüften...;* Be 8884; 0-4819; 1)RO 20113 (later PO 152); 2)4066; 3)20282; 5)B 503; 8)139; o & c see 149; LP: 17, 15, 70.

172 LOHENGRIN: *Einsam in trüben Tagen* (Wagner); Be 8885 other data see 171; LP: 15, 42.

173 *Ich grolle nicht* (Schumann); 17 Jun. '30; Be 9044; 0-4825; 1)RO 20185; 2)4092; 3)20378; instrumental trio directed by Weissmann; LP: 5.

174 *Der Erlkönig* (Schubert); Be 9045; 0-4825; 1) 20292; 2)4092; 6)15005; p. Weissmann; LP: 2, 42.

175 FAUST: *Es war ein König...* (Gounod); 18 Jun. '30; xxB 8494; 0-8747; 1)20137; 2)9082; Hungary: NM 7060; o & c 165 LP: 68

176 MIGNON: *Kennst du das Land* (Thomas); xxB 8495; all other data see 175; LP: 68, 73.

177 a)DIE WALKÜRE: *Du bist der Lenz* b)TRISTAN UND ISOLDE: *Mild und leise* (first half of *Liebestod*) (Wagner); xxB 8497; 0-8745; 1)20122; 2)9049; 3)25807; 8)1045; Odeon 177216; o & c see 165; LP: a)68, 74.

178 TRISTAN UND ISOLDE: *Seht ihr's nicht;* (Part 2); xxB 8498; 0-8745; other data see 177; LP: 177 b) & 178: 1, 17, 20, 74, (& Seraphim 60274?).

179 *Ein feste Burg* (Luther, Bach); 23 May '31; Be 9488; 0-4828; 1)RO 20368; 3)20338; male chorus and organ conducted by Weissmann; LP: none.

180 *Ich bete an die Macht der Liebe* (Russian trad.); Be 9489-2; 0-4828; other data see 179; arr. Bortniansky; LP: none.

181 *Die Mainacht* (Brahms); Be 9490; 0-4829 (later 0-4847); 1)RO 20159; 2)4094; 3)20285; xxRek 22-0; trio directed by Weissmann; LP: 68;

182 *Wiegenlied* (Schlaf Herzenssöhnchen) (Weber); 23 May '31; Be 9491-2; 0-4838; 1)RO 20185; 3)20378; LP: none.

183 *'s Zuschau'n* (Bavarian folksong) (Böhm); Be 9492; 0-4838; trio dir. by Weissmann; LP: none.

184 MIGNON: *Dort bei ihm ist sie* (Thomas); 26 May '31; Be 9493; 0-4826; 1)RO 20174; o & c see 165; LP: 68.

185 MIGNON: *Kam ein armes Kind;* Be 9494; 0-4826; 1)RO 20174; o & c see 165; LP: 20, 70.

186 DIE FLEDERMAUS: *Klänge der Heimat* (Joh. Strauss); Be 9495-2; 0-4831; 1)RO 20171 (later

PO 163); 2)4101; 3)20280; 5)B 504; date, o & c see 165; LP: 16, 42.
187 DIE FLEDERMAUS: *Mein Herr...*(Joh. Strauss); 26 May '31; Be 9496 other data see 186;
　　LP: 1, 16, 68, 71.
188 *Vergebliches Ständchen* (Brahms); 26 May '31; Be 9497; 0-4829; 1)RO 20159; 2)4090; 3)20285;
　　with instrumental trio (c. Weissmann?); (w/added instrumental introduction); LP: 50.

Recorded on 23, 25, 26 and 28 Apr. '32; Gurlitt cond. Berlin State Opera Orchestra (or members).

189 DIE ZAUBERFLÖTE: *Ach, ich fühl's* (Mozart); Be 9905; 0-4832 (later 0-4851); 1)RO 20194
　　(later PO 157); 3)20279; 8)194; LP: 15, 20, 50.
190 DIE LUSTIGEN WEIBER VON WINDSOR: *Nun eilt herbei* (Nicolai); 23 April '32; Be 9906;
　　0-4833;1)RO 20303; 3)23025; LP: 1, 17, 20, 42, 74.
191 DIE LUSTIGEN WEIBER...; *Ha, er wird mir glauben*; Be 9907 other data see 190.
192 MADAME BUTTERFLY: *Über das Meer* (Puccini); 23 Aprl '32; Be 9908; 0-4832 (later 0-
　　4849); 1)RO 20194 (later PO 157); w/chorus; LP: 15, 68, 70.
193 OTELLO: *Sie sass mit Leide...*(Verdi); Be 9909; 0-4834; 1)RO 20248; LP: 20, 70.
194 *Die Lotosblume* (Schumann); Be 9910; 0-4839; 1)RO 20207; 2)4049; 3)20377; LP: 5, 50, 68.
195 a)*An den Sonnenschein* b)*Marienwürmchen* (Schumann); Be 9911; O-4839; 1)RO 20207; 2) 4090;
　　3) 20377; chamber orch.; c. Gurlitt; LP: 5, 23, 50.
196 *Die Trommel gerühret* (from Egmont) (Beethoven); 28 Apr. '32; Be 9912; 0-4835; 1)RO 20196;
　　3)20276; 8)217; Odeon Chamber Orchestra; LP: none.
197 *Freudvoll und leidvoll* (Egmont) (Beethoven); 28 Apr. '32; Be 9913 other data see 196.
198 *Sandmännchen* (Brahms); Be 9914; 0-4836 (also 0-4847); 1)20403; 2)4087; 3)20286; LP: 50.
199 a)*Leise zieht durch mein Gemüt* (Mendelssohn) b)*Der Schmied* (Brahms); inst. trio dir. by Gurlitt;
　　Be 9915; 0-4836; 1)RO 20403; 2)4087; 3)20286; LP: a)none b)50.
200 MADAME BUTTERFLY: *Eines Tages seh'n wir* (Puccini); 25 May '32; Be 9935; 0-4834
　　(also 0-4849); o & c see 165; LP: 20, 50.
201 DIE TOTE STADT: *Glück das mir...*(Korngold); reported: 13 May '33, xxB 8558-0, 0-8613,
　　dubbing with electrically recorded orchestra, c. Weissmann; 1)20258 dubbing from acoustic: xxB
　　6993-4-0; 3)29012; LP: see 062.

Recorded 20 Jun '33; Weissmann cond. Berlin State Opera Orchestra.

202 WERTHER: *Werther, Werther...*(Part 1)(Massenet); Be 10384; 0-4845; 1)RO 20240;
　　LP: 1, 68 (both contain 202-203).
203 WERTHER: *Zum Fenster...*(Part 2)(Massenet); Be 10385 all other data see 202.
204 HOFFMANNS ERZÄHLUNGEN: *Sie entfloh* (Offenbach); Be 10386; 0-4844; 1)RO 20263;
　　LP: 68, 70.
205 MANON: *Nützet die schönen...*(Massenet); Be 10387; 0-4844 (also 0-4850); 1)RO 20248;
　　LP: 20, 70, 72.
206 DIE TOTEN AUGEN: *Psyché wandelt...*(d'Albert); Be 10388; 0-4841; 1)RO 20229 (later PO
　　158); LP: 1, 15, 20.
207 FIGAROS HOCHZEIT: *O säume länger nicht* (Mozart); Be 10389; 0-4841 (also 0-4850) (later
　　0-4851); 1)RO 20229 (later PO 158); 3)20279; LP: 1, 15, 68.
208 ARABELLA: *Mein Elemer!* (Part 1) (R. Strauss); 11 Nov. '33; Be 10468; 0-4842; 1)RO 20237
　　(later PO 171); 8)234; c. Richard Jäger; LP: 16, 19, 68, 69, 70.
209 ARABELLA: *Wie sagt die Zdenka* (Part 2)(R. Strauss); Be 10469; all other data see 208.
210 ARABELLA: *Er ist der Richtige*; Be 10470; 0-4843; 1)RO 20236; 3)23048; 8)233;
　　LP: 20, 69, 70.
211 ARABELLA: *Ich weiss nicht* .(Part 2); w/Kate Heidersbach; Be 10471; all other data see 210.

HIS MASTER'S VOICE (HMV)
1933-1935 in Vienna. Matrices followed by a catalogue number, a slash and then a "coupling" number.

212 DER ROSENKAVALIER: *Heut' oder Morgen* (R. Strauss); 21 Sep. '33; First of 17 listings of
　　abridged opera. Underlined numbers are takes used. Cast: Richard Mayr, Maria Olszewska, Vic-
　　tor Madin, Elisabeth Schumann, Bella Paalen, Karl Ettl, William Wergnick. Vienna Phil. Orch.; c.
　　Robert Heger; comp. sets: HMV DB 2060-72 (auto. coupling 7547-59), Victor albums: M 196

(7917-29), AM (7930-42), DM (17119-31); HMV matrices begin with 2WX, Victor's with CVS. Only Lehmann recordings; CVS 81440/2WX 585-1-1A-2A-3-3A; DB 2071/7928; LP: 80.

213 *Marie Theres*; CVS 81441/2WX 586-1-1A-2-2A; DB 2071/7928.

214 *Wie du warst!*; CVS 81419/2WX 587-1-1A; DB 2060/7917.

215 *Lachst du mich aus*; CVS 81420/2WX 588-1-1A-2-2A; DB 2061/7918.

216 *Der Feldmarschall sitzt*; CVS 81421/2WX 589-1-1A-2-2A; DB 2061/7918.

217 *Ah, du bist wieder da...*; CVS 81425/2WX 590-1A-2-2A; DB 2063/7920; (LP: 18, 20=217).

218 *Da geht er hin...*; CVS 81424/2WX 591-1-1A-2-2A; DB 2063/7920.

219 *Wo sie mich da hat...*; CVS 81426/2WX 592-1-2; DB 2064/7921.

220 *Weiss bereits nicht...*; CVS 81438/2WX 593-1-1A; DB 2070/7927.

221 *Hat sie schon einmal...*; 2WX 594-1 unpublished; see 226.

222 *Ich hab' halt schon einmal.*; 23 Sep. '33; CVS 81439/2WX 600-1-2-3-3A; DB 2070/7927.

223 *Die Stimm'* !; 23 Sep. '33; CVS 81422/2WX 601-1-2-2A; DB 2062/7919.

224 *Ich werd' jetzt*; 23 Sep. 33; 2WX 603-1-1A unpublished; see 227.

225 *Muss jetzt partout*; CVS 81437/2WX 604-1-2A; DB 2069/7926.

226 *Hat sie schon einmal...*; 24 Sep. '33; CVS 81423/2WX 594-2A-3-3A; DB 2062/7919.

227 *Ich werd' jetzt*, CVS 81427/2WX 603-2A-3-3A; DB 2064/7921.

228 *Sind halt also..(Ja, ja)*; CVS 81443-1-1A-2-2A; (2WX 584-1-2-3-4-5 unpublished, Schumann is reported to have sung the *Ja, ja*.)

229 DIE WALKÜRE: *Ein fremder Mann* (Wagner); 20 Jun. '35; First of 18 listings of act 1 & scenes from act 2; HMV matrices begin 2VH; Victor's CVS. Cast: Lauritz Melchior, Emanuel List, Ella Flesch, Alfred Jerger. Vienna Phil. Orch.; c. Bruno Walter. Catalogue numbers for act 1: HMV: DB 2636-43 (auto. coupling: DB 8039-46); Ger. Col.: LWX 105-112; It.Col GQX 10889-96; Victor albums M 298 (8932-39), AM (8940-47), DM (16933-40); Only Lehmann recordings. 2VH 95-2/CVS 95834; DB 2636/8932; LP: 81.

230 *Kühlende Labung*; 2VH 96-2/CVS 95835; DB 2637/8933.

231 *Einen Unseligen labtest du*; 2VH 97-1/CVS 95836; DB 2637/8933.

232 *Müd' am Herd*; 2VH 98-3A/CVS 95837; DB 2638/8934; LP: TC 9048=232.

233 *Trägst du Sorge*; 2VH 99-2/CVS 95838; DB 2638/8934.

234 *Wunder und wilde Märe*; 21 Jun. '35; 2VH 100-1/CVS 95839; DB 2639/8935.

235 *Die so leidig loos*; 2VH 101-1/CVS 95840; DB 2639/8935; LP: TC 9048=232, 235.

236 *Was gleisst dort hell*; 2VH 104-2A/CVS 95843; DB 2641/8937.

237 *Der Männer Sippe*; 2VH 105-2/CVS 95843; DB 2641/8937; Victor 14205 M-329; LP: 73 & RCA LM 1909=237.

238 *Dich selige Frau*; 2VH 106-1A/CVS 95845; DB 2642/8938; Victor 14204 M-329, HMV D2202, Electrola EJ 475; 238-241=1C147.

239 *Du bist der Lenz*; 2VH 107-1/CVS 95846; DB 2642/8938; Victor 15817 M-633; LP: LCT 1001, LCT 1=239=239.

240 *Wie dir die Stirn*; 2VH 108-1/CVS 95847; DB 2643/8939.

241 *Siegmund heiss' ich*; 22 Jun. '35; 2VH 109-1/CVS 95848; DB 2643/8939; Victor 15817 M-633; 241=LVT 1003, LCT 1001, WCT 2.

242 *Raste nun hier*; Scenes from act 2 w/same cast on Lehmann recordings; HMV DB 3719-28 (auto. coupling 8737-46); Victor: M-582 (15506-15), AM (15516-25), DM (16058-67) (16933-40). Only Lehmann recordings; same prefix numbers apply to HMV & Victor as in 229. 2VH 110-2/CVS 037525; DB 3724/15511; LP: 81 lists which reissues are act 2 or act 1.

243 *Hinweg! Hinweg!*; 2VH 111-1/CVS 037526; DB 3725/15512; LP: 20, 42.

244 *Horch! Horch!*; 2VH 112-1/CVS 037527; all other data as 243.

245 *Zauberfest bezähmt ein Schlaf*; 2VH 113-2A/CVS 037532; other data see 246.

246 *Wehwalt! Wehwalt!*; 2VH 114-2/CVS 037533; DB 3728/15515.

VICTOR

1935 & 1940. Victor matrices begin "BS"(10") or "CS" (12"); HMV: "OA." Matrix number is followed by Victor order number, HMV and Australian HMV (EC & ED), Japanese resleases (NF, SF & SD), then Victor sets "M" (where applicable). Underlined number is take used (when known). All with piano accomp; "p. B." refers to Ernö Balogh; "p. U.," to Paul Ulanowsky.

247 *An Chloe* (Mozart); 17 Oct. '35; p. B.; BS 95611-1-2; 1730; DA 1466; M-292; LP: 58, 60.

248 *Die Verschweigung* (Mozart); BS 95612-1-2; 1730; DA 1466; M-292; LP: 58, 60.

249 *Ungeduld* (Schubert); BS 95613-1-2; 1731; DA 1467; NF 4196; M-292; used to complete "Die
 schöne Müllerin" cycle on Columbia lp in 1964; LP: 58, 60.
250 *Im Abendrot* (Schubert); p. B.; BS 95614-1-2; 1731; DA 1467; NF 4196; M-292; LP: 6, 58, 60.
251 *Die Kartenlegerin* (Schumann); p. B.; BS 95615-1-2;1732; DA 1468; NF 4203; M-292; LP: 58, 60.
252 *Waldesgespräch* (Schumann); p. B.; BS 95616-1-2; 1732; DA 1468; NF 4203; M-292; LP: 58, 60.
253 *Der Tod, das ist die kühle Nacht* (Brahms); 17 Oct. '35; BS 95617-1-2; 1733; DA 1469; M-292;
 LP: 2, 58, 60.
254 a)*Therèse* b)*Meine Liebe ist grün*: BS 95618-1-2; 1733; DA 1469; M-292; LP: 3, 20, 42, 62.
255 *Anakreons Grab* (Wolf); p. B.; BS 95619-1-2; 1734; DA 1470; M-292; LP: 4, 55, 57, 62.
256 *In dem Schatten meiner Locken* (Wolf); BS 95620-1-2; 1734; DA 1470; M-292; LP: 4, 55, 57.
257 *Do not chide* (Eng.) (Balogh); 13 Mar. '36; p. B.; BS 99451-1-2 unpublished.
258 a)*My native land* (Gretchaninoff) b)*Midsummer* (Worth) (Eng.); BS 99452-1-1A; 1893; DA 1617;
 LP: none.
259 *Fa la nanna, bambin* (It.) (Sodero); 13 Mar. '36; p. B.; BS 99453-1-2 unpublished.
260 *Canta di primavera* (It.) (Cimara); 13 Mar. '36; p. B.; BS 99454-1-1A unpublished.
261 *Ich liebe dich* (Beethoven); p. B.; BS 99455-1-1A-2; 1995; DA 1733; LP: 55, 57.
262 *Schlafe, mein süsses Kind* (arr. Alwin); p. B.; BS 99456-1; 1995; DA 1733; LP: none.
263 *D'une prison* (Fr.) (Hahn); 13 Mar. '36; p. B.; BS 99457-1-1A; 1972; LP: none.
264 *Vierge d'Athènes* (Fr.) (Gounod); 13 Mar. '36; p. B.; BS 99458-1-2-2A unpublished.
265 *Botschaft* (Brahms); 16 Mar. '37; p. B.; BS 0957-1-2; 1857; DA 1604; M-419; LP: 55, 57, 62;
 take 1 (unpublished) recorded 16 Oct. '36.
266 *Gretel* (Pfitzner); 16 Mar. '37; p. B.; BS 06656-1; 1858; DA 1572; M-419; LP: 55, 57.
267 *Selige Nacht* (Marx); 16 Mar. '37; p. B.; BS 06657-1-2; 1858; DA 1572; M-419; LP: 57.
268 *Storchenbotschaft* (Wolf); p. B.; BS 06658-1; 1860; DA 1602; M-419; LP: 4, 62.
269 a)*Der Gärtner* b)*Du denkst mit einem Fädchen*; BS 06659-1-2; all other data see 268.
270 a)*Für Musik* b)*Gute Nacht* (Franz); p. B.; BS 06660-1; 1861; DA 1573; M-419; LP: 58.
271 *Lehn' deine Wang'* (Jensen); BS 06661-1-2; all other data see 270; LP: 57;
272 *Alte Laute* (Schumann); p. B.; BS 06662-1; 1859; DA 1571; M-419; LP: 58, 60.
273 a)*Du bist wie eine Blume* b)*Frühlingsnacht* (Schumann); BS 06663-1-2; 1859; DA 1571; M-419;
 LP: b=58, a & b=60.
274 *Gretchen am Spinnrade* (Schubert); p. B.; BS 06664-1; 1856; DA 1603; M-419; LP: 6.
275 *Wiegenlied* (Schlafe, schlafe, holder) (Schubert); BS 06665-1-1A; all other data see 274.
276 a)*Das Mädchen spricht* b)*Mein Mädel hat einen Rosenmund* (Brahms); p. B.; BS 06666-1-2; 1857;
 DA 1604; M-419; LP: 55, 57, 62.
277 *Tonera (Visions)* (Eng.) (Sjøberg-Balogh); p. B.; BS 06667-1-1A; 1972; DA 1612; LP: none.
278 *Drink to me only* (Eng.) (Calcott; arr. Cohen); p. B.; BS 06668-1-1A;1893; DA 1612 &1617; LP: 85.
279 *Gebet* (Wolf); 6 Jan. '39; p. Ulanowsky; BS 031403-1-1A-2-2A only LP: 62.
280 *Nun lass uns Frieden schliessen* (Wolf); 6 Jan. '39; p. U.; BS 031404-1-1A only LP: 62.
281 *Frühling übers Jahr* (Wolf); BS 031405-1-2; (1969) (DA 1734); 2029; M-613; LP: 4, 62.
282 *Auf ein altes Bild* (Wolf); BS 031406-1-2; 2030; DA 1723; M-613; LP: 4, 57, 62.
283 *In der Frühe* (Wolf); BS 031407-1-2; (1969) (DA 1734); 2029; M-613; LP: 4, 62.
284 *Auch kleine Dinge* (Wolf); BS 031408-1-2; 2031; DA 1724; M-613; LP: 4, 55, 57, 62.
285 *Und willst du deinen Liebsten…* (Wolf); 6 Jan. '39; p. U.; BS 031409-1 only LP: 62.
286 *Peregrina I* (Wolf); BS 031410-1-2; 2031; DA 1724; M-613; LP: 4, 57, 62.
287 *Der Knabe und das Immlein* (Wolf); 6 Jan. '39; p. U.; BS 031411-1 only LP: 62.
288 *Heimweh* (Wolf); BS 031412-1-2; 2030; DA 1723; M-613; LP: 4, 62.
289 *Er und Sie* (Schumann); 30 Jan. '39; first of 4 listings containing duets with Lauritz Melchior &
 Victor Orchestra; c. Bruno Reibold; album M-560; BS 031860-1-2; 1906; DA 1716; EC 72; SF
 730; LP: 59, 55 (289-292).
290 a)*So wahr die Sonne* b)*Unterm Fenster*; BS 031861-1; 1907; DA 1717; SF 731; other data: 289.
291 *Familien-Gemälde* (Schumann); BS 031862-1-2; 1907; DA 1717; SF 731; other data see 289.
292 *Ich denke dein* (Schumann); BS 031863-1; 1906; DA 1716; EC 72; SF 730; other data see 289.
293 *Die Nebensonnen* (Schubert); 26 Feb. '40; p. Ulanowsky; first of 8 listings containing songs from
 Die Winterreise; in album M-692 (2108-09) (17190-91); cycle completed later with Columbia albums M-466 & M-587; 293, 295, 296, 297, 298 released as "Tribute To Lotte Lehmann" in 1952;
 BS 047267-1; 2108; EC 124; LP: 6 (comp. cycle).
294 a)*Die Post* b)*Der stürmische Morgen*; BS 047268-1; other data see 293.
295 *Der Lindenbaum*; CS 047269-1; 12"-17190; ED 265, SD 3136; (DB 5767); other data see 293 +

LP: 58=295, 296, 297, 299.
296 *Der Wegweiser;* CS 047270-1; 17191; ED 266; (DB 5768); SD 3137; other data see 293 + LP: 58.
297 *Die Krähe;* BS 047271-1-2; 2109; EC 125; see 293 + LP: 58.
298 *Das Wirtshaus;* CS 047272-1-2; all other data see 296.
299 a)*Täuschung* b)*Mut!;* BS 047273-1; all other data see 297.
300 a)*Rückblick* b)*Im Dorfe;* CS 047274-1; all other data see 295.

COLUMBIA

1941-1943; p. Ulanowsky, (except for *Dichterliebe* and *Frauenliebe und Leben* with Bruno Walter,
pianist); matrices that begin CO are 10", XCO are 12"; matrix is followed by catalogue number divided
by a slash; the second is an automatic coupling number; when applicable, an album number follows.

301 *Gefrorene Tränen* (Schubert); 14 Mar. '41; p. Ulanowsky; first of 10 listings of songs from Die
     Winterreise in 2 sets completing the cycle begun on Victor. One album (M-587) is 10"; the sec-
     ond (M-466) is 12"; CO 29948-1-1A; 17367/17564; M-587; LP: 6 (compl. cycle.)
302 *Wasserflut;* XCO 29949-1-1A; 71174/72071; Canadian Columbia 15485.
303 *Der greise Kopf;* CO 29950-1-1A-1B; 17369/17466; M-587.
304 a)*Die Wetterfahne* b)*Letzte Hoffnung;* XCO 29951-1-1A; 71175/72072; M-466; Canadaian Co-
     lumbia 15486.
305 *Auf dem Flusse;* XCO 29952-1-1A all other data see 304.
306 *Rast;* XCO 29953-1-1A-1B; 71176/72073; M-466; Can. Col. 15487.
307 *Einsamkeit;* CO 29954-1-1A-1B-1C-1D-1E; 17368/17465; M-587.
308 *Irrlicht;* CO 29955-1-1A-1B-1C-1D; 17368/17465; M-587.
309 *Frühlingstraum;* XCO 29956-1-1A all other data see 306.
310 *Die Mainacht* (Brahms); 19 Mar. '41; p. U.; XCO 30005-1-1A; 71060/71980; M-453; LP: 3, 11.
311 *Feinsliebchen, du sollst mir nicht;* XCO 30006-1-1A; 71059/71979; M-453; LP: 3, 9, 11.
312 *An die Nachtigall* (Brahms); CO 30007-1-1A; 17274/17439; M-453; 10-1551A; LP: 3, 11.
313 *Auf dem Kirchhofe* (Brahms); CO 30008-1-1A; 17274/17439; M-453; LP: 3, 11.
314 *Wie bist du, meine Königin* (Brahms); CO 30009-1-1A; 17273/17438; M- 453; LP: 3, 11.
315 *Wir wandelten* (Brahms); CO 30010-1-1A; 17273/17438; M-453; LP: 3, 11.
316 a)*Erlaube mir* b)*Da unten im Tale* ; XCO 30011-1-1A; 71059/71979; M-453; LP: 3, 9, 11.
317 a)*Sonntag* b)*O liebliche Wangen* (Brahms); XCO 30012-1-1A; 71060/71980; M-453; LP: 3, 11
318 *Die junge Nonne* (Schubert); 4 Mar. '41 ?; XCO 30013-1-1A; 71509; LP: 6, 9, 13.
319 *Der Leiermann* (Schubert); 19 Mar. '41; CO 30014-1-1A-1B; 17369/17466; M-587; LP: 6.
320 *Erstarrung;*19 Mar. '41; CO 30015-1-1A; 17367/17464; Die Winterreise M-587; LP: 6.
321 *Der Doppelgänger* (Schubert); 4 Mar. '41?; p. U.; XCO 30016-1-1A; 71509; LP: 6, 9, 13.
322 *Liebesbotschaft* (Schubert); 19 Mar. '41; p. U.; CO 30017-1-1A; only LP: 6.
323 *Gute Nacht* (Schubert); XCO 30018-1-1A; 71174/72071; M-466; Can. Col. 15485; LP: 6.
324 *Seit ich ihn gesehen* (Schumann); 24 Jun. '41; p. Walter; first of 8 listings of the complete Frauen-
     liebe und Leben; CO 31508-1-1A; 17362; M-539; LP: 12 (w/Dichterliebe).
325 *Er, der Herrlichste von allen;* CO 31509-1-1A; 17362; M-539.
326 *Ich kann's nicht fassen;* CO 31510-1-1A; 17363; M-539.
327 *Du Ring an meinem Finger;* CO 31511-1-1A; 17363; M-539.
328 *Helft mir, ihr Schwestern;* CO 31512-1-1A; 17364; M-539.
329 *Süsser Freund;* CO 31513-1-1A; 17364; M-539.
330 *An meinem Herzen;* CO 31514-1-1A; 17365; M-539.
331 *Nun hast du mir;* CO 31515-1-1A; 17365; M-539.
332 a)*In der Fremde I* (Aus der Heimat...) b)*Wenn ich früh in den Garten gehe* (Schumann);
     26 Jun. '41; p. Ulanowsky; CO 31485-1-1A only LP: 7.
333 *Aufträge* (Schumann); CO 31486-1-1A only LP: 7, 9, 13 (XLP 57265)?.
334 *Die Lotosblume* (Schumann); CO 31487-1-1A unpublished.
335 *Morgengruss* (Mendelssohn); 30 Jun '41; CO 31699-1-1A; 17344; LP: 9.
336 *Venetianisches Gondellied* (Mendelssohn); CO 31700-1-1A; LP: 13.
337 *Neue Liebe* (In dem Mondenschein); CO 31701-1-1A only LP: 7 (mislabeled as by "Wolf").
338 *Der Nussbaum* (Schumann); CO 31702-1-1A only LP: 9, 13.
339 *Wonne der Wehmut* (Beethoven); CO 31703-1-1A only LP: 7.
340 *Andenken* (Beethoven); CO 31704-1-1A only LP: 7.
341 a)*Der Kuss* b)*Die Trommel gerühret* (Beethoven); CO 31705-1-1A only LP: a) 9, 13, b) 7.

342 *In questa tomba oscura* (It.) (Beethoven); CO 31706-1-1A only LP: 9, 13.
343 *Verborgenheit* (Wolf); CO 31707-1-1A only LP: 4.
344 *Zur Ruh', zur Ruh'* (Wolf); CO 31708-1-1A only LP: 4, 13.
345 *Gesang Weylas* (Wolf); CO 31709-1-1A only LP: 4, 7.
346 a) *Wiegenlied* b)*Ständchen* (Brahms); CO 31710-1-1A became a) CO 32035-1
    b) CO 32036-1.
347 *Wiegenlied* (Brahms); CO 32035-1 17300; LP: 3, 11, 13.
348 *Ständchen* (Der Mond steht über…) (Brahms); CO 32036-1; 17300; LP: 3, 11, 13.
349 *Auf Flügeln des Gesanges* (Mendelssohn); 2 Jul. '41; CO 31693-1-1A; 17344; LP: 9, 44.
350 *Allerseelen* (R. Strauss); CO 31694-1-1A; 17385; X-270; LP: 9, 11.
351 *Morgen* (R. Strauss); CO 31695-1-1A; 17384; X-270; LP: 9, 11, 13.
352 *Zueignung* (R. Strauss); CO 31696-1-1A; 17385; see 351.
353 *Ständchen* (R. Strauss); CO 31297-1-1A; 17384; see 351.
354 *Schmerzen* (Wagner); CO 31698-1-1A only LP: 9, 11, 13.
355 *Der Engel* (Wagner); 9 Jul. '41; CO 31488-1A only LP: 7.
356 a)*Sehnsucht nach dem Frühling* b) *Warnung* (Mozart); CO 31489-1-1A only LP: 7.
357 *Das Veilchen* (Mozart); CO 31490-1-1A only LP: 7.
358 *Träume* (Wagner); XCO 31491-1-1A-1E; 71469; LP: 9, 11, 13.
359 *Im Treibhaus* (Wagner); XCO 31492-1-1A-1B; 71469; LP: 11.
360 *Wer tat deinem Füsslein weh* (Wolf); CO 31493-1-1A only LP: 4.
361 *Wien, du Stadt meiner Träume* (Sieczynski); CO 31494-1-1A; 17304; M-494; LP: 44.
362 *Da draussen in der Wachau* (Arnold); 14 July '41; CO 31521-1-1A; 17302; M-494; LP: 44.
363 *Im Prater blüh'n wieder…* (Stolz); CO 31522-1-1A; see 362.
364 *Wien, sterbende Märchenstadt* (Leopoldi); CO 31523-1-1A; all other data see 368.
365 *My lovely Celia* (Eng.) (Munro); CO 31524-1-1A only LP: 44.
366 *She never told her love* (Eng.) (Haydn); CO 31525-1-1A only LP: 44.
367 *Ich muss wieder einmal…* (Benatsky); CO 31526-1-1A see 361.
368 *Heut' macht die Welt* (after Joh. Strauss by Dostal); CO 31527-1-1A; 17303; M-494; LP: 44.
369 a)*C'est mon ami* b)*Maman dites-moi* (Fr.) (folksongs); XCO 31528-1-1A-1B only LP: 44.
370 a)*La vierge a la crèche* b)*La mère Michel* (Fr.) (folksongs); XCO 31529-1-1A only LP: 44.
371 a)*Wenn ich in deine Augen seh'* b)*Ich will meine Seele tauchen* (Schumann); 13 Aug. '41;
    p.Walter; first of 8 listings for Dichterliebe; CO 31377-1; 17295/17440; M-486;
    LP: 12 (& Frauenliebe und Leben).
372 a)*Ich hab' im Traum geweinet* b)*Allnächtlich in Träume* ; CO 31378-1; 17296/17441.
373 *Aus alten Märchen winkt es*; XCO 31379-1A-1B; 71309/72078.
374 a)*Im wunderschönen Monat Mai* b)*Aus meinen Tränen spriessen* c)*Die Rose, die Lilie*;
    CO 31380-1; 17295/17440.
375 a)*Und wüssten's die Blumen* b)*Das ist ein Flöten und Geigen* c)*Hör' ich das Liedchen*;
    XCO 31381-1A; 71308/72077.
376 *Die alten bösen Lieder*; XCO 31382-1; 71309/72078.
377 a)*Im Rhein, im heiligen Strome* b)*Ich grolle nicht*; XCO 31383-1; 71308/72077; M-486.
378 a)*Ein Jüngling liebt ein Mädchen* b)*Am leuchtenden Sommermorgen*; CO 31384-1;
    17296/17441.
379 a)*Das Wandern* b) *Wohin* (Schubert); 22 Jun. '42; p. Ulanowsky; first of 14 listings for Die schöne
    Müllerin, withoutUngeduld see: 249; XCO 32966-1-1B; 71771/71778; M-615; LP:14 (all).
380 a)*Halt!* b)*Danksagung an den Bach*; XCO 32967-1-1B-1E; 71771/71779.
381 a)*Morgengruss* b)*Des Müllers Blumen*; XCO 32970-1C; 71773/71783.
382 *Tränenregen* (Schubert); XCO 32971-1A-1C; 71773/71783.
383 *Pause*; XCO 32972-1A; 71774/71784; M-615; LP: 14.
384 a)*Mit dem grünen Lautenbande* b) *Mein!*; XCO 32973-1A; 71774/71784; LP: 14.
385 *Die liebe Farbe*; XCO 32975-1B-1C; 71775/71782; M-615; LP: 14.
386 *Die böse Farbe*; XCO 32976-1; 71776/71781; M-615; LP: 14.
387 *Am Feierabend*; 25 Jun. '42; XCO 32968-1; 71772/71780; LP: 14.
388 *Der Neugierige*; XCO 32969-1A-1C; 71772/71781; LP: 14.
389 a)*Der Jäger* b) *Eifersucht und Stolz*; XCO 32974-1B-1C-1D; 71775/71783; LP: 14.
390 *Trock'ne Blumen*; XCO 32977-1A; 71776/71780; M-615; LP: 14.
391 *Der Müller und der Bach*; XCO 32978-1A; 71777/71779; LP: 14.
392 *Des Baches Wiegenlied*; XCO 32979-1A-1B; 71777/71778; LP: 14.

VICTOR

1947-1949; p. Ulanowsky. The matrices are followed by catalogue numbers (10- are 10" 78 rpm's, 49- are 7" 45 rpm's). Japanese releases: SF. When known, takes that were used are underlined.

393 *Ständchen* (Schubert); 26 Jun. '47; D7-RB-560-1-1A; 10-1498; 49-0699 or 49-1498; SF1; LP: –.

394 *Der Erlkönig* (Schubert); 26 Jun. '47 (takes 1, 1A); 11 Jul. '47; (takes 2, 2A); test pressing of 2A at UCSB; D7-RB-561-1-1A-2-2A; 10-1448; 49-1033; (DA 1919); SF 1; LP: 55, 57.

395 a)*He Zigeuner* b)*Hochgetürmte Rimaflut* (Brahms); first of 4 listings for Zigeunerlieder; D7-RB-562-1-1A; 10-1391 in M 1188; 10-1393 in DM 1188; 49- 0846 in WDM 1188; LP: 3, 62.

396 a) *Wisst ihr, wann...* b)*Lieber Gott, du weisst* ; D7-RB-563-1-1A; 10-1394 in DM 1188; 10-1391 in M 1188; other data see 395.

397 a)*Brauner Bursche* b)*Röslein dreie in der Reihe* (Brahms); D7-RB-564-1-1A; 10-1392 in M 1188; 10-1394 in DM 1188; 49-0847 in WDM 1188; LP: 3, 62.

398 a)*Kommt mir manchmal in den Sinn* b)*Rote Abendwolken* (one verse); D7-RB-565-1-1A; 10-1392 in M-1188; 10-1393 in DM-1188; 49- 0846 in WDM 1188; LP: 3, 62.

399 *An den Mond* (Geuss, lieber Mond) (Schubert); 26 Jun. '47; D7-RB-566-1-1A; 10-1498; 49-0699 or 49-1498; LP: none.

400 *An die Musik* (Schubert); D7-RB-567-1-1A; 10-1448; 49-1033; (DA 1919); LP: 57.

401 *Feldeinsamkeit* (Brahms); 26 Jun. '47; D7-RB-568-1-1A; 10-1405; LP: 3, 62.

402 a)*Der Kranz* b)*Der Schmied* (Brahms); D7-RB-569-1-1A; 10-1405; LP: 3, 62.

403 *Ave Maria* (sung in Latin); (Bach-Gounod); 30 Jun. '47; first of 4 listings with RCA-Victor Orchestra; c. Richard Lert; D7-RB-578-1-1A only LP: 56 (45 rpm).

404 *O come all ye faithful* (Eng.) (trad.); D7-RB-579-1-1A; 10-1367; 49-0793; MO-1226; LP: 56.

405 *Stille Nacht...* (Eng. & Ger.) (Gruber); D7-RB-580-1-1A; 10-1367; 49-0793; MO-1226; LP: 56.

406 *Es ist ein Ros' entsprungen* (Eng. & Ger.) (Praetorius); D7-RB-581-1-1A only LP: 56.

407 a)*Der Jüngling an der Quelle* b)*An die Nachtigall;* (Schubert); 11 Jul. '47; D7-RB-1300-1-1A-2-2A; 10-1551; 49-1277; M-1342; LP: 6; test pressing of 1A at UCSB.

408 *Die Männer sind mèchant;* D7-RB-1301-1-1A; 10-1551; 49-1277; M-1342; LP: 55, 57.

409 *Nacht und Träume;* D7-RB-1302-1-1A-2A; unpublished, but test pressings of 1A & 2A at UCSB; 2B, 2C, 2D "electrical transfer from 1302-2 to furnish new master".

410 *God bless America* (Eng.) (Berlin); 22 Dec. '47; first of 4 recordings made for MGM's film: "Big City" (see 460); MGM Orchestra; c. Robert Armbruster; St. Luke Choristers; D7-RB-2733-1-1A-2-2A; 10-1433; MO-1226; LP: 86; also test pressing (26 Nov. '47) w/piano, then orch. & chorus, one verse only, 80 rpm, at UCSB.

411 *The Kerry dance* (Eng.) (Molloy); D7-RB-2734-1-1A; 10-1433; MO-1226; LP: none.

412 *Träumerei* (as a vocalise) (Schumann); D7-RB-2735-1-1A-2-2A-3-3A; 10-1432; MO-1226; (HMV DA 1909); LP: none.

413 *Wiegenlied* (Eng.) (Brahms); D7-RB-2736-1-1A-2-2A; all other data see 412.

414 *L'enamourée* (Fr.) (Hahn); 9 Mar. '49; p. U.; first of 6 entries: all A, B, C's, are transfers from 1; D9-RB-263-1-1A-1B-1C; 10-1509 & DM-1342; 49-0769 & WDM-B342 (45 rpm); LP: none; 78 rpm test pressing of 1C at UCSB.

415 *Infidèlité* (Fr.) (Hahn); D9-RB-264-1-1A-1B-1C; 10-1510 & DM-1342; 49-0770 & WDM-B342 (45 rpm); LP: none; 78 rpm test pressing of 1C at UCSB.

416 *La vie anterieure* (Fr.) (Duparc); D9-RB-265-1-1A-1B-1C; 10-1510 & DM-1342; 49-0770 & WDM-B342 (45 rpm); LP: none; 78 rpm test pressing of 1B at UCSB.

417 *Psyché* (Fr.) (Paladilhe); D9-RB-266-1-1A-1B-1C; 10-1508 & DM-1342; 49-0768 & WDM-B342 45 rpm; LP: none.

418 a)*Die Zeitlose* b)*Wozu noch* (R. Strauss); D9-RB-267-1-1B-1C; 10-1509 & DM-1342; HMV DA 1943; 49-0769 & WDM-B342 45 rpm; LP: none; 78 rpm test pressing of 1C at UCSB.

419 *Du meines Herzens Krönelein;* D9-RB-268-1-1B-1C; 10-1508 & DM-1342; HMV DA 1943; 49-0768 & WDM-B342 45 rpm; LP: none; 78 rpm test pressing of 1C at UCSB.

CAEDMON

Two lp recordings spoken by Lotte Lehmann.

420 "Lotte Lehmann Reading German Lyric Poetry" (in German); October 1956; TC 1072; Goethe: *Mignon; Ganymed, Wanderers Nachtlied, Geheimes, Als ich auf dem Euphrat schiffte;* Mörike: *Peregrina I, Gebet, Im Frühling, Der Genesene an die Hoffnung, Begegnung, Nimmersatte*

Liebe, Verborgenheit; Heine: *Dichterliebe;* Rilke: *Ich lebe mein leben in wachsenden Ringen;*
von Hofmannsthal: DER ROSENKAVALIER monologue from act 1; Müller: *Die Winterreise.*
421 "Rainer Maria Rilke: *Die Weise von Liebe und Tod; Marienleben;* Read by Lehmann;" (in Ger.);
late Feb.-Mar. '58; TC 1128; OL-222-CD (CBS Japan).

NON-COMMERCIAL   RECORDINGS

This section contains a mixture of private recordings of live performances, "air-checks," tapes of radio and tv performances, film and video documentation of Lehmann's work. The dating is often only
approximate and the contents, especially of the master classes, is open to conjecture. How much is
there of Lehmann demonstrating and teaching, and how much of students' efforts? She usually introduces the aria by telling some of the story; she recites a *Lied* in English. During the class she inter-
rupts to make suggestions and comments. If no lp format exists, there follows a possible location of
an acetate, tape or cassette. UCSB has all listings unless another location is indicated. In this section,
spoken entries are in English unless otherwise stated.

422 TANNHÄUSER: *Dich teure Halle* (Wagner); 11 Jan. '30; Chicago Opera Company; with Paul
   Althouse, Hans Nisson; c. Giorgio Polacco; opening of act 2; LP: 31; poor sound.
423 FIDELIO: *Komm Hoffnung* (Beethoven); 11 Feb. '34; General Motors Symphony Orch.; c. Arturo Toscanini broadcast on "Cadillac Hour;" LP:—; Rodgers & Hammerstein Rec. Sound Archive.
424 TANNHÄUSER: complete opera?; 24 Feb. '34; Metropolitan Opera; w/Melchior,Olszewska,
   Ludwig Hoffmann, Hans Clemens; c. Arthur Bodanzky; broadcast by American Tobacco Co.
   (Lucky Strike); LP: none; existence ?
425 OTHELLO: excerpts: act 1 duet, act 4 Willow Song & Ave Maria; (Verdi); 1 Jun. '35; Vienna
   Opera; with Gotthelf Pistor; c. Walter; LP: none; UCSB: fragments, poor sound.
426 FIDELIO: act 1 (to end of Komm Hoffnung) (Beethoven); 31 Aug. '35; Vienna Phil. at Salzburg;
   w/Alfred Jerger, Anton Baumann; Luise Helletsgruber; c. Toscanini; LP: 76 (shortwave noise.)
427 DIE MEISTERSINGER: Quintet (Wagner); 20 Sep. '35; Vienna State Opera Orchestra;
   c. Felix Weingartner; LP: 87.
428 Broadcast: a)LOHENGRIN: *Einsam in trüben Tagen* (Wagner) b) *Wiegenlied* (R. Strauss); 24 Oct.
   '35; RCA Magic Key; NBC Orchestra; c. Frank Black; LP: none; Museum of Broadcasting.
429 DER ROSENKAVALIER: excerpts (R. Strauss); Apr. 22 '36; Vienna Opera; w/Schumann, Jarmila Novotna; c. Hans Knappersbusch; LP: 29 (mixture of 2 performances, perhaps no Lehmann.)
430 Broadcast (contents unknown); 27 Feb. '36; Kraft Phoenix Cheese Corp.; LP: none; existence ?
431 DIE MEISTERSINGER: act 1 (Wagner); 8 Aug. '36; Vienna Phil at Salzburg; w/Kerstin Thorborg, Nissen, Charles Kullmann, Hermann Wiedemann; c.Toscanini; LP: 78 (shortwave noise.)
432 Broadcast (contents unknown); 26 Oct. '36; Kraft Phoenix Cheese Corp.; LP: none; existence ?
433 DIE WALKÜRE: act 2 (Wagner); 13 Nov. '36; San Francisco Opera; with Kirsten Flagstad,
   Friedrich Schorr, Melchior, Emanuel List, Kathryn Meisle; c. Fritz Reiner; LP: 28.
434 LOHENGRIN: excerpts;10 Jan. '37; RCA Magic Key; NBC Orch.; c. Black; LP: none; LOC.
435 Broadcast interview on "Let's Talk It Over;" 30 Dec. '37; NBC radio; Lehmann discusses her art &
   recent book: *Eternal Flight;* LP: none; Library of Congress.
436 *Lieder* recital; 18 Jan. '38; Town Hall, New York City; p.U.; LP: 77; (Wolf unless noted); a)*Kennst
   du das Land* b)*Frühling übers Jahr* c)*Und willst du deinen* d)*Wenn du, mein Liebster*
   e)*Verborgenheit* f)*In der Frühe* g)*Auch kleine Dinge* h)*Der Knabe und das Immlein* (repeated)
   i)*Peregrina I* j)*Er ist's* (Schumann) (encore) k)*Storchenbotschaft* (encore) l)*An eine Äolsharfe*
   m) *In dem Schatten meiner Locken* n)*Gebet* o)*Nun lass uns Frieden* p)*Der Gärtner* q)*Ständchen*
   (R. Strauss) (encore) r)*Thérèse* (Brahms) (encore) s)*Auf ein altes Bild* t) *Du denkst mit einem
   Fädchen* (repeated) u)*Heimweh* v)*Schweig einmal still* w)*Ich hab' in Penna* x)*Zueignung*
   (R. Strauss) (encore) y)*Heimkehr vom Fest* (Blech) (encore) z)*Vergebliches Ständchen* (Brahms)
   (encore); aa)*Anakreons Grab* from this recital not on lp, only acetate at UCSB.
437 Broadcast (discussing the role of Marschallin); 5 Feb. '38 Met. Opera Intermission Feature; LP:-.
438 DER ROSENKAVALIER: complete (R. Strauss); 5 Feb. '38 Metropolitan Opera Orch.; w/ Emanuel List, Kerstin Thorborg, Friedrich Schorr; c. Bodanzky; LP: 33 (poor sound.)
439 Broadcast (contents unknown); 24 Feb. '38; Kraft Phoenix Cheese Corp.; LP: none; existence ?
440 Broadcast: 3 Apr. '38; a)TOSCA: *Vissi d'arte* (It.) (Puccini) b)*Zueignung* c)*Traum durch die
   Dämmerung* d) *Ständchen* (R. Strauss); RCA Magic Key; NBC Orchestra; c. Black; LP: 7.

*Lohengrin- nearly complete 1935   CAS.   , < 0

441 Broadcast: reading excerpts from her book *Eternal Flight*; 13 Apr. '38; WHN.

442 Broadcast (contents unknown); 8 Sep. '38; Kraft Phoenix Cheese Corp.; LP: none; existence ?

443 Broadcast (contents unknown); 2 Oct. '38; RCA Magic Key; NBC Orch.; c. Black; LP: none; LOC.

444 DER ROSENKAVALIER: complete (R. Strauss); 7 Jan. '39; Metropolitan Opera; w/List, Risë Stevens, Martita Farell, Schorr, Dorothea Manski; c. Bodansky; LP: 39.

445 Broadcast (contents unknown); 17 Aug. '39; Kraft Music Hall; LP: none; existence ?

446 Broadcast interview by Roy Miller; 18 Sep. '39; RCA Magic Key; LP: none; LOC.

447 Broadcast (contents unknown); 14 Mar. '40; Kraft Music Hall; LP: none; existence ?

448 DIE WALKÜRE: complete (Wagner); 30 Mar. '40; Metropolitan Opera (on tour in Boston); with Melchior, Schorr, Margarie Lawrence, Thorborg; c. Erich Leinsdorf; LP: 27.

449 Broadcast interview; 18 Jan. '41; Metropolitan Opera Intermission Feature; LP: none; LOC.

450 Broadcasts for Columbia: "Electrical Transcription licensed only for radio broadcasting;" aired 3 Oct. '41 through 24 Dec. '41; Frank Gallop host; p. U; Lehmann introduces each song; a)*Andenken* b)*Wonne der Wehmut* c)*Die Trommel gerühret* d)*Der Kuss* (Beethoven); e)*An die Musik* f)*Ständchen* g)*Der Erlkönig* (Schubert); h)*Auf Flügeln des Gesanges* i)*Neue Liebe* j)*Venetianisches Gondellied* (Mendelssohn); k)*Abendempfindung* l)*Das Veilchen* m)*Warnung* n)*Gute Nacht* o)*Frühlingstraum* p)*Der Leiermann* (Schubert); q)*In der Fremde II* r)*Ich grolle nicht* s)*Der Nussbaum* t)*Aufträge* (Schumann); u)*Die Mainacht* v)*Ständchen* w)*Wiegenlied* x)*O liebliche Wangen* (Brahms); y)*Schmerzen* z)*Im Treibhaus* aa)*Träume* (Wagner); bb)*Zur Ruh*; cc)*Gesang Weylas* dd)*Verborgenheit* ee)*Wer tat deinen Füsslein weh* (Wolf); ff)*Allerseelen* gg)*Zueignung* hh)*Ständchen* (Strauss); ii)*Sehnsucht nach dem Frühling* jj)*Sei du mein Trost* kk)*Dans un bois solitaire* (Mozart); ll)*Der Doppelgänger* (Schubert); mm)*Die Lotosblume* (Schumann); nn)*Wiegenlied* (Flies); oo)*Vergebliches Ständchen* (Brahms); pp)*Es ist ein Ros' entsprungen* (Praetorius); qq)*O du Fröhliche* rr)*O Tannenbaum* (trad.); ss)*Silent night* (Eng.) (Gruber); LP: orig. 33 rpm, 16".

451 TRISTAN UND ISOLDE: *Liebestod* (Wagner); 1943; San Francisco Symphony; c. Pierre Monteux; LP: 7.

452 Recital: 1944; p. U.; a)*She never told her love* (Haydn); b)*Widmung* (Schumann); c)*Londonderry air* d)*Drink to me only* (trad.); e)*Ständchen* (Schubert); f)*Auf Flügeln des Gesanges* (Mendelssohn); all Eng.; (possibly miss-dated, see 463); LP: 34.

453 DER ROSENKAVALIER: *Ich sag': Pardon mein hübsches Kind* (R. Strauss); 23 Feb. '45; Metropolitan Opera; with List, Stevens, Conner; c. Szell; excerpt from live performance; LP:(?); acetate; existence ?

454 DER ROSENKAVALIER: act 3 (R. Strauss); 18 Oct. '45; San Francisco Opera; w/Stevens, Lorenzo Alvary, Nadine Conner, Walter Olitzki; c. George Sebastian; LP: 32.

455 Recital: *Frauenliebe und Leben* (Schumann); 20 Jan. '46; p. Ulanowsky; LP: 83.

456 Recital: 10 Feb. '46; Town Hall; p.Ulanowsky; a)*An eine Quelle* b)*Der Tod und das Mädchen* c)*Der Jüngling und der Tod* d)*Auflösung* e)*Die Forelle* f)*Dass sie hier gewesen* g)*Schwanengesang* (Wie klag' ich's aus) h)*Die Männer sind mèchant* (Schubert); i)*Zigeunerlieder* (8 songs) j)*Wie bist du, meine Königin* k)*Die Kränze* l)*Es träumte mir* m)*Frühlingslied* n)*Willst du, dass ich geh'* (Brahms); LP: 82.

457 Recital: 11 Aug. '46; Seattle Symphony Orchestra; c. Carl Bricker; a)*Die junge Nonne* b)*Der Jüngling an der Quelle* c)*Der Erlkönig* (Schubert); d)*Träume* (Wagner); LP: 34.

457.1 DER ROSENKAVALIER: (part of act 1) (R. Strauss); Oct. 8, '46; San Francisco Opera; w/ Lorenzo Alvary; (begins w/*Pardon mein hübsches Kind*); Wm. Moran collection.

458 Broadcast: radio sketch: "Duffy's Tavern;" 13 Oct. '46; sings a little and speaks (English); LP: 35.

459 Recital: 9 Feb. '47 or 7 Mar. '48; Town Hall; p. U.; a)*Venetianisches Gondellied* b)*Die Liebende schreibt* (Mendelssohn); c)*An die ferne Geliebte* (6 songs) (Beethoven); LP: 82.

460 Film: MGM's "Big City;" released in 1948; with Karin Booth, Margaret O'Brien, George Murphy, Danny Thomas, Rbt. Preston; see 410.

461 Recital: 5 Aug. '48; Hollywood Bowl Orch.; c. Eugene Ormandy; a)*Morgen* (vn. solo: Sascha Jacobson) b)*Allerseelen* c)*Traum durch die Dämmerung* d)*Zueignung* (R. Strauss); Encores: e)*Ständchen* (Schubert) f)*Wiegenlied* (Brahms); w/piano acc.; LP: Armed Forces Radio Serv.

462 Recital: 27 Feb. '49;Town Hall; p. U.; a)*Als Luise die Briefe* b)*Abendempfindung* c)*Dans un bois solitaire* (Fr.) d)*Die Verschweigung* (Mozart); e)*Dein blaues Auge* f)*Komm' bald* g)*Bitteres zu sagen* h)*Schön war, dass ich dir weihte* i)*Am Sonntagmorgen* j)*Der Gang zum Liebsten* k)*DerTod, das ist der kühle Nacht* l)*Liebestreu* m)*Frühlingstrost* n)*Der Kuss* o)*O wüsst' ich doch den Weg zurück* p)*Wie froh und frisch* (Brahms); LP: 83.

463 Broadcast: 8 Jan. '49; a)*Ständchen* (Schubert) b)*Londonderry air* (trad.) c)*Widmung* (Schumann) d)*Drink to me only* (trad.); (all Eng.); Lionel Barrymore host; LP: none (see 452).

464 Recital: 1950; p. Walter; a)*Ständchen* (Schubert) b)*Auf Flügeln des Gesanges* (Mendelssohn) c)*Wiegenlied* (Brahms) d)*Aufträge* (Schumann); LP: 7, 8.

465 Interview (including E. Schumann) by James Fassett; 5 Feb. '50; N. Y. Philharmonic Intermission Feature; on B. Walter & his importance in their careers; anecdotes.

466 Interview by M. Mc Bride; 13 Feb. '51; ABC's Mary Margaret Mc Bride Show; LP:—; LOC.

467 Recital (NY Farewell): 16 Feb. '51; Town Hall; p. Ulanowsky; a)*Widmung* b)*O, Ihr Herren* c)*Ständchen* d)*Wer machte dich so krank* e)*Alte Laute* (Schumann); f)*Der Mond* g)*Venetianisches Gondellied* (Mendelssohn); h)*Ein Ton* i)*Wiegenlied* (Cornelius); j)*Träume* (Wagner); k)*Für Musik* l)*Ständchen* m)*Gute Nacht* n)*Weisst du noch* o)*Dies und das* (Franz); p)*Wohin* q)*Danksagung an den Bach* r)*Der Neugierige* s)*Tränenregen* t)*Die liebe Farbe* u)*Des Baches Wiegenlied* v)*An die Musik* (encore-incomplete) (Schubert); w)Farewell speech; LP: 47.

468 Recital (Santa Barbara Farewell): 7 Aug. '51; Lobero Theatre; p. Gwendolyn Koldofsky; a)*An mein Klavier* b)*Der Neugierige* c)*Fischerweise* d)*Im Abendrot* e)*Seligkeit* (Schubert); f)*Der Mond* g)*Venetianisches Gondellied* (Mendelssohn); h)*Ein Ton* i) *Wiegenlied* (Cornelius); j)*Träume* (Wagner); k) *A nos morts ignores* l)*Pholoe* m)*Phillis* n)*Offrande* o)*Le rossignol des lilas* p)*Si mes vers* (Hahn)(Fr.); q)*Die Mainacht* r)*Lerchengesang* s)*Es träumte nur* t)*Botschaft* (Brahms); u)*Morgen* (encore) (R. Strauss); LP: 79.

469 Master Classes: Pasadena; from 4 Mar. '52 to 2 Apr. '52; p. Koldofsky; a)*Heimkehr* b)*Cäcilie* c)DER ROSENKAVALIER: Marschallin's Monologue (R. Strauss); d)*Ich grolle nicht* (Schumann); e) *Tu lo sai* (Torelli); f)*La flute de pan* (Debussy); g)*Gesang Weylas* (Wolf); h)*Im Abendrot* (Schubert); i)*Der Kuss* (Beethoven); j) *Warnung* (Mozart); k)*Les cloches* (Debussy); l)*Das Veilchen* (Mozart); m)*Hat dich die Liebe* (Marx); n)*Anakreons Grab* (Wolf);o) *Waldesgespräch* (Schumann); p)*Heimliche Aufforderung* (R. Strauss); q)*Requerdo* (Castelnuovo-Tedesco); r)*Chanson d'amour* (Chausson); s)*Die Verschweigung* (Mozart); t)LA BOHEME: *Mi chiamano Mimi* (Puccini); u)*Zur Ruh'* (Wolf); v)*Hist!* (Arnold); w)*Zueignung* (R. Strauss); x)*Maman, dites moi* (folksong); y)*Ein junger Dichter denkt* (Marx); z)*Feast of lanterns* (Bartok); aa)*In dem Schatten* bb)*Über Nacht* (Wolf); cc)*Der Nussbaum* (Schumann); dd)HERODIADE: *Il est doux* (Massenet); ee)LOHENGRIN: *In fernem Land* (Wagner); ff)*Nicht mehr zu dir* (Brahms); gg)*Stresa* (Watts); hh)*Im wunderschönen Monat Mai* ii)*Aus meinen Tränen* jj)*Die Rose, die Lilie* (Schumann); kk)*Die Nachtigall* (Brahms); ll)*Die heisse schwüle Sommernacht* (Wolf); mm)*Aufenthalt* (Schubert); nn)*Le tombeau des Naïades* oo)*Mandolin* (Debussy); pp)*Psyché* (Paladilhe); qq)*Carnaval* (Fourdrain); rr)DER ROSENKAVALIER: Duet (R. Strauss); ss)*Fischerweise* (Schubert); tt)*Das Mädchen spricht* (Brahms); uu)*Träume* (Wagner); vv)*Wiegenlied* ww)*Ruhe, meine Seele* (R. Strauss); xx)OTHELLO: *Credo* (Verdi); yy)*Auf einer Wanderung* (Wolf); zz)*D'une prison* (Hahn); aaa)*Du denkst mit einem Fädchen* (Wolf); bbb)DIE WALKÜRE: *Du bist der Lenz* (Wagner); ccc)*Immer leiser* (Brahms); ddd)*Die Nacht* (R. Strauss); eee)LA BOHEME: *Che gelida manina* (Puccini);fff)*A nun takes a veil* (Barber); ggg)*Die Krähe* hhh)*Der Jüngling an der Quelle* (Schubert); iii)*Unbewegte laue Luft* (Brahms); jjj)What is sentimentality? kkk)Opening & concl. remarks by Lehmann; LP: priv. rec. & issued by John Campbell.

470 Master class: Music Academy of the West; 28 Aug. '52 contents unknown; LP—; at MAW.

471 Master class: see 470; 30 Aug. '52.

472 Master class: see 470; 15 Aug. '53.

473 Master class: see 470; 21 Aug. '53.

474 Master class: see 470; 22 Aug. '53.

475 TV Interview by Dr. Jan Popper on "Spotlight on Opera;" discusses career; includes master class, 1954 or 3 Sep. '61?

476 TV Master class: "An Evening With Lotte Lehmann;" 8 May '54; 30 minute film; p. Zweig.

477 Interview by Louis Palmer; 30 Sep. '55; on her life, career, MAW, opera in U.S., requirements for singers, about DER ROSENKAVALIER, accompanists, translating opera.

478 Interview by Walter Todds for BBC; 20 Oct. '56; on her first visit to London in 19 years, impressions of recent trip to Vienna, her shock on seeing the modern opera house in Hamburg, recalls first visit to Covent Garden which she finds unchanged, describes recording DER ROSENKAVALIER with anecdote of E. Schumann singing "*Ja, ja,*", memories of working with Strauss & his consideration for singers, her role as Composer in ARIADNE AUF NAXOS, favorite roles, present life teaching in Calif., forthcoming master classes at Wigmore Hall, modern Bayreuth productions, anecdote about Tauber & a bar of chocolate; BBC.

479 TV show: "This Is Your Life, Constance Hope;" 6 Feb. '57; tape possibly with the Hope estate.
480 Interview by John Gutman; 22 Feb. '58; Met. Opera Intermission Feature on her interpretation
    of the role of the Marschallin in DER ROSENKAVALIER, Strauss, teaching.
481 Master class at MAW; Aug. '58; on DER ROSENKAVALIER: "play-by-play" interpretation.
482 TV show: "This Is Your Life, Lauritz Melchior;" 10 Dec. '58; tape possibly w/ Melchior estate.
483 Interview by Roy Plomley for BBC; 14 May '59; from series called "Desert Island Discs," where
    he introduces his castaway who queries anyone's ability to swim ashore carrying 8 records. Leh-
    mann's first choice is the *Prelude* to DIE MEISTERSINGER which reminds her of singing Eva
    at Salzburg with Toscanini; next Mahler's *Um Mitternacht*, for the artistry of Kathleen Ferrier
    & Walter; recalls singing as a child, earliest professional experience, admiration for E. Schumann,
    experience with Vienna Opera, London, first big roles, what opera and *Lieder* have meant to her,
    her "14 day retirement," then teaching, of young singers today; chooses a recording of Gerard
    Souzay, then one conducted by Franz Schalk which reminds her of his kindness, then the trio
    from DER ROSENKAVALIER to remind her of Vienna; a luxury (on the desert island) would
    be a box of paints and a book... Goethe's *Faust*; BBC.
484 Interview by Irene Slade on BBC program in a series called "People Today;" 26 Jul. '59; compares
    London of 1914 with that of today, tribute to London audiences, on early studies, career at Ham-
    burg, Freia under Nikisch, Elsa under Klemperer, necessity of losing oneself in a role, Vienna in
    1916, its claques, role of Composer, memories of first visit to US, *Lieder* singing & its technique,
    teaching, impressions of Toscanini, preferences for Romantic composers & her feeling that she
    lacked the control for Mozart, tribute to Melchior & E. Schumann, her tastes in dress & food,
    hobbies; BBC.
485 Interview by Studs Terkel; 18 Apr. '60; on *Lieder*, master class series at Northwestern Universi-
    ty, career, what she learned from the Marschallin, retirement, goal as a singer, today's singers,
    MAW, Grace Bumbry, modern opera productions, opera in translation, advice to young singers.
486 Master class: NWU; 25, 27, 29 Apr. '60; a) *Die junge Nonne* b)*Am Grabe Anselmos* (Schubert);
    c)*An den Sonnenschein* d)*Aufträge* e)*Geisternähe* (Schumann); f)*Eine gute, gute Nacht* (Brahms);
    g) *Heb' auf dein blondes Haupt* (Wolf); h)*Der Mond* (Mendelssohn); i)*Mit einem gemalten Band*
    (Beethoven); j)*Fleur Fanée* (Hahn); k)*Wozu noch, Mädchen* (Strauss); l)*Paysage* (Hahn); m)Nuits
    d'été (complete) (Berlioz); n)Schéhérezade (complete) (Ravel); o)Poème d'un jour (complete)
    (Fauré); p)TANNHÄUSER: *Dich teure Halle* (Wagner); q)SUOR ANGELICA: *Senza madre*
    (Puccini); r)CARMEN: *Habanera* (Bizet); s)MIGNON: *Connais-tu le pays* (Thomas);
    t)WERTHER: *Les larmes* (Massenet); u)LOHENGRIN: Duet (act 3) (Wagner); v)DIE ZAU-
    BERFLÖTE: *O Isis und Osiris* (Mozart); w)MERRY WIVES OF WINDSOR: Anna's aria
    (Nicolai); x)DIE MEISTERSINGER: *Wahnmonolog* (Wagner); y)DER FREISCHÜTZ: Agatha's
    aria (Weber); z)MANON: Duet of Manon & des Grieux (act 1); p. Donald Isaak; NWU.
487 Interview by Peter Jacobi; WRMQ; 1 May '60; on retirement, teaching (interpretation not imi-
    tation); her career, Bumbry, Vienna, technique, many other roles besides the Marschallin.
488 Interview by Dick Johnson; KDB; 14 Jun. '60; on MAW, teaching in Europe in 1959, plans for
    production of ARABELLA at MAW.
489 Interview by John Gutman; 21 Jan. '61; for Met. Opera Intermission on ARABELLA, its similari-
    ties to DER ROSENKAVALIER, reason for not creating title role, MAW performance, its
    English translation (by Gutman.)
490 TV Master classes at MAW; 28 Jul '61; a)*O Liebliche Wangen* b)*Waldeinsamkeit* (Brahms);
    c)*Benedeit die selge Mutter* (Wolf); d)*Die liebe Farbe* (Schubert); e)DER ROSENKAVALIER:
    Monologue (Eng.), Lehmann sings in German, (R. Strauss); f)MARRIAGE OF FIGARO: *Dove
    sono* (Mozart); g)*Ich kann's nicht fassen* h)*Schöne Wiege* i)*Nun hast du mir* (Schumann); p. Kol-
    dofsky; original series "Master Classes in Opera & *Lieder*" for NET totaled 4 hours.
491 Interview for KPFK; 6 Oct. '62; on Bruno Walter.
492 TV Tribute by NDR-German TV: *Besuch bei Lotte Lehmann*, Santa Barbara, 1963.
493 Interview by John Gutman; WQXR; Jan. 1963; Met. Opera Intermission Feature; on her stage
    direction of DER ROSENKAVALIER.
494 Interview with Maria Jeritza by Gutman; aired: 2 Feb. '63; taped Nov. 1962; for Met. Opera In-
    termission Feature of ARIADNE AUF NAXOS; on this opera's premiere, Strauss & his other
    operas, technique, singers in jet age, MAW; LP: 75.
495 Master class at Wigmore Hall, London; BBC; 14 Mar '64; a)*An die Geliebte* (Wolf); b)*Heimliche
    Aufforderung* (R. Strauss); c)*Gretchen am Spinnrade* (Schubert); d)*Schöne Wiege* (Schumann);
    e)*Das Wirtshaus* (Schubert); f)DIE WALKÜRE: act 2 (Wagner); p. Ivor Newton.

496 Master class at Wigmore Hall, London; BBC; 15 Mar '64; a)*Liebst du um Schönheit* (Mahler); b)*Gute Nacht* (Schubert); c)*Mausfallen-Sprüchlein* (Wolf); d)SUOR ANGELICA: excerpts (Puccini); p. Newton.

497 Master class at Wigmore Hall, London; BBC; 29 Mar '64; a)*Warnung* (Mozart); b)*Um Mitternacht* (Mahler); c)*Von ewiger Liebe* (Brahms); d)ANDREA CHÉNIER: excerpts (Eng.) (Giordano); p. Newton.

498 Interview by Joan Cross & John Amis; BBC; 29 Mar '64; on master classes, her early studies, talent; used as the introduction to the broadcast of the master classes listed above.

499 Presentation of Honorary Ring of Vienna by Franz Jonas, Mayor; 10 Jun. '64; (Ger.); in short speech Lehmann accepts; happiest years of her life as woman & artist were in Vienna.

500 Speech (short); 10 Jun. '64; feels at home in US, loves Austria, thinks of Vienna with the longing of youth; (Ger.).

501 Interview (Ger.) on the centennial of R. Strauss' birth; 1964; his demands as conductor of his own works, on Schalk, B. Walter, Toscanini, why the latter liked her in spite of musical errors, Hoffmansthal, DER ROSENKAVALIER as both comic and tragic, Marschallin as a worldly wise person, sees stylized FIDELIO as robbing it of its living drama, Strauss probably wouldn't mind modern interpretations, her discussion with Desmond Shawe-Taylor on the state of technique, on value of ensemble such as Vienna was, singing/acting should come from inside a person, Hermann Prey as example of one who sings from his soul, how one controls the emotions when singing (horse riding given as an example).

502 Interview by Malloch; KPFK; aired 16 Jan. '65; recorded in her home; on state of opera & *Lieder* singing past & present.

503 Reading from her book, *Five Operas and Richard Strauss* at Faulkner Gallery, Santa Barbara; KPFK; aired 16 Jan '65.

504 Interview by Robert Chesterman; "Music Diary;" CBC; 30 May '65.; on her "retirement," teaching, today's singers, state support for arts, Bumbry, modern opera productions, secret of her success.

505 Interview: 11 Nov. '65; on Bruno Walter.

506 Interview: April 1966; Met. Opera's "Singers Roundtable;" Bidu Sayão, Richard Crooks, Giovanni Martinelli, Lily Pons & Lehmann reminisce, tell anecdotes; Lehmann on new roles, acting, modern Wagnerian productions, jet-age singers, MAW, advice to students, early studies, Old Met.

507 Interview by Peter Lehmann (stage director of 1967 Met. production of Wagner's LOHENGRIN) for WQXR; 21 Jan. '67; contents unknown; Rodgers & Hammerstein Archives.

508 Interview by Olin Downes; 1967; for Met. Opera Int. Feature; on Toscanini, their performances, anecdotes, fear & fondness for him.

509 Interview by Calhoun; Feb. '67; for "Hall of Song;" on first appearances in US, Met., early career, Vienna, Strauss as a person, acting, Wagnerian roles, Convent Garden roles, B. Walter, anecdotes at Met., Melchior, other greats, her work on Met. production of DER ROSENKAVALIER, present activities.

510 Master class at NWU; 1 May '67; Die schöne Müllerin (except # 10 & # 17); p. Laurence Davis.

511 Master class at NWU; 3 May '67; a)*Shéhérazade* (Ravel); b)*Nuits d'été* (Berlioz); c)*L'invitation au voyage* d)*La vie antérieure* e)*Sérénade Florentine* (Duparc); f)Songs and dances of death (Moussorgsky); p. Davis.

512 Master class at NWU; 5 May '67; a)*Geisternähe* b)*Schöne Wiege meiner Leiden* c)*Er ist's* d)*In der Fremde I* (Aus der Heimat) e)*Intermezzo* f)*Waldesgespräch* g)*Die Stille* h)*Mondnacht* i)*Lust der Sturmnacht* j)*Frühlingsnacht* k)*Stille Liebe* l)*In der Fremde II* (Ich hör' die Bächlein) m)*Schöne Fremde* n)*Wehmut* o)*Auf einer Burg* p)*Sehnsucht nach der Waldgegend* (Schumann); p. Davis.

513 Master class at NWU; 8 May '67; a)*Blumengruss* b)*Um Mitternacht* c)*Nimmersatte Liebe* d)*Schlafendes Jesuskind* e)*Die Spröde* f)*Die Bekehrte* g)*Harfenspieler III* h)*Frühling über's Jahr* i)*Er ist's* j)*Denk es, o Seele* k)*Der Knabe und das Immlein* l)*Der Schäfer* m)*An eine Äolsharfe* n)*Elfenlied* o)*Lebe wohl* (Wolf); p. Laurence Davis.

514 Master class at NWU; 10 May '67; a)*Nachtigallen schwingen* b)*Unbewegte, laue Luft* c)*Bitteres zu sagen...*(Brahms); d)*Neue Liebe* (Mendelssohn); e)*Sommerabend* f)*Mondenschein*(Brahms); g)*Und gestern hat er mir Rosen gebracht* (Marx); h)*Es traümte mir* i)*Die Mainacht* (sung by Lehmann) (Brahms); j)*Selige Nacht* (Marx); k)*Der Mond* l)*Die Liebende schreibt* (Mendelssohn); m)*Ruhe, Süssliebchen* (Brahms); n)*Hat dich die Liebe berührt* (Marx); o)*Dämmerung senkte sich*

p)Wenn du nur zuweilen lächelst q)Lerchengesang (Brahms); p. Davis.

515 Master class at NWU; 12 May '67; a)Pace, pace (not attributed); b)Amour, viens aider (SAMSON ET DALILA) (Saint-Saëns); c)Wo berg' ich mich (EURYANTHE) (Weber); d)Wie nahte mir (DER FREISCHÜTZ) (Weber); e)Che faro (ORFEO ED EURIDICE) (Gluck); f)Und ob die Wolke (DER FREISCHÜTZ) (Weber); g)Eri tu (UN BALLO IN MASCHERA) (Verdi); h)Pleurez mes yeux (LE CID) (Massenet); i) Vissi d'arte (TOSCA) (Puccini); j)Avant de quitter ces lieux (FAUST) (Gounod); k)Gavotte (MANON) (Massenet); w/short speech of protest; p. Davis.

516 Interview (Ger.) by Marcel Prawy; 1960's; on Vienna, jet set vs. ensemble, Schalk, Jeritza, farewell recital, books, MAW, her vocal technique, interpretation, "retirement."

517 Speaking (Ger.); 1960's; 2 bands of LP: 42; original source (?); on early studies & career, Vienna, the Marschallin, US & the Met., Lieder, farewell recital, Walter, Schalk, Toscanini, favorite role (Sieglinde), other roles in Vienna, ensemble missing today, modern "stylised" productions.

518 Master class; UCSB "College of Creative Studies;" 6 Jan. '68; a)Dichterliebe (Schumann); b)Gretchen am Spinnrade c)Die Krähe (Schubert); d)Widmung e)Er, der Herrlichste (Schumann); p. La Verne Dayton.

519 Master class; UCSB (see 518); 13 Jan. '68; a)AIDA: Ritorna vincitar (act 1) & Romanza (act 3) (It.) (Verdi); b)EUGEN ONEGIN: Letter scene (act 1) (Eng.)(Tchaikovsky); p. Dayton.

520 Master class; UCSB (see 518); 20 Jan. '68; a)DER ROSENKAVALIER: Presentation of the rose b)ARABELLA: Duet (act 1) (R. Strauss); p. Dayton.

521 Master class; UCSB (see 518); 27 Jan. '68; a)Lieder eines fahrenden Gesellen (Mahler); b)Allerseelen c)Heimkehr d)Zueignung (R. Strauss); e)Gesang Weylas f)In dem Schatten (Wolf); g)Morgen h)Ständchen (R. Strauss); p. Dayton.

522 Interview (Ger.) by a Vienna radio station; 25 Jun. '68; mc sent questions which Lehmann answered in her hotel at Bad Gastein; on early career, Vienna, roles, teaching, writing.

523 Master class; UCSB (see 518); 12 Oct. '68; Die Winterreise (first 5 songs) (Schubert) (remarks that it is ok for women to sing songs originally written for men). p. Dayton.

524 Master class; UCSB (see 518); 19 Oct. '68; a)DIE WALKÜRE: Duet (act 1) (Wagner); b)LA BOHEME: Che gelida manina (Puccini); p. Dayton.

525 Master class; UCSB (see 518); 26 Oct. '68; a)DER ROSENKAVALIER: Monologue (Strauss); b)LA BOHEME: Mimi (act 3) (Puccini); p. Dayton.

526 Master class; UCSB (see 518); 2 Nov. '68; a)Liebestreu b)Am Sonntag Morgen c)Der Tod, das ist die kühle Nacht d)Auf dem Kirchhofe (Brahms); e)DER FREISCHÜTZ: Scene & aria (act 2) (Weber); f)DIE LUSTIGEN WEIBER VON WINDSOR: Duet (act 1) (Nicolai); p. Dayton.

527 Interview by Gutman; 8 Feb. '69; Met. Int. feature; dub of earlier interview; 3 different sopranos who sang the Marschallin.

528 Interview by Hans Fischer Karwin; Summer? '69; on Wessling's Lehmann biography, Mehr als eine Sängerin; great names associated with her, technique vs. personality, early Lieder attempts probably too "operatic," early period in Vienna as a "wild Prussian;" then became more at home and finally "Viennese;" (Ger.).

529 TV Interview in Salzburg by Karwin; Summer? '69; on her life, early studies, career, anecdotes, fate, Vienna, early roles there, husband, Strauss as director, as a conductor, ensemble, B. Walter, Schalk, Toscanini, Isolde, Nazis, US, return to Vienna, most exciting event in career.

530 Master class; UCSB (see 518); 11 Oct. '69; a)FIDELIO: from act 1 (Beethoven); b)Die Georgine c)Wiegenlied d)All' mein Gedanken e)Zueignung (R. Strauss); p. Dayton.

531 Master class; UCSB (see 518); 25 Oct. '69; a)DIE MEISTERSINGER: from act 2 (Wagner); b)Es muss ein Wunderbares sein c)Die Lorelei (Liszt); d)Ich bin der Welt e)Ich atmet' einen linden Duft f)Um Mitternacht (Mahler); p. Dayton.

532 Master class; UCSB (see 518); 1 Nov. '69; a)CARMEN: part of act 1 (Bizet); b)DER FREISCHÜTZ: from act 2 (Weber); c)INTERMEZZO: from act 1 d)DER ROSENKAVALIER: Trio (act 3) (R. Strauss); p. Dayton.

533 Interview for "Singer not the Song;" BBC; 1969; on early career when everything slower than for today's "stars," giving all until end, farewell recital when public still wanted more.

534 Interview for BBC; 1969; recollections of Strauss; that he was not bothered by her vocal & musical imperfections; Dresden premiere of INTERMEZZO; his wife & the story of their engagement, preparation for FRAU OHNE SCHATTEN, singing Strauss' Lieder for him.

535 Interview by Miles Castendique & Milton Cross; WBUR's "Hall of Song" story of Met.; for NPR; aired Jan. '71; prog. #22=1933 season; she talks of her early efforts at the Met.

536 TV Interview by Neville Cardus from Hyde Park Hotel, London; BBC; Aug. 1971; on her recent

book on *Lieder* cycles, teaching, his recollections of her from 1925; Strauss, role of Eva with Toscanini; Schalk anecdote, Beecham, Walter as teacher of opera & *Lieder* understanding roles, interpretation, DER ROSENKAVALIER as theater, Hoffmansthal, her hobbies, favorite roles.

537 Interview by Sylvia Vickers from Hyde Park Hotel, London; BBC; Aug. '71; Vickers makes many embarrassing errors; on early career, INTERMEZZO, working with a composer, how she brought a role to life, relinquishing teaching, how to recognize talent, intelligence vs. voice, jet-set stars of today, technique, Toscanini, teaching interpretation, Bumbry, critics from country to country, future of opera.

538 Interview: aired 16 Sept. '71; contents unknown.

539 Interview by Gary Hickling for 85th birthday tribute; WBAI; taped 18 Dec. '72; on favorite roles & recordings, students.

540 Interview by Hickling for Melchior memorial program; WBAI; 15 Aug. '73; on singing with Melchior, his Siegmund, anecdotes.

541 Interview (Ger.) by Frieda Jahre for "Kultur Interview;" 22 Aug. '73; on Vienna in 1914, 1916, first roles there, at first not fitting in, Strauss, Puccini, Toscanini, *Lieder* as another world, third career as teacher, Vienna as "home," no "stars" then, writing a book on *Lied* interpretation.

542 Coaching Jeannine Altmeyer in the role of Eva; Salzburg; 1973; on stage movement, important words, psychological interpretation.

LATE RECORDINGS WITH INCOMPLETE DATA (some possibly taken from Columbia radio broadcasts; see 450.)

543 *Es weiss und rät es* (Mendelssohn); no date, 1940's?; p. Ulanowsky; VOA 16" acetate, 33 rpm.
544 *Pagenlied* (Mendelssohn); see 543.
545 *Schilflied* (Mendelssohn); see 543..
546 *Neue Liebe, neues Leben* (Beethoven); see 543.
547 *Das Veilchen* (Mozart); live; no date, possibly mid 1940's; p. Ulanowsky?; no data.
548 *Andenken* (Beethoven); see 543.
549 *Freiheit, die ich meine* (C. Groos); no date, possibly early or mid 1940's; p. ?; OWI Series.
550 *Frühlingstraum* (Schubert); see 543.
551 *Gute Nacht* (Schubert); see 543.
552 *Abendemfindung* (Mozart); see 543.
553 *Anakreons Grab* (Wolf); see 543.

UNDATED INTERVIEW/CLASS
553 Interview/class by Jan Popper; no date; DER OPERNBALL: *Im chambre separé*; (Heuberger); Lehmann sets the scene.

■ ■ DISCOGRAPHY INDEX ■ ■

Numbers refer to discography's listings. When the number is preceded by "mc" it refers to a master class, in which Lehmann taught the selection but may have sung or demonstrated only a portion.

Wehmut (Schumann) mc 512
Weisse und rote Rose (Eulenburg) 076
Weisst du noch (Franz) 467 n
Wenn dein ich denk (Zauberlied) (Meyer-
 Helmund) 110
Wenn du einmal dein Herz verschenkst (Rosen)
 147
Wenn du, mein Liebster (Wolf) 436 d
Wenn du nur zuweilen lächelst (Brahms) mc514
Wenn ich früh in den Garten geh' (Schumann)
 332 b
Wenn ich in deine Augen seh' (Schumann) 371 a
Wer machte dich so krank (Schumann) 467 d
Wer tat deinem Füsslein weh (Wolf) 360,
 450 ee
Werther, Werther..(WERTHER) (Massenet)
 202
What is sentimentality? (speaking) mc 469
Widmung (Schumann) 153, 467 a; in Eng. 452 b
 & 463 c, mc 518
Wie bist du, meine Königin (Brahms) 314, 456 j
Wie froh und frisch (Brahms) 462 p
Wie nahte mir der Schlummer (DER
 FREISCHÜTZ) (Weber) 007, 022, 064,
 143, mc 486, mc 515; see Und ob die
 Wolke
Wie sagt die Zdenka (ARABELLA) (R. Strauss)
 209
Wiegenlied (Brahms) 346 a or 347, 450 w,
 461 f, 464 c; in Eng. 413
Wiegenlied (Cornelius) 467 i, 468 i
Wiegenlied (Flies formerly attr. to Mozart)
 450 nn
Wiegenlied (Schlaf' Herzenssöhnchen) (Weber)
 182
Wiegenlied (Schlafe, schlafe, holder)
 (Schubert) 275
Wiegenlied (Träume, träume…) (R. Strauss)
 054, 428 b, mc 469, mc 530
Wien, du Stadt meiner Träume (Sieczynski)
 361
Wien, sterbende Märchenstadt (Leopoldi) 364
Wilde Rose (Eulenburg) 075 b
Willst du, das ich geh (Brahms) 456 n
Wir glauben all' an einen Gott (Bach) 161
Wir wandelten (Brahms) 315
Wisst ihr, wann mein Kindchen (Brahms) 396 a
Wo berg' ich mich (EURYANTHE) (Weber)
 mc 515
Wo du hingehst (Rössel) 134
Wohin (Schubert) 379 b, 467 p
Wonne der Wehmut (Beethoven) 339, 450 b
Wozu noch Mädchen (R. Strauss) 418 b,
 mc 486
Zauberlied (Meyer-Helmund) 110
Zigeunerlieder (Brahms) 395-398, 456 i
Zueignung (R. Strauss) 063.4 a, 352, 436 x, 440
 b, 450 gg, 461 d, mc 469, mc 521, mc 530

Zum Fenster…(WERTHER) (Massenet) 203
Zur Drossel sprach der Fink (D' Albert) 120
Zur Ruh' (Wolf) 344, 450 bb, mc 469
Zuschau'n (Böhm) (Bavarian folksong) 183

LP: REFERENCE

LP: 1 COLO (or COLH) 112 (ANGEL)=PMA
 1057 PARLOPHONE-ODEON (EMI)=GR
 2046 (TOSHIBA JAPAN).
LP: 2 77307 (ANGEL JAPAN).
LP: 3 ARTPHONE C22 G0008 (JAPAN).
LP: 4 CS22 G0009 (JAPAN).
LP: 5 YD 3016 (JAPAN).
LP: 6 YD 3017/18 (JAPAN).
LP: 7 BRUNO WALTER SOCIETY BWS
 729.
LP: 8 BWS 1009.
LP: 9 CBS (SONY) MASTERWORKS 20 AC
 1915 (JAPAN).
LP: 10 20 AC 1914 (JAPAN).
LP: 11 SONC 15117 (JAPAN).
LP: 12 Frauenliebe und Leben & Dichterliebe:
 COLUMBIA MS 4788=ML
 4788=PHILIPS A01265L=ODYSSEY 32
 16 0315=CBS (SONY) MASTERWORKS
 SONC 15112, CBS (SONY) SOCF 134 &
 CBS 20AC 1913 (JAPAN); only Frauen-
 liebe und Leben: ML 2182=XLP 15249=
 ARTPHONE YD 3016 (JAPAN); Dichter-
 liebe only: CBS 72250=ML 4788=ML
 2183=C 1020 (UK)=FC 1034 (FRANCE).
LP: 13 COLUMBIA ML 5778=CBS-BRG
 72073 (UK).
LP: 14 ML 5996=CBS-BRG 72209 (UK).
LP: 15 DECCA DL 9523.
LP: 16 DECCA DL 9524.
LP: 17 EMI CD
LP: 18 EMI 0-83396.
LP: 19 EMI 1C 137-30707/05=SERAPHIM
 1B-6105.
LP: 20 EMI 1C 147-29116/117M.
LP: 21 EMI 1C 147-30226/27M.
LP: 22 EMI HLM 7027.
LP: 23 EMI RLS 154 7003.
LP: 24 EMI RLS 743.
LP: 25 EMI RLS 766.
LP: 26 GAO EJS 100.
LP: 27 GAO EJS 178.
LP: 28 GAO EJS 234=BWS/DISCOCORP
 RR-426 (E80 686/88WC 634/36)
 =EDIZIONE LIRICA 004-2=PEARL
 GEMM 228/9 (excerpts).
LP: 29 GAO EJS 332.
LP: 30 GAO EJS 425.
LP: 31 GAO EJS 444.
LP: 32 GAO EJS 462.
LP: 33 GAO EJS 496.

LP: 34 GAO EJS 536.
LP: 35 LEGENDARY RECORDINGS LR
142-5.
LP: 36 LR 212.
LP: 37 MET OPERA 206.
LP: 38 MET OPERA 403.
LP: 39 MET 5 SORIA SERIES.
LP: 40 ODEON OBL 1072(3)/20479=7xBe 169/
170 (45rpm).
LP: 41 ODEON-BELCANTODISC ORX 123
(45rpm) (FRANCE).
LP: 42 ODEON (EMI) 0-83396.
LP: 43 ODEON OPX 503/505.
LP: 44 ODYSSEY (CBS-COLUMBIA) 32 16
0179.
LP: 45 OPERA DISC 3086.
LP: 46 PEARL GEMM 259/60.
LP: 47 PEMBROKE=PELICAN 2009
(incomplete) =EMI 1C 027 60386.
LP: 48 PREISER COURT OPERA CLAS-
SICS CO 387.
LP: 49 CO 410.
LP: 50 PREISER LEBENDIGE VERGAN-
GENHEIT LV 22.
LP: 51 LV 94.
LP: 52 LV 180.
LP: 53 LV 294.
LP: 54 LV 1336.
LP: 55 RCA 430.661 (FRANCE).
LP: 56 RCA CAMDEN CAE 438 (45rpm), LR
212 (only 405).
LP: 57 RCA CAMDEN CAL 378=CDN 1015
(UK)=RS 7 (JAPAN).
LP: 58 RCA LCT 1108=430.529S (FRANCE).
LP: 59 RCA LM 2763=RB 6604 (UK)=HR
GEMM 219.
LP: 60 RCA RS 12 (JAPAN), RCA LM 6130
only An Chloë.
LP: 61 RCA CD?
LP: 62 RCA VICTROLA VICS 1320 E.
LP: 63 ROCOCO 5217.
LP: 64 ROCOCO 5356.
LP: 65 ROCOCO 5257.
LP: 66 RUBINI RDA 003.
LP: 67 SCALA 837, SCALA 1435, ETERNA
494.
LP: 68 SERAPHIM 1B-6105=EMI 137-30704/
05.
LP: 69 SERAPHIM 1C-6041.
LP: 70 SERAPHIM 60060=EMI HQM
1121=GR 2198 (TOSHIBA JAPAN); EMI
2902123/PM 663 & SERAPHIM 6130-1G
(only 171)
LP: 71 SERAPHIM 60013.
LP: 72 TOP ARTISTS PLATTERS T 306.
LP: 73 T 318.
LP: 74 TOP CLASSICS 9052.
LP: 75 TMC 100.

LP: 76 UORC 218.
LP: 77 UORC 235.
LP: 78 UORC 257.
LP: 79 UORC 306=LOBERO LL
1=AQUITAINE MS90420 (no A nos
morts)
LP: 80 DER ROSENKAVALIER (abridged):
VICTOR LCT 6005=VICTOR WCT 6005
(45 rpm)=LVT 2002=ANGEL GRB 4001=E
80630-1= FRENCH S 0014-5=HMV
COLH 110-111=ELECTROLA E 30 (80)
630-6, WCLP 697-8=SERAPHIM 1C
6041(which includes Strauss arias from
other operas)=WORLD RECORD CLUB
(EMI) SH 181-2=EMI RLS
7704=REFERENCE 143 2943=EMI C 187-
29225 M/26; LCT 1=217 & 226 only;
(WCT 5=LCT 1 =218 & 227?); act 1 monologue EMI CD: see LP: 17.
LP: 81 DIE WALKÜRE: VICTOR LVT
1003, LCT 1001, WCT 2 (45 rpm) (only
238); EMI ELECTROLA 1C 047-29 116/
117 & SERAPHIM 1C 6140 (only 242-
243); TC 9048 (only 234 & 240); 1C 147
01259 (only 233, 237-239); LCT 1003,
WCT 58, SERAPHIM 60190, HMV
COLH 133, EMI ELECTROLA 1C 049-
03023M, FALP 50013 & REFERENCE
2C 051 03023M (PM322) (FRANCE) (act
1); ODEON ELECTROLA (EMI) E 80686
88, WCLP 734-6, DANACORD DACO
171-176 (acts 1 & 2); EMI TURNABOUT/
VOX THS 65163 (act 2 scenes 3 & 5);
EMI ELECTROLA C 147-30 636 m/37,
ANGEL 1G 6130 (excerpts); EMI
2902123/PM 663 (act 2).
LP: 82 VOCE 69.
LP: 83 VOCE 99.
LP: 84 VRCS 1968.
LP: 85 VRCS 1974.
LP: 86 VRCS 1976.
LP: 87 BELVEDERE 120747 (120841) &
TELDEC 6.43333.

That which would not be forgotten survives
and thrives, in type as well as song.
American type designer Frederic Goudy
created Goudy Newstyle in 1921 as a literary
alphabet with phonetic pretensions (20 extra
characters). The Grabhorn Press used it for
several fine letterpress books. The matrices
were burned in a fire in the 1930's and the
design became one of Goudy's "lost faces,"
until Judy Sutcliffe redrew it in 1986 using a
Macintosh computer and Fontographer software by Altsys Corporation. Roger Levenson
supplied a Grabhorn-Hoyem type specimen
and good advice. The body type for this book
is 11 pt. Goudy Newstyle with 10 pt. Goudy
Oldstyle Italic (also drawn with Fontographer). The notes, index and discography
were set in 8 pt. Goudy Newstyle with a
Macintosh-generated oblique italic. Type and
page formatting were done by Judy Sutcliffe
using ReadySetGo3 software on a Macintosh
computer with camera-ready copy printed on
an Apple LaserWriter.